Sugar Islands

THE 165-YEAR STORY OF SUGAR IN HAWAIʻI

OTHER BOOKS BY WILLIAM H. DORRANCE

Viscous Hypersonic Flow

Fort Kamehameha: The Story of the Harbor Defenses of Pearl Harbor

Oʻahu's Hidden History

Sugar Islands | THE 165-YEAR STORY OF SUGAR IN HAWAI'I

William Henry Dorrance
Former President, OCS, Inc.

Chapter Introductions by
Francis Swanzy Morgan
Former Proprietor, Hamakua Sugar Co.

Mutual Publishing

Copyright © 2000 by William H. Dorrance

No part of this book may be reproduced in any form or by any electronic or mechanical means, including information storage and retrieval devices or systems, without prior written permission from the publisher, except that brief passages may be quoted for reviews.

All rights reserved
Library of Congress Catalog Card Number: 00-111766

Softcover ISBN 1-56647-339-X
Hardcover ISBN 1-56647-503-1

Design by Julie Matsuo

First Printing, June 2001
Second Printing, June 2005
2 3 4 5 6 7 8 9

Mutual Publishing, LLC
1215 Center Street, Suite 210
Honolulu, Hawaii 96816
Ph: (808) 732-1709
Fax: (808) 734-4094
e-mail: mutual@mutualpublishing.com
www.mutualpublishing.com

Printed in Taiwan

Contents

	Preface	vii
1	An Overview of Sugar in Hawai'i	1
2	Sugar in Hawai'i Before Reciprocity (1802-1875)	9
3	Sugar on Kaua'i (1876-2000)	23
4	Sugar on O'ahu (1876-1996)	39
5	Sugar on Moloka'i & Lāna'i (1876-1901)	53
6	Sugar on Maui (1876-1991)	59
7	Sugar on the Island of Hawai'i (1876-1996)	75
8	Independent Farmers and Independent Sugarmills (1876-1996)	115
9	The Plantation Workers	123
10	Factors, then Agencies	135
11	Cooperation in the Industry	149
12	Sugar-Related Industries	159
13	Sugar and Science	175
14	Competition and Price Supports	189
15	Sugar's Future in Hawai'i (2000)	199
	Appendix A. Monarchs and Missionaries	207
	Appendix B. Sugar Prices	210
	Appendix C. How Sugar Is Manufactured	212
	Glossary	215
	Chapter Notes	216
	Bibliography	236
	Index	252
	About Francis S. Morgan	264
	About William H. Dorrance	265

Waimanalo Sugar Co.
(Hawai'i State Archives)

PREFACE

My interest in plantation farming stems from youthful experiences. In the Depression year of 1938, during the summer months between my sophomore and junior years in high school, I worked as a field hand on a large Ford Motor Company soybean plantation in southern Michigan. I hoed weeds, spread fertilizer, and, just before returning to school, earned a coveted "sit down" job driving a Fordson tractor that pulled a disc harrow. This experience left me with a lasting impression of, and curiosity about, large-scale plantation farming.

When I retired to Hawaiʻi after a career in science and business, I found the farming industry that had meant so much to Hawaiʻi was changed in fundamental ways. For the sake of efficiency, the plantation railroads and hordes of machete-wielding cane-cutters I'd read about had disappeared. Plantations had been combined and sugarmills were being dismantled. If the trend continued, it seemed that soon there would be few reminders of the industry that was once "king" in Hawaiʻi.

In the early 1900s, there were over 50 sugar plantations, most of which had their own mill and railroad. In 1993, when the first draft of this book was completed, there were twelve survivors and the number was dwindling. Now only four plantations are left. My research answers a number of basic questions: Where were all the original plantations and on which island? When did they start, and when and how did they end? Who established and managed them? Which were unique and in what way? Which plantations survive to this day? What industries owe their existence to sugar? What are the problems confronting the industry and the prospects for sugar?

I visited every surviving plantation, many of them several times, and observed operations while taking photographs. I interviewed retired sugar workers, active and retired managers, and active and retired executives. I located and photographed the remains of sugarmills; many of these pictures illustrate grinders, steam engines, boiling pots, and structures long retired but demonstrating "the way it used to be," in several cases over a century ago. Some structures that I photographed, like the mill house of Hutchinson Sugar Plantation Company in Kau, have since been removed. I supplemented my field trips with archival research, including the Hawaiian Sugar Planters' Association in Aiea. Librarian Anne Marsteller helped me locate documents and was patient with my many questions. (On October 3, 1996, some of the archives I consulted were transferred to the Hamilton Library on the campus of the University of Hawaiʻi-Mānoa.)

I spent days studying and copying documents from the extensive collection at the Hawaiʻi State Library in Honolulu. Many hours were also spent plumbing the records at Lyman House Memorial Museum in Hilo. I read everything in the bibliography related to Hawaiʻi's sugar industry. The guide to historical resources for the sugar industry, prepared by Susan M. Campbell and sponsored by the Humanities Program of the State Foundation on Culture and the Arts in cooperation with the

Hawaiian Historical Society, helped beyond measure in locating documents. The state library system's on-line accessions list helped locate documents from off-island branches. I made an effort to verify every secondary source by searching the various libraries and archives for back-up data. I cited primary sources when appropriate, and when restrictions placed on back-up documents permitted this.

  The following people read all or portions of the manuscript and were generous with helpful comments and suggestions: retired sugar executives Robert H. Hughes, former vice president, C. Brewer & Company, Ltd. and former president of HSPA; Robert Vorfeld, former manager of Pioneer Mill Company on Maui; L. A. "Tony" Faye, former manager of Kekaha Sugar Company on Kauaʻi; David Morgan, former manager of Hamakua Sugar Company on Hawaiʻi; and J. I. Frederick Reppun, M.D., retired plantation physician on Lānaʻi and Molokaʻi. Archivist Susan M. Campbell also made several helpful suggestions after reading my first draft. I owe thanks to all of them.

  I am especially grateful to Stephanie A. Whalen, President and Director of the Experiment Station at the Hawaiʻi Agriculture Research Center, for her comments. Every effort has been made to accommodate all suggestions. My wife, Jan, earned my particular gratitude for her constant encouragement.

  It was early in my field trip activity that I first met Francis S. Morgan, then owner of Hamakua Sugar Company on the Big Island of Hawaiʻi. "Frannie" to all who know him, he made a lasting impression on me when he set aside the better part of a day at his headquarters in Paʻauilo to answer my questions. This took place at a time when he was in the midst of the struggle to save his plantation. I vowed to myself to somehow incorporate Frannie's experiences and enormous wealth of information into the history of the industry. This book is the result.

William H. Dorrance

✦ ✦ ✦

  I have been involved in Hawaiʻi agriculture for my entire life. Kualoa Ranch on Oʻahu is a family-owned business which has been in operation since 1850. I grew up with an appreciation of this property, and a strong commitment to its preservation and continuation. Beginning when I was a boy, all my spare time when not in school was spent working with cattle, clearing pastures, fixing fences and water pipes, and many other chores. Along with my family, I feel that Kualoa Ranch was instrumental in forming my personality and beliefs.

  As an adult, I was hired by Theo H. Davies & Co., Ltd., and assigned to its Plantation Department with responsibility for labor and union relations. I had to spend considerable time at the Davies sugar plantations to learn the plantation operations, the work involved, and existing working relationships. Being from an agricultural background, I was fascinated with the extremely high agricultural and operational expertise practiced at the plantations, and I spent a lot of time with employees, managers, and other supervisors going through the fields, factories, garages and other operations. I became interested in current activities and also the history and development at these plantations. I heard about past experiences and exploits and encouraged old-timers to tell me about them. I also found that all the records and annual reports at these companies had been preserved since their founding. So, when not otherwise occupied, I read and absorbed these documents.

After almost twenty years in the business I was promoted to Group Vice President for Agriculture, with responsibility for Davies' four plantations on the North Hilo and Hāmākua Coast, and at Kūkaʻiau Ranch. We gradually merged the operations and eventually became the second largest sugar plantation in Hawaiʻi, and among those with the lowest costs.

In 1973 a series of business events resulted in a decision to liquidate these plantations. I felt it would be devastating to Hawaiʻi and, in particular, to the employees and families of Davies Hamakua Sugar Co. In order to preserve this operation as long as possible, I borrowed heavily, put up my life savings, and purchased one plantation. I renamed it "Hamakua Sugar Company." At the time I was 65 years old, and, to assure continuity beyond my lifetime, my son David and daughter Patricia started to work there, intending to learn the business from the ground up. I am pleased to say they performed in a highly satisfactory manner. However, a number of further events occurred outside my control and these, together with some unfortunate timing, combined to make it impossible to continue full debt service. The impatient bankers called the loan and threw Hamakua Sugar Company into bankruptcy. Nevertheless, I was able to prolong the life of this large-scale plantation for over nine years, and believe I demonstrated that, with adequate financial resources and an appropriate management philosophy, elements of the Hawaiʻi sugar industry can, and will, survive well into the future.

When contemplating the history of Hāmākua Coast plantations, I realized that in their approximately 100 years of existence, I had been personally involved for almost half that time. Together with knowing long-time employees and researching old company files, I was as knowledgeable as anyone about the history of these operations. In addition, I have been on the board of directors of the Hawaiian Sugar Planters' Association (HSPA) since 1963 and continue as honorary director of its successor, the Hawaiʻi Agriculture Research Center. I also served for a number of years as either president of HSPA or chairman of the board. During this time I made congressional appearances, attended industry meetings, and got to know its leaders, in Hawaiʻi as well as on the mainland United States and abroad.

Many of them urged me to write my memoirs so that all this information would be saved for posterity. At this point Dr. William H. Dorrance approached me and proposed we collaborate on a book about Hawaiʻi's sugar industry. I was impressed with the research Bill had already done, and further impressed by articles he had published, one about me and Kualoa Ranch. I decided that with his research and writing ability and my knowledge of the industry, we could produce a work that was interesting and would preserve some valuable knowledge. For me, it was a happy solution, and this book does much to fill the need.

Francis Swanzy Morgan

Hakalau Sugar Mill, Hawai‘i
(Van Dyke Collection)

CHAPTER 1

AN OVERVIEW OF SUGAR IN HAWAI'I

Native Hawaiians first brought sugarcane to the Islands many centuries ago. Archibald Menzies, a naturalist who visited with Captain Vancouver in 1793, was amazed by the high level of sophistication in the construction of their ponds and fields. He felt the Hawaiians were more advanced than European and American farmers, and described irrigation ditches and the use of fish remains for fertilizer. They accomplished successful cultivation with very primitive tools. Lacking any metal, a flat-ended wooden stick-like implement, the 'ō'ō, was used for digging. Constructing an irrigation system involved a cooperative effort with large numbers of workers. So, in the early 1800s, newcomers to the Islands built a cane-farming industry on a firm agricultural foundation.

Westerners brought modern machinery and ran what became the most efficient sugar plantations in the world. Eventually, steam was used to power the mills and steam locomotives and, later, trucks fueled by gasoline hauled the harvests from the fields. Long ditches and tunnels were dug to distribute irrigation water. Hawai'i's cane farmers learned to match the fertilizers to the different soils on the islands. When local labor sources proved insufficient, workers were imported from the Orient and elsewhere, thus setting the stage for the diverse ethnic makeup of modern Hawai'i.

The most significant advance was the application of engineering and science, via the Hawaiian Sugar Planters' Association (HSPA) and innovative plantation managers. The HSPA developed disease-resistant cane, methods of weed and pest control, and cultivating and harvesting equipment best suited to the unique environment of Hawai'i. Plantation managers developed techniques and field equipment that were far ahead of those used elsewhere. I am proud to have participated in Hawai'i's sugar industry for over 50 years, and am pleased to help tell the story of the industry's 165-year history.

⊕ ⊕ ⊕

MAN HAS A voracious sweet tooth that for centuries could be satisfied only with sugar. Sugar (chemical name sucrose) is a substance made up of carbon, hydrogen, and oxygen, and is most abundant in honey, maple syrup, sugar beets, and sugarcane. Per capita annual consumption of sugar in the

United States has averaged about 65 pounds in recent decades. The romance shows no sign of cooling.[1]

Until cultivated in the Western world, sugar was a rare commodity sold by apothecaries. Sugarcane, a member of the grass family (genus saccharum), originated in India and southern Asia centuries before Christ. The conqueror Alexander saw sugarcane in about 325 B.C., and called it "honey-bearing reeds." Later it migrated to the islands of the South Pacific but was unknown to Europeans until early historic times. Sugar from cane made its way to the Near East, then the Arabs brought cane plantings from ancient Persia to the Mediterranean countries. Columbus took sugarcane to the Caribbean on his second voyage.[2] To this day it flourishes on islands throughout the Caribbean, most notably in Cuba, and is big business for otherwise impoverished islands.

Hawai'i is a latecomer to the sugar industry. By 1778, when the explorer Capt. James Cook (1728-1779) discovered Hawai'i for Europeans, centuries of Mediterranean and Atlantic island cane cultivation had come and gone. The industry was mid-way in a 300-year period of growth in South America and the Caribbean.[3] Nevertheless, sugar helped to make modern Hawai'i.

And how did sugarcane arrive here? The origin of the archipelago is volcanic. Over millennia lava fields eroded and broke down into soils rich in minerals (but not in hydrocarbons or metals). All flora came from elsewhere. An occasional coconut washing ashore may account for lush palm groves, but it is unlikely that a vital sugarcane stalk would survive after drifting thousands of miles in the Pacific. Sugarcane was brought to Hawai'i.

Ancient Polynesians first came here from the Marquesas Islands about A.D. 750.[4] Some of the richest varieties of sugarcane are found in the South Pacific. Over a thousand years later Captain Cook recorded in his journal, "We saw...a few trees about the villages; near which...we could observe several plantations of plantains and sugar-canes."[5] Since it is unlikely that Hawaiians cultivated sugarcane on a large scale, this observation raises questions of what was meant by "plantations." However, Cook had visited Tahiti, where cane was abundant, so he knew sugarcane when he saw it.

Further observations come from the Russian explorer, Captain Iurii F. Lisianskii (1773-1837), whose *Neva* dropped anchor in June 1804 off Kealakekua on the island of Hawai'i, where Cook met his death at the hands of Native Hawaiians in 1779. Captain Lisianskii and his accompanying scientist Georg H. Langsdorf (1774-1872) were impressed with the quality and amount of sugarcane growing in the area. Langsdorf wrote, "If this [sugarcane] were cultivated to any degree of perfection in time...all of Siberia might be supplied with sugar thence." Lisianskii was more far-seeing when he recorded, "Sugar cane alone, which grows in great abundance and without the slightest supervision, might give [the Hawaiians] huge wealth if they saw fit to turn it into sugar or rum. Both products, after all, are sold on the coasts of America in great quantity."[6]

The Hawaiian sugar fields were all within a few miles of the ocean because cane grows slowly in the coolness of higher elevations. They were easily seen from offshore. More evidence that the Hawaiians planted and used sugarcane for food is provided by the early planter George W. Wilfong. In 1863 he was hired to manage the Kohala Sugar Company plantation in North Kohala on the island of Hawai'i. Curious about the abundance of wild cane growing for several miles around, Wilfong* asked a Hawaiian, Naihie, to explain, and received this reply:

> *After the Kamehameha war (i.e. after 1790 on Hawai'i) the konohiki* [headmen of land divisions] *were ordered to plant cane about the land; so when their chiefs came that way with their many followers, which was the custom of the chiefs of that day, they could have cane to eat.*[7]

The eight principal islands of the Hawaiian archipelago showing where sugarcane has been cultivated at one time or another.
(CULTIVATED AREAS NOT TO SCALE)

In other words, a chewed stalk provided energy and sustenance.

Rev. Artemas Bishop (1795-1872) arrived in Hawai'i with the second company of missionaries in 1823, and was stationed at Kailua, Hawai'i. From there he undertook exploratory expeditions to remote areas of the island. In 1825 he wrote in a letter: "...We then came to a fertile region [in Kohala] presenting a very beautiful sloping landscape, upon which grew the taro, banana and sugar cane in abundance...."[8]

Although the Hawaiians enjoyed a healthy existence before the European discovery of the Islands, they lacked metal tools necessary to hew stone, cut metal, and cultivate soil, or manufacture even a rudimentary sugarmill. No metals are indigenous to Hawai'i. Western tools and ingenuity made harvesting Hawai'i-grown sugarcane a profitable undertaking. Sugarcane resembles corn and bamboo with a long, noded stalk topped with blossoms when mature. Typically, in Hawai'i the stalks grow from 15 to 20 feet in length, with a

---

* Sometimes spelled "Willfong" in sources. However, he apparently spelled his surname "Wilfong." See his article in the October 1882 issue of The Planter's Monthly as cited herein.

diameter of up to two inches. Unlike hollow bamboo, the stalk is filled with pulp saturated with sugar juice. When mature, much of the cane forms a dense matting along the ground. The stalk's growth develops in narrow leaves arranged in two rows along the length of the stalk. Energy from sunlight produces growth by a chemical process, photosynthesis, using carbon dioxide from the oxygen and water from the soil. A stalk matures in 24 to 36 months. Sugarcane has the most efficient photosynthesis of any plant, produces more vegetative material and oxygen, and consumes more carbon dioxide than the trees in tropical rain forests.

Sugarcane, *genus saccharum*.

Early sugarmakers found several varieties of wild cane: red, greenish-red, purple, green, yellow-striped, and variegated.[9] The first Western cane farmers erected a mill amidst a large patch of cane, hired native workers, and harvested the surrounding field. The cane would be trimmed of leaves, hauled away by oxen and fed by hand into the wooden or stone grinders of an animal-powered mill. The extracted, sugar-laden juice was drained off to a series of large iron kettles arranged in a cascade, then concentrated by boiling off water and impurities. The sugar master, with a trained eye, drained the last pot in the array (i.e., "made a strike") to a cooling trough exactly when the sugar would crystallize as it cooled. This actually consisted of molasses floating in crystallized sugar. The molasses was drained off over a period of days and weeks, a crude process that produced a brown sugar because not all of the molasses could be removed. It was a labor-intensive business.

The population of Hawai'i declined to a minimum of 56,897 in December 1872.[10] At the same time the number of plantations increased from 14 in 1862[11] to 32 in 1872.[12] The competition for sugar workers was fierce, and the reduced number of Native Hawaiians was not inclined to work in the fields. The desperate Kingdom responded by importing contract workers. They came in waves: first the Chinese, then the Portuguese and northern Europeans, the Japanese, and, after annexation by the United States in 1898, the Filipinos. The die was cast for Hawai'i's ethnic mix.

In the last half of the nineteenth century, Hawai'i sugar planters adopted a scientific approach to cultivation. Depletion of soil nutrients was controlled with fertilizers tailored to each plantation by chemical analyses. Vulnerability to erratic rainfall (each pound of sugar produced requires a ton of water during its growth) was eliminated with irrigation. The Hawaiian Sugar Planters' Association, a cooperative, was formed in 1885 to apply scientific methods to solving problems, develop new varieties of cane, and make improvements in sugar farming. Insect and rodent infestations were controlled with their natural enemies. Consequently, by 1897 Hawai'i's sugar producers were the most efficient in the world, with an average yield of over four tons per acre, compared to their chief competitors, Louisiana with one ton per acre, and Cuba with two tons.[13] Eighty years later, ten tons per acre was the norm in Hawai'i.

The costs of harvesting and transporting cane to the mill were studied. Fluming the harvested cane to some mills (i.e., conveying by water in a trough), was cost-competitive, compared to animal carts, as was the use of bundles attached to trolleys suspended from wire cables. On other plantations, railroads replaced oxen and mules. By the mid-twentieth century all these were supplanted by trucks and tournahaulers. Simple three-roller mills were replaced with more crushers and, in some cases, the sugar-beet industry's diffusion extraction method was used.

The industry's five-year average annual production grew to one million tons in 1930 and stayed there for 50 years, beginning a decline only in 1988.[14] During this period the New York price of sugar ranged from 2.78 cents a pound to 23.36 cents a pound. Using a reasonable average figure of 20 cents a pound ($400 per ton), Hawai'i sugar became a $400 million per year industry based on sugar production alone. An additional $60 million per year came from sales of molasses. From 1980 on, revenue from sugarmill-generated electricity to the commercial power grids totaled another $40 million annually.

Before and after World War II, sugar and molasses sales were by far the major source of Hawai'i's favorable balance of payments. A large portion of the excess funds were invested in making the industry grow and, after about 1930, keeping it competitive. The sugar industry supported many a white-collar job in Honolulu and was the source of many a family fortune.

As shown in Table 1, by 1900 the number of plantations was 59 allocated among six of the islands.[15] At the same time the average plantation size was 2,169 acres, and the average annual production was a modest 4,907 tons. The producers introduced plantation railroads and more crushers in the sugarmill. Yields improved with the introduction of steam plows and irrigation. The Honolulu sugar factors saw advantages in combining neighboring plantations, and in time their ownership stakes increased. After 1900 the number of plantations steadily decreased, although the total area under cultivation grew as these practical businessmen reaped the economies of scale.

The number of plantations declined from 52 in 1910 to 14 in 1980. During this time the overall figure for cultivation held firm at some 215,000 acres, and the average acres per plantation increased from 2,169 to 15,551. Tons of sugar produced per harvested acre increased from 4.50 to 10.51 during this same period. Much of this improvement came from pest and disease control, fertilization, efficient irrigation, improved mechanical cultivators, more efficient sugarmills, and richer sugarcane varieties.

TABLE 1 | HAWAI'I SUGAR PLANTATIONS: NUMBER, CULTIVATED ACRES, AND ANNUAL SUGAR PRODUCTION 1856-1994

YEAR	NUMBER OF PLANTATIONS	ACRES IN SUGARCANE	ACRES PER PLANTATION	TONS PRODUCED	TONS ACRE*
1856	7	2,150	392	277	.20
1867	29	10,006	345	12,115	1.21
1880	62	28,200	420	28,200	2.00
1882	72	39,350	546	57,088	2.90
1884 (most)	80	unk.	unk.	71,327	unk.
1890	63	87,016	1,381	129,899	3.00
1900	59	128,024	2,169	289,544	4.40
1910	52	214,312	4,121	582,196	4.50
1920	49	236,510	4,826	546,273	4.91
1930	46	251,533	5,468	1,129,899	7.02
1939	36	235,227	6,534	994,173	7.18
1949	28	213,354	7,619	955,890	8.76
1962	26	228,926	8,804	1,120,011	10.31
1974	20	224,227	11,211	1,128,529	10.86
1980	14	217,718	15,551	1,059,735	10.51
1990	12	161,991	13,499	819,631	11.38
1995	9	83,810	9,812	492,346	10.16
1997	5	unk.	unk.	357,000	unk.

* Note: Tons per harvested acre is about twice the tons per cultivated acre because of the two-year Hawai'i sugar-crop cycle. Table 1 Sources: *All About Hawai'i*, 1948, 1974; Judd; HSPA, *Sugar Manual*, 1965, 1981, 1991; HSPA, *Annual Report*, 1995: HSPA, *Sugar in Hawai'i*, 1949; Kuykendall, 1953, 1967; Lind; Schmitt; Thrum, 1875-1939; *Honolulu Advertiser*, 1999.
Sources: *All About Hawai'i*, 1948, 1974; Judd; HSPA, Sugar Manual, 1965, 1981, 1991; HSPA, Annual Report, 1995; HSPA, Sugar in Hawai'i, 1949; Kuykendall, 1953, 1967; Lind; Schmitt; Thrum, 1875-1939; *Honolulu Advertiser*, 1999.

The plantation was the heart and soul of the Hawai'i sugar industry. These large enterprises were equipped with the most modern machinery, especially designed to minimize the costs of production. A private cane-haul road system replaced the private railroad and/or flumes to haul harvests from the widespread thousands of acres to the factory. Specially designed mechanical harvesters replaced human cane-cutters. Fertilizers were spread in combination with efficient drip irrigation at scientifically determined times in scientifically determined compositions and amounts. Spreading involved using special high, wide tractors and, later, when the cane closed in, aircraft. The vast field operations were monitored by radio and telephone with nothing left to chance. The harvests were delivered to a computer-controlled factory by trucks or tournahaulers over a private road system. Pollution control devices purified the stack gases issued from the factory, and soil was recovered from water discharged to the ocean.

In 1980 producers began to take low-yielding fields out of production. Further reductions occurred as plantations on O'ahu, Kaua'i, and Maui sold land for urban growth. Considered by sugar industrialists to be a premature statement at the time, in 1985 the former chairman of Castle & Cooke (renamed Dole Food Co. in 1991) called sugar "a dying industry" and said, much to the disgust of many managers, that the sooner it was allowed to expire, the sooner real progress would be made to find alternatives.[16]

Most of Hawai'i's plantations started as independent enterprises and, when merged or shut down, were owned by, or controlled by, one or another of the sugar factors in Honolulu. By 1945 this handful of large agencies was known as the "Big Five"—Alexander & Baldwin (now A & B-Hawai'i, Inc.); American Factors, Ltd. (today's Amfac/JMB-Hawai'i, Inc.); C. Brewer & Company, Ltd.; Castle & Cooke, Ltd. (today's Dole Food Company); and Theo H. Davies & Co., Ltd. (acquired by Jardine Matheson & Co. in 1973, and no longer a sugar factor). They were joined by the smaller F.A. Schaefer & Co., Ltd., representing wholly owned Honokaa Sugar Company, and Bishop Trust Company, representing Gay & Robinson's plantation on Kaua'i.

These agencies acted as bankers for the plantations they represented. They advanced operating funds secured by future sugar sales and financed the plantations by buying shares of primary or secondary stock issues. Frequently, in lean times, plantation debt to the agency was discharged by an exchange of stock. As a consequence, when it came time to merge or shut a plantation down, an agency controlled or wholly owned the stock, and action was taken on the agency's authority.

Until 1893 the growth of the sugar industry in Hawai'i took place in a small kingdom on an isolated archipelago 2,300 miles from the mainland United States. The population was less than 150,000 until 1900, and interisland communication depended on slow-moving coastal shipping.[17] It wasn't until 1901 that a low-power radio-telegraph that was too weak for communicating to the mainland connected the islands to each other.[18] A cable to the mainland began operation in 1903.

The Hawai'i sugar industry endured for over 165 years. Its life span exceeded the telephone, telegraph, radio, TV, airplane, automobile, railroad, and the electronics and computer industries. The constant application of cost-saving developments enabled Hawai'i sugar producers to compete, while at the same time paying the highest wages in the world to agricultural workers, and absorbing the costs of shipping product to mainland refineries. The industry and the plantations that supported it were a modern industrial wonder. The stories of its people are woven into the history that follows.

(Hawai'i State Archives)

CHAPTER 2

SUGAR IN HAWAI'I BEFORE RECIPROCITY (1802-1875)

My great-great-grandfather, Dr. Gerrit P. Judd, came to O'ahu in 1828 with the third company of American missionaries. His business acumen caught the eye of King Kamehameha III, and in 1842 Doctor Judd became a leading court counselor. He renounced his U.S. citizenship, swore allegiance to the monarchy, and served as minister of finance, interior minister, and minister of foreign affairs.

During the Great Mahele (division of the land) of 1848-1850, King Kamehameha III reserved the ahupua'a (land division) of Kualoa for himself. He sold 635 acres to his loyal servant Doctor Judd, and it remains in my family to this day as Kualoa Ranch, Inc. Back in 1863, however, it was planted in sugarcane.

The Civil War, 1861-1865, boosted the price of sugar because the northern and western states and territories were cut off from cane growers in the South. Doctor Judd's son, Charles Hastings Judd, and his son-in-law, Samuel G. Wilder, established Kualoa as a sugarcane plantation in 1863. The equipment they installed was modern for those times, the very first steam-driven sugarmill on O'ahu, with belt-driven centrifugals.

The mill's foundation was dug by Native Hawaiians who had no prior experience at digging with a shovel. Used to the 'ō'ō, little more than a flat-ended, pointed stick, they struggled with the unaccustomed turning motion involved in casting a shovelful of dirt to one side. "Wili ka 'ā'ī," (turn the neck) implored their foremen. This refrain was repeated until they developed the smooth motions needed for digging with a shovel. The location of the mill's foundation was thereafter known as Wili Ka 'Ā'ī.

The workmen were excellent stonemasons and erected stout walls. They also built a chimney for the boilers, but the height of the scaffolding bothered them and they refused to lay more stone. At last Charles Judd and Sam Wilder had to complete the upper half of the chimney with brickwork. It survives to this day along Kamehameha Highway.

In the primitive sugar-making process, animals and sometimes waterwheels powered the grinders. The resulting juices were boiled in a cascade of large iron pans or basins. Vacuum boiling (which occurs at a lower temperature, minimizing the chance of burning the sugar) was unheard of. Liquid from the last basin passed into a trough pierced by holes that allowed the molasses to slowly drip out, and cool and settle over several weeks' time. Centrifugals later did this in a matter of minutes.

To conserve fuel, bagasse—the residue of the grinding process—was burned for the boiling process. Unfortunately, the grinders were inefficient and the squeezed cane stalks contained considerable moisture and would not burn until dried. So the bagasse was left to dry in a storage house. Unfortunately, many burned down from spontaneous combustion. Modern grinders squeeze almost all the sugar from the stalks and the bagasse is dry enough to burn immediately.

In the 1860s, barrel staves had to be imported and a cooper employed to assemble containers for transporting sugar. Shipping was often a perilous adventure without railroads or even roads of any size. Barrels of sugar usually had to be lightered from shore on rowboats, or hauled by overhead cable trolley to a ship anchored offshore. Further transport was also subject to changes in the weather. I have nothing but admiration for those old-timers who were able to make a go of it under such adverse circumstances. The problems they faced make some of my operating problems pale in comparison.

During the plantation's short life, Willie, Samuel Wilder's 10 year-old son, visited the mill. While crossing a narrow catwalk over the sugar vats, a workman approached from the opposite direction. The boy stepped aside to let him pass, lost his balance, and fell into a boiling vat. He was pulled out promptly, but his burns were extensive. His father rushed from his office in Honolulu at such speed that his horse died of exhaustion when they arrived on the other side of the island. Willie lingered for days and during one lucid moment was heard to ask, "Am I being a good little soldier?"

The boy's death had a dampening effect on the enthusiasm of the two entrepreneurs. The lands were also too dry, the sugar yield was poor, and prices dropped when the Civil War ended in 1865. After a terrible drought, the last cane was cut and ground on July 21, 1871. The lease was terminated and the lands given back to cattle ranching.

What Kualoa Plantation mainly lacked was irrigation water. Runoff from the Koʻolau mountain range has been collected since then for the cattle. Had this water been used for crop irrigation and supplemented with fertilizers, cane farming might have been profitable for decades longer.

A curious remnant of the Kualoa mill, and of earlier sugar grinding, is still visible. In the early 1970s, when the HSPA, now Hawaiʻi Agriculture Research Center, or HARC, moved to Aiea, an appropriate monument to the early days of sugar farming in Hawaiʻi was sought. That piece of history was discovered half-buried at the old Kualoa mill site.

The mill's centrifugals (whirling baskets that separate the lighter sugar from the heavier molasses, just as cream is separated from milk) had been mounted on two heavy, cylindrical stones. These crushers of an animal-powered grinder were fitted with wooden cogs and a superstructure to represent the mechanism that rotated them. Formerly this was done by oxen, mules, or horses tethered to a shaft.

Today the stones look surprisingly small, only a yard in diameter compared to modern centrifuges of six feet and more in width. Properly restored, the stones are accurate replicas of the kind of sugarmills that first appeared in Hawai'i, usually with Chinese operators.

Kualoa Plantation faced a typical problem of its time: how to efficiently haul harvests in from the fields. My great-grandfather used mule and oxen carts, but the slow pace was a severe handicap, and limited the distance from the mill at which crops could be planted. Cane, once cut, must be promptly ground or it ferments in transit or while piled in the mill yard. Animals required acreage for pasture and stables, and a veterinarian or skilled trainer; all costly additions. Kualoa Plantation shut down 15 years before railroads became available. This was a revolutionary change because the fields serving the mill could be extended further, and plantations could be combined, thus allowing a mill to reap the benefits of economies of scale.

Labor was a continuing problem. In the mid-nineteenth century the Hawaiians were dying off, and it took years of experimentation before 1876 until a steady and reliable work force was developed by importing Chinese, Japanese, Portuguese, Korean, and Filipino workers. Hawai'i's plantation workers became the highest-paid agricultural employees in the world, a fact that contributed to the difficulty of staying competitive in the marketplace. The "labor problem" was met by using labor-saving machinery in the fields and by automating the factories.

⊕ ⊕ ⊕

MAKING SUGAR IN Hawai'i was a continual struggle before 1876. Machinery was primitive and growers had to be innovators to survive. Sugar shipped to the United States and other markets was subject to import tariffs. Selling prices oscillated with events beyond the growers' control. Despite all, the industry survived this era to enjoy well over a century of prosperity.

The years before 1850 were especially difficult because all land was owned by the Hawaiian Kingdom. The best a sugar manufacturer could do was win a rare lease, or rely on cane grown by natives. Finally, in 1846, King Kamehameha III (1813-1854) formed a land commission leading to the Great Mahele. Titles to the Kingdom's lands were apportioned among the royal family, the government, and the chiefs. An 1850 act broadened the Mahele to include land titles for commoners. The way was opened for foreigners to purchase land to cultivate sugarcane.

Up to this time producers came and went as the market for sugar fluctuated. With the settlement of California in the 1830s, this territory became a principal market for Hawai'i's sugar. The Gold Rush of 1849 created an especially strong, profitable demand. However, when California became a state in 1850, an import tariff was imposed, profits declined, and by 1857 the number of plantations in Hawai'i dwindled to five.[1]

The U.S. Civil War of 1861-1865 created a new strong market for a few years when the northern states were cut off from Louisiana-grown sugar. This demand didn't outlast the war. By 1872 the plantations in Hawai'i numbered 32, but at least seven had gone out of business in the previous decade.[2]

A list of Hawai'i sugar producers before 1875 depends on scattered journal entries and brief newspaper accounts. In 1867 Dr. Gerrit P. Judd toured the Islands to obtain data for sugar plantations. He published his own list, at the same time disclaiming "...all responsibility for any imperfections which may be found in the statistics or for the deductions that may be made from them."[3] An attempt to compile a list some 130 years later shares Judd's disclaimer.

Table 2 is limited to those plantations with mills that ceased operations before the Reciprocity Treaty of 1876. Plantations that started before 1876 and continued operations beyond that year are described in subsequent chapters.

TABLE 2 | SOME EARLY MILLS AND PLANTATIONS NO LONGER OPERATING BY 1876

ISLAND	PLANTATION/MILL	FIRST DATE*	LAST DATE*	LOCATION
Lāna'i	Unknown Chinese	1802	1803	Windward Lāna'i
O'ahu	"The King's Mill"	1811	1811	Honolulu
	Don Francisco Marin	1813	1819	Pearl Harbor
	Livinia	1823	1823	Honolulu
	Wilkinson (Boki)	1825	1826	Mānoa Valley
	Nu'uanu (Boki)	1828	1828	Nu'uanu Valley
	Kualoa (Judd/Wilder)	1863	1871	Kualoa
	L.&W. Chamberlain	1862	1874	Waialua
	Nu'uanu (Wood)	1863	1871	Nu'uanu Valley
	Halawa Plantation	1867	1872	Hālawa Valley
Kaua'i	Whitney & Ruggles	1820	1820	Waimea
	William French	1835	1838	Waimea
	Randall & Young	1839	1839	Hanalei
	Kaikioewa	1839	1840	Līhu'e
	Titcomb	1838	1862	Hanalei
	Waipa (Titcomb)	1862	1872	Near Kīlauea
Maui	Catalina	1823	1823	Wailuku
	Silva	1823	1828	Wailuku
	Hungtai (Atai)	1828	1841	Wailuku
	Malo (Hawaiians)	1837	1850	Lahaina
	Kamehameha III (Apung)	1839	1844	Wailuku
	Ahpong	1843	1843	Lahaina
	'Ulupalakua (Torbert)	1846	1856	'Ulupalakua
	Parsons	1848	1849	Lahaina
	Miner & McLane (Gower)	1838	1850s	Makawao
	Hali'imaile (Reynolds)	1841	1856	Hāli'imaile

SUGAR IN HAWAI'I BEFORE RECIPROCITY

FIRST ISLAND	LAST PLANTATION/MILL	DATE*	DATE*	LOCATION
Maui, cont.	Howe (Judd)	1852	1854	Hāna
	Hali'imaile (Brewer)	1857	1863	Hāli'imaile
	Lahaina Company	1859	1867	Lahaina
	Bailey & Son	1867	1869	Wailuku
Hawai'i	Goodrich	1829	1836	Hilo
	Lihue (Aiko+others)	1835	1843	Waimea
	Ponahawai (Chinese)	1839	1855	Hilo
	Kuakini (Aiko)	1839	1850	N. Kohala
	'Amauulu (Aiko)	1840	1867	Hilo
	Pu'u'eo (Akina)	1840	1851	Hilo
	Ahpong	1843	1843	Waimea
	Ahpong	1843	1843	N. Kohala
	Pi'ihonua (Aina)	1843	1843	Hilo
	Makahanaloa (Asing)	1847	1847	Papa'ikou
	Paukaa (Akau)	1857	1864	N. Hilo
	Utai & Company	1857	1857	Hilo
	Samsing & Company	1856	1859	Hilo
	Kaiwiki	1857	1872	O'okala
	Metcalf Plantation	1858	1862	Hilo
	Kona Plantation	1867	1872	Kona

* Note: "First Date" and "Last Date" are first and last dates given in a source. Mills and/or plantations may have operated before the First Date and after the Last Date, but names were absent from all post-1877 listings.

Sources: Baldwin, 1928; Cushing; Char; Damon, Vol. 1, 1931; Dye; The Friend, 1862; Jarves, 1872; Judd, 1867; Kai; Kelly, Nakamura, and Barrere; Kuykendall, 1938; Maclennan; Nellist, 1925; Silva; Simpich; Smith; Sterling, Summers; Thrum, 1875; Wilfong, 1882.

THE FIRST SUGAR MADE IN HAWAI'I

The Royal Hawaiian Agricultural Society was organized in August of 1850. This came in response to the king's call for a meeting of all farmers, planters, grazers, and other persons interested in the formation of a society for the promotion of Hawaiian agriculture.[4] Annual meetings were held for a number of years at which papers were read and discussions held. Seven years of transactions were published (1850-1856), covering the vital era of this society.

Linton L. Torbert (1816-1871), Pennsylvania-born, had immigrated to the Islands and, by 1851, was established as a sugar planter on Maui. He read a paper before the society's meeting in January 1852, giving the date and location of the earliest manufacture of sugar in Hawai'i. In 1851 Torbert was managing his plantation at 'Ulupalakua, Maui, and his aged father-in-law, John White (1767?-1857), lived on the estate. White had come to the Islands in 1797, settled in Lahaina, Maui, and became a landowner after the Mahele.

Barely eight miles across the 'Au'au channel from Lahaina is the island of Lāna'i. As Torbert reported, White said a Chinese sugarmaker had arrived on Lānaʻi in 1802, set up his stone mill and boiling pots, ground a crop of cane, and returned to China the following year.[5]

Trading in Hawaiʻi-grown sandalwood began about the turn of the nineteenth century, and it is likely that an itinerant Chinese sugar master, of which there were many in China at the time, saw an opportunity in tales he heard about plentiful sugarcane growing on the "sandalwood mountain." Lānaʻi was an unfortunate location, however. The rainfall is insufficient to support a rich growth of sugarcane, as subsequent events have amply demonstrated. Nevertheless, an unknown Chinese sugar master can lay claim to having been the first to make sugar in Hawaiʻi.

DON FRANCISCO DE PAULA MARIN'S CONTRIBUTIONS

The settlement of Honolulu was enlivened in 1793, when Don Francisco De Paula Marin (1774-1837) arrived. A deserter from the Spanish navy, Marin was determined to make a new start. During the rest of his life in Hawaiʻi he had at least three wives and fathered at least 23 children.[6] Working his way into the confidence of King Kamehameha I (1758?-1819), he lived on to enjoy the affection of King Kamehameha III, as well. Aside from his vigorous matrimonial attentions and wise counsel, Marin found time to farm and build a substantial ship supply business.

Marin kept a journal from 1809 through August 1826 with details on his many agricultural projects. He had a substantial vineyard, coffee plants, and gardens of imported exotica. For a time he occupied Ford Island and used it to raise livestock for his ship supply business. Journal entries in 1813, 1817, and 1819 refer to his making molasses or sugar. The entry of March 7, 1819 states, "This day I was grinding cane and I made 45 gallons."[7] Clearly, Marin was an early Hawaiʻi sugar manufacturer. From his journal it can be assumed that his cane grew in an area near Pearl Harbor, perhaps on Ford Island itself. If so, he anticipated the Oahu Sugar Company by some 98 years.

Marin left us more than his journal and numerous descendants. He had the reputation with Native Hawaiians for being a skinflint, because his Western concept of ownership did not include sharing with the community. The Hawaiian version of his name was "Manini," a common small fish, but also a common insult meaning "stingy."

MANOA VALLEY PLANTATION

High Chief Boki (died 1830?), Governor of Oʻahu, travelled to England in 1824 with King Kamehameha II (1796-1824) and Queen Kamamalu (1802-1824) and their retinue. While the royal couple unfortunately died in London from measles, the visit resulted in one of the first organized efforts to grow cane and manufacture sugar and molasses in Hawaiʻi. Boki made the acquaintance of a consumptive English agriculturalist, John Wilkinson (died 1826), who agreed to cultivate cane

A primitive sugarmill of the kind employed by early sugar-makers. Traces attached to a mule, horse, or ox supplied power. Displayed here at the entrance to the Hawaii Agriculture Research Center headquarters, ʻAiea, Oʻahu. (W. H. Dorrance)

and make sugar in the Islands.[8] Wilkinson had experience as a sugar planter in the West Indies.

Back in Hawaiʻi with Boki as his sponsor, Wilkinson laid out a plantation in Mānoa Valley on Oʻahu in 1825. He began cultivation with native labor supplied by the governor and supervised by High Chief Mataio Kekuanaoʻa (1794-1868).[9]

A mill was erected and the feverish Wilkinson made ready to grind the first crop in 1826. But the work had weakened him and he died in September of the same year. Shortly before this setback, Governor Boki had reassigned Kekuanaoʻa to oversee the king's guards, so the enterprise now lacked leadership.[10]

Boki then enlisted the aid of prominent local businessmen, including Stephen Reynolds (1782-1857) and William French (1765-1861). They succeeded in grinding a crop by 1829. Their plans included using the mill's product for the highly profitable manufacture of rum. But the Queen Regent Kaʻahumanu (1768?-1832) got word of this, and ordered the cane fields destroyed, thus permanently frustrating the enterprise. Much to his disgust, French lost $7,000 that he had invested in the distillery.[11]

HUNGTAI PLANTATION

By 1828 Honolulu was an established reprovisioning port for east- and west-bound merchants in the sandalwood, fur, and spice trades. Both Hawaiians and Chinese were among passengers and crews. Sometime before 1828 two Chinese, Ahung (died 1845) and Atai (died 1841), arrived in Honolulu, joined forces and established a retail store, the Hungtai Company. They sold locally grown commodities and goods from China. Sugar was in great demand, so Atai went to Wailuku on Maui to start a sugar-making operation in the firm's name.[12]

An Italian by the name of Catalina, and a Portuguese named Silva, about whom nothing more is known, had made sugar in Wailuku between 1823 and 1828, so the area was promising.[13] In 1828 Atai set up his mill and ground cane grown by Hawaiians. The enterprise thrived and, as late as May 1841, this advertisement ran in the Honolulu paper:

HUNGTAI

Have for sale, at their plantation, at Wailuku, East side of Maui, a quantity of superior WHITE SUGAR, not inferior to the best imported Loaf Sugar. Also WHITE* SYRUP, a superior article for family use. For the information of merchants...they are enlarging their business, having now 150 acres of Sugar Cane under cultivation, and...will have 250 acres.[14]

*Note: The emphasis on "white" indicates using a sugar-making process that included clarification.

But Atai, ill and suffering financial reverses, took his life in 1841, and little is known about the fate of his business. Two years earlier his brother, Apung, had also gone into the sugar-making business in the same vicinity. That enterprise, which Apung entered on a share basis, was established by King Kamehameha III.[15] Despite this advantage, the venture was short-lived, possibly because in 1842 Apung committed suicide, as well.

GOODRICH'S HILO SUGARMILL

About the same time, sugar-making began on the island of Hawai'i. Hilo enjoys heavy rainfall (170 inches per year) and cane grows abundantly. Joseph Goodrich (1794-1852) and his wife had arrived in Hawai'i in 1823 with the second company of missionaries. After he was ordained at Kailua-Kona in 1826, the Goodriches were sent to Hilo to establish a missionary station.[16] He was an accomplished farmer, soon constructed a sugarmill and, by 1829, was grinding cane to make sugar for the mission. He became so successful that when the church recalled him in 1836, he was offered the manager's position of Koloa Plantation on Kaua'i. He accepted it, then the church made clear that such secular employment would conflict with his religious duties, and the Goodriches returned to the United States.[17]

WILLIAM FRENCH'S KAUA'I MILL

All of these early entrepreneurs—Marin, Atai, Ahung, Reynolds, French—were contemporaries, and had many interactions. William French arrived originally in 1819, and, after an interlude in the Orient between 1820 and 1825, he returned to Honolulu as a businessman. One venture was making sugar at Waimea, Kaua'i.

In 1835 French and Atai sent a sugarmill and several Chinese men to Waimea to "make sugar on shares" (splitting the proceeds between the grower and the miller). This was successful, using harvests of native-grown cane. French and Atai were emboldened to import four sugar masters and a second mill from Canton, China. While their success on Kaua'i continued, they were unable to buy land. This shortcoming forced the mills to shut down in 1838. The apparatus was returned to O'ahu and its disposition is unknown.[18]

GOVERNOR KUAKINI'S BIG ISLAND PLANTATIONS

One of the four Chinese sugar masters brought to Hawai'i by French and Atai was Aiko (1799-1895). When the mill at Waimea, Kaua'i shut down, he went to the island of Hawai'i. In 1837 Aiko settled in South Kohala on land that Governor Kuakini (1791-1844) had planted in cane. He erected and operated a mill on shares with Kuakini until 1843, when he moved to North Kohala to run Kuakini's plantation located there.[19]

Aiko had supervised both these operations since 1839. During this time, Governor Kuakini, with Chinese help, started another mill in Hilo on Ponahawai Hill. A year later, in 1844, Aiko moved there with his family.[20] Then after the Mahele (land division) that began in 1848, he acquired considerable property of his own. In 1849 Aiko went back to the North Kohala plantation, closed it down in 1850, and returned to Hilo. For the next two decades, until 1869, he lived there and devoted his time to helping several other Chinese run the mill and plantation at 'Amauulu.[21]

An eyewitness of its operation is worth quoting. As a boy in 1864, Rev. John M. Lydgate (1854-1922) moved to Hilo with his parents. In his reminiscences he described visiting the mill at 'Amauulu at the age of 10 (condensed here):

> It was a very primitive affair. The crusher was water driven, by means of a large overshot water-wheel. The rollers were iron about fifteen inches in diameter, by perhaps two and a half feet long. There was no provision for reversing.
>
> From the mill a scanty stream of juice ran in an open spout to the boiling house. Here was installed the open train, a series of four or five pots, five or six feet in diameter, diminishing in size to the final one. They were coupled, lip to lip, the whole forming a range, under [which] a fierce fire was kept going. The liveliest job on the plantation was that of the stoker who was always being stirred up, in language sometimes profane. A Hawaiian attendant, nearly nude and sweating like a Turk, stood by to sweep off the scum. The vision through the open doorway into the dim interior with the dusky naked figures silhouetted against the great volumes of steam, would have been worthy of a modern Rembrandt.
>
> As the density was increased by evaporation, in the last pot it was boiled to the density necessary for graining. When [the time for a strike] was reached, the mass in the last pot was bailed out [and] conveyed to the coolers, where it was allowed to remain for weeks leaving a lake of molasses over grained sugar below. The grained mass was shovelled into tubs and slid to the centrifugals. The sugar resulting was packed in kegs and shipped to Honolulu by schooner.[22]

Whaler's trypot. This iron basin was used by whalers to boil the oil out of whale blubber and was used by Hawaiian sugar-makers to boil off water and impurities from the syrup. This rare artifact is at the Kauai Museum in Lihue, Kaua'i.
(W. H. Dorrance)

AHPONG'S PLANTATIONS

For a few months in 1843, the flag of the British Empire flew over Hawai'i when Lord George Paulet (1790-1864) of the Royal Navy seized control of the government in an unauthorized adventure.[23] During this time, all foreigners were requested to register their claims to property. The Chinese immigrant Ahpong, a principal in Samsing & Company, registered sugarcane acreage in Waimea and Kohala, on the island of Hawai'i, and a sugarmill in Lahaina, Maui.[24] In that era of time-consuming and uncertain travel by interisland schooner, Ahpong was often absent—tending to business—and carefully gave power of attorney to a company colleague while gone.[25] This emphasizes the fact that before 1850, the Chinese were a force in sugar manufacturing in Hawai'i.

MALO'S CANE, AND JUDGE PARSONS' AND GOWER'S MAKAWAO MILL

George W. Wilfong, mentioned earlier, took his discharge as an officer of a whaling ship at Lahaina, Maui, in October 1849.[26] He rented a room from Judge Alfred W. Parsons, then residing in the David Malo house. Parsons operated a sugarmill that ground cane grown nearby. In the same year, John L. Gower visited Lahaina, purchased Parsons' mill, and, with Wilfong's help, took it back to Makawao.[27]

David Malo (1793?-1853) was an educated Hawaiian raised in the household of high chief Kuakini, brother of the Queen Regent Ka'ahumanu. Malo had grown sugarcane on the land harvested by Judge Parsons for 10 years beginning in 1840.[28] Wilfong had a longer involvement with sugar-making, and more will be heard about him later.

HALI'IMAILE PLANTATION/BREWER PLANTATION

When Linton L. Torbert read his paper before the Royal Hawaiian Agricultural Society in 1852, he was managing his plantation at 'Ulupalakua,

Maui. Several years later events overwhelmed him, and his plantation was sold in 1856. Torbert then took over management of Haliimaile Plantation in East Maui, formerly a Stephen Reynolds enterprise from 1849 to 1856.

C. Brewer & Company's interests in Maui-grown sugarcane started in 1856, when Charles Brewer, 2d (1823-1863) and Capt. James Makee (1812-1879) bought Haliimaile Plantation from the Reynolds estate for $14,000. It had a mule-powered mill, and from 1856 to 1858 was managed by Torbert, and known as the "Brewer Plantation." In 1859 Brewer became sole owner of the operation, which by then had an annual production of about 200 tons of sugar.[29] He died in 1863, and his estate sold the plantation to Charles H. Judd (1835-1890) and Samuel G. Wilder (1831-1888).[30]

STEPHEN REYNOLDS

Another early settler in the Islands, Stephen Reynolds came in 1811. It was he who referred to "the king's mill" he saw on arriving. After working in Honolulu as a clerk for William French from 1823 to 1829, Reynolds established his own store a block away. The two men became friendly competitors. Atai's store, Hungtai Company, did business directly across Merchant Street from French. A little later Samsing & Company was established, also only a block away.[31] All of these stores were located in the section of Honolulu now known as Chinatown.

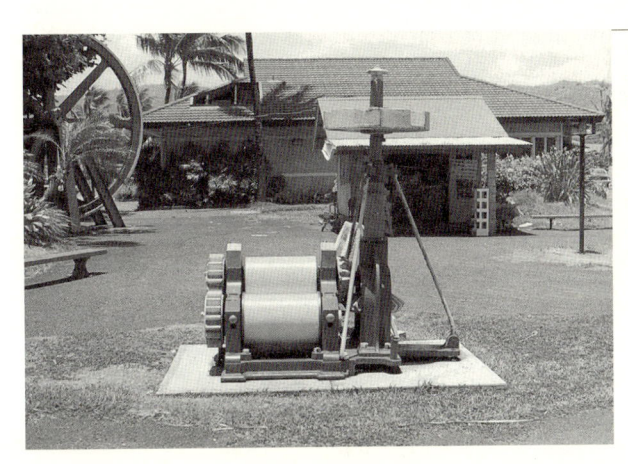

An early animal-powered sugar mill made by the Honolulu Iron Works for Puakea Ranch, Kohola, Island of Hawai'i (Hind, p. 91). This rare artifact is exhibited in the Kahuku plantation mill yard.
(W. H. Dorrance)

It was a small world before 1850.

Stephen Reynolds from Boxford, Massachusetts, was a remarkably versatile man. Another early settler recorded that, when the vessel bringing him to Honolulu approached the harbor mouth in 1841, Reynolds came out in a whale boat rowed by Native Hawaiians, climbed aboard the ship, and piloted it safely through the narrows and into the harbor. This same observer reported that, in the absence of a resident attorney, Reynolds represented defendants in the courts. One such case resulted in the manslaughter conviction of his client, Linton L. Torbert, who had shot and killed a Maui man. Apparently there was provocation and Torbert got off with payment of a $200 fine under existing law.[32]

The same observer went on to describe Reynolds' appearance and his store:

> He was very peculiar in his dress as well as his thinking. His clothes were cut in his own fashion, generally what we know as the jacket and trousers and made of light colored nankeen. His shirt was always of unbleached cotton cloth, destitute of any linen bosom, buttoned in front at the throat with a wide turned over collar, white stockings and low shoes, and a Panama hat destitute of any ribbon completed his costume....The simplicity of the costume was somewhat characteristic of the man. A visitor to his store went up a half dozen well worn planks to the somewhat rickety veranda and entering within found a most miscellaneous assortment of dry goods and notions in what would be to him an indescribable confusion, yet the kindly gentleman, past middle life, with a very pleasant manner to his native customers, found no difficulty in meeting their wishes, and enjoyed a large share of their confidence.[33]

This interesting man's stay in Hawai'i came to an end in 1855, when he fell ill and returned to his home in Massachusetts to live out his life.[34]

NUUANU VALLEY PLANTATION

Massachusetts-born John W. Wood (1816-1892) came to Honolulu as a passenger on the brig *Henry* in 1846. His finances were secure, and he erected the first brick building in the city, and established a successful mercantile business. In 1863 he operated a sugar plantation on his land in Nu'uanu Valley, one of the first on the Honolulu side of the Ko'olau mountain range.[38]

By 1871 sugar prices had fallen and the venture was unprofitable, so Wood closed his mill and converted his acreage into a stock and dairy farm. He had two married daughters, one of whom, Florence Wood Jones, became the lifelong friend and confidant of the dowager Queen Emma (1836-1885), widow of King Kamehameha IV (Alexander Liholiho, 1834-1863).[39]

THE BEGINNING OF IMPORTED LABOR

Contract laborers first came to the Islands in 1852, when about 300 single men arrived from South China in two shiploads.[35] While their help was welcome, they created new problems for many planters: feeding, housing, and otherwise caring for new employees. Prior to imported labor, Native Hawaiians supplied the muscle for day-to-day work in the cane fields and mills. Many lived off the plantation in settlements of their own, and required little in the way of support when not working.

The plantations now had to face the implications of relying on imported labor. A situation of mutual dependency existed and, in the ensuing years, this led to the concept of the plantation community.

After mid-century, the animal-driven sugarmill became a thing of the past. There were rivers and streams to tap, and mills in the West Indies and New England had demonstrated how water power could be harnessed. According to Doctor Judd's 1867 report from Kualoa Plantation, 18 of 29 mills in the Islands were wholly or partially driven by water power. Only two still used animals for grinding, and 13 were wholly or partially driven by steam.[37]

This single set of statistics suggests that by 1867, the Hawai'i sugar industry was in the midst of an industrial revolution. For almost seven decades, a group of hardy entrepreneurs had showed the way for numerous ventures that followed. They did not survive to enjoy the benefits of the 1876 Reciprocity Treaty with the United States. Their sugar sold for six cents a pound on the mainland, and they paid an import tax of two cents per pound. Thus, when the treaty was signed, Hawai'i's producers gained an immediate 50-percent increase in sales proceeds, netting the full six cents instead of four. This overnight increase encouraged a growth in the industry.

During these early years Hawai'i was ruled by a monarchy, a small kingdom sparsely populated with Native Hawaiians, and a tiny minority of immigrant missionaries, merchants, court officials, stranded sailors, and adventurers. From this handful of foreigners came the entrepreneurs who, against unfavorable odds, established Hawai'i as a major sugar producer. By the time that the 1876 Reciprocity Treaty was ratified, allowing duty-free importation of sugar into the United States, precedents had been set, lessons learned, labor was imported, several plantations were poised to thrive, and over 120 years of prosperity followed.

Kilauea Mill, Kaua'i,
Hawai'i, 1887.
(Hedemann Collection/Bishop Museum)

CHAPTER 3

SUGAR ON KAUA'I (1876-2000)

My grandfather, Francis M. Swanzy, first got involved in sugar farming on Kaua'i as managing director of Theo H. Davies & Co. After Hawai'i's annexation by the United States in 1898, sugar farmers no longer faced the threat of import tariffs. Benjamin F. Dillingham, the O'ahu railroad builder, and other business leaders of the time saw annexation as an opportunity for starting up new, profitable plantations. One of his promotions was the McBryde Sugar Company on southwest Kaua'i.

This venture was incorporated in 1899 with an initial investment of about $1.8 million. In those days crops were harvested after a year of growth, and in the meantime money was spent to build a mill, cultivate the crop, and install a railroad to haul harvests to the mill. For the first year, it was all money going out and none coming in.

Theo H. Davies & Co. agreed to serve as the new plantation's agent, and purchased some of the stock issue. My grandfather was a careful executive but McBryde plantation proved to be a thorn in his side.

In its first nine years of operation, Kaua'i suffered two droughts that stunted harvests. Runoff water was insufficient for irrigation, so deep wells were dug, and coal-fired pumps installed to bring water to the surface. Expenses mounted, the plantation couldn't pay, and Theo H. Davies & Co. made sizable loans to McBryde. The plantation incurred further large expenses in constructing a system to transport hydroelectric power across the Wai'ale'ale mountains for new electric well pumps.

By this time, McBryde Sugar owed Theo H. Davies & Co. almost $2 million, an enormous sum for that era. Finally Davies sold the agency contract to Alexander & Baldwin and regained stability, but it was a painful experience for my grandfather.

One lesson learned was that creating a sugar plantation involved a leap of faith and considerable investment before the first returns came in after one or two years of cane growth. Once Hawai'i plantations shut down, they were unlikely to be started up again.

During my time I developed a healthy respect for managers of the C. Brewer plantations throughout the Islands. Many started out managing the company's

Kilauea Sugar Company plantation on the east coast of Kaua'i, a very difficult job. Kīlauea is gulch-ridden, dry, and shipment of product was complicated by the distance from the nearest harbor. If a manager could make it at Kīlauea, he was a good candidate for promotion to one of Brewer's larger plantations.

Hawai'i sugar farmers owe much to the drip irrigation system developed at C. Brewer's Olokele plantation on Kaua'i. This very economical method delivered the proper amount of water to the proper places at the proper times during cane growth. Expenses were considerably reduced and fertilizer could be introduced at the distribution head for additional savings. It proved to be a tremendous advance.

In 1994, C. Brewer & Company sold its profitable Olokele plantation and mill to landowners Gay & Robinson. The lease was to expire within a year or so, and required upgrading the mill, a considerable expense. While the operation was successful, C. Brewer did not feel the future of sugar in Hawai'i was bright enough to justify spending large sums. Therefore, the mill and planation equipment were sold to the families who owned most of the land.

Gay & Robinson had been farming sugar on adjacent land since the beginning, with the Olokele mill processing their cane. They know sugar farming and do a good job of it.

⊕ ⊕ ⊕

KAUA'I'S SUGAR PRODUCERS

Located 98 miles northwest of Honolulu, Kaua'i is the oldest, wettest, and greenest of the Hawaiian sugar islands. The Wai'ale'ale mountain range at its center rises to 5,080 feet, where the annual rainfall averages almost 500 inches. The runoff is the source of the island's plentiful hydroelectric power and irrigation water. This small island of 547 square miles is home to three of Hawai'i's four remaining sugar plantations.

The 31 plantations that existed on Kaua'i after 1876 are shown in Figure 1. Their years of production are given in Table 3. During the 1990 harvest, the five remaining Kaua'i plantations were collectively responsible for 24.4 percent, or 200,356 tons, of the 819,631 tons of sugar produced in Hawai'i.[1]

Location of sugar plantations on Kaua'i after 1876. See Table 3 for identification of plantations.
(NOT TO SCALE)

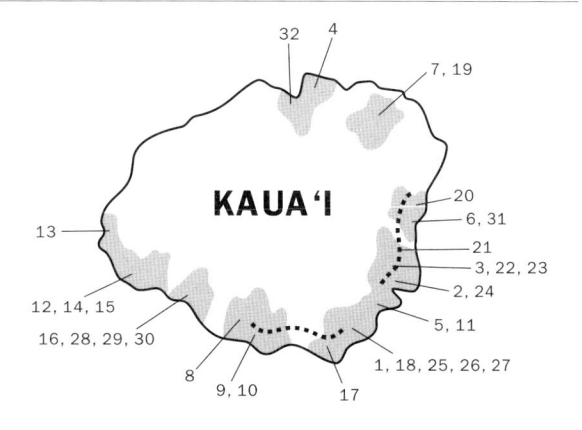

TABLE 3 | SUGAR PLANTATIONS ON KAUAʻI 1876-1996

NO.	NAME	FIRST DATE*	LAST DATE*	OR OPERATING IN 1996 AS
1.	Koloa Sugar Company	1835	1948	
2.	Lihue Plantation Company	1849		Amfac Sugar/East
3.	Hanamaulu Plantation (A. Wilcox)	1870	1898	
4.	Princeville Plantation Company	1862	1894	
5.	Grove Farm Plantation	1864	1974	See Note (1)
6.	Makee Sugar Company	1877	1933	
7.	Kilauea Sugar Company	1877	1971	
8.	Gay & Robinson	1885		Gay & Robinson
9.	Hawaiian Sugar Company	1889	1941	
10.	Olokele Sugar Company	1942	1994	See Note (2)
11.	V. Knudsen & Estate	1894	1927	
12.	Meier & Kruse	1886	1898	
13.	H. P. Faye & Company	1886	1898	
14.	Kekaha Mill Company	1880	1898	
15.	Kekaha Sugar Company	1898		Amfac Sugar/West
16.	Waimea Sugar Mill Company	1884	1969	See Note (3)
17.	Eleele Plantation	1880	1898	
18.	McBryde Sugar Company	1899	1996	
	Numbers 19 through 32 are not described in the text			
19.	Grant & Brigstock	1882	1884	
20.	Kealia Plantation	1879	1885	
21.	Wailua Plantation	1879	1880	
22.	Hanamaulu Mill Company	1870	1880	
23.	Ch. L. L'Orange	1882	1888	
24.	Kipu Plantation	1907	1942	
25.	Koloa Ranch	1882	1886	
26.	Koluahonu Company	1883	1888	
27.	Smiths: Jared K. Smith	1870	1880	
	A. H. Smith & Company	1880	1886	
	J. K. Smith & Company	1886	1898	
	Koloa Agricultural Company	1898	1900	
28.	Fr. Bindt	1882	1884	
29.	C. Borchgrevink	1885	1887	
30.	Faye & Meier	1886	1886	
31.	Hui Kawaihai	1877	1881	
32.	Hanalei Sugar Mill Company	1889	1893	

*Notes: "First Date" and "Last Date" are the first and last years, respectively, that a plantation is listed in a source. The dates are believed to be within two years of the years of organization or shutdown, respectively.
    (1) In 1974 Grove Farm Plantation's sugarcane lands were leased in two parcels—one to Lihue Plantation Company, the other, including the mill, to McBryde Sugar Company.
    (2) Mill and equipment were sold to Gay & Robinson in 1994.
    (3) In 1969 Waimea Sugar Mill Company's sugarcane lands were leased to Kekaha Sugar Company.
Sources: Alexander; L. A. Faye; Listing 1878-1940, *Hawaiian Almanac and Annual*; *Historic Hawaiʻi*, March 1990; listing, dates of charter, *The Planters' Monthly*, Aug. 1882; Damon, Vol. 1, 1931; listing 1895-1945, HSPA Annual Meeting, Dec. 10, 1945; Wilcox; citations 1945-date, corporation annual reports and newspapers.

The post-1876 history of sugar starts on Kaua'i because the first plantation, Koloa Sugar Company, number 1 on the map, was located here. It was eventually merged into McBryde Sugar Company, and shut down in 1996, ending 161 years of continuous sugarcane cultivation on the island.

Kaua'i was the last island to be incorporated into the Hawaiian kingdom by King Kamehameha I. In 1795 he had completed a series of conquests with O'ahu, and assembled a fleet of war canoes with the intention of invading Kaua'i. The weather in the stormy channel separating it from O'ahu continually thwarted his expeditions.

Finally, in 1810 American Capt. Nathan Winship (1778-1820), having a stake in establishing a peaceful kingdom with which to trade, persuaded Kaua'i's King Kaumuali'i (1780?-1824) to go to O'ahu to make peace with Kamehameha. This was arranged, and Kaumuali'i, overwhelmed by the sight of Kamehameha's fleet, capitulated and agreed to be his subject. But only after Kaumuali'i's death was his island to become an integral part of the Kingdom of Hawai'i.[2]

Perhaps because of this background, an admirable spirit of independence prevailed in the operation of Kaua'i's plantations. The more significant and/or long-lasting plantations are described in the order listed on Table 3.

KOLOA SUGAR COMPANY (1)

William Hooper (1809-1878), accompanied by Peter Allen Brinsmade (1804-1859) and William Ladd (1807-unk.), arrived in Honolulu from England on the *Hellespont* in July 1833. Two years later the young men established a mercantile business in Honolulu, naming it Ladd & Company. They obtained a rare 50-year lease from King Kamehameha III on 980 acres of rich land on Kaua'i, intending to create a sugar plantation employing Native Hawaiians. Hooper, lacking any experience in farming, moved to Kaua'i to manage the start-up of the plantation. It was to be a turbulent time.

Hooper's initial efforts to hire natives were met with fierce resistance by local chiefs. They were not about to allow a young foreigner to weaken their hold over local commoners, the king's lease-grant notwithstanding. But by the end of the year Hooper had made peace with the chiefs, hired natives, obtained tools, built a rudimentary mill and thatched huts for his workers, and planted a nursery of indigenous cane. Koloa Plantation then began 113 years of almost continuous operation.

Despite his remarkable accomplishments, Hooper knew he was in over his head. He pleaded with his partners to hire Reverend Goodrich of Hilo, or some other man with sugar farming expertise. Goodrich being unavailable, the qualified manager James Burnham replaced Hooper in 1839.[3]

The chief characteristic of Koloa Plantation that deserves attention here is its longevity. The full history of the plantation is recorded elsewhere, and this chapter will offer few incidents to illustrate early plantation management.[4]

Financial trouble developed quickly. Less than 300 tons of sugar were produced annually, and soon the plantation was hopelessly in debt to the government and private investors. In 1847, Dr. Robert W. Wood (died 1892) discharged the debt to the Kingdom and took over the plantation. He was the first investor to make profits from Hawaiian sugar. A Honolulu medical man, Wood had a good understanding of what was needed to run a successful business in Hawai'i. He offered a one-half ownership of his plantation enterprises to his managers to ensure their commitment. This had worked with his East Maui plantation, where Ambrose H. Spencer was partner and manager, and Wood was confident of finding the right man for Koloa.[5]

Nevertheless, manager-owner candidates were hard to find. In 1848 feisty young Gorham D. Gilman (1821-1909) managed Koloa for several months. Some hint of his nature is revealed by an incident that occurred during a visit from Dr. Gerrit Judd. Apparently Judd, several chiefs, and Kōloa neighbor and independent planter Lt. Van R. Morgan, U.S. Navy (ret.), took over the manager's house as guests. One evening, while Gilman and Morgan were on the veranda, Morgan took exception to a remark by Gilman and a vigorous fight broke out. Judd, hearing the scuffle and thinking the manager was "killing rats," rushed out to observe the fun. Judd broke up the fight and restored an uneasy peace. Gilman departed in September, leaving Doctor Wood with some pithy suggestions about what he could do with a job that paid $550 a year.[6]

In 1848 when Doctor Wood purchased the inter-island schooner *Chance* from Linton L. Torbert, it was yet another example of close-knit cooperation

Memorial to sugar workers erected on the site of the old sugarmill in Kōloa town. All ethnic groups that worked on Hawai'i's plantations from the beginning are represented.
(W. H. Dorrance)

among the early planters. The *Chance* had been built a year earlier at Lahaina, Maui to service Torbert's plantation.[7] By 1848 his plantation was strapped for funds and Wood's purchase helped to ease Torbert's financial pressures.

Wood continued his search for a manager-partner. In March 1868 he encountered George W. Wilfong in the Boston office of C. Brewer & Company. (One marvels at how these early sugar pioneers got around.) Wilfong had completed a tour as manager of Kohala Sugar Plantation in 1866, and gone to the mainland to sell holdings in cattle and sheep in Vermont, and to study sugar beet manufacturing in Illinois. Doctor Wood offered him one-half ownership of Koloa Plantation if he would manage it. The deal was set to be closed in Honolulu. Wilfong returned to the Islands first and, when Wood failed to appear, the anxious Wilfong contracted to manage Wailuku Sugar Plantation on Maui. Thus Wood lost his chance to obtain an experienced manager-partner.[8]

In 1872 Doctor Wood sold Koloa to the manager of neighboring Lihue Plantation, Paul Isenberg (1837-1903), and two partners. These three new owners incorporated as Koloa Sugar Company in 1878, which lasted until 1948, when it merged into Grove Farm Plantation.[9] After 1881, millions in dividends were paid to the owners of Koloa Sugar Company, and by 1925 annual production exceeded 10,000 tons of sugar.

LIHUE AND HANAMAULU PLANTATION COMPANIES (2 & 3)

The longevity of Koloa Plantation has been eclipsed by still-operating Lihue Plantation Company, organized in 1849 by Henry A. Pierce (1808-1885) & Company. In 1850 Pierce returned to Boston, where he became a partner in the enterprise that was created, owned, and represented by C. Brewer & Company, Ltd. in Honolulu. Then, in 1854, he sold his interest in Lihue Plantation to partners, including manager William Harrison Rice (1813-1862). In 1869 Pierce moved back to the Islands as United States minister to Hawai'i, serving until 1878.[10] Since the Reciprocity Treaty of 1876 was ratified during his tenure, his appointment was clearly advantageous for Hawai'i's cane farmers.

William H. Rice had come to Hawai'i with the ninth company of American missionaries in 1841. He served out his contract in 1854 as a teacher at Punahou School in Honolulu, and took his family to Kaua'i to work as manager of Lihue Plantation until his death in 1862. The plantation thrived under his stewardship. The first irrigation ditch in Hawai'i was dug in 1857, and in 1859 the first steam engine in a Hawai'i mill was installed at Lihue Plantation.[11]

In the late 1850s Rice hired Paul Isenberg as overseer, and he became manager upon Rice's death. Isenberg also became a power in the Kingdom. He bought Koloa Plantation in 1872 and managed both plantations until he resigned in 1878. With partners, he organized Kekaha Mill Company in 1880, and in 1881 became a half-share partner in H. Hackfeld & Company, destined to become today's Amfac/JMB-Hawai'i, Inc.. Possessing enormous energy, he also represented Kaua'i in the legislature of King David Kalākaua (1836-1891).[12]

After 1878, Isenberg managed to spend several months a year at his family estate in Bremen, Germany, usually returning to Hawai'i in time to attend sessions of the legislature. Because of his efforts, and subsequent changes of ownership, Amfac/JMB-Hawai'i, Corporation still owns Lihue Plantation Company, currently called Amfac Sugar/East.

In 1870, during Isenberg's reign, Lihue Plantation Company purchased about 17,000 undeveloped acres in the neighboring Hanamā'ulu ahupua'a. These were set aside for growing cane and using the water runoff to irrigate both Lihue Plantation and Hanamā'ulu lands. This venture, Hanamaulu Plantation, was placed under the management of experienced planter and missionary son Albert Spencer Wilcox (1844-1919).[14]

In 1898 Hanamaulu Plantation was merged into Lihue Plantation, and Wilcox ran his own stock ranch in Līhu'e and served in the Kingdom's House of Representatives from 1891 to 1892. His father, Abner Wilcox (1808-1869), had arrived in Hawai'i in 1837 with the eighth company of American missionaries. Until 1844 he was stationed at Hilo, Hawai'i, where Albert Spencer was born. Transferred to O'ahu, Abner worked there until 1846 then went to Wai'oli, Kaua'i, where he served until his death.[15] His career again shows the influence of a strong missionary background in an early plantation enterprise.

In 1912 Lihue Plantation Company, following a pioneering advance made in 1907 by Kekaha Sugar Company, helped establish the use of hydroelectric power in Hawai'i. Two 240-kw generators were installed in a station above the cane fields on the slopes of Kilohana Crater.[16] Eventually enough power was produced to run all the mill machinery, irrigation pumps, and to illuminate every house and building on the plantation.

A second 500-kw station was added in 1931. Half a century later, by 1981 the total hydroelectric-generating capacity had increased to 1,300 kilowatts. An additional 20,000 units were generated by burning bagasse (the residue of ground cane). Sixty to 78 percent of this power was sold to the electric utility on Kaua'i. By 1987 Lihue Plantation supplied over 25 percent of the island's electricity.[17]

In 1923, Lihue Plantation's manager, R. D. Moler, and his chief engineer, Olaf R. Olsen, began building up the machine shop by installing heavy-duty lathes and metal working tools. Until this shop reached full strength in 1924, all of Kaua'i's mills were dependent on the Honolulu Iron Works on O'ahu for repairing mill machinery. Lihue Plantation intended to do this work on site.[18] The other Kaua'i cane farmers also wanted to minimize their dependence on Honolulu businesses.

PRINCEVILLE PLANTATION COMPANY (4)

Robert Crichton Wyllie (1798-1865), a Scottish bachelor, came to Hawai'i in 1844. His talent for business attracted attention and he served as minister of foreign affairs for Kings Kamehameha III, IV, and V.[19] In 1853 he purchased crown lands at Hanalei, Kaua'i. By 1862 Wyllie had added to his holdings, named the plantation "Princeville" in honor of the heir to the throne, Prince Albert Kauikeaouli (1858-1862), and planted sugarcane.[20]

A well-educated man, Wyllie had built up businesses in South America and made a fortune in London's financial world. He was a prolific letter writer and record keeper, and provided a valuable source of information on his era through dispatches to various foreign ministries. Wyllie found and translated Don Francisco De Paula Marin's journals, the original of which only partially survives.[22] Although multitalented and devoted to the beauty of Hanalei, producing sugar proved to be one of Wyllie's least successful ventures. Like other early entrepreneurs, he was eventually plagued by money problems.

Princeville Plantation changed hands many times after Wyllie's death and was shut down in 1894 by C. Brewer & Company.[21] The name of his former estate lives on at the world-famous golf resort and residential development in Princeville.

GROVE FARM PLANTATION (5)

George Norton Wilcox (1839-1933), son of missionary Abner Wilcox, had one of the longest and most successful careers in sugar production on Kaua'i. At the instigation of Samuel Wilder, Honolulu agent for the American Guano Company, the young Wilcox spent most of 1859 recovering guano on Jarvis Island, 1,300 miles south of Hawai'i. Guano was a rich, valuable fertilizer and it wasn't until the early 1880s that other plantations in Hawai'i recognized its usefulness. Wilcox followed that adventure with two years at Yale University, where he earned a certificate in civil engineering.[23] By then he was eager to put his training and experience to work on his beloved Kaua'i.

In 1864, G. N. Wilcox, as he came to be known, took over as manager of Grove Farm Plantation. A bachelor, he immersed himself in running and improving his operation, performing good works in the community, and participating in Hawai'i's politics. In 1890, harking back to his youthful Jarvis Island experience, he and several co-investors founded the Pacific Guano & Fertilizer Company to recover guano on Laysan Island, 700 miles northwest of Hawai'i. He enlarged the acreage of Grove Farm Plantation, served as a member of every legislative body from 1888 until 1898, and as prime minister of Queen Lili'uokalani's (1839-1917) cabinet in 1892.[24]

When Wilcox died in 1933, control of Grove Farm Plantation passed to his nieces and nephews. It ceased sugar operations in 1974, when its cane lands were leased in two parcels: 2,800 acres to Lihue Plantation, and 7,200 acres with mill (formerly the Koloa Plantation mill) to McBryde Sugar Company.

MAKEE SUGAR COMPANY (6)

One morning in 1843 the deranged cook of the whaler *Maine*, en route from Lahaina to Honolulu, attacked the ship's captain with a cleaver and inflicted serious injuries. Fortunately for Capt. James Makee (1812-1879), the H.M.S. *Carysfort* was at anchor in Honolulu harbor, and its surgeon and Dr. Robert Wood were able to save his life.[25] The episode was pivotal for Hawaiian sugar because Makee faced a long period of recovery in Hawai'i. Taken by the beauty of the surroundings and hospitality of the people, he sent for his wife and resolved to settle in the Islands.

After running a successful trading business in Honolulu, in 1856 Makee purchased Linton L. Torbert's moribund plantation and mill at 'Ulupalakua, Maui, intending to make the estate his home.[26] In 1858 he planted sugarcane and ordered a modern mill.

In 1876 Makee purchased Waihee Sugar Company on Maui in partnership with J.D. Spreckels, and in 1878 he bought Spreckels' share, becoming the sole owner. Then, in 1877, Captain Makee started his third plantation with King Kalākaua, the Makee Sugar Company, located near Kapa'a, Kaua'i.

Under the management of his son-in-law, Col. Z.S. Spalding (1837-1907), in 1855 the plantation's mill became the first in Hawai'i to improve productivity by operating at night.[27] Spalding was a benevolent and respected manager. In 1940, 23 years after his death, retired and active Japanese employees

Monument erected in 1930 in memory of former Makee Sugar Company manager and owner Col. Zephian Swift Spalding. The monument was erected by "his Kealia Japanese friends." (W.H. Dorrance)

erected a substantial monument on the plantation in his memory. This monument has survived, but today it stands in lonely neglect overlooking the former Makee cane fields inland from Kealia.

In 1933 the Makee Sugar Company plantation was merged into Lihue Plantation, which had a railroad system that made hauling widespread crops to the Līhu'e mill a cost-effective improvement.[28] The entire Makee mill was also moved to Līhu'e to increase its production capacity. Because of space limitations, the Makee mill had to be installed at an angle to the original one in Līhu'e, resulting in an unusual arrangement of the two buildings.

KILAUEA SUGAR COMPANY (7)

In 1877 the ranch lands at Kīlauea were purchased by Capt. James Ross (1838-1903) and E.P. Adams, and converted into a sugarcane plantation.[29] Located 26 miles from Līhu'e and never larger than 5,000 acres, Kilauea Sugar Company was among the smallest in the Islands. Nevertheless, it survived for 94 years and was the site of innovations and unique events.

In 1881, at the invitation of part-owner and manager R.A. Macfie, Jr., Princess Regent Lili'uokalani drove the first ceremonial spike for the plantation's railroad.[30] Sister of King Kalākaua (1836-1891) and heir to the throne, she was serving as regent while he took a historic and precedent-setting world tour.

Macfie, a British subject, retired in 1891 to England, where he engaged in political maneuvers. He urged the Foreign Office to press the Kingdom of Hawai'i to grant the Royal Navy a concession for a coaling station at Hilo because the U.S. had one at Pearl Harbor. His proposal pointed out that Hilo Bay was a superior location, true at the time because the entrance to Pearl Harbor had yet to be dredged. The Foreign Office referred the suggestion to the Admiralty, whose experts concluded that a coaling station in the Sandwich Islands would be of little advantage to British naval interests.[31]

The two-foot, narrow gauge railroad inaugurated by Princess Lili'uokalani hauled cane to Kilauea's mill until replaced by trucks in 1942. In 1910 the plantation was the first in Hawai'i to employ a gasoline-powered tractor for field cultivation.[32] C. Brewer shut the plantation down in 1972.[33]

GAY & ROBINSON (8)

In 1840 Eliza McHutchinson Sinclair (1803-1895) emigrated to New Zealand with her husband, Capt. Francis S. Sinclair. Widowed after he was lost at sea, in 1863 she packed up family, property, and livestock and sailed on her son-in-law's vessel *Corsair* to find a new home. After intermediate stops in Tahiti and Canada, she arrived in Hawai'i with her family and possessions. Mrs. Sinclair made the acquaintance of King Kamehameha V (1830-1872), and in 1864 persuaded him to sell her the island of Ni'ihau and over 6,000 acres on Kaua'i's west side, in the name of her sons.[34]

Grandson Aubrey Robinson (1853-1936), with his cousin Francis Gay, pioneered a stock ranch and sugarcane fields on the land in Makaweli. Mrs. Sinclair made her home on Kaua'i and preserved the island of Ni'ihau for its native residents by carefully controlling visits by outsiders in the way that survives to this day.

In 1889, Gay & Robinson leased lands to the Hawaiian Sugar Company and reserved hundreds of acres for its own cane. The Hawaiian Sugar Company mill ground this cane, taking payment from a share of the sugar produced. This arrangement survived when Olokele Sugar Company took over the land lease in 1940. In 1944 C. Brewer & Company sold the Olokele mill and equipment to the landowners Gay & Robinson, who continue to operate the plantation.

HAWAIIAN SUGAR COMPANY (9)

In 1889, a corporation controlled by pioneer planters Henry Baldwin (1842-1911) and Samuel Alexander (1836-1904) leased the Makaweli land from Gay & Robinson.[35] Baldwin was a son of missionary Dwight Baldwin (1793-1886), who arrived in Hawai'i in 1831 with the fourth company of missionaries. Alexander was the son of William Alexander (1805-1884), who arrived in Hawai'i in 1832 with the fifth company.

By 1891 the Hawaiian Sugar Company, Inc. was grinding its first crop at the mill in Makaweli. For years the plantation was managed by Benjamin D. Baldwin (1867-1928), nephew of Henry and known as a first-class mill builder and operator. He also enjoyed a good reputation for taking care of the company's employees. The plantation was among the first to construct family housing with modern amenities, and attend to the medical and social needs of workers and their dependents.[37]

The plantation's day began when the mill blew a loud wake-up whistle. This set the workday's starting time, as early as 4:30 a.m., and was adjusted by the manager to coincide with the sunrise. (Similar to today's daylight savings time, but more frequent.) This custom was the basis for a friendly rivalry between neighboring plantations. Around 1930, Douglas Baldwin (son of Benjamin) managed at Makaweli, and Frank A. Alexander (1869-1938), grandson of William Alexander, managed the neighboring McBryde Sugar Company plantation. One day each man adjusted his start times according to the time in the nearby coastal town of Port Allen. Of course the result was the same. When they discovered the coincidence the next day, both changed the timing of their whistles to differ from each other's, and from clock time in Port Allen. The practice of maintaining independent "plantation time" was discontinued in the early 1940s.[38]

The red-dirt Makaweli plantation was reputed to be the dustiest of all Hawai'i plantations in what is by nature a dirty business. Visitors confirmed this opinion. Manager B.D. Baldwin met complaints from the workers about it with the observation, "Never mind. This is ten-ton dust."[39] The rich lands consistently yielded an admirable ten tons of sugar or more per acre.

The nearest towns to the labor camps at Makaweli and Kaumakani were Hanapēpē, two miles east, and Waimea, four miles west. In the early 1900s, a plantation worker was very unlikely to have a horse or automobile, and was dependent on home-grown produce and the company store. In 1923 Hawaiian Sugar built up a herd of cows to meet the demands for dairy products. It turned out to be a slow process. Of the first 40 calves dropped, 33 were male, and the plantation's veterinarian complained bitterly of his poor luck.[40]

OLOKELE SUGAR COMPANY / GAY & ROBINSON (10)

Hawaiian Sugar Company's lease with Gay & Robinson expired in 1938, and was extended by two years to allow for renegotiation of terms. The owners wanted to retain more lands under the proposed new lease, but Hawaiian Sugar didn't want to give up any fields. Negotiations reached an impasse in 1940 and Hawaiian Sugar Company, Inc. dissolved. The lease and operations were taken over by Olokele Sugar Company, Inc. organized for the purpose by C. Brewer & Company.[41]

This plantation enjoyed decades of highly profitable years from its first harvest in 1891. Usually producing the highest, or near highest, sugar yield per acre of all Hawai'i plantations, the Hawaiian Sugar Company began paying dividends even before the installments of stock subscriptions were fully paid.

Over the years Hawai'i's sugar farmers struggled to remain competitive with producers on the continental United States. Saddled with the costs of transportation to mainland refineries, they offset the disadvantage by reducing their own production costs and increasing yields per acre. A significant

Dusty Olokele Sugar Company mill at Makaweli in 1991.
(W. H. Dorrance)

improvement came with the introduction of drip irrigation. Related to the domestic lawn soaker, drip irrigation brought down the cost of water and pumping while dramatically improving water distribution. From 1979 to 1987 drip-irrigated fields averaged 13.34 tons of sugar yield versus 10.74 tons per acre averaged in fields using other methods.[42]

Drip irrigation was first used in 1972, when C. Brewer & Company executive Donald J. Martin (1919-1991) pioneered its installation at Olokele Sugar Company. In 1982 he was honored by the Hawai'i Sugar Technologists for this contribution. During World War II, Martin served with the U.S. Army Air Forces and was awarded the Distinguished Flying Cross and Croix de Guerre, among other decorations, for distinguished combat service.[43]

In 1994, C. Brewer & Company, faced with a lease renewal in the year 2000, and questioning the future of sugar farming in Hawai'i, sold Olokele Sugar Company's mill and equipment to the landlord, Gay & Robinson. As part of the terms of the sale, Olokele Sugar Company's employees were retained. Since they belonged to the ILWU before the sale, and Gay & Robinson's employees did not, after the sale the Gay & Robinson employees also joined the union, a first for this plantation that continues to operate as Gay & Robinson.

V. KNUDSEN & ESTATE (11)

In 1853 Valdemar Knudsen (1820-1898) arrived in Hawai'i, looking for a warm, hospitable climate to recover his health. His initiation into the Hawai'i sugar industry began with a short term as manager of Grove Farm Plantation, then he began acquiring cane fields of his own. In 1867 Knudsen married Anne McHutchinson Sinclair, daughter of Gay & Robinson matriarch Eliza Sinclair, and added Anne's portion of Kaua'i lands to his leased property.[44]

After Knudsen's death, his two sons carried on with sugarcane planting and harvests that were ground in shares at the Koloa Sugar Company mill. By 1927 the Koloa Sugar Company leased their lands, and the Knudsen family was no longer in the sugar business.

KEKAHA SUGAR COMPANY (12, 13, 14 & 15)

In 1898 the lands of Meier and Kruse, H.P. Faye & Company, and Kekaha Mill Company—all located near Waimea, Kaua'i—were combined into Kekaha Sugar Company, Inc.[45] Organized under the auspices of pioneer Honolulu sugar factor H. Hackfeld & Company, the plantation operates today as Amfac Sugar/West, owned by Hackfeld successor Amfac/JMB-Hawai'i, Inc..

In the early decades of the twentieth century, Kekaha Sugar Company was managed by H.P. Faye (1859-1928). A veteran sugar planter who owned Waimea Sugar Mill Company, and also ran Kekaha's plantation from 1898 to 1928, he believed that most Hawai'i sugar lands were underproducing.

To minimize expenses, Faye used "ratooning," growing second and succeeding crops from the roots of the first, much as lawns are allowed to grow back after being mowed. The opposite method was to replant the fields after each harvest, a costly expense. Replanting was done where a new crop was expected to yield enough sugar over that of the ratoon to offset the added expense. In Faye's opinion, under proper management both the first and succeeding ratoons could be almost as rich in sugar as the original crop.[46]

WAIMEA SUGAR MILL COMPANY (16)

At his own Waimea Sugar Mill plantation, H.P. Faye demonstrated how good management could improve production. This small operation in the valley of the Waimea river was hemmed in by the lands of the Kekaha Sugar Company. Under the guidance of his sons Lindsay and, later, Alan, the fields were doubled in size by leaching out the salt in the muddy marsh land at the estuary of the Waimea river.[47] Thus the plantation outlived numerous larger plantations under the astute management of generations of Fayes.

ELEELE PLANTATION AND MCBRYDE SUGAR COMPANY (17 & 18)

Another "annexation plantation" was McBryde Sugar Company, Inc., formed by combining the lands of Koloa Agriculture Company (not to be confused with Koloa Sugar Company), Eleele Plantation, and the estate of Judge Duncan McBryde (died 1878). Promoted by Oʻahu railroad magnate Benjamin Dillingham, McBryde's mill produced its first sugar in 1899, with Theo H. Davies & Co. as agent. A new mill purchased to replace the one at the ʻEleʻele mill was a curiosity because it was originally intended for the American Sugar Company on Molokaʻi, which failed before its first crop could be harvested.[48]

McBryde Sugar Company, owned by Alexander & Baldwin, Inc., ground its last crop in 1996. Since then, agricultural diversification has become a prominent goal, and now much of the land is planted in coffee.

Kauaʻi Electric Company, which serves the island's 50,000 inhabitants, owes most of its success to McBryde Sugar Company. In 1905 McBryde hired a contractor to build a hydroelectric generating station at the head of Wainiha Valley in northern Kauaʻi, some 34 miles from the plantation. By 1906 the station was delivering electrical power on lines erected over the spine of the Waiʻaleʻale mountain range to electric irrigation pumps. Leftover power ran the mill and supplied the labor camps, and was sold to neighboring plantations, the Kauaʻi Railway Company, and Kauaʻi Electric Company.[49] For over 90 years this dependable generating station has served Kauaʻi as a public utility.

The Koloa Agricultural Company, integrated into the McBryde plantation, was the last of several farms operated by the Smith family. This

Kauaʻi clan consisted of the descendants of Dr. James Smith (1810-1887), who arrived in Hawaiʻi in 1842 with the tenth company of missionaries. He lived out his life in Kōloa and for many years was the only physician on Kauaʻi.

KAUAʻI MUSEUMS

Three institutions on Kauaʻi are worth a visit to complete a study of this island's history of sugar. Kauaʻi Museum on Rice Street in Līhuʻe has well-designed exhibits that portray the roles played by prominent families and workers. The contributions of the Wilcox family are chronicled at their own Grove Farm Homestead, in a beautiful setting with a unique library available to the serious researcher. Both museums have exhibits that carefully document the contributions of plantation workers. The story of sugar farming on Kauaʻi is completed with the excellent Kōloa Museum diorama in the restored old town of Kōloa.

In 1992, representatives of Kauaʻi's five surviving plantations stated their determination to remain in sugar. The former Olokele Sugar Company, under its new owner Gay & Robinson, continues to operate and may add a bagasse-burning electric power generator. In 1996 McBryde Sugar Company converted much of its cane acreage to coffee and macadamia nuts, and discontinued sugar farming. The management of Kekaha Sugar Company and Lihue Sugar Company have been combined and streamlined to reduce expenses.[50]

It is clear that the island where, in 1835, the first commercial sugar manufacturing began, may well be the island—along with Maui—where the last Hawaiʻi sugar plantations reside. Several smaller planters came and went before annexation, and their contributions were significant in one way or another to Kauaʻi's development. Many of these pioneers are described in Ethel M. Damon's work, to which the interested reader is referred.[51] This work moves on to describe the history of sugar farming on the other islands in the Hawaiian archipelago.

'Aiea Mill, Oʻahu, Hawaiʻi
(Hawaiʻi State Archives)

CHAPTER 4

SUGAR ON OʻAHU (1876-1996)

When I drive from my home in Kaʻaʻawa to my office in Honolulu, I can't escape reminders of my family's tie to sugar. I pass our Kualoa Ranch at the head of Kāneʻohe Bay, then the ruins of the stone chimney on the mauka (inland) side of the highway, the remains of my great-grandfather's sugar mill that closed down in 1871. A little further along I drive by land where Theo H. Davies ran Kaalaea Plantation until he sold his interest in 1880 and recruited my grandfather to help manage his firm. My father, James, also worked for Theo H. Davies & Company, so my family's involvement in the sugar business goes back continuously for over 135 years, beginning with Kualoa Plantation.

We shared an interesting coincidence: In 1920 my father was involved in the construction of a new Theo H. Davies building in downtown Honolulu. Half a century later, in 1970, I oversaw the construction of the present Davies Pacific Center Building on the same site.

After I was named Davies' Group Vice President for Agriculture, I divided my time between duties on the Big Island and my family's operations at Kualoa Ranch.

My uncle George Bennett, assistant manager of Hilo Sugar Company, later managed the Waimanalo Sugar Company on Oʻahu. On weekends and holidays there were exchange visits between the Morgans and the Bennetts. I remember the Waimānalo plantation railway system, and Uncle George explaining that all the sugar the plantation produced went by truck to the refinery in ʻAiea. C. Brewer & Company was agent for both the Waimānalo plantation and Honolulu Plantation Company (that operated the ʻAiea refinery), and the Honolulu production of raw sugar was insufficient for the refinery's needs. So the trucking was arranged to replace the shortfall.

Oʻahu wasn't the best location for sugar farming. Only after introducing the collection of mountain water, and digging deep wells with heavy-duty pumps, was cultivation even possible on the west side of the island.

Where it was wet, there was too little arable land, and where there was sufficient land, there was not enough rainfall. When the water shortage was solved by tunnels, ditches, and wells, economies of scale were often denied because of the limited geography. The little Waianae Company plantation on Oʻahu's leeward coast produced some of the highest yields per acre in the world, yet it couldn't survive. There was just no room for necessary expansion.

The heartbeat of our sugar industry, the agencies, was located on the one of the islands least hospitable to sugar farming. But Honolulu became the commercial center of Hawaiʻi long before sugar production was important. Mercantile firms had established credit with mainland suppliers. An isolated, independent sugar farmer relied completely on his agency for both credit and supplies.

Only the agencies could afford branch offices in San Francisco and New York. They also got better prices on machinery and plantation goods because of repeat and large-quantity orders. In addition, they negotiated the highest price for raw sugar and arranged for shipment on the best terms. When I joined Davies in 1946, no plantation in Hawaiʻi was large enough to survive without the help of the Big Five agencies that represented them.

⊕ ⊕ ⊕

OʻAHU IS 2,100 miles from San Francisco. The island is roughly 25 miles wide and 25 miles long, the third largest in the state. Two mountain ranges, Koʻolau to the east and Waiʻanae to the west, line the coasts and create a central plain largely devoted to pineapple cultivation.

Honolulu is on the southern shore, and for decades had the only sheltered harbor in the archipelago. This attracted commercial activity that eventually resulted in a single large city that spread out from the harbor area. The island was slow to participate in large-scale cane farming. It took the 1879 discovery of well water in the ʻEwa District, and heavy-duty pumps, to convert desert land into cane fields. In 1990 Oʻahu's last two plantations produced 139,480 tons of sugar, 17 percent of Hawaiʻi's total production that year.[1]

Location of sugar plantations on Oʻahu during the years after 1876. See Table 4 for identification of the numbered plantations. Not to scale.
(W.H. Dorrance)

TABLE 4 | SUGAR PLANTATIONS ON OʻAHU 1876-1996

NO.	NAME	FIRST DATE*	LAST DATE*
1.	Kaneohe Sugar Plantation Co.	1865	1891
2.	Laie Plantation	1872	1931
3.	Gordon and Halstead & Sons	1874	1898
4.	Heeia Agricultural Company	1878	1902
5.	Waimanalo Sugar Company	1878	1947
6.	Waianae Company	1879	1947
7.	Ewa Plantation Company	1890	1970
8.	Apokaa Sugar Company, Ltd.	1902	1932
9.	Kahuku Plantation Company	1891	1971
10.	Koolau Agriculture Company	1909	1925
11.	Waialua Agricultural Company	1898	1996
12.	Oahu Sugar Company	1898	1994
13.	Honolulu Plantation Company	1899	1947
(numbers 14 through 18 are not described in the text)			
14.	Keaahala Plantation	1872	1879
15.	Kaalaea Plantation	1865	1880
16.	Ahuimanu Plantation	1882	1883
17.	Rose & Company	1882	1883
18.	Makaha Plantation	1884	1890

* Notes: "First Date" and "Last Date" are the first and last years a plantation is cited in a source. The dates are believed to be within two years of the organization or shutdown.
Sources: Listing 1878-1940, *Hawaiian Almanac* and *Annual*; listing, dates of charter, *The Planter Monthly*, Aug. 1882: listing 1895-1945, HSPA Annual Meeting, Dec. 10, 1945; citations 1945-date, corporation annual reports, newspapers, and HSPA library.

The Hawaiian Islands stretch out in a diagonal line running from the northwest to the southeast, and the prevailing winds come from the east by northeast. The eastern sides of the Islands receive the most rainfall as the trade winds sweep onto shorelines backed by mountains within a few miles of the coast.

Early post-Mahele plantations (after 1850) were located in these wet regions on every island. This was especially true on Oʻahu.

KANEOHE SUGAR PLANTATION COMPANY (1)

One of the earliest Oʻahu plantations was owned by Charles Coffin Harris (1822-1881), who came to Hawaiʻi in 1850 determined to practice law.[2] In 1865, while serving as the Kingdom's Minister of Finance and Minister of Foreign Affairs, he established the Kaneohe Sugar Plantation Company. This was in partnership with Harriet Kalama (1817-1870), widow of Kamehameha III, on 7,000 acres she owned. After her death, Harris purchased the land from her heirs. From 500 acres under cultivation, the plantation's mill produced 500 tons of sugar in 1880.

Eventually the yield was inadequate to support the operation, and it shut down in 1891. Harris had more success as a lawyer. In 1877 he became Chief

Justice of the Supreme Court and Chancellor of the Kingdom, posts he held until his death.[3]

Judge Harris' daughter and heir incorporated the lands as Kaneohe Ranch and converted it to stock farming. Beginning in 1907, James Castle (1855-1918) purchased stock in the corporation and eventually owned all of it. Castle was the son of Samuel Castle (1808-1894), who arrived in Hawai'i in 1837 with the eighth company of missionaries, and later co-founded the Big Five sugar factor firm Castle & Cooke.

Kaneohe Ranch was to play a part in James B. Castle's dream of converting all of Windward O'ahu to profitable agricultural pursuits. By the time he acquired Kaneohe Ranch, his holdings already included several established plantations.

LAIE PLANTATION (2)

Lā'ie is the Windward O'ahu location of a magnificent Mormon temple and community surrounded by church-owned land. In 1872 its leaders set aside 6,000 acres for sugarcane, rice, and pasturage.[4] A quarter century later, in 1896, the railroad at neighboring Kahuku Plantation Company was extended two miles to Laie Plantation. This allowed Lā'ie's cane to be ground at the Kahuku mill. The arrangements lasted for decades but the operation was a small one. In 1930 Lā'ie's sugar production peaked at 4,788 tons. At this point the corporation was dissolved and the lands assigned to the Kahuku Plantation Company.

GORDON AND HALSTEAD & SONS (3)

Robert Halstead (1836-1900) came to Lahaina, Maui in 1865. For seven years he managed the Pioneer Mill Company for Campbell and Turton. In 1874, under the partnership name Halstead & Gordon, he purchased the moribund Chamberlain plantation on O'ahu's north shore. After Gordon's death in 1888, he continued to manage the plantation with his sons, Edgar and Frank, as Halstead Brothers.[5] In 1898 the enterprise was acquired by the Waialua Agricultural Company.

Hāpai kō (carrying cane) was the most demanding and dangerous work on the plantation. Many injuries in the field were attributed to carrying 100- to 125-pound bundles of stalks up the ramp. The planters welcomed mechanical loading when it appeared. (Dorrance Collection)

HEEIA AGRICULTURAL COMPANY (4)

John McKeague was one of the first planters to exploit the opportunities presented by the 1876 Reciprocity Treaty. In 1878 he established the Heeia Agricultural Company on 2,500 leased acres in Heʻeia ahupuaʻa on Windward Oʻahu.[6] By 1883 the plantation had a modern mill, a 20-inch narrow gauge railroad, and a pier to receive supplies and ship its product to the mainland United States. Never a large producer, this plantation reached its maximum output of 2,309 tons of sugar in 1900. Traceable to its small size, Heeia Agricultural Company was often in financial trouble and went bankrupt years before being shut down in 1903.

WAIMANALO SUGAR COMPANY (5)

John Adams Cummins (1835-1913) was the son of a prosperous Englishman and a Native Hawaiian mother of the chiefly class. Born on Oʻahu and educated at the Royal School with future rulers of the Kingdom, he settled down as a gentleman farmer on his father's estate in Waimānalo. Both father and son were gracious hosts and their home became a favorite getaway for Kings Kamehameha V and Kalākaua, and Queen Liliʻuokalani.[7]

Following ratification of the Reciprocity Treaty, in 1878 Cummins used his connections in the monarchy to lease 7,900 acres of crown lands in Waimānalo ahupuaʻa to cultivate sugarcane. By 1880 Waimanalo Sugar Company was producing 500 tons of sugar a year. In 1885 control passed to William G. Irwin (1843-1914), and in 1910 to C. Brewer & Company, Ltd., when Irwin's enterprise merged with the powerful sugar factor.

Despite giving up 3,000 acres to the government in 1917, eventually named Bellows Army Air Field, the plantation reached a peak production of 12,060 tons in 1936.[8] But over a decade later, after several years of losses, C. Brewer shut down the plantation in 1947.

WAIANAE SUGAR COMPANY (6)

Another entrepreneur who took advantage of the Reciprocity Treaty was Judge Hermann A. Widemann (1823-1899). In 1879, along with partners—including Kauaʻi planters G.N. Wilcox and A.S. Wilcox—he started the Waianae Sugar Company on land owned by J.I. Dowsett (1829-1898).[9]

Judge Widemann had been an associate justice of the Supreme Court, and was serving King Kalākaua as Minister of the Interior at the time. The plantation was 35 miles from Honolulu on the west coast of Oʻahu. It occupied 6,132 acres in the Mākaha, Waiʻanae, and Lualualei Valleys, of which some 2,000 acres were suitable for planting cane. This small plantation was unique in that it was serviced by its own 30-inch narrow gauge railroad from its beginning to its demise over 65 years later.

The Waianae Sugar Company enjoyed smooth labor relations throughout its existence because of its comparative isolation and careful attention to employee welfare. Production increased dramatically in the early decades of the 1900s after long tunnels were constructed to collect mountain water, and wells were sunk to tap ground water for irrigation. In pre-irrigation 1915, sugar production stood at 5.24 tons per acre. This increased to 8.57 tons by 1930, and culminated in a remarkable 13.79 tons per acre in 1935.[10] These simple statistics demonstrate the powerful effect of irrigation.

From 1931 to after 1940 the Waiʻanae plantation was managed by Robert Fricke, inventor of a patented chain-side cane car. When mechanical (derrick-grab) loading became feasible, Fricke's innovation supplanted the old-style cane cars with sides made of wooden stakes. Stakes broke if accidentally struck by a heavy cane bundle, replacing them was a big expense, and chains were resilient. Fricke was head overseer of Kauaʻi's Kīlauea plantation at the time of his invention. Honolulu Iron Works made tidy profits selling the new-style cane cars while paying royalties to Fricke.

Unfortunately, production efficiency wasn't everything. Average annual production of sugar at the Waianae Sugar Company never exceeded 12,000 tons. The plantation was limited by the amount of water available, and hemmed in by the surrounding mountain ridges that prevented enlarging the operation. Amfac, Inc. purchased it and then closed it down in 1947.[11] Makaha Resort and two golf courses now occupy much of the former plantation lands.

CAMPBELL AND DILLINGHAM

The next four Oʻahu plantations owed their existence to the business acumen of James Campbell (1826-1900), the vision and entrepreneurship of Benjamin Franklin Dillingham, and the cooperation of King David Kalākaua.

James Campbell was a seafaring man who settled in Lahaina, Maui, in 1850. A decade later he started the Pioneer Mill Company in partnership with Henry Turton and James Dunbar. In 1876 he purchased 15,000 acres at Kahuku on the northern tip of Oʻahu. A year later he sold his interest in Pioneer Mill Company to Turton and moved to Oʻahu. He also purchased 41,000 dry acres at Honouliuli on the ʻEwa plains west of Pearl Harbor.[12]

Campbell visualized supplying his desert-like land with water from artesian wells. A successful drilling in 1879 in the ʻEwa District changed the future of Oʻahu. Additional wells were drilled and supplied millions of gallons daily with no diminishing of the source. The aquifer is still maintained by rainfall from the upper regions of the island's mountain ranges.

Benjamin F. Dillingham saw opportunity in Campbell's success on the ʻEwa plains. King David Kalākaua had cooperated in 1878 by signing the Railway Act that made it possible to obtain a railroad right-of-way by eminent domain. Dillingham secured an option to lease Campbell's lands, and sold bonds to build a line from Honolulu to Kahuku. His 36-inch narrow gauge railroad, incorporated as the Oʻahu Railway and Land Company (O.R.& L.), was begun in 1886 and completed at Kahuku in 1890.[13] By then, Dillingham had exercised his option to lease Campbell's land and was well into the next phase of his grand scheme.

EWA PLANTATION COMPANY (7)

Dillingham persuaded the Castle & Cooke partnership to underwrite a sugar plantation on Campbell's 'Ewa lands. The Ewa Plantation Company was organized in conjunction with several investors, including Samuel Castle and his son James.[14] The plantation negotiated a sublease with Dillingham on 11,000 acres of the Campbell lands and began sugarcane cultivation in 1890. Sugar was transported to the docks in Honolulu on Dillingham's O.R.& L. railroad. A modern nine-roller crusher was installed in the mill after a false start with an inefficient diffusion process. The plantation grew to become a model of efficiency and earned a reputation for concern with the welfare of its employees.

Underwriting Ewa Plantation turned out to be a heroic effort for Castle & Cooke. In 1890, in the midst of fundraising, the McKinley tariff law was passed and removed all tariffs on sugar imported into the United States. This killed the competitive advantage over other overseas producers that Hawai'i had enjoyed since the Reciprocity Treaty of 1876. Investors turned skittish and were reluctant to loan money or buy bonds for financing Ewa Plantation. While Castle & Cooke's Kohala Sugar Company was a profitable source of funds, these weren't enough. In desperation Castle & Cooke turned to its archenemy and competitor Claus Spreckels (1828-1908). He drove a hard bargain, supplying money in return for ownership of Castle & Cooke's profitable Ha'ikū and Pā'ia plantations on Maui, among other acquisitions.[15] Castle & Cooke put its future in the hands of Ewa Plantation Company and was rewarded for the sacrifices it made.

Numerous new wells provided irrigation water. From its start in 1890 until 1947, when trucks took over, the plantation's railroad hauled harvested cane to the mill. Production reached 50,000 tons of sugar a year in 1925, with a remarkable yield of over 12 tons per acre.[16] When fertilized and irrigated, the 'Ewa desert lands were among Hawai'i's most productive. Scientific farming was used, and bungalows with indoor plumbing were built for employees' families. Japanese and Filipino workers lived in separate, carefully laid-out communities. A plantation hospital, properly staffed, served all. A professional social worker presided over a kindergarten and preschool, freeing mothers to work if they wanted to.

The management of Ewa Plantation was quick to incorporate innovations. The nine-roller mill installed in 1895 was Hawai'i's first. Sugar extraction improved as the number of grinders was increased, and at the time all other mills used six rollers or less. In 1937 the arduous manual labor of cutting by machete and loading by hand was completely replaced by mechanical harvesting. Ewa Plantation was the first to use a plant to wash the mechanically harvested cane before it entered the mill. Eventually every Hawai'i mill used this kind of cleaning process. Liquid ammonia fertilizer was also first used on the fields at 'Ewa in 1953.

By 1970 Ewa Plantation was entirely controlled by sugar factor Castle & Cooke, small by modern standards, and denied economies of scale. The neighboring Oahu Sugar Company plantation, controlled by Amfac, Inc., suffered the same disadvantage. Ewa Plantation's lease was due to expire in 1978, and renewal terms were uncertain because the Campbell Estate foresaw a more profitable use for some of the land. The solution was obvious. In 1970 Castle & Cooke sold Ewa Plantation to Oahu Sugar Company, which added a portion of 'Ewa's lands to its own, and the 'Ewa mill shut down.[17]

Today the old mill town is surrounded by a residential development. Preservationists have managed to insure continued use of many buildings, and the camp housing is often occupied by retired sugar workers. A glimpse of this bygone life is possible through a visit to the Hawai'i Plantation Village in 'Ewa, a 25-minute drive from downtown Honolulu.

APOKAA PLANTATION COMPANY (8)

In 1898, when Hawai'i was annexed to the United States, local contract labor laws became nonbinding under American law. Some method of encouraging labor stability was needed. Ewa Plantation Company met the challenge with a new approach: land was allocated to labor teams or contractors who would be responsible for cultivating and harvesting the cane. The company supplied equipment, railroad transport to the mill, fertilizer and tools, and housing for the workers. The rest was up to the contractor-worker team to accomplish. The proceeds of the sugar produced were to be shared with the workers.[18]

An independent but wholly-owned corporation, Apokaa Sugar Company, Ltd., was formed in 1902. Five hundred acres of 'Ewa plantation lands were allocated to the enterprise. However, the effort never produced more than 1,400 tons of sugar in any given year. After an experiment that lasted three decades, in 1932 Apokaa was shut down and absorbed by its parent corporation.

KAHUKU PLANTATION COMPANY (9)

When Frank Dillingham promoted Ewa Plantation, he was far from done. He had leased Campbell's Kahuku lands and by 1890 his railroad was extended to O'ahu's north shore. Kahuku was ripe for development. James Castle agreed and, with several others, including prominent lawyer Lorrin Thurston (1858-1931), organized the Kahuku Plantation Company. In 1891 it subleased 2,800 acres of Campbell's lands from Dillingham for farming sugarcane. Thurston's participation was another example of the role played by early missionaries and their descendants. His grandfather, Asa Thurston (1787-1868), arrived in Hawai'i in 1820 with the first company of American missionaries.

Just a year after being organized, Kahuku Plantation's first crop was ground in 1892. It was a complete operation from the start, with a mill and a railway system. After more than three decades of success, in 1924 Kahuku was the first Hawai'i plantation to use a mechanical derrick for loading harvested cane.[19] Yet its managers had to struggle to compete in an area severely limited by the surrounding rugged terrain. The fields of the Koolau Agricultural

Company as far south as Kahana Bay were bought in 1925. In 1931 an additional 2,700 acres of Laie Plantation were purchased, but peak production never exceeded the 21,873 tons of sugar in 1935.[20] A decade later, Kahuku still remained small by post-World War II standards. Shipping costs went up when the O.R.& L. railroad ceased operations in 1947. Denied the economies of scale, the owner, sugar factor Alexander & Baldwin, Inc., shut down the plantation in 1971.

KOOLAU AGRICULTURAL COMPANY (10)

Kahuku fit into James Castle's grand vision for the development of the Windward side of O'ahu. His dream of industrial transport included extending the O.R.& L. railroad from its terminus at Kahuku with his own railroad leading south, down the eastern coast of O'ahu to Kāne'ohe, then back through the Ko'olau range to Honolulu, where it would join his Honolulu Rapid Transit railway. He planned to revitalize the Heeia Agricultural Company plantation at the railroad's southern end, and establish new agricultural enterprises along the way between Kahuku and He'eia.[21] Castle made considerable progress in fulfilling this dream before his death in 1918.

In 1905 the Territory of Hawai'i issued a charter for the Koolau Railway Company to the James Castle interests. By 1908 the 36-inch narrow gauge railroad was operating 11 miles south of Kahuku to Kahana Bay. In 1909 Castle established the Koolau Agricultural Company plantation south of Kahuku, between Lā'ie and Kahana Bay, and was transporting harvested cane to the Kahuku mill on his railroad. The plantation was hemmed in by the nearby ridges of the Ko'olau range and never produced more than 1,500 tons of sugar in any one year. After the 1924 harvest, it sold out to the Kahuku Plantation Company.[22] This affected the viability of the Koolau Railway Company, which was also sold to Kahuku plantation in 1931. By 1952 the railroad was out of business and Castle's dream died with it.

WAIALUA AGRICULTURE COMPANY (11)

On its way to Kahuku, Dillingham's O.R.& L. railroad crossed the Halstead Brothers plantation and mill at Waialua, near O'ahu's north shore. This small sugar farm didn't generate much freight, and was surrounded by thousands of uncultivated acres divided into small parcels with numerous owners, many of them Native Hawaiians. Dillingham encouraged Castle & Cooke, then benefiting from rich profits of Ewa Plantation, to acquire the Halstead properties and the small parcels. Dillingham had already leased much of the surrounding land. Castle & Cooke formed Waialua Agricultural Company, Ltd. in 1898, subleased the lands held by Dillingham, leased other lands from Bishop Estate, and had its lawyers negotiate leases or buy the adjacent parcels.[23] By the end of 1898, the small Halstead mill was replaced, and a year later Waialua Agricultural Company's first crop was harvested, producing 1,741 tons of sugar.

This plantation got off to a good start because of its initial manager. William Goodale was hired in 1898 and served for 25 prosperous years. Before coming to Waialua he spent five years at the Pāhala plantation on Hawai'i, one year each at Pā'ia and Wailuku plantations on Maui, and 13 years at the Onomea plantation (ten as manager) on the island of Hawai'i.[24] Goodale's knowledge of sugar farming showed in his astute management. By 1905 production rose to 19,722 tons.

In 1920 Goodale pioneered the use of mechanical (derrick) loading for harvested cane. He had purchased a self-propelled drag-line excavator for ditch digging, and experimented with it to lift harvested cane bundles onto the railway cars in the field. His method worked, and the dangerous, exhausting task of carrying 125-pound bundles of cane up a ramp to load (hāpai kō or "carrying cane") became a thing of the past.

Goodale also took the innovative step of installing a 450-kilowatt hydroelectric plant in the uplands. The generating frequency was the same as the Hawaiian Electric Co., so excess power could be sold.[25] This was the first deliberate matching of plantation output to a domestic utility with power sales in mind.

By 1925, sugar production had grown to 32,585 tons, a rising trend that continued. Over a decade later, in 1936, as irrigation reservoirs and wells were introduced, sugar production stood at 54,671 tons.[26] In all the years of its existence, Waialua Agricultural Company never ranked lower than sixth among Hawai'i producers.

Waialua Agricultural Company locomotive number 6 hauling cane to the Waialua mill in 1935. (Dorrance Collection)

In 1990 the plantation, now owned by Dole Food Co., Inc., successor to Castle & Cooke, produced 62,555 tons of sugar with 12,074 acres under cultivation.[27] But times had changed, and following the 1996 harvest, Waialua was shut down, the last plantation to operate on Oʻahu.

OAHU SUGAR COMPANY (12)

After Kahuku Sugar Company was launched, Frank Dillingham looked at the lands adjacent to Ewa Plantation Company, and at others on the central, elevated plains of the island. These areas were ripe for cultivation, providing well pumps located at sea level could lift irrigation water a considerable distance. In 1897 he promoted the Oahu Sugar Company, Inc., which leased property from the John Papa ʻIʻi, Bishop, and Robinson Estates, and subleased land from Dillingham, for a total of about 12,000 acres.[28] This included Ford Island and Waipiʻo Peninsula, which projects into Pearl Harbor.

A plantation railroad brought harvests to a mill built at Waipahu, and the raw sugar was transported down to the Honolulu docks by the O.R.& L. railroad. Irrigation water was obtained by some of the largest steam pumps ever manufactured, which provided a lift of 300 to 400 feet.

Innovation was encouraged and flourished at Oahu Sugar. In 1907 a 12-roller mill was installed, the first in Hawaiʻi. In 1913 the plantation's chemist, P. A. Messchaert, invented a method of grooving that was machined into rollers to permit juice to flow while maintaining pressure on the cane being processed. This was adopted throughout the industry. Also in 1913, a wholly-owned subsidiary, Waiahole Water Company, was formed to dig a tunnel through the Koʻolau range to transport runoff from the eastern side of the mountains. Completed in 1916, this engineering marvel had a capacity to supply up to 125 million gallons of water daily,[29] although this enormous figure was never realized. In the following decades the average flow of water was 32 million gallons developed daily in the tunnels. In 1926 the first Oliver filter, which removed impurities during processing, was installed.

Sugar production increased from 29,983 tons in 1915 to 50,005 tons in 1918, and after that was never less than 43,980 tons. Mechanical loading of harvested cane began in 1924, followed by mechanical harvesting during World War II, and trucks replacing the railroad in 1950.

Oahu Sugar Company gave up its lease on Ford Island in 1917, and the last crop there was harvested a year later. Cut cane had been loaded onto cars, barged to a landing on Waipiʻo Peninsula, and hauled by train to the Waipahu mill. At best, it was a burdensome form of transport. Ford Island became the site of Army and Navy facilities, including a large runway that covered the center of the island.

In 1970, when Ewa Plantation shut down, much of its acreage was acquired. Two decades later, in 1990, Oahu Sugar Company was still producing with remarkable efficiency: 11,526 cultivated acres resulted in 76,925 tons of sugar with a yield of 13.66 tons per acre.[30] Owned by Amfac/

JMB-Hawaiʻi, Oahu Sugar Company was one of the largest and best-run operations in Hawaiʻi, but by 1993 both the plantation and the mill were surrounded by urban growth. One lease was due to expire in 1995, another in 1996. Faced by these changes, Oahu Sugar Company shut down after the 1995 harvest.

HONOLULU PLANTATION COMPANY (13)

Today it is difficult to visualize the thousands of acres of sugarcane that once covered the well-developed region close to Honolulu. This was formerly the Honolulu Plantation Company, now the home of Hickam Air Force Base, Honolulu International Airport, Pearl Harbor naval base facilities, a state correctional facility, the Humane Society reservation, shopping centers, Aloha Stadium, the community of ʻAiea, and acres of urban sprawl.

It wasn't always that way. In 1899 San Francisco investors, including Suessmann and Wurmser, producers of S&W canned foods, organized the Honolulu Plantation Company. They leased 6,500 acres in and around Pearl Harbor, and erected a mill and plantation railroad.[31]

The first harvest in 1901 yielded a respectable 10,008 tons of sugar. In 1906, the mill was converted to a refinery, the only one in Hawaiʻi. Refined sugar was produced for local consumption, including soft drink bottlers and pineapple canneries, with any excess shipped to the mainland.[32] Although a peak production of 36,552 tons was achieved in 1928, the average annual output was about 20,000 tons of refined sugar.

Despite being a mere seven miles from downtown Honolulu, the company owners maintained employee housing and a hospital. Camps were distributed throughout the plantation, and management made an effort to keep its workers. Longtime manager James Gibb complained that his camps were the first place that recruiters showed up whenever there was a labor shortage in Honolulu.[33]

The plantation had to balance increased yields per acre against surrendering its lands to the U.S. government. In 1907 it gave up a sizable portion for expansion of the U.S. Navy facilities at Pearl Harbor. Three decades later, in 1935, all of the Puʻuloa lands, roughly 15 percent of the plantation, were turned over for the construction of Hickam Air Field. Additional land was given up during World War II. Post-war urban growth supplied the final blow, and on January 1, 1947, Honolulu Plantation Company went out of business. Its equipment was sold to the neighboring Oahu Sugar Company, the refinery was sold to California & Hawaiian Sugar Company, the remaining lands were acquired by Oahu Sugar Company, and the mill was dismantled and shipped to the Philippines.[34]

The refinery continued to operate for almost half a century. Its machinery was upgraded in 1993 to provide a liquid product for canners and bottlers. However, when the Hawaiʻi bottlers switched to corn syrup, the operation shut down in 1996. Surrounded by urban shopping centers and residential areas, the refinery building is now home to the Hawaiʻi Agriculture Research Center.

O'AHU MUSEUMS

In 1973 the City and County of Honolulu and the State of Hawai'i purchased about 40 acres opposite the sugar mill to establish the Waipahu Cultural and Garden Park. The park matured into the Hawai'i Plantation Village. This well-planned series of exhibits includes a museum and examples of plantation housing, going all the way back to an authentic Native Hawaiian worker's grass house. A restored Oahu Sugar Company steam locomotive and attached cane haul car are displayed on a section of railroad track. There is no better place in Hawai'i to see and experience the significance of the everyday lives of early plantation workers and their families.

Kahuku Sugar Mill has been converted into a community center and marketplace. The old mill house serves as its centerpiece, and the grinding machinery is on display; the only place on O'ahu where it's possible to inspect the impressive apparatus used to manufacture sugar. After the mill shut down in 1971, the machinery and other artifacts were renovated by a public-spirited group of preservationists.

The Hawai'i Railway Society maintains a train yard at the end of Renton Road in 'Ewa District, next to the fence surrounding the former Barbers Point Naval Air Station. Visitors can see locomotives and rolling stock used by the O.R.& L. railroad to haul supplies to the mills, and sugar and molasses to the Honolulu sugar dock. A former Ewa Plantation Company locomotive is displayed on a section of track.

O'ahu was late to become a major sugar producer, but after 1900 made up for lost time. For nearly a century, until 1992, the island's two surviving plantations contributed between 15 and 20 percent of Hawai'i's sugar production. Considering the pressures of urban growth that occurred in post-war years, this lengthy record of the industry's survival on O'ahu is all the more remarkable.

Irrigation Ditch on Hawaiian sugar plantation. (Van Dyke Collection)

CHAPTER 5

SUGAR ON MOLOKAʻI AND LĀNAʻI (1876-1901)

In my time, sugar on Molokaʻi and Lānaʻi was long gone and pineapple was the cash crop. Both islands were far too dry for sugar farming, as the early planters soon discovered. Deep wells on Molokaʻi turned out to be brackish when heavy-duty pumps were installed to bring up irrigation water.

A few plantations started on Molokaʻi and Lānaʻi in the years immediately after annexation. One Lānaʻi operation barged their harvests across the channel to a mill at Olowalu, Maui. This may seem unusual, but harvested cane had to be transported to the mill somehow, and moving it by barge was relatively inexpensive. The method could be easily compared to barging pineapple harvests from Lānaʻi to the cannery in Honolulu, which was done for decades. Barging also compared favorably with the cost of trucking harvests when vehicle and road maintenance was included.

⊕ ⊕ ⊕

MOLOKAʻI IS THE fifth largest Hawaiian Island, with an area of 261 square miles; Lānaʻi is the sixth largest at 139 square miles. Molokaʻi lies within eyesight of Oʻahu, some 20 miles to the southeast at the nearest point; Lānaʻi lies 12 miles south of Molokaʻi, eight miles west of Maui, and is visible from both islands. In 1900, the heyday of sugar on the two islands, the population of Molokaʻi was 2,504; Lānaʻi had 619 residents. Today there is no sugarcane cultivated on either island. Their last cash crop grown on a plantation scale was pineapple. In 1982 Molokaʻi's pineapple operation was shut down, and pineapple departed from Lānaʻi in 1992. In both cases, ranching and the visitor industry have taken over.

The locations of sugar plantations operating on Molokaʻi and Lānaʻi in the years after 1876 are given on the following map. Table 5 identifies the plantations and specifies the years of sugar production.

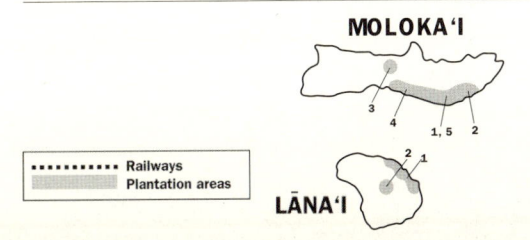

Location of sugar plantations on Molokaʻi and Lānaʻi in the years after 1876. See Table 5 for identification of the numbered plantations. (NOT TO SCALE)

TABLE 5 | SUGAR PLANTATIONS ON MOLOKAʻI AND LĀNAʻI 1878-1996

NO.	NAME	FIRST DATE*	LAST DATE*
	MOLOKAʻI		
1.	Kamalo Plantation	1878	1891
2.	Moanui Plantation	1878	1887
3.	R.W. Meyer	1878	1895
4.	American Sugar Co.	1900	1901
5.	Kamalo Sugar Company	1900	1901
	LĀNAʻI		
1.	Maunalei Sugar Company	1900	1901
2.	Palawai Development Company	1900	1900

*Notes: "First Date" and "Last Date" are the first and last years a plantation is listed in a source. The dates are believed to be within two years of organization or shutdown.
Sources: Hackler; Listing 1878-1895, *Hawaiian Almanac and Annual*; listing 1895-1945, HSPA Annual Meeting, Dec. 10, 1945.

Molokaʻi is not a hospitable place to grow sugarcane. The northern region gets the most rainfall, but the land is elevated and broken up by volcanic outcroppings and deep gulches. The southern region consists of sloping plains and richer land but receives little rainfall. In the past, school children were told in geography class that, "Owing to the lack of water in its desirable sections, Molokaʻi is of no great commercial value."[1] Nevertheless, there have been several attempts to grow sugarcane on the island.

KAMALO PLANTATION (1)

In 1878 Kamalo Plantation harvested its first crop. Located on the southern slopes of the island, 44 laborers cultivated about 100 acres of cane.[2] Its mill was managed by D. McCorriston, and struggled to produce 250 tons of sugar in any one year. In 1891 the plantation harvested its last crop and became a historical footnote.

MOANUI PLANTATION (2)

Moanui Plantation started in 1878 and lasted through 1887. It was situated along the southern shore of the island on 1,000 acres, of which only 100 to 200 were planted in sugarcane. The plantation and mill were managed by Eugene Bal and the Honolulu agent was Wong, Leong & Company.[3] The mill was located near the shore and the manager's house overlooked it, with vistas of the islands of Maui, Lānaʻi, and Kahoʻolawe in the distance. Despite the pleasant surroundings, the plantation was out of business in slightly over a decade.

R.W. MEYER (3)

Beginning in 1878, R.W. Meyer planted cane on less than a hundred acres of the 1,000 he owned near Kala'e in north central Moloka'i. This was one of the island's few locations with plentiful rainfall, but crops suffered from being at an elevation of 1,500 feet and higher. Sugarcane matures slowly in a cooler environment so Meyer's yields were very low. He constructed a mill and produced sugar until 1895, but it remained a family operation on a modest scale.[4]

AMERICAN SUGAR COMPANY (4)

The last attempts to grow sugar on Moloka'i came after the annexation of Hawai'i by the United States in 1898. A group of prominent Honolulu investors, including Charles Cooke (1849-1909), second son of missionary Amos Cooke (1810-1871) and later president of C. Brewer & Company, Ltd., incorporated American Sugar Company. Seventy-five hundred shares were sold for $750,000 to be used for building a plantation on the southern flanks of Moloka'i.[6] C. Brewer & Company, Ltd. invested $300,000 in the stock. The owners of Moloka'i Ranch exchanged their shares for shares in the new corporation, thus contributing land for the plantation. Machinery for a mill was purchased and railroad equipment was ordered from the Baldwin Locomotive Works. The plantation was initially managed by Patrick McLane (born 1861), and the Honolulu agents were C. Brewer & Company.[7]

McLane was an experienced Hawai'i sugar man. He came to the Islands in the early 1880s and worked for ten years at various Maui plantations; six years as head overseer at Hana Plantation, then Kipahulu Plantation, followed by four years as manager of Hamoa Plantation.[8] He managed the buildup of the Moloka'i plantation and installed large steam pumps to lift and distribute well water for irrigation. The first crop had been planted by the time the pumps began supplying water. But the cane was stunted and the well water seemed to contribute to this condition. Studies revealed that the heavy-duty pumps were exhausting the fresh water in the aquifer, salt water was seeping in, and the brackish result was too salty to grow cane.[9] This fact doomed the enterprise just two years after it started.

The organizers moved quickly to salvage what they could. For a bargain price Cooke offered the mill, already located on Moloka'i but not fully assembled, to the new McBryde Sugar Company on Kaua'i. The offer was accepted.[10] The two locomotives were returned to the Baldwin Works distributor in Honolulu, who sold one to Ewa Plantation and the other to Honolulu Plantation Company. C. Brewer & Company lost $300,000 in the venture.[11]

One account from the time claims that when an investor learned of the disaster on his hands, he caught the next boat to Honolulu and unloaded his stock in the enterprise before word got out.[12] Before the plantation shut down, Patrick McLane was succeeded by D. Center. McLane went on to briefly manage Kamalo Sugar Company on Moloka'i, then to manage Koloa Plantation on Kaua'i from 1900 to 1906. He ended his lengthy career in the sugar with the highly successful Central Aguirre Plantation in Puerto Rico.[13]

KAMALO SUGAR COMPANY (5)

Little is known about the short-lived Kamalo Sugar Company. It was incorporated in 1899 with $250,000 of paid-in capital. Patrick McLane was listed as manager and the agent was F. Hustace.[14] By the end of 1900, McLane had joined Koloa Plantation on Kaua'i, and Kamalo Sugar Company was out of business. This signaled the end of sugarcane plantations on Moloka'i.

MOLOKA'I MUSEUM

The restored Meyer Sugar Mill on Moloka'i is well worth a visit. Historians and industrial archaeologists discovered the remains of this small mill that had shut down in the 1890s. Restoration began about 1974, using contributions from enthusiasts and preservationists throughout the industry and the state. The restored mill has been placed on the National List of Historic Places, with the state of Hawai'i supplying maintenance funds. The mill is an excellent example of the equipment used in the late nineteenth century, and is complete with steam-driven centrifugals, all restored.

The mill is also listed on the Historic Engineering Record of the National Park Service.[5] It was dedicated in March 1988, and serves as the Moloka'i Museum and Cultural Center.

R.W. Meyer Sugar Mill in 1995.
(W. H. Dorrance)

SUGAR ON LĀNA'I

In 1861 Walter Murray Gibson (1822-1888) and his daughter came to Hawai'i from Salt Lake City, where he had been converted to the Mormon Church. Presenting himself as president of the church in Hawai'i, he purchased considerable acreage on Lāna'i. He was busy proselytizing converts and settlers when the Mormon elders in Utah sent a delegation to investigate. Gibson was excommunicated in 1864 and turned his energies to ranching and politics in the Kingdom of Hawai'i. He served King Kalākaua as Premier and Minister of Foreign Affairs from 1882 to 1887, when he was deposed during the constitutional revolution of 1887.[15] Through it all, Gibson held on to his Lāna'i property. Yet another missionary had played a role in Hawai'i's sugar industry. Although Walter Gibson wasn't "official," he did begin as a representative of the Mormon Church.

MAUNALEI SUGAR COMPANY (1)

Gibson's only daughter, Talula (died 1903), married Frederick Heyselden (1851-1924), who inherited the Lāna'i property following Gibson's death. In 1899 Heyselden and others incorporated the Maunalei Sugar Company with $100,000 of paid-in capital.[16] Cane was planted in and around Keōmuku on the northeast coast of the island. A 24-inch narrow gauge railroad was laid down to transport harvests to a wharf at Halepalaoa Landing. From there the sugarcane was to be transported by barge across the eight-mile channel for grinding by the Olowalu Company mill on West Maui.[17]

Records show that the production at the Olowalu Company mill peaked slightly in 1899 and 1900, indicating that one or two crops were taken off Lāna'i.[18] Yet the sugar produced there could not have been more than 200 to 300 tons for each year. The plantation had inadequate rainfall, well water was insufficient to bridge the gap, and transporting harvested cane to Maui was a burden. The operation closed down by the end of 1901.

The plantation had been managed by engineer William Stodart. McBryde Sugar Company on Kaua'i ran into problems erecting the mill they had purchased from the moribund American Sugar Company, and hired Stodart to oversee its construction. He stayed on to manage McBryde Sugar until 1911.[19]

PALAWAI DEVELOPMENT COMPANY (2)

Little is recorded of the short-lived Palawai Development Company on Lāna'i. Apparently it existed for only one year, 1900. Palawai was located on Heyselden's land, the manager was W.F. Hasson, and the Honolulu agent was W.H. Pain, then manager of the Hawaiian Tramways Company, Ltd.[20] The plantation failed for the same reason that every sugar-growing enterprise on Lāna'i failed—insufficient water.

Pu'unene Mill, Maui,
Hawai'i, 1912

(Baker/The Hawaiian Historical Society)

CHAPTER 6

SUGAR ON MAUI (1876-1991)

I remember when Maui Agricultural Company was merged into the Hawaiian Commercial & Sugar Company (H.C.& S.) plantation in 1948, making it the largest plantation in Hawai'i. Asa Baldwin became manager of the combined operation. He attended many HSPA meetings and could be counted on to make helpful observations that drew on his experience as a large-scale sugarcane farmer.

Asa was descended from a line of Maui plantation managers. His grandfather was pioneer planter Henry P. Baldwin, a remarkable man in his own right. In 1878 he supervised the digging of the ditch to bring Haleakalā runoff to his Ha'ikū sugar plantation. The ditch had to cross the deep Māliko Gulch and a large metal siphon was assembled. One side of the gulch was a near-vertical precipice and the workers refused to rappel down to assemble the siphon. Baldwin had lost an arm in a terrible sugarmill accident, but he clutched the rope with his legs and his one good arm, and worked himself down to the bottom of the gulch. The workers were impressed. Soon they followed his example and the siphon was completed.

When Theo H. Davies & Co. decided to modernize the Haina, Hawai'i, mill, they had a choice: install a modern roller-based crusher, or a diffusion extractor. The diffusion plant extracted a little more sugar but used a little more energy because the bagasse had to be run through a crusher to remove the water before it could be burned. Both Pioneer Mill Company and H.C.& S. had installed diffusion plants on Maui that we studied before making our decision. However, I was much impressed by the South African technology. They were producing refined sugar at mills which all used conventional crushers. I decided to install those because I planned to do the same.

H.C.& S. was the first to completely automate an entire factory, the mill at Pu'unēnē, Maui. Automation was the only answer to reducing the number of employees, and labor was at least 50 percent of the cost of running a plantation. When we modernized our Haina factory, we followed H.C.& S. and installed automation as much as possible.

⊕ ⊕ ⊕

MAUI LIES 72 miles southeast of Oʻahu, and is 48 miles long and 31 miles wide. Its surface area of 728 square miles makes Maui the second-largest island in the archipelago. Most of its cane was cultivated in the central valley between the mountainous heights at both ends of the island.

After deep wells and large-scale irrigation ditches were introduced, Maui blossomed as a major sugar producer. As on the other islands, before irrigation its plantations were small and concentrated in the wettest areas. Over the years Maui managed to increase its share of Hawaiʻi's sugar production despite the inroads of urban and resort development.

In 1935 its five plantations produced 198,753 tons, or 20.63 percent, of the Territory's sugar.[1] Over half a century later in 1990, the two remaining Maui plantations produced 267,271 tons, or 32.61 percent, of the state's total.[2]

Locations of Maui sugar plantations that existed after 1876; not to scale. See Table 6 for identification of the numbered plantations.

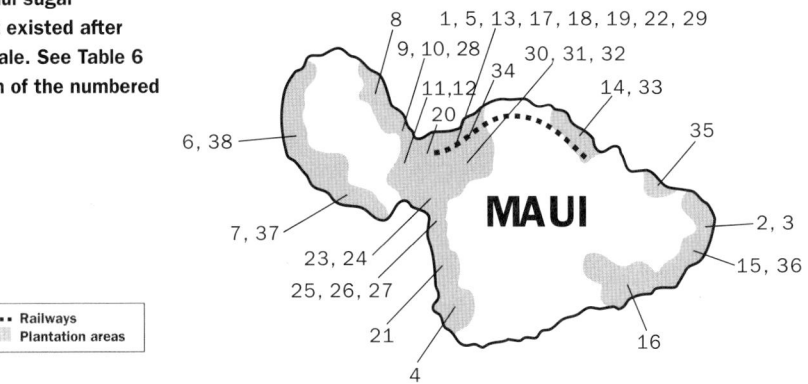

TABLE 6 | SUGAR PLANTATIONS ON MAUI 1876-1996

NO.	NAME	FIRST DATE*	LAST DATE*	OR OPERATING IN 1996 AS
1.	E. Maui Plantation Company	1850	1886	
2.	Hana Plantation Company	1850	1904	
3.	Kaeleku Plantation Company	1905	1944	
4.	Ulupalakua Plantation (Makee)	1858	1883	
5.	Haiku Sugar Company	1858	1921	
6.	Pioneer Mill Company	1863	1999	
7.	Olowalu Company	1881	1931	
8.	Waihee Sugar Company (Lewers)	1862	1894	
9.	Wailuku Sugar Co., includes	1862	1988	
10.	Bailey Brothers	1884	1884	
11.	Bal & Adams	1865	1877	
12.	Waikapu Sugar Company	1862	1894	
13.	Grove Ranch Plantation	1863	1889	
14.	Huelo Plantation	1879	1894	
15.	Reciprocity Sugar Company	1883	1898	
16.	Kipahulu Sugar Company	1879	1925	

NO.	NAME	FIRST DATE*	LAST DATE*	OR OPERATING IN 1996 AS
17.	Alexander & Baldwin, includes	1872	1883	
18.	Paia Plantation Company	1883	1921	
19.	J.M. Alexander	1882	1884	
20.	Hwn. Cmml. Co.,then H.C.& S. Co.	1878		Hwn. Cmml.& Sgr. Co.
21.	Kihei Sugar Company	1899	1908	
22.	Maui Agricultural Co., includes	1904	1948	
23.	Kula Plantation Company	1903	1921	
24.	Makawao Plantation Co.	1903	1921	
25.	Pulehu Plantation Co.	1903	1921	
26.	Kailua Plantation	1903	1921	
27.	Kalianui Plantation Co.	1903	1921	
(numbers 28 through 38 are not described in the text)				
28.	Barnes & Palmer	1884	1886	
29.	Lilikoe Sugar Plantation	1878	1880	
30.	Piiholo Sugar Plantation	1879	1880	
31.	E. Maui Stock Company	1884	1889	
32.	Brewer & Associates	1884	1886	
33.	Maui Sugar Company	1902	1904	
34.	Hamakua Plantation	1878	1880	
35.	Nahiku Sugar Company	1900	1901	
36.	Hamoa Plantation	1900	1902	See Note (2)
37.	West Maui Plantation	1871	1878	
38.	Y.W. Horner, Planter	1883	1891	

*Notes: (1) "First Date" and "Last Date" are the first and last years a plantation is listed in a source. The dates are believed to be within two years of organization or shutdown. (2) Hamoa Plantation operated as Reciprocity Sugar Company 1883-1898. See No. 15 listed above.
Sources: Listing 1878-1940, *Hawaiian Almanac and Annual*; listing, dates of charter, *The Planters Monthly*, Aug. 1882; listing 1895-1945, HSPA Annual Meeting, Dec. 10, 1945; Dean; Sullivan; Wilfong; citations 1945-1996, corporation annual reports, newspapers, and HSPA library.

The following descriptions concentrate on plantations which had a life of six or more years, or some noteworthy feature. As in previous chapters, the descriptions proceed chronologically.

EAST MAUI PLANTATION (1)

In about 1850 Dr. Robert W. Wood, long-time owner of Koloa Plantation on Kauaʻi, entered into a partnership with Ambrose H. Spencer to start a plantation on the western slopes of Mount Haleakalā, near the town of Makawao. East Maui Plantation occupied about 2,000 acres, of which 500 acres were cultivated, and was managed by veteran sugarcane-planter Spencer.[3] In 1852 its mill became the first to use centrifugals to separate sugar from molasses in the sugar manufacturing process.[4] By 1880 the estate had changed hands and was yielding about 500 tons of sugar annually.

In 1886 the agency/owner C. Brewer & Company found itself in financial straits. The East Maui Plantation holdings were auctioned off, and

Henry Baldwin purchased the majority of the acreage, then resold it at cost to the neighboring Haiku Sugar Company.[5]

HANA PLANTATION COMPANY (2)

About the time East Maui Plantation got its start, another early business was established in remote Hāna, on the island's eastern shore on the other side of Mount Haleakalā. Hana Plantation had a checkered existence. George Wilfong wrote of how he and Dr. Gerrit Judd traveled to Hāna in 1851 to assess the prospects of the small plantation. They agreed that Wilfong would take over the operation for Mr. A.B. Howe, who had acquired the holdings from the founder, a Mr. Lingrin.

Wilfong acted as manager for two years and produced about 50 to 60 tons of sugar annually from some 60 acres of native cane. When his sugar and boiling houses burned down (a common occurrence in early days), at a loss of 50 tons of sugar, in discouragement he turned the plantation over to Doctor Judd, who closed it down.[6]

By 1861 Hana Plantation was back in operation in the hands of August Unna (died 1885). He successfully expanded the acreage under cultivation, and installed a 20-inch narrow gauge railroad in 1883. Following Unna's death, the plantation entered another era of uncertainty. However, by 1890 the lands had grown to 950 acres under cultivation, and 2,290 tons of sugar were produced by its manager D. Center.[7] In 1905 the operation changed hands again and became the Kaeleku Plantation Company.

KAELEKU PLANTATION COMPANY (3)

This was one of a very few sugar farms on Maui that survived without irrigation because most of the time rainfall in the Hāna vicinity was sufficient. In 1907 manager John Chalmers changed the gauge of the plantation's railroad to a more workable 36 inches and made other improvements, including transport of cane by flumes in the more rugged areas.[8] By 1939 Kaeleku Plantation was producing 7,536 tons of sugar annually from 3,362 acres under cultivation.[9] Its last crop was harvested in 1945, and C. Brewer & Company sold the plantation to Paul Fagan, who closed it down.

ULUPALAKUA PLANTATION (MAKEE PLANTATION) (4)

In 1856 Capt. James Makee purchased the moribund Linton Torbert plantation at 'Ulupalakua in southeast Maui. He planted cane in 1858 and created Makee Plantation. In addition he developed the area as his residence and put in an abundance of trees and shrubbery around the estate that he named "Rose Ranch."[10] In 1867 its steam-powered mill produced 800 tons of sugar from a harvest of 800 acres. This level of production was sustained through at least 1872.[11] Following Makee's death in 1879, the plantation lingered on until it shut down after the harvest of 1883, and was converted to cattle ranching.

HAIKU SUGAR COMPANY (5)

Another early venture began in 1858, when Richard Armstrong (1805-1860) proposed that Amos Cooke buy stock in a company to develop a plantation and mill at Ha'ikū, in northeast Maui.[12] Both men had arrived in Hawai'i as missionaries—Armstrong with the fifth company in 1832, and Cooke as a teacher with the eighth company in 1837. Armstrong purchased the Ha'ikū property when King Kamehameha III offered to sell land cheaply to missionaries. By 1858 Cooke had discharged his teaching obligations and was doing business in partnership with the former manager of missionary secular affairs, Samuel Castle. The Castle & Cooke partnership invested in Haiku Plantation, a steam-powered mill was erected, and the first crop of 260 tons was harvested in 1862.[13]

By 1872 Haiku Sugar Company's production had risen to 650 tons.[14] In 1880 it had expanded to 6,000 acres, with 1,200 acres under cultivation in two parcels separated by a deep gulch. These parcels produced 2,600 tons of sugar.[15] In 1884 Samuel Alexander and Henry Baldwin bought the majority of the stock and took control of the company. Two decades later in 1904, they merged Haiku Sugar Company with their Maui Agricultural Company, and Haiku Sugar Company ceased to exist.[16]

PIONEER MILL COMPANY (6)

Lahaina entrepreneurs James Campbell and Henry Turton, in partnership with Hilo merchant Benjamin Pitman (died 1888), established Pioneer Mill Company in 1863. The land belonged to Pitman and had been occupied by the Lahaina Sugar Company.[17] Campbell had arrived in Lahaina in 1850 as a ship's carpenter on a New Bedford whaler after an adventurous voyage that included being shipwrecked and taken prisoner by natives on a South Pacific island. Working for 12 years as a carpenter in Lahaina gave him the capital he needed to enter the sugar business. His fellow entrepreneur Turton was a mason by trade, and owner of a billiard parlor and bowling alley in Lahaina.

They started with a steam-powered mill and 126 acres under cultivation. Annual production was 500 tons of sugar in 1866, using their own cane and what was grown by independent planters like Henry and Dwight Baldwin.[18] Henry Baldwin had entered the sugar business in 1863 at age 21, when he joined his brother in raising cane to be ground at Pioneer Mill.[19] By 1872 the mill's yield was 1,000 tons and the plantation continued to grow.[20]

Eventually Pitman, Campbell, and Turton sold their interests, and in 1885 H. Hackfeld & Company, predecessor of today's owner, Amfac/JMB-Hawai'i, Inc., bought control.[21] Pioneer Mill has succeeded over the years against obstacles that killed off many a competitor.

Pioneer Mill's land was honeycombed with boulders and stones that were cleared in the 1950s. Irrigation water is transported by ditches from distant watersheds and lifted from wells by heavy-duty pumps. Much of the land is leased and not owned. Nevertheless, production grew over the years from 2,

132 tons in 1895 to 10,316 tons in 1900. A decade later this increase of almost 500 percent in five years was almost tripled, to 27,299 tons in 1910. The total rose again to 35,691 tons in 1925, followed by decades of stable production leading to a record of 63,000 tons in the 1960s.[22]

In recent decades some of the most attractive areas were given up to resort development at Kāʻanapali. Pioneer Mill Company was not large, with only 6,867 acres under cultivation, and was only marginally profitable. It owed its continued survival to the contributions it made to tourism on the island. The mill represented what had once been Hawaiʻi's dominant industry, and the lush green fields of sugarcane provided a pleasant background for the Kāʻanapali resort hotels and golf courses. The last operating railway in Hawaiʻi—the Lahaina, Kaanapali and Pacific Railroad, which offered a recreational ride over a surviving roadbed on the old plantation—owed its existence to Pioneer Mill.

In 1999 Amfac/JMB-Hawaiʻi announced that Pioneer Mill would shut down after the last harvest, and Maui lost one of its historic visitor attractions.

OLOWALU COMPANY (7)

In 1881 Olowalu Company was organized on the lands given up by the West Maui Plantation. Never a large producer, Olowalu's mill produced the maximum of 2,969 tons of sugar in 1931.[24] Its 24-inch narrow gauge cane haul railroad was considered a curiosity because of its "watch-charm" locomotives, although they were not unique in Hawaiʻi.

Half a century after its founding, Olowalu Company's mill and lands were purchased in 1931, when Pioneer Mill added to its acreage.[23] As a result, the former plantation lost its separate identity.

WAIHEE SUGAR COMPANY (8)

When a steam-powered mill was assembled in 1862, at Waiheʻe on the northeast coast of Maui[25], the Waihee Sugar Company was also established. The plantation had 800 acres of cane under cultivation. Linton Torbert managed it from 1863 until 1865, then Samuel Alexander took over and persuaded his old friend and schoolmate Henry Baldwin to join him as head luna.[26]

The plantation prospered and was soon producing 1,000 tons of sugar annually. But Alexander & Baldwin were anxious to strike out on their own, and in 1869 they left. Waiheʻe Plantation survived their departure, and by 1877 was owned by Capt. James Makee.[27]

The Waiheʻe mill had a diffusion extractor installed in 1890 and reported it to be satisfactory. If so, it was the only satisfactory diffusion plant in Hawaiʻi at that time. The processing method was highly efficient at extracting sugar from the cane, but required an inordinate amount of heat. The residue (bagasse) was too wet to burn, and imported coal was expensive. Ewa Plantation on Oʻahu, Hawaiian Sugar Company and Makee Sugar Company on Kauaʻi, and Haiku Plantation on Maui also installed diffusion plants about this time, but soon replaced them with conventional crushers for better overall efficiency.

Despite its choice of processing technique, Waihee Sugar Company's production never exceeded 1,200 tons. In 1894 Wailuku Sugar Company purchased the plantation and it ceased to be an independent enterprise.[28]

WAILUKU SUGAR COMPANY (9, 10, 11 & 12)

In 1862 a group of partners, including C. Brewer & Company, Ltd., established Wailuku Sugar Company in north central Maui. Rev. Edward Bailey (1814-1903) managed it from the beginning until he quit to run his own plantation. Bailey had arrived in Hawaiʻi in 1837 with the eighth company of missionaries, and left the mission in 1850 to take up farming. He was succeeded by others, including George Wilfong in 1868.[29]

By 1867 Wailuku Sugar Company was producing 800 tons of sugar from 500 acres of cane.[30] The plantation incorporated in 1875 and C. Brewer & Company was a major shareowner. Two years later in 1877, William Bailey, son of Edward, sold his neighboring 420-acre plantation to Wailuku Sugar Company. He and his father had been planting cane there for over ten years. Also in 1877, Bal & Adams, who had set up a mill and begun planting in 1865, sold out to Wailuku Sugar Company.[31] The combined plantations produced 1,550 tons of sugar in 1880, with a minority shared among independent planters.[32]

Steam plows lined up for a parade in Wailuku early 1910. (Wailuku Sugar Company)

The first Wailuku Sugar Company mill was water-powered and lasted until 1890, when it was replaced with a steam-powered six-roller mill.[33] That year the plantation employed 275 workers and produced 2,400 tons of sugar.[34] In 1894 Wailuku Sugar Company purchased Waikapu Sugar Company and Waihee Sugar Company, and combined production was 4,349 tons of sugar.[35] Teams of oxen hauled harvests to the mill until 1895, when the plantation installed a narrow gauge railroad.

Wailuku Sugar Company continued to grow by acquiring nearby plantations. By 1939 it was producing 20,475 tons of sugar from 4,450 acres under cultivation. In the 1970s it averaged over 30,000 tons[36], the maximum production, as C. Brewer & Company began to give up land to macadamia nuts, followed by pineapple planting and urban growth.

By 1986 the sugar yield had dropped to 19,885 tons. Milling was contracted out to the Hawaiian Commercial & Sugar Company in Puʻunēnē.[37] The end was near for Wailuku Sugar Company. Two years later in 1988 C. Brewer & Company, Ltd. shut down the sugarcane operations.

GROVE RANCH PLANTATION (13)

In 1863 Capt. H.T. Hobron of Makawao took over planting and milling at the former Brewer plantation at Hāliʻimaile in northwest Maui. He named the new enterprise Grove Ranch Plantation. By 1880, members of the Kauaʻi "Smith clan" were its main proprietors and W.O. Smith was manager.[38]

The three brothers—Jared, A.H. and W.O.—were sons of the missionary Dr. James Smith, who began cultivating cane at Kōloa, Kauaʻi, in 1879. Another investor was Judge Alfred Stedman, who was also attorney general at the time. Some 110 men were employed and produced 800 tons of sugar from 350 acres under cultivation.[39]

Grove Ranch Plantation operated independently until 1889, when it was merged into the neighboring Paia Plantation Company.[40]

HUELO PLANTATION (14)

In the wake of the Reciprocity Treaty, Huelo Plantation was established in northeast Maui in 1878 by T. Akanaliilii, proprietor and manager. This 1,500-acre plantation employed 120 men and produced 900 tons of sugar in 1880.[41] It was situated in a beautiful, but rugged, coastal region about 25 miles from Wailuku, one of very few post-Mahele plantations owned and operated by a Native Hawaiian.

Flumes were used to transport much of the harvested cane to the mill. The plantation had its own inter-island steamer landing at Huelo Point, one of the most beautiful spots on the island. But, hemmed in by the surrounding terrain and unable to expand, Huelo Plantation harvested its last crop in 1894.

RECIPROCITY SUGAR COMPANY (15)

Another post-treaty plantation was owned by the aptly named Reciprocity Sugar Company, Inc. In 1883 it was established in Hāna with W.G. Irwin & Co. as agent. By 1890 the plantation had 500 acres planted in cane, employed 260 laborers, and produced 2,200 tons of sugar.[42]

Fifteen years later, in 1898, the plantation reported its last harvest. Agent C. Brewer & Company, Ltd., shut it down, and its manager Patrick McLane went on to work at the new American Sugar Company plantation on Molokaʻi.

KIPAHULU SUGAR COMPANY (16)

This business was unusual in the sense that it was incorporated with all shares of stock owned by German nationals. The plantation was located on the rugged southeast shore below the slopes of Mount Haleakalā. Its first reported harvest in 1879 had H. Hackfield & Company as the Honolulu agent. For several years the plantation was managed by Oscar Unna. Maximum production was 2,699 tons in 1915.[43]

American Factors, Ltd., successors to H. Hackfield & Company, sold out to Haiku Fruit & Packing Corp. and shut down Kipahulu Sugar Comapny following the harvest of its 1925 crop.

ALEXANDER & BALDWIN (17, 18 & 19)

In about 1869 Samuel Alexander and Henry Baldwin began to purchase land with the goal of assembling a sizable plantation. They bought over 600 acres in east Maui and entered into an agreement with Robert Hind (1832-1901), who built a mill capable of producing up to 500 tons of sugar per year from cane grown by Alexander & Baldwin. The proceeds were divided equally between the miller and the planters.[44] While the fledgling operation was being developed, Alexander contracted to manage nearby Haiku Plantation to give his household some financial security.

In 1872 the partnership became officially established as the Alexander & Baldwin Plantation, with Baldwin as manager. The milling agreement with Hind was cancelled by paying him $22,000.[45] Curiously, his son John (1858-1933) remembers the amount in his memoirs as $23,000.[46]

Four years later, in 1876, Henry Baldwin was involved in a tragic and nearly fatal accident. W.H. Wilkinson, manager of the mill at the time, described what happened to Baldwin's son, Arthur, who used the story in a biography of his father. Baldwin and Wilkinson were adjusting the clearance of the old mill's rollers in an attempt to get them to press out more sugar. In Wilkinson's words:

"Mr. Baldwin came up and stepped up on the plank where the man stood when he fed the mill. He...showed me by slipping his fingers in between the rollers where it was widest....The mill was going pretty fast. He reached over and slipped his hand in the place where the rollers were closest together. The rollers...caught his finger and I knew a pair of cattle couldn't pull him out and I ran...to the engine intending to throw it out of gear." [Baldwin called to

Wilkinson to reverse the engine at once. Wilkinson did so just in time to save Baldwin's life.] "I called out to him 'Are you all right?' He did not answer…I called to Charlie to shut off the steam. I…went out to see how Mr. Baldwin was and met him walking into the engine house. He was white as a sheet…The mill had stripped all the flesh from his hand and his arm to some distance above the elbow. The arteries were not severed and there was very little bleeding…."[47]

Baldwin never lost consciousness and called for the nearest doctor some ten miles away, who fortunately, came quickly. Baldwin's right arm was amputated between the elbow and shoulder. Within weeks he was back on horseback managing the plantation.

In November 1876 the Hamakua Ditch Company was formed, owned in shares by Haiku Plantation, Alexander & Baldwin Plantation, T.H. Hobron (representing Grove Ranch Plantation), and independent planter James Alexander, a brother of Samuel Alexander.[48] This pioneering irrigation effort was designed to bring water several miles from the slopes of Mount Haleakalā to the four plantations. The project was completed in two years, the first large-scale irrigation system on Maui. Along with the Reciprocity Treaty, it vastly increased the prospects of success for the Alexander & Baldwin enterprise.

Through purchases from Haiku Sugar Company and several small parcels, mostly native kuleana, by 1877 Alexander & Baldwin Plantation had grown to slightly over 2,000 acres. In 1883 it was incorporated as Paia Plantation and the former name was no longer used.[49]

That same year Samuel Alexander resigned as manager of Haiku Plantation and moved to California for health reasons. He was replaced by Henry Baldwin, who managed both Paia and Haiku Plantations for a time. The move to San Francisco resulted in the formation of the Alexander & Baldwin agency, which survives to this day.

HAWAIIAN COMMERCIAL & SUGAR COMPANY (20)

Negotiation of the Reciprocity Treaty in 1876 had the expected result of attracting outside investors to Hawai'i. Claus Spreckels was a prime example. By 1876 he had become enormously wealthy through his 13-year monopoly of sugar refining in California. His San Francisco refinery processed sugar purchased from China, the Philippines, and Hawai'i.[50] If sugar from Hawai'i were to enter the United States duty free, Spreckels reasoned, then making sugar in the Islands would be quite profitable. Spreckels came to Hawai'i in August of 1876 to investigate the possibilities. It was an epochal visit for Hawaiian sugar.

Spreckels lost no time ingratiating himself with King Kalākaua. He leased thousands of acres of crown lands in central Maui and purchased a half-interest in 16,000 acres of adjacent, privately owned lands. In 1878 he formed Hawaiian Commercial Company in order to raise capital to develop these sprawling lands.[51] The plantation was to be modern in all respects, including a 24-inch narrow

The Hawaiian Commercial & Sugar Company mill at Puʻunēnē, Maui, in 1990.
(W. H. Dorrance)

gauge railroad. The mill was constructed with two parallel crushing trains to accommodate the large harvests.

In 1882 the Hawaiian Commercial & Sugar Company, a California corporation, was formed to take over the assets of the Hawaiian Commercial Company. The plantation was soon the largest producer in the Islands, beginning with 9,000 tons of sugar in 1889.[52]

Several lasting innovations were first introduced at the Spreckels plantation. The mill was the first to have a five-roller crusher at a time when all other mills employed three rollers. The resulting improvement in extraction efficiency produced bagasse dry enough to be directly burned in the mill's boilers. The first large-scale plantation railroad was installed at H.C.& S. The plantation's many worker camps were the first to have electric lighting. Steam plows were first used here beginning in 1880. In addition, between 1878 and 1880 Spreckels spent thousands of dollars to construct an irrigation ditch above the Hāmākua ditch to bring in much-needed water for the fields.[53] It was only the second such irrigation ditch constructed on Maui.

For a time the H.C.& S. plantation prospered at the expense of preventive maintenance and improvements. But, by 1898, the entire operation was run down and in debt. When its stock sold at a new low, James Castle initiated a quiet move to buy control. Alexander & Baldwin agreed to advance the funds, a partnership with Castle interests was formed, the controlling stock purchase was made, and Claus Spreckels was out of the picture.[54] Henry Baldwin took over as president.

KIHEI SUGAR COMPANY (21)

Henry Baldwin and partner Lorrin Thurston owned thousands of acres of ranch land hear Kīhei in south central Maui. In 1899 they organized the Kihei Sugar Company to grow cane to be ground under contract at the H.C. & S. Company mill in Puʻunēnē. It was one of very few Baldwin projects that turned out poorly. The problem was lack of water.

While production grew to 5,609 tons in 1903, it was not enough to cover costs. In 1908 all property except the land was sold to H.C.& S. Company, and Kihei Plantation lost its identity as a cane grower.[55]

These were years of furious activity for the indefatigable Henry Baldwin. One of his sons described a typical, busy two-day stretch: "I remember on one occasion he left Maui in the afternoon by the *James Makee* for Honolulu, arriving there the next morning about ten o'clock. He attended to some business there and returned the same afternoon about three o'clock on one of the small boats, the *Iwalani* I think it was, arriving at Kīhei the following morning. There he got a horse from Mr. Pogue, who was then manager of the Kihei Plantation, rode over the Kihei Plantation, arriving at my house at Paliuli, just above the Paia church. He had lunch with us, got a fresh horse, rode over to Hamakuapoko [in East Maui] and looked over the fields and mill. He then rode over to Haiku and got another horse and rode up to Olinda, arriving there about half past six that evening. After dinner, so I am told, he sat up until about half past nine, apparently 'as fresh as a daisy.'[56]"

This remarkable one-armed man earned the respect of his peers. However, Hubert Edson, a sugar chemist for Baldwin's mills at Pāʻia and Hamākua Poko, offered some observations that provide an interesting contrast. "After a month's idleness [in 1894] Paia and Hamakuapoko began to grind again, and I took up the chemical work at these two factories. While each had a fairly well equipped laboratory, the management didn't have any more understanding of what a chemist was supposed to do than [the management] during my first year at Calumet [Louisiana]…My routine was to make in the morning analyses of samples collected at Paia and then in the early afternoon ride horseback to Hamakuapoko and repeat the performance there…as far as I could tell, little attention was paid to my analytical work by the managing partner [Baldwin], who made his residence on the property. This partner, a descendant of a missionary family was a man of tremendous energy, generally directed more to the agricultural side of the business than to the factory. He was a deeply religious man and there was a general impression among employees that his favor was secured as much by going to church on Sunday as by doing your work efficiently…However, it seemed to me that his actions, like those of many zealots, contradicted the religion in which he professed to believe. An example of this was his unrelenting attitude toward the indentured labor force… The contract contained a clause…inflicting a severe penalty—a long term on government road work—when they failed to report for work…The resident manager attended court proceedings to insist on the enforcement of this penalty, which in effect kept the workers indefinitely in slavery. Just how his religion countenanced this attitude I couldn't understand...."[57]

MAUI AGRICULTURAL COMPANY (22, 23, 24, 25, 26 & 27)

From a business perspective, sugar planters saw the 1898 annexation of the Republic of Hawai'i by the United States as a mixed blessing. On the one hand, abolishing the possibility of tariffs imposed on Hawaiian sugar was a favorable development. On the other, United States laws forbade the enforcement of binding clauses in labor contracts, and the importation of Oriental labor. There were other considerations.

The Organic Act of 1900, which determined the powers of the Territorial Legislature, imposed a limitation that affected the growers. Section 55 of the Act stated: "...no corporation, domestic or foreign, shall acquire and hold real estate in Hawai'i in excess of one thousand acres...but existing vested rights in real estate shall not be impaired." As a consequence of this restrictive clause, very few new plantation corporations were formed until Congress deleted the clause in 1921.[58] By 1900 it was a recognized fact that a plantation must be far larger than 1,000 acres in order to be profitable.

Planters on Maui did not feel inhibited by the restriction. They wanted to combine plantations, reap economies of scale, and their lawyers found a way to do it. The Maui Agricultural Company, a co-partnership, was formed in 1903. It owned seven plantations, two of them well established in 1900, with well over 1,000 acres each—Paia Plantation Company, formed in 1883, and Haiku Sugar Company, formed in 1858. Both came into the partnership complete with mills. In 1904 the five others—Kula Plantation Company, Makawao Plantation Company, Pulehu Plantation Company, Kailua Plantation and Kalianui Plantation Company—each with 1,000 acres, were newly formed by carving up the lands of Kihei Plantation.[59]

As co-partner and owner of all seven, Maui Agricultural Company delegated management to a board of managers that included H.P. Baldwin, T.H. Hobron, W.O. Smith, J.B. Castle, C.W. Dickey, and S.M. Damon (1845-1924).[60] Damon represented Haiku Sugar Company and was the son of Samuel Damon (1815-1885), who arrived in 1842 and became chaplain of the American Seaman's Friend Society in Honolulu.[61]

In 1905 a mill at Hāmākua Poko ground the Maui Agricultural Company's cane. A year later this arrangement was consolidated with the Pā'ia mill, creating a tandem operation that was then replaced for several years with a 21-roller mill. In 1917 a striking, different kind of innovation was introduced by chemist J.P. Foster. He made ethanol from molasses by a process he developed himself. Management welcomed the idea of using it for fuel, a production plant was constructed, and for years the plantation's fleet of trucks and automobiles ran on ethanol.[65] This effort was far ahead of its time.

Main street of the sugar town Pā'ia, Maui in 1991. (W. H. Dorrance)

In 1921 the Maui Agricultural Company was incorporated and the seven subsidiary corporations disbanded. Production peaked at 63,280 tons of sugar in 1932.[62] The 21-roller mill was eventually replaced with two tandem mills until they, in turn, were also replaced by a diffusion extractor in the 1970s.

After World War II, in 1948 corporate leadership realized many cost savings were possible, as well as more efficient use of irrigation water. Shareholders agreed. The two plantations were combined under the banner of H.C.& S. Company, and Maui Agricultural Company went out of existence.[63] In 1990, 225,555 tons of sugar were produced from 35,501 acres under cultivation, an admirable rate of 13.2 tons per acre harvested that year.[64]

Today H.C.& S. Company operates two mills, the grinder at Pu'unēnē and a diffusion plant at Pā'ia. It is one of the strongest of the remaining plantations in Hawai'i and its future seems secure. Whatever the future brings, there can be no denying that for over 150 years the face of Maui was determined by sugar cultivation.

A MAUI MUSEUM

No visit to the Valley Isle is complete without stopping at the Alexander & Baldwin Sugar Museum, located in a former supervisor's residence next to the Puʻunēnē mill. Visitors can examine scenes from the Maui sugar industry ranging from the life of the workers to operations at the mill. An outdoor exhibit will include the 1882 locomotive named after Claus Spreckels. Restoration of the engine is complete and there are plans to put it on display. This excellent memorial to the past opened in 1982 and is among the most outstanding sugar museums in the world.[66]

Papaaloa Mill and Village,
1933, Hawai'i.
(Baker/Van Dyke Collection)

CHAPTER 7

SUGAR ON THE ISLAND OF HAWAI'I (1876-1996)

In the days before World War II, the Morgan family traveled by inter-island steamer to visit the Big Island. We usually stayed at least two weeks to see various attractions. The roads were rough and narrow, so it was a long trip from Hilo to Kona, a drive that today lasts no more than four hours. My first trip took place when I was very young, and my Uncle George Bennett was assistant manager of Hilo Sugar Company (until 1936, when he became manager of Waimanalo Plantation on O'ahu). Particularly memorable was the large flume that transported harvests to the mill.

The Kaiwiki plantation north of Hilo had a more unusual method of transporting harvested stalks from the field. A pulley with slings of cane suspended from a cable ran downhill, where the bundles struck a backboard that triggered a release to dump them into railroad cars for the rest of the journey to the mill. The pulley whined as it sped down the inclined cable, a special variety made by a German supplier. No loose strands formed and the cable never unraveled; I've never seen another like it.

On the Big Island my grandmother's chauffeur was a retired sugar employee named Alfred Medeiros. He'd worked at the Hamakua Mill Company on the railroad that zigzagged up the foothills into the farthest reaches of the plantation. It crossed several gulches, one especially deep with a bridge not strong enough to support a locomotive. So the cane cars were hauled by mules from the distant fields, and over the bridge to where a locomotive finished the journey to the mill. Alfred's job was to drive the mules over the bridge. One day the cars tipped about half-way across, throwing him and everything else into the gulch. Alfred landed on trees that had been recently trimmed, exposing many sharp branches. At first he was blinded by the fall, then realized that the back of his scalp had been torn open and folded forward over his eyes. He pushed the skin back in place but found his abdomen punctured, exposing a length of gut. Stuffing that back into his stomach cavity, he climbed the bank of the gulch where other workers rushed him to the plantation clinic. Physicians sewed him up "good as new," and within a few weeks he returned to work. For me this incident always underscored the tough constitution of plantation workers, and the superior medical attention they received in those relatively early times.

In 1946 I rejoined Theo H. Davies & Co. after a leave of absence for Navy service during World War II. I knew little about sugar farming but had experience as a cowboy at Kualoa Ranch, and a degree from Stanford University. Although other agencies hired mainland labor experts to deal with the unions, my job was now labor relations. A strike was a possibility in 1946, and to prepare for it I made frequent visits to the Big Island, where Davies' agricultural operations were located. There I toured the fields and discussed labor problems with overseers, fertilizer foremen, and plantation and factory managers. At Kūkaʻiau Ranch on the gentle slopes of Mauna Kea, I verified the cattle count during the annual roundup, checked the condition of animals and pastures, and roped and branded calves. It all gave me a healthy respect for the workers, and served me in good stead for labor relations.

In 1946 the island of Hawai'i had sixteen sugar plantations, more than on any other island. North of Hilo was known as the "Scotch Coast" because its plantations were mostly managed by Scotsmen—like W.F. Robertson of Hamakua Mill Company; Andrew Walker and, later, Robert Bruce of Laupahoehoe Sugar Company; also Sandy Hossack of Paauhau Sugar Plantation Company; Douglas Ednie of Pepeekeo Plantation; and Martin Black of Hilo Sugar Company. Many Scots were factory superintendents and field overseers as well, some of the most competent men I ever encountered; hard-working, fair with employees, and shrewd at making money. I once asked a retiree why so many of his countrymen ended up in Hawai'i, and he answered, "Any Scotsman with any brains left Scotland." By 1946 they belonged to a second and third wave of emigrants to the Big Island. All started as field luna and rose into management by dint of hard work. They were easy to identify because each spoke with a thick brogue. Regular Sunday cricket matches were held up and down the Scotch Coast, and Andrew Walker once performed the traditional "Sword Dance" for me at his home in Pāpaʻaloa.

One report by Hamakua Mill Company's manager to the Davies agency in Honolulu exemplified the practical approach to the job during the early twentieth century. This occurred in about 1913. The Hāmākua manager's valued factory superintendent was inclined to roam, and visited the Hawaiian Agricultural Company in Kaʻū. There he befriended the Kaʻū superintendent's family, then enthusiastically seduced the wife of his host. When the cuckolding was discovered later, the Kaʻū superintendent announced he was taking the train up to Paʻauilo to "shoot the son of a bitch."

The Hāmākua manager learned about this plan for revenge, but didn't want to lose his competent factory superintendent. He rounded up men, gave them guns, and met the train from Kaʻū. The vengeful husband got off, also armed, but was surrounded by the Hāmākua posse, then disarmed, and told to reboard the train "and don't come back." All of this was thoroughly explained in the report, and justified by insisting that "good factory superintendents are hard to find." Evidently this satisfied the Davies executives.

Another early story concerned the mill built for Laupahoehoe Sugar Company. It was to be constructed on a high bluff at Pāpaʻaloa, some six miles down the coast from Hilo. The rugged shoreline prevented vessels from docking, so the mill's boilers were plugged up, lowered over the side of the ship, and floated ashore. They landed at Laupāhoehoe Point, a flat peninsula a few feet above sea level. A wagon and three pairs of mules were driven down a narrow, winding cliff-side path to get the first boiler. Part-way up, the team encountered a sharp switch-back turn. The first four mules would have gone around and pulled the last two and the wagon over the cliff. But the muleskinners stopped the train, took crowbars and leveraged the wagon around the sharp turn. All six mules continued on without incident. Such were the problems connected with erecting mill machinery on the remote, inaccessible Hāmākua Coast.

An old-timer told me how money was raised to build a huge irrigation ditch, finished in 1906, to distribute water from Waipi'o Valley down the coast to Pa'auilo. In those days the world financial market was in London. The Hamakua Ditch Company was organized, bonds were issued to raise construction funds, and a representative sent from Honolulu to England. The first day he made the rounds of the investment houses without making a single sale. Nobody was interested. He returned to his hotel and slumped into a chair in the lobby. A stranger asked what his trouble was. and the salesman described his failure. On being assured that the company was in Hawai'i, and that at least part of the water would be used for irrigation, the stranger said, "Your problem is the name. Everybody in London knows about Hawai'i but nobody has heard of Hāmākua. And why would anyone want to invest in a ditch? You should call it The Hawaiian Irrigation Company." The next day the salesman took the advice, resumed his rounds, and soon sold every bond. A cable back to Honolulu took care of quickly renaming the ditch company.

A geologist was hired to recommend where water-collecting tunnels at the head of Waipi'o Valley should be dug into the face of the cliffs. These were to be connected to a water-distributing ditch that served the downstream plantations. Without any records of stream flow or rainfall, he estimated the maximum, minimum, and average flow for tunnels located on high, middle, and low elevations. The middle elevation was chosen for construction, and was remarkably successful.

Irrigation water was distributed by running it within furrows to prevent it from spreading before it reached the end of a cane row. The soil at Pā'auhau plantation held the water, but at Pacific Sugar Mill, Honoka'a, and Hāmākua, the soil was too porous to prevent leaking through the walls of the furrows. The Hamakua Ditch was used mostly to supply flume and factory water. Years ago several Big Island plantations flumed cane harvests down the slopes of Mauna Kea from fields unreachable by plantation railroads. By the end of my time, trucks hauled harvests to the mill, and the ditch water was used entirely for irrigation, cane cleaners, and the factory. Eventually, with sprinklers and drip irrigation, 7,000 acres could be watered from the Hāmākua Ditch. The tunnels were inspected in a rowboat. Once I took one of those trips—it was an eerie voyage!

Fluming cane required stalks cut and trimmed by hand to a size that would float in the flume. Laupahoehoe Plantation was the last of the Davies plantations to use this kind of transport. Until the early 1950s, field crews wielding machetes cut and trimmed the cane, then Davies replaced manual labor with a mechanical harvester developed by the HSPA. C. Brewer & Company hired the cane cutters for their north Hilo operations. Its Hakalau, Onomea, Pepeʻekeo, and Hilo Sugar Company plantations had the last hand harvesting in Hawaiʻi.

Davies' holdings on the Big Island changed after I joined the company. First to go was Waiakea Mill Company, the land so rock-filled that it could not be plowed for replanting cane. Ratoon crops were grown, but no new varieties of cane could be planted except by hand, which was expensive. Harvesting had to be done by hand because numerous rock outcropping prevented the use of mechanical equipment and hindered off-road work with trucks. Field operations were simply too costly. After 68 years, the Waiākea mill was shut down in 1947, and the land sold to C. Brewer & Company, who constructed a resort hotel.

We went through an evolution of mechanical cane harvesters before eventually using push rakes. After some experimentation, the local Steubenberg Company studied an Australian machine, then designed and built the "short cane harvester." This deposited cut and stripped stalks into "buggies" mounted on a self-propelled crawler that loaded the cane into storage trailers parked at the edge of the fields. Cane haul trucks periodically replaced the full trailers with empties, and took the filled trailers to the mill, where an air blast cleaner removed leaf trash and soil before the stalks entered the mill. The short cane harvester increased sugar production and reduced cleaning costs, but was unsatisfactory. The sequencing of harvester, buggies, and cane haul trucks was a difficult schedule to maintain without an excessive investment in trailers to supply necessary storage. Steubenberg then built a terrain-following push rake harvester mounted on a Caterpillar tractor. This cut the cane at its root tops and pushed it into piles. A self-propelled mechanical grab loaded these into the cane haul trucks and trailers, eliminating the need to unhitch the trailers. No scheduling problems arose, but the cane still had to be washed before entering the mill. We used this push rake harvester exclusively until the plantation was shut down in 1993.

Theo H. Davies & Co. had been shipping product through the Hilo port ever since the railroad was extended to Paʻauilo in 1913. An interruption occurred on April 1, 1946, when disaster in the form of a tsunami struck the North Hilo Coast. Lengths of track and several bridges and trestles were wiped out. The Paʻauilo branch of the railroad was shut down for good. Trucking product over the narrow, winding government road to Hilo was too costly. So the Davies plantations in Hāmākua turned to shipping sugar from Kukuihaele Landing, a high promontory adjacent to the southern entrance of Waipio Valley. Molasses was shipped from Honokaʻa landing, which had been used for decades by Honokaʻa Plantation.

Loading the bagged sugar from Kukuihaele involved a trolley system that suspended a cargo sling on two cables running from the cliff down to vessels anchored offshore. A donkey engine pulled the sling to and from the landing. The ships picked up stevedores at Hilo before anchoring at Kukuihaele, and, with the trolley system, these men loaded the bagged sugar bundles faster than by crane at any other Hawaiian port. The trolley could transport heavier bundles with more bags, and the trolley winch gang kept cargo moving to and fro at a rapid rate. The molasses shipped from Honoka'a Landing was warmed up to reduce the viscosity, and pumped out through a large hose to transport vessels anchored offshore.

The Matson company supplied Liberty ships as sugar transports, and shipping to the refinery was done directly from Kukuihaele. Then in 1949, the Hilo port facilities were prepared and the industry began to ship bulk sugar rather than bagged sugar. The road from Hāmākua to Hilo was also improved so that truck transport of bulk sugar and molasses was feasible. The Davies plantations employed contractors for this work. Soon I became quite concerned about the trucking costs and C. Brewer's charges for storing and loading Davies' sugar at the Hilo wharf. I met with C. Brewer's representatives but had no success in negotiating better terms. At the time Brewer had a bulk sugar shipping monopoly on the island.

I decided to find a less costly method. Castle & Cooke had considered developing the port at Kawaihae to handle bulk shipments. They proposed a joint venture to Theo H. Davies. Together, we developed the port, shared the costs of the sugar warehouse and loading machinery, and from 1959 on, our product was trucked to Kawaihae with a large savings.

In 1963, when I became Davies' Vice President for Agriculture, their plantations had a reputation for being expensive to run because of unfavorable climate and difficult terrain. I encouraged managers' suggestions for improvements and greater efficiency. We mechanized all harvesting, introduced sprinkler irrigation, then drip irrigation. This produced dramatic increases in yields on land subjected to droughts every summer. We built cane haul roads and bridges so our trucks avoided public highways as much as possible. Commercial trucks had difficulty with slow, heavy-duty movement through muddy fields, followed by a rapid run to the mill. These conflicting requirements were met by manufacturers, but we were able to assemble vehicles ourselves at a much lower cost, using components from different suppliers. The 30 to 40 cane haul trucks we put together were continuously serviced by our plantation garage, and lasted until replaced by new technology.

The HSPA developed a new variety of cane that would grow at higher elevations. Because of cooler temperatures, it matured in three years rather than in two, but we saw great potential in it. Davies had thousands of forested acres inland and upwards from Honoka'a, so we cleared the fields and planted the new variety of cane. Harvests had the same yield per acre as lower fields at a comparable cost per ton of sugar. The cane required little attention beyond occasional aerial fertilizing. Rainfall through the year was sufficient and no irrigation was needed.

For years Davies contracted with a crop-dusting company to fertilize the fields. When the cane was young, they used a high, wide Steubenberg tractor spreader, but after the stalks became densely clumped or closed in, planes were used. We had three landing strips in the upper reaches of Hamakua plantation. [It is cheaper to haul fertilizer up in trucks than to load airplanes at a lower level and fly them up to the fields.] Crop dusters were also used to inspect mature fields to determine whether fertilizing and/or irrigation was needed.

Once I inspected the forested uplands slated for planting with the new variety of cane. We needed to know how rugged the area might be under its canopy of trees.

Were there many gulches and streams? Outcroppings of rocks? What kind of terrain was covered by the trees? The owner of the crop-dusting company took me up, but the first few passes were too high to see much. When I complained, a few minutes later we were flying so low that tree branches were whipping by on both sides of the plane. After I got used to that frightening sensation, I saw things clearly and concluded that the land would be profitable for cane. These pilots were used to flying "low and slow," and dodging trees and power lines at the borders of the fields. In all the years we used them, they never had an accident while delivering fertilizer, and were important contributors to our high yields over the years.

By 1972 Davies had three separate plantations, each with its own mill, so I began consolidating operations. The intervening Paauhau Plantation Company was bought from C. Brewer & Company and merged into our adjacent Honokaa Sugar Plantation. The Environmental Protection Agency had been pressing C. Brewer to improve trash and dirt removal from the cane-wash water discharged into the ocean. Its plantation wasn't large enough to justify the cost, but we could combine ours and spread the cost around.

However, Theo H. Davies & Co. still had three old sugar mills in operation. In 1974 I persuaded executives to merge Hamakua Mill Company into Laupahoehoe Sugar Company. Years earlier Kaiwiki plantation had been merged into Laupahoehoe Sugar, and the last consolidation took place in 1979, when Davies combined Laupahoehoe and Honokaa Sugar Company to make Hamakua Sugar Company. Five old sugar mills were replaced by two modern mills of greater capacity to serve one large plantation. Additional savings came with the reduction of garages, offices, field departments, and medical facilities required for separate plantations. The mills now had larger capacity crushers, electrical generators with new boilers, and larger capacity boiling houses. But gulches separated the formerly independent plantations, so we did a lot of road and bridge building with our employees.

For the 1979 consolidation I resurrected the Hāmākua name to avoid morale problems that followed earlier mergers. When Paauhau Sugar Company was combined with Honokaa Sugar Company in 1972, the Paauhau name disappeared. When Kaiwiki Sugar Company and, later, Hamakua Mill Company were merged into Laupahoehoe Sugar Company, the Kaiwiki Sugar Company and Hamakua Mill Company names also disappeared. An unanticipated result was that Honokaa and Laupahoehoe employees felt superior to the former Paauhau, Kaiwiki and Hamakua Mill employees. So I was careful not to name the latest combination after either of the companies entering the merger.

When we reduced the factories to two, I retained the Haina mill near Honoka'a because of its proximity to Hāmākua Ditch, which supplied water for washing the cut cane. The other site was the old Kaiwiki mill at 'Ōkala at the opposite end of the plantation. Both mills were renovated with more modern crushers, higher pressure boilers with topping turbines, electric generators, and expanded boiling houses. 'O'ōkala factory had an extra boiler for burning the cane trash (after the old grinders first squeezed out the water). The boiler provided steam to *generate excess electricity sold to the local utility, adding considerably to the plantation's income. Otherwise we took advantage of recent advances made elsewhere. HSPA technicians had toured the world's sugar-producing countries to inspect production methods, and returned from South Africa with a glowing report. Refining there was done in the raw mills at the back end of the boiling house, at a sizable savings over using a separate refinery. All heat needed to boil sugar in the refinery was obtained from vapor produced by the raw sugar factory, thus avoiding the significant costs of fuel in a free-standing refinery.*

I persuaded Davies to employ South African engineers to design and oversee construction of our new Haina mill, and incorporate the refining process. But we had contracted to supply raw sugar to the C & H refinery in California, so had to wait until that contract expired to do our own refining. As a result of all these efforts, Davies Hamakua Sugar Company (and its successor, Hamakua Sugar Company), consistently had among the lowest production costs in Hawai'i. Before my time, Theo H. Davies, Co. was the first to replace steam plows with Caterpillar tractors, and the Kaiwiki plantation was the first to convert completely to truck cane hauling. The spirit of innovation was well established, and that made it easier to accept my changes.

In 1973 the Hong Kong-based Jardine, Matheson & Co. purchased Theo H. Davies & Co. My duties remained the same, but, when the year 1984 approached, I would be 65 and was expected to retire. Instead of replacing me, my superiors decided to harvest the last crop and sell the plantation to provide critically needed cash. As a result, I offered to buy Davies Hamakua Sugar Company, and in January 1984 became the sole owner of the plantation I named Hamakua Sugar Company. I operated it until events beyond my control overtook us and, in 1992, declared bankruptcy. For nine years I prolonged the life of sugarcane farming along the Hamakua Coast, but in the end adverse developments, including a disastrous decline in sugar prices, ended a sad chapter in the picturesque history of the sugar industry on the Big Island of Hawai'i.

⊕ ⊕ ⊕

THE BIG ISLAND is located 130 miles southeast of O'ahu, and measures 90 miles long by 74 miles wide. With a total of 4,015 square miles, it is the largest island in the archipelago. Its landscape is dominated by the volcanoes Mauna Kea and Mauna Loa, and it has the state's only current volcanic activity. The summit of inactive Mauna Kea, at 13,784 feet, is its highest point.

The island of Hawai'i has seen a greater diversity of plantations than any other sugarcane-growing region in the world. Cane was planted at high elevations and transported over rugged terrain with the utmost difficulty. Irrigation was slow to come to the plantations, if it came at all, and for decades cane was cultivated only with rainfall and runoff. The island's sugar history encapsulates the diversity shown by all of Hawai'i's sugarcane farmers since the beginning.

Two statistics can give an idea of the importance this one island played in the industry as a whole. In 1936 the 16 mills then operating on Hawai'i produced

318,163 tons of sugar, 34.66 percent of the Territory's total production.[1] In 1990 Hawai'i's three remaining mills produced 212,524 tons, 25.93 of the state's total production.[2] The last of the Big Island's plantations was shut down in 1996.

The following Tables 7 and 8 summarize an impressive list of operations that spanned more than a century. They are divided into north and south regions on the island.

Location of sugar plantations on Hawai'i after 1876. See Tables 7 and 8 for identification of numbered plantations. Not to scale.

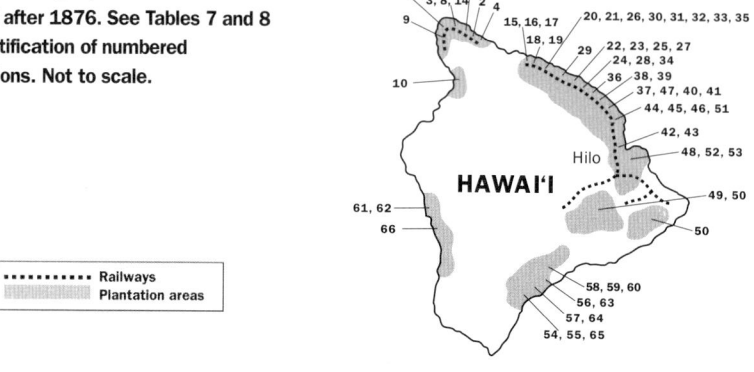

TABLE 7 | SUGAR PLANTATIONS ON HAWAI'I— NORTH KOHALA AND HĀMĀKUA DISTRICTS 1876-1996

NO.	NAME	FIRST DATE*	LAST DATE*
	NORTH KOHALA		
1.	Kohala Sugar Company	1863	1975
2.	Halawa Mill and Plantation	1873	1928
3.	Union Mill & Plantation Company	1874	1937
4.	Niulii Mill & Plantation Company	1877	1932
5.	Hawi Mill, later	1878	1885
6.	Hawi Mill & Plantation Company	1886	1931
7.	Beecroft Plantation	1879	1901
8.	Star Mill Company	1879	1889
9.	Puakea Plantation	1886	1931
10.	Puako Plantation	1903	1913
(numbers 11 through 14 are not described in the following text)			
11.	Thompson & Associates	1882	1888
12.	G.F. Holmes	1883	1883
13.	Kynnersley Brothers	1883	1887
14.	Puehuehu Plantation Company	1889	1897
	HĀMĀKUA COAST		
15.	Honokaa Sugar Company/mills for:	1876	1979
16.	J.R. Mills, and	1882	1882
17.	W.H. Rickard	1887	1891

NO.	NAME	FIRST DATE*	LAST DATE*
	HĀMĀKUA COAST, cont.		
18.	Pacific Sugar Mill	1879	1928
19.	Paauhau Plantation Company	1879	1972
20.	Hamakua Mill Company/	1883	1974
	Davies Hamakua Sugar Company/	1979	1984
	Hamakua Sugar Company	1984	1994
21.	Kukaiau Plantation Company	1884	1917
22.	Ookala Plantation	1879	1909
23.	Kaiwiki Sugar Company	1909	1957
24.	Lidgate & Campbell/	1876	1884
	Laupahoehoe Sugar Company	1884	1979
(numbers 25 through 35 are not described in the following text)			
25.	Soper Wright & Company	1882	1883
26.	Aamano Plantation	1882	1889
27.	R.M. Overend	1883	1891
28.	Kaiwilahilahi	1883	1900
29.	J.N. Wright	1886	1891
30.	W.H. Purvis	1887	1890
31.	J.M. Horner & Sons	1887	1891
32.	J.Marsden	1887	1891
33.	Paty & Parker	1887	1889
34.	A.Lidgate	1888	1889
35.	J.T. Broderick	1891	1891

* Note: "First Date" and "Last Date" are the first and last years a plantation is listed in a source. The dates are believed to be within two years of organization or shutdown. Many plantations were consolidated with others that continued to operate.
Sources: Bowser; Hansen; HSPA library; Hind; Hoyt; Listing 1878-1895, *Hawaiian Almanac and Annual*; listing, dates of charter, *The Planters Monthly*, Aug. 1882; listing 1895-1945, HSPA Annual Meeting, Dec. 10, 1945; Wilfong; citations 1945-date, corporate annual reports, and newspapers.

TABLE 8 | SUGAR PLANTATIONS ON HAWAI'I— HILO, PUNA, KA'Ū, AND KONA DISTRICTS 1876-1996

NO.	NAME	FIRST DATE*	LAST DATE*
	HILO AND PUNA		
36.	Hakalau Plantation Company	1878	1967
37.	Honomu Sugar Company	1880	1946
38.	Ka'upakuea Plantation	1861	1880
39.	Pepeekeo Sugar Company	1880	1973
40.	Onomea Sugar Company	1867	1965
41.	Paukaa Sugar Company	1867	1894
42.	Hitchcock & Company	1877	1886
43.	Papaikou Sugar Company	1886	1888
44.	Amauulu Plantation/Spencer's Pltn.	1867	1884
45.	Hilo Sugar Company	1880	1965

NO.	NAME	FIRST DATE*	LAST DATE*
46.	Wainaku Plantation	1882	1884
47.	Mauna Kea Sugar Company	1965	1994
48.	Waiakea Mill Company	1879	1947
49.	Olaa Sugar Company	1900	1960
50.	First Puna Sugar Company/	1899	1908
	Second Puna Sugar Company	1960	1982
(numbers 51 through 53 are not described in the following text)			
51.	Nakahanaloa Plantation	1879	1880
52.	Hilo Portuguese Sugar Company	1896	1901
53.	Hawai'i Mill Company	1901	1923
	KA'Ū AND KONA		
54.	Naalehu Plantation	1878	1884
55.	Hutchinson Sugar Company	1885	1972
56.	Hilea Sugar Company	1878	1891
57.	Honuapo Plantation	1879	1884
58.	Hawaiian Agricultural Company	1876	1972
59.	Ka'u Sugar Company	1972	1986
60.	Kau Agribusiness Company	1986	1996 (Sugar)
61.	Kona Sugar Company	1891	1904
62.	Kona Development Company	1908	1926
(numbers 63 through 66 are not described in the following text)			
63.	Charles Wall	1882	1883
64.	H. M. Whitney	1882	1884
65.	L. Chong	1895	1899
66.	Holualoa Sugar Mill Company	1897	1898

*Note: "First Date" and "Last Date" are the first and last years a plantation is listed in a source. The dates are believed to be within two years of the years of organization or shutdown. Some plantations were consolidated into others.
Sources: Bowser; Listing 1878-1895, *Hawaiian Almanac and Annual*; HSPA library; dates of charter, *The Planters Monthly*, Aug. 1882; listing, HSPA Annual Meeting, Dec. 10, 1945; Smith; Sullivan; citations 1945 to 1993, corporation annual reports, and newspapers.

Sugar survived on Hawai'i for 120 years following the Reciprocity Treaty because of astute owners and managers. Over the decades plantations were combined advantageously to better transport remote harvests, use improved mills, and reap the resulting economies of scale. Brief histories of the most significant plantations are given in the order listed on Tables 7 and 8.

SUGAR IN KOHALA

For decades the North Kohala District plantations were cosolidated again and again until in 1937 there was one efficient survivor. The following text describes the growth and combination of its plantations from 1863 until 1975, when the Kohala Sugar Company was shut down.

KOHALA SUGAR COMPANY (1)

Today a visitor to Kohala on the northwest corner of Hawai'i would see it as a difficult location for large-scale sugar farming. The eastern and wettest region is broken up by gulches, and the western region is a wind-swept, dry slope of the Kohala mountain range that retains little rainfall. Nevertheless, sugarcane farming came to Kohala in 1863 and stayed for over a hundred years.

Rev. Elias Bond (1813-1896) and his wife arrived in Hawai'i in 1842 with the ninth company of missionaries, and settled in Kohala to build a mission and school. For the next 55 years the couple devoted themselves to the welfare of the natives. Kohala had few employment opportunities, and Reverend Bond was dismayed to see Hawaiians depart for the attractions of Lahaina and Honolulu. He considered sugarcane cultivation a way to keep his congregation in Kohala, and decided to farm cane and employ Native Hawaiians.

In 1862 Bond turned to former mission manager Samuel Castle for help. Castle and his advisor, Dr. John Mott-Smith (1824-1895), a Honolulu dentist and friend of Prince David Kalākaua, visited Kohala to assess its prospects. They were encouraging, and Castle & Cooke raised $40,000 from the sale of Kohala Sugar Company stock. Reverend Bond received shares in the corporation.[3]

Dr. James Wight, Kohala's only physician, also acquired stock by exchanging 3,282 acres of his land for it. Castle ordered a sugarmill from the Mirlees, Tate & Watson machine works in Scotland.[4] Planting began in 1863 and an experienced manager, George Wilfong, was hired to supervise assembly of the mill. He stayed on to complete construction of workers' housing and manage the plantation.

Wilfong was a strict disciplinarian and had little patience with the native laborers so beloved by Reverend Bond. He demanded a hard day's work for a day's pay and was determined to get it, whereas Bond occasionally called the workers out of the fields to attend prayer meetings. The team of Bond and Wilfong was a mismatch, and in 1866 Wilfong was discharged after an incident that involved a native being flogged for thieving.[5]

Nevertheless, the plantation owed much to Wilfong's enterprise. He had begun to build a stock of working animals and dairy cattle within days of his arrival in Kohala. Then, as now, Parker Ranch was the logical source of cattle, and Wilfong lost no time riding over the Kohala mountain range to Waimea to negotiate with James Parker, Esq. (1790-1864), owner of the ranch and one-time employee of King Kamehameha I. Wilfong bought 100 steers, milk cows, and calves. Parker set an agreeable price, then allowed Wilfong to pick out the animals he wanted from the herd of thousands. Wilfong hadn't chosen many before Parker interrupted, told him his choices were poor, and suggested Wilfong let Parker's son John finish the job. Wilfong gladly deferred and ended up with a fine selection.[6] Such was the aloha of James Parker.

Loading sugar at Māhukona landing, circa 1930s. Bagged sugar was lightered out to the anchored transport that shipped it to the refinery in San Francisco. (Kohala Sugar Company)

Following Wilfong's departure in 1866, Dwight Baldwin, brother of Henry, came over from Maui to manage the plantation. Over the next six years Baldwin struggled to get the plantation out of debt. Finally, after more years of uncertain operation under a succession of managers, in 1880 the plantation had grown to 2,000 cultivated acres with a mill producing 1,200 tons of sugar annually.[7] By now it was paying dividends. Reverend Bond was embarrassed by the profits and contributed most of his share to the American Board of Foreign Missions in Boston.

In 1880 three steam traction engines were used to pull loaded carts to the mill, replacing the slow teams of oxen or mules used by other plantations.[8] For a time the processed sugar was shipped via schooners anchored offshore at Kohala Landing, going directly to the refinery in San Francisco. The Hawaiian Railroad Company, owned by Samuel Wilder, was completed in 1881, and after that product was transported by rail from the port of Māhukona some 20 miles southwest of the plantation.[9]

Kohala Sugar Company was destined to become the sole survivor in the entire district. Half a century later, the process of merging began. In 1929 Halawa Plantation was dissolved and its lands divided between Kohala Sugar Company and Niulii Mill & Plantation Company. In 1931 Hawi Mill & Plantation Company merged with Union Mill & Plantation Company. Union Mill then acquired Niulii Mill & Plantation Company in 1932. But in 1937, Union Mill & Plantation Company was bought by Kohala Sugar Company, bringing with it ownership of The Hawaiian Railroad Company. This purchase combined all sugar operations in the district under the banner of Kohala Sugar Company, with the majority owner being Castle & Cooke.[10]

The enlarged Kohala Sugar Company had 12,115 acres under cultivation and produced 35,124 tons of sugar in 1938.[11] During World War II the port at Māhukona was closed, never to reopen. Product was trucked 50 miles to the railhead of the Hawaiian Consolidated Railway Limited in Paʻauilo, for transport to the open port at Hilo. Maximum production before shutdown was 41,501 tons in the war year of 1943.[12] In 1945 The Hawaiian Railroad Company ceased operations due to lack of freight. From 1959 until the plantation closed in 1975, sugar was shipped from Kawaihae.

Mechanical harvesting in a Kohala Sugar Company field, circa 1960s. During and after World War II, throughout the Islands machines and trucks replaced hand harvesting and transport by flumes and railroads. (Kohala Sugar Company)

During its lifetime, Kohala Sugar Company was a marginally profitable operation, depending on the weather. In 1971 Castle & Cooke decided to shut it down. The last crop was ground in 1975, and an era passed for North Kohala.[13]

HALAWA MILL AND PLANTATION (2)

In 1851 Dr. James Wight arrived in North Kohala from New Zealand. He prospered as the only medical man in the district, and also ran a successful country store. At a time when land was cheap, he purchased thousands of acres in east Kohala in the region known as Hālawa. In 1873, emboldened by the example of Kohala Sugar Company, Doctor Wight established Halawa Mill and Plantation.[14]

By today's standards, the original Hālawa mill was primitive. A water wheel supplied power for grinding, and a visitor who observed the simple, three-roller mill recorded: "The canes are badly bent, but few are broken."[15] The mill was the last to employ open boiling of its product, since the vacuum pan had been widely introduced into Hawai'i mills. However, by 1891 the plantation had a new mill and 380 of its 1,500 acres were producing 650 tons of sugar yearly.[16] Maximum production was 3,250 tons in 1925.[1] In 1928 Halawa Mill and Plantation company harvested its last crop, and the Wight estate leased part of the land to Kohala Sugar Company and the rest to Niulii Plantation and Mill Company.[10]

UNION MILL AND PLANTATION COMPANY (3)

In 1873 Robert W. Hind visited Kohala to examine sugar farming prospects. He had recently completed his milling contract with Alexander and Baldwin on Maui, and was looking for a promising location. He leased a large tract in north central Kohala, then in partnership with others purchased machinery and erected a mill. The Union Mill & Plantation Company got off to a disastrous start. Before the first crop was ground, a fire destroyed the new building. (In the days before corrugated sheeting and steel beams were used for construction, fires were spectacular and much more common.) Fortunately,

Theo H. Davies, Honolulu agent for the plantation, had insurance that covered much of the loss. Hind rebuilt the mill, and the first crop was harvested. Then another devastating fire took its toll. The discouraged Hind sold out to a group that included James Renton and Theo H. Davies.[17]

Renton restored the mill again, and this time the Union Mill Company, incorporated in 1881, went on to prosper. By 1890 the plantation was cultivating 1,260 acres and producing 2,500 tons of sugar. This continued, under Renton's long-term management that lasted until 1904.[16] More than a quarter century later, in 1932, the mill was merged into Niulii Mill & Plantation Company to increase the land under cultivation to over 5,000 acres. Out of this merger, the Union name was retained. The maximum produced in any one year was 11,239 tons of sugar in 1935.[1] Two years later in 1937, Union Mill & Plantation Company was purchased by Kohala Sugar Company and subsequently all cane processing was done at a new mill.[18]

NIULII MILL & PLANTATION COMPANY (4)

In 1877, encouraged by the Reciprocity Treaty, and in partnership with Theo H. Davies, Judge C. F. Hart founded Niulii Mill & Plantation Company on some 2,000 acres in North Kohala.[19] Davies had recently inspected the Kohala lands and was convinced that the Hāmākua and North Kohala districts were the most promising areas in Hawai'i for sugar farming. Hart's plantation was at the end of The Hawai'i Railroad Company's eastern line. By 1891 the Niulii mill was producing 1,000 tons of sugar from 740 acres under cultivation.[16] Never a large producer, it nevertheless stayed in business and 40 years later, in 1931, ground its maximum yield of 3,902 tons of sugar.[1] After the 1932 harvest, the plantation lands were added to those of the Union Mill & Plantation Company, and Niulii Mill & Plantation Company ceased to exist.[10]

HAWI MILL (5 & 6)

In 1881, when Robert Hind sold his interests in Union Mill, he had already begun a new, nearby business named Hawi Mill. By 1890 this plantation had 1,155 acres under cultivation, with another 625 acres cultivated by suppliers, and produced 2,200 tons of sugar.[16] Hind's son, John (1858-1933), managed Hawi Mill & Plantation & Company for four decades, from 1884 to 1923. During his tenure a maximum of 9,426 tons was produced in 1915.[1]

John Hind did much for Kohala sugar interests. In 1904 he formed the Kohala Ditch Company to build 21 miles of ditches and tunnels to bring irrigation water to the north Kohala region. All the district's plantations subscribed to use the water, but only Hawi Mill & Plantation Company invested in the ditch company. The irrigation system was completed in 1906, and delivered between 20 million and 70 million gallons of water each day. Kohala plantations significantly increased their yields owing to Hind's farsightedness and industry.[20] The Kohala ditch did more than just supply irrigation water for sugar farmers because almost all the cultivated land was below the ditch. Each plantation constructed reservoirs to collect their share of water, and built flumes to transport harvested cane to the downstream mills. When harvesting began, on a signal to gate tenders, the sluice gates at the reservoirs were opened and cane was flumed directly to the mill. This method was so successful that plantation railroads were never used extensively in Kohala.

Fluming cane to the mill. This method of transporting harvests was employed by almost every Big Island plantation. (Hawaiian Sugar Planters' Association)

John's brother Henry took over Hawi Mill & Plantation Company in 1924. In the wet year of 1925 a total of 10,689 tons of sugar were produced.[1] This yield was never matched, and in 1931 the Hind family sold the plantation to Kohala Sugar Company.

BEECROFT PLANTATION (7)

In 1879 the Englishman Henry Beecroft Jackson, in partnership with a fellow Britisher and former employee, Theo H. Davies, established Beecroft Plantation.[10] Back in England, Davies had worked as a clerk for Jackson before coming to Honolulu, where he also worked as a clerk for the R.C. Janion firm. The plantation's harvests were processed by the neighboring Hawi Plantation mill. Production never exceeded the 800 tons reported for 1890[16], and the operation's last reported harvest in 1901 yielded 320 tons of sugar.[21]

STAR MILL COMPANY (8)

Also in 1879, Daniel Vida, one of the partners who purchased Robert Hind's interest in Union Mill and Plantation Company, established the nearby Star Mill Company.[22] Squeezed between Union Mill's lands to the west and Kohala Sugar's lands to the east, the plantation was forced to cultivate upper stretches cut by gullies and rock outcroppings. In 1880 Star Mill was still a small plantation with only 32 workers.[7] By the end of the decade in 1889, the operation had closed down.[10]

PUAKEA PLANTATION (9)

The James Wight estate owned Puakea Ranch. Located on the gentle slopes of the Kohala range near the northwest tip of the island, the lands were a prime location for planting sugar. His daughter and heir, Mrs. H.R. Bryant of Kohala, leased the property with sugarcane farming in mind. John Hind secured a 50 percent ownership of Puakea Plantation for Hawi Mill & Plantation Company in return for grinding rights at Hawi Mill. It was a modest but profitable investment.[23] Puakea Plantation paid regular dividends and always produced between 600 and 1,700 tons of sugar each year. But, like many small operations, it didn't survive beyond a certain point. After harvesting the 1930 crop, Puakea Plantation was shut down.[24]

PUAKO PLANTATION (10)

In 1903 this disastrous venture was undertaken by Robert and John Hind. Land at Puakō was obtained from Parker Ranch in exchange for Hind-owned land at Waipunalei in the Hāmākua District southeast of Kohala. Located some 80 miles south of Hawi Mill, Puakō Plantation had its own mill.

The Hinds counted on water from a flume constructed eight miles into the uplands. But the water never materialized on a regular basis, and frequent, heavy windstorms quickly evaporated any rainfall. Puako Plantation's peak production during its lifetime was 839 tons in 1909. Four years later it shut down after the 1913 harvest, and the equipment was brought to the Hawi mill or sold elsewhere. In 1929 the mill machinery was again sold, this time to the Ormoc Sugar Company of Leyte, Philippine Islands. In 1950 it was still operating, 50 years after being manufactured at the Fulton Iron Works in St. Louis, Missouri.[25]

Today little evidence remains of sugar farming in Kohala. The brick mill chimney erected by Robert Hind in 1878 still dominates the rural Hāwī scenery. The magnificent Kohala Sugar Company mill built in 1937-1938 lies in ruins that are fast being obscured by vines, weeds, and mesquite. The offices of The Hawaiian Railroad Company have become a residence next to the little-used harbor at Māhukona. The landing is deserted and being battered into rubble by Pacific storms. The plantation economy that dominated the Kohala scene for over a hundred years has passed into history.

SUGAR ON THE HĀMĀKUA COAST

The premiere site for sugar growing on the island of Hawai'i ran 20 miles southeast from Waipi'o Valley to the town of 'O'ōkala. This coastline contained some of the most gulch-ridden acreage on the entire island. But the gully-divided lands above the shore cliffs had rich soil blessed with heavy runoff from the slopes of Mauna Kea. Reaching, cultivating, and harvesting these lands challenged sugarcane farmers. Eventually the many small plantations along this coast were combined into one large operation. When the end came in 1993, there was one survivor, Hamakua Sugar Company.

The Reciprocity Treaty of 1876 encouraged sugarcane farming in this rugged terrain. Roads were primitive and no train tracks led to a seaport until the line to Hilo was completed in 1913. Nevertheless, beginning in 1877 large-scale planting began along the Hāmākua Coast. Each mill had a landing. Using lighters, raw sugar and plantation supplies were delivered to and from vessels anchored offshore.

HONOKAA SUGAR COMPANY (15, 16 & 17)

Frederick A. Schaefer (1836-1920) arrived in Hawai'i from Bremen, Germany, in 1857. After clerking in Honolulu for ten years for Melchers & Co., merchants and importers, he re-established the firm as F.A. Schaefer & Co. In 1878 it took control of land some 51 miles north of Hilo, farmed for two years by Messrs. Siemson and Marsdon, and incorporated it as Honokaa Sugar Company.[26] Several other planters, including W.H. Rickard and J.R. Mills, farmed cane on nearby parcels for processing by the Honokaa Sugar Company mill.[7] By 1890 most of these parcels were consolidated into Honokaa Sugar Company, and the mill was producing 1,600 tons annually.[16]

The Honoka'a plantation experienced difficulties that were typical of operations along the Hāmākua Coast. Its fields extended from a narrow plateau along a six-mile shoreline to two miles inland, where the foothills of Mauna Kea began at elevations of 1,500 to 1,800 feet. The mountain slope consisted of a series of ledges divided by gullies, but the soil was rich in nutrients. For 25 years ratoon crops were grown on several parcels because reaching the fields to replant was so difficult. Eventually harvesting was done using a complicated combination of hand labor, flumes, and railroad transport.

Two narrow gauge tracks were constructed, one the width of the plantation at the level of the mill, and the other the width of the plantation below the level of the mill. Cane harvested in the fields above the upper rail line was flumed down to receiving stations, and washed into railroad cars that carried the crop to the mill. The flume water was then diverted to lower fields for irrigation. Cane harvested in the lower fields was both flumed or hand-loaded into railroad cars along the lower tracks. These were pulled by a cable to the upper level tracks using a shunt line with a Fowler steam tractor-powered winch[1], then hauled by locomotives to the mill.

In the 1880s, transporting product to the refinery in San Francisco was a challenge. Bags of raw sugar were loaded onto lighters at Honoka'a landing and taken to inter-island vessels anchored offshore. These schooners and steamers then proceeded to Honolulu for trans-shipment. In 1929 this cumbersome system was changed to direct shipment to San Francisco, when the shipping facility was moved to Kukuihaele, some six miles north, near Waipi'o Valley. The large freighters anchored offshore and a cable and trolley system hauled the bagged sugar out over the water. In 1936 the Honoka'a plantation obtained a large portion of its electricity from a water-driven 55-

kw generator. At that time, almost every Hāmākua Coast and North Hilo Coast plantation had a hydroelectric plant.[1]

When the landing at Kukuihaele was shut down in World War II, product was trucked to the railhead at Pa'auilo for transport to Hilo. After the tsunami of 1946 shut down the railroad, shipment resumed from Kukuihaele. Then in 1949 Kukuihaele was again abandoned when it was decided to ship bulk sugar instead of bagged sugar. The road to Hilo was improved, Hilo's port prepared, and product went by truck to the Hilo wharf.

The history of mergers in this area followed a somewhat predictable pattern. Honokaa Sugar absorbed neighboring Pacific Sugar Mill Company plantation in 1928, after having ground that plantation's cane since 1913. As a result, Honokaa's yield increased from 10,714 tons in 1925 to 23,005 tons in 1930, and land under cultivation increased to over 9,000 acres.[1] Theo H. Davies & Co., Ltd. bought F.A. Schaefer & Company in 1951 to get control of Honokaa Sugar Company. In 1979, Theo H. Davies merged Honokaa Sugar Company with Laupahoehoe Sugar Company to form Davies Hamakua Sugar Company, and the Honokaa Sugar Company name was no longer used.

John Watt (born 1862) managed Honokaa Sugar Company from 1892 until 1904, replacing W.H. Rickard, who gave up independent planting at the same time. Watt increased the annual yield from 1,700 tons in 1893 to 8,000 to 10,000 tons and was promoted to an executive position at the new Olaa Sugar Company southwest of Hilo in the Puna district. Watt was one of several Scotsmen who managed Hāmākua Coast plantations. His background well illustrated why Hāmākua was called the "Scotch Coast." Born and raised in Scotland, Watt arrived in Hawai'i in 1887. For the next five years he gained experience as a field overseer with Waiakea Plantation, and head overseer at the Paauhau Plantation Company. Beginning with the Honoka'a plantation, he embarked on 21 highly successful years as a manager and, at 'Ōla'a, as senior on-site executive.[27] His career spanned over four decades of exemplary service in the Hawai'i sugar industry.

PACIFIC SUGAR MILL (18)

In 1879 Dr. George Trousseau (1833-1894) and William Purvis (1858-1950) consolidated several parcels of land to establish the Pacific Sugar Mill. This plantation lay on the rugged coastline between the northern boundary of the Honokaa Sugar Company and isolated Waipi'o Valley. F.A. Schaefer & Company served as their Honolulu agent.[7] Dr. Trousseau was a Frenchman who arrived in Honolulu in 1872, and acted as personal physician to King William Lunalilo (1833-1874).[28] A year after being established the plantation produced 800 tons of sugar in 1880.[7]

In 1907 Mr. Purvis, former co-owner and manager, was employed by Schaefer as a consultant. He visited the plantation to study its operations with a view toward improvements. His observations included: "The railway has been built in a most suitable place for the respective managers of Honokaa and Kukuihaele (Pacific Sugar Mill) running over it to visit, and dine with one another, but certainly not where it should be to transport cane to the mill."[29] Following these pointed remarks, the railroad's location was changed.

Beginning in 1913 the plantation shut down its mill, connected its railroad to the neighboring Honokaa plantation, and had its cane ground by the Honokaa Sugar Company. Production figures increased to more than ten times the amount of the original harvest; in 1926 the yield was 8,690 tons.[1] Then in 1928 F.A. Schaefer merged the plantation into its neighbor, Honokaa Sugar Company, and this remotest of the Hāmākua Coast plantations lost its separate identity.[30]

PAAUHAU PLANTATION COMPANY (19)

In 1879 Samuel Parker and other backers, including Claus Spreckels and William Irwin, established Paauhau Sugar Plantation Company. Its 2,000 acres lay south of Honokaa Sugar Plantation Company.[7] The land was difficult to work, but its sticky soil made Paauhau the only plantation on the Hāmākua Coast that could use furrow irrigation. By the 1900s, over 50 small homestead parcels planted and worked by independent operators were embedded in its center. Their crops were ground on shares by Paauhau Plantation's mill, but coordinating this was complicated. A combination of mule-drawn carts, a cable and gravity-powered tramway (known as the "gravity road"), flumes, and a railroad hauled harvests to the mill. In 1935 the mill produced 12,552 tons from 4,500 acres under cultivation, including 1,000 acres cultivated by 55 independent planters.[1]

Despite its awkward structure, Paauhau Sugar Plantation produced a steady annual 11,000 to 15,000 tons well into the twentieth century. Until the onset of World War II, product was loaded from the plantation's landing via a cable and trolley system on the shore cliffs, then shipped directly to the refinery in San Francisco. During and after the war, its sugar went to Hilo by train until the tsunami of 1946 shut down the railroad. For three years product was shipped from Kukuihaele, then after the 1949 switch to bulk sugar, was trucked to the port at Hilo.

In 1972 Theo H. Davies & Co., Ltd. bought Paauhau Plantation Company from C. Brewer & Company, Ltd. and merged it with Honokaa Sugar Company.[31]

HAMAKUA MILL COMPANY / DAVIES HAMAKUA SUGAR COMPANY (20)

During a visit to the Big Island, Theo H. Davies met another fellow Englishman, Charles Notley. Along with Frederick Jackson, son of former Davies' employer Henry Beecroft Jackson, they established Hamakua Mill Company and Hamakua Plantation Company. The land was in and around Pa'auilo at the southern border of the Pā'auhau plantation. Davies and Jackson erected the mill and Notley grew the cane. Hamakua Mill Company ground its first crop in 1885.[32] In 1889 it integrated land from the short-lived Aamano plantation. When Notley wanted to sell out in 1896, Davies bought his land and combined it with the Hamakua Mill Company. Twenty years later in 1917, Kukaiau Plantation Company lands were also added to increase the acreage.[33] By 1935 the plantation had some 6,000 acres under cultivation.[1]

Hāmākua plantation shared all the rigors of its northern neighbors, and added a creative method of bringing harvests to the mill—transport by gravity on trolleys suspended from cables. Fields in the Kūkaʻiau section sloped up from the shoreline cliffs for three miles to an elevation of 3,000 feet. A considerable number of gulches cut through the cultivated fields, making direct access impossible. The harvest was gathered on sleds or carts, and drawn by mules to aerial loading stations. There the cane was assembled into 250-pound bundles and attached to slings on trolleys that slid down taut overhead cables, sometimes as far as two miles. The upper loading stations could be moved to minimize upper-end crop transport by sled or cart. At the lower end, the crop was deposited in railroad cars and hauled to the mill by locomotive.[1] This elaborate system was replaced with trucks, and by the end of World War II the most difficult fields were abandoned. In the Hāmākua section of the plantation, things were a little easier: a zigzag railroad system up the inland slopes was used to haul harvests back down to the mill.

Receiving station for cable-trolley cane transport system. Here the cane was transferred to carts for moving to the mill. A luna on horseback oversaw the operation. (Hawaiian Sugar Planters' Association)

Beginning in 1913, Paʻauilo was the northernmost terminus of the Hawaiian Consolidated Railway Limited. Hāmākua Mill Company's product was shipped to Hilo via this railroad until it was shut down in 1946 after a tsunami destroyed much of the tracks and several trestles. The mills at Honokaʻa, Pāʻauhau, Hāmākua, Kaiwiki, and Laupāhoehoe then shipped product to the Kukuihaele landing, where it was loaded by the cable and trolley system on Matson-owned Liberty ships.[34] By 1949 the Hilo port facilities were modified to handle bulk shipments. Sugar was trucked to Hilo starting that year, and to Kawaihae in 1959.[35]

Two years earlier, in 1957, Laupahoehoe Sugar Company had absorbed Kaiwiki Sugar Company, but it wasn't until 1974 that Hamakua Mill Company was merged into the Laupāhoehoe operation. Five years after that in 1979, Theo H. Davies & Co., Ltd. purchased the Davies' family ownership of the Laupahoehoe Sugar Company, and combined it and Honokaa Sugar Company to form Davies Hamakua Sugar Company.[36] Then, after another five years, in 1984 Davies executive Francis Morgan purchased the company and dropped "Davies" from the name.

HAMAKUA SUGAR COMPANY (20)

From 1984 to 1993, this plantation proved to be a last holdout in a climate of strong economic change. After eight years of consistently low-cost operations, in August 1992 Hamakua Sugar Company filed for Chapter 11 protection in bankruptcy court.[37] Subsequent events led to harvesting the fields a last time and closing the plantation down in March of 1993.[38] It was the end of a 36,000-acre estate that in 1990 had produced fully 12.7 percent of sugar made in Hawai'i that year.[39]

Francis Swanzy Morgan (1919-1999)

Francis Swanzy Morgan (1919-1999) was a fifth-generation descendant of missionary Dr. Gerrit Judd. His maternal grandfather, Francis Swanzy (1850-1917), served as Managing Director of Theo H. Davies & Co., Ltd. Morgan had been involved in Hawai'i sugar production since World War II, and in 1992 he was also chairman of the Hawaiian Sugar Planters' Association. The author visited his headquarters in Pa'auilo, and interviewed him in the elegant former manager's residence. The nearly century-old house overlooks plantation fields and the ocean, and is surrounded by generous lawns and gardens.

Forty-seven years of experience and a farmer's wisdom entered into Morgan's statements—for example, one subtle problem he encountered in growing sugar on the Hāmākua Coast was the constant presence of weeds.

The gulch and gully-separated fields were relatively small, and the acreage had unusually long borders. "Weeds grow on the borders," he said simply, "and that makes a lot of weed killing to do." In addition, for a long time mechanical harvesting could not be used on wetter fields.

Frequent rains during the harvesting season also created problems. Wet ripe cane leaves would not burn, so, after cutting unburned cane, a lot of trash leaves got into the mill. This created a large problem. Morgan said, "Not burning off the leaves before milling costs one ton per acre in yield because the trash absorbs that amount of sugar."[40]

After so many years of valiant struggle, Hamakua Sugar Company was the sole remaining plantation on this fertile coast. Yet, as Morgan put it sadly, "We just ran out of steam."[41]

KUKAIAU PLANTATION COMPANY (21)

In 1884 Theo H. Davies had his hand in another sugar venture. Kukaiau Plantation Company and Kukaiau Mill Company were established, and Davies erected the mill and J.M. Horner grew the sugarcane. When Horner dropped out, Davies took over in order to keep the mill busy. Before being closed down in 1917, the Kūkaʻiau mill produced its largest yield of 5,056 tons of sugar from the plantation's last harvest.[43]

OOKALA PLANTATION / KAIWIKI SUGAR COMPANY (22 & 23)

Bordering on the Kūkaʻiau plantation was the Ookala Sugar Company, Ltd. Two years earlier, in 1879, it had been incorporated to grow cane on 4,000 acres near the village of ʻOʻōkala.[7] Seventy percent of the shares were British-owned, and by 1890 the plantation's mill was producing 1,500 tons of sugar.[16] Ocean frontage was four and a half miles of cliffs at 300 feet above sea level. Cultivated land extended back up into the foothills some two and a half miles to an elevation of 1,800 feet. A cable and sling gravity system was used to deliver most of the harvests to a lower level railroad line that went to the mill. Some cables extended two miles up the slopes.[1]

Ookala Sugar Company railroad circumventing Kaʻula Gulch, circa 1880s. By 1913 railroad trestles had made a direct crossing possible. The terrain is typical of the Big Island's gulch-ridden northeast coastline. (Hawaiʻi State Archives)

In 1909 Ookala Sugar Company went broke, and Theo H. Davies & Co., Ltd. gained control and changed its name to Kaiwiki Sugar Company, Ltd.[44] Maximum production was 13,884 tons in the war year of 1944.[11] Kaiwiki Sugar Company was the first in Hawai'i to haul all its harvests by truck, on the initiative of its manager Leslie Wishard (1894-1993). In 1957 the lands were merged with Laupahoehoe Sugar Company, but Davies shut down the Laupāhoehoe mill and enlarged the O'ōkala mill to continue operations.[36]

LIDGATE & CAMPBELL / LAUPAHOEHOE SUGAR COMPANY (24)

In 1876 William Lidgate and Thomas Campbell entered into an agreement to start a sugar business on land in and around Laupāhoehoe that Lidgate owned. In a style common at the time, Lidgate planted the cane and Campbell built the mill. This was constructed on Laupāhoehoe Point using a loan from Theo H. Davies. After operating as Lidgate & Campbell, then Laupahoehoe Sugar Mill & Plantation Company, the enterprise was incorporated by 1883 as Laupahoehoe Sugar Company, with the Davies family as principal shareholders.[45]

By 1880 the Laupāhoehoe mill produced 600 tons of sugar from 900 acres under cultivation.[7] Steady growth continued through the following decades, and an additional mill was constructed on the bluffs above the ocean at Pāpa'aloa. From 1931 until 1957 annual production stood at about 20,000 tons of sugar from some 7,000 acres under cultivation, with both mills operating for only a fraction of a year. Production increased after 1957, when Kaiwiki Sugar Company was merged into Laupahoehoe Sugar Company.

This substantial operation added one more cane transport technique to methods used along the Hāmākua Coast. Fluming was the principal means because the difficult topography didn't allow for a railroad. But flumes to skirt deep ravines were not feasible at Maulua Gulch, where a long depression divided the plantation with the harvest on one side and the mill on the other. So cane was flumed to the bottom of the gulch, then hoisted up 450 feet by a cable car tramway. A sump collected the flume water at the bottom and heavy-duty pumps raised it to the top, where it was used to flume the cane the rest of the way to the mill.[1] Because of this method the Laupāhoehoe operation was the last Davies plantation to use hand harvesting.

In 1979 Theo H. Davies & Co., Ltd. purchased the Davies family ownership of Laupahoehoe Sugar Company and merged its acreage with Honokaa Sugar Company to form Davies Hamakua Sugar Company. After a life of almost 100 years, Laupahoehoe Sugar Company ceased to exist.[36]

It is likely that the sugar industry on the Hāmākua Coast has ended forever. Most of the 20 miles of former cane fields are awaiting decisions about alternative crops so that weeds and scrub do not take over.

SUGAR IN THE NORTH HILO, HILO, AND PUNA DISTRICTS

If Theo H. Davies & Co., Ltd. dominated sugar production in Hāmākua, along the North Hilo Coast that role was first played by W.G. Irwin & Company, and after 1910 by its successor, C. Brewer & Company. Conditions were quite different in certain ways. No Hilo Coast plantation had a railroad, so fluming was used extensively until roads were constructed to allow for truck hauling. No Hilo Coast plantation was irrigated, and the rains frequently prevented burning the cane to remove the leaves and trash before harvesting it.[46]

By 1994 cost-saving efforts were no longer possible. All milling was done in a modern factory operated by C. Brewer's Hilo Coast Processing Company, but cane farming still came to an end in the district.

HAKALAU PLANTATION COMPANY (36)

Hakalau Plantation Company's estate, 14 miles north of Hilo, was established on 9,000 acres by Claus Spreckels in 1878, with W.G. Irwin & Company as agent.[7] By 1890 the plantation's mill, located on the shore at the foot of a 200-foot bluff, produced 5,000 tons of sugar yearly.[16] Maximum production was 26,509 tons during the war year of 1944.[11] By this time 40 percent of the cane was grown by over 300 independent or contract planters on individually or company-owned small plots.[1]

A 60-kw hydroelectric plant made use of mountain ground water and supplied all electrical power demands of the mill. Until 1913, when the railroad was completed, product was shipped to Honolulu via inter-island vessels that anchored offshore. After the railroad was shut down in 1946, product was trucked to the Hilo dock.

In 1943 the neighboring Wailea Milling Company was merged into Hakalau Plantation Company. Two decades later, in 1962, its owner C. Brewer & Co. merged the combined plantations into their southern neighbor, Pepeekeo Sugar Company. The Hakalau mill was shut down, and Hakalau Plantation Company no longer existed.[36]

HONOMU SUGAR COMPANY (37)

Honomu Sugar Company was established on 2,400 acres by M. Kirchoff & Company in 1880, with C. Brewer & Company, Ltd. as agent.[7] By 1890 the plantation was producing 2,000 tons of sugar yearly.[16] Maximum production reached 10,218 tons during wartime in 1942.[11] Until 1913 the sugar was shipped directly from the plantation's landing, then went by railroad to Hilo Port, and, after April 1946, by truck.

For many years the Honomū plantation depended on a 200-kw hydroelectric plant in a nearby gulch for its electricity. In 1938 this plant was replaced with a diesel-powered generator.[1] The mill was located at the shore and flumes extended four miles up into the rain forest. The upper region was interspersed with small-farm homesteaders growing cane that was milled for them on shares. An employee rest house provided breathtaking views overlooking Kolekole Canyon and ʻAkaka Falls.

Before 1923, for over 20 years this efficient little plantation never missed paying a dividend. From 1929 to 1936 Honomu Plantation Company was managed by Andrew T. Spalding (born 1890).[47] After serving as an Army officer during World War I, Spalding organized the first National Guard company on the Big Island. Later he organized and commanded the 299th regiment. During World War II Colonel Spalding commanded the First Regiment Hawaiian Rifles[48], and was one of several Spaldings prominent in the history of the sugar industry.[49]

In 1946 C. Brewer & Company closed down the Honomū mill, and merged operations into the neighboring Pepeekeo Sugar Company.[36]

KAʻUPAKUEA PLANTATION (38)

Sometime between 1857 and 1861, the highly successful Honolulu businessman Chun Afong (1825-1906) acquired Kaʻupakuea Sugar Plantation and Mill. It consisted of 1,500 acres ten miles north of Hilo.[50] In addition, in 1879 he acquired Makahaula Plantation on 7,600 acres at the southern border of Kaʻupakuea Plantation. By 1882 Afong had combined the two into Pepeekeo Sugar Mill & Plantation Company.

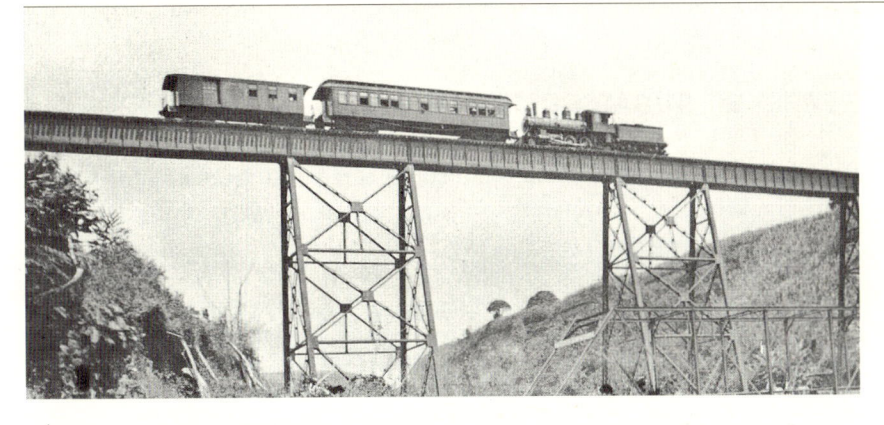

Hawaiian Consolidated Railroad Limited trestle crossing the gulch where Kamaee Stream enters Hakalau Bay, 1915. The railroad transported far more sugar than passengers until it was shut down following the tsunami of April 1, 1946. (Dorrance collection)

Chun Afong came to Hawaiʻi from China in 1849 to work in his uncle's store. He soon became a successful merchant on his own, and also invested in coffee and sugar plantations. His stature increased to the point that in 1879 King Kalākaua appointed him a noble of the Kingdom. But a decade later, in 1889, the weary and aging Afong returned to his homeland, leaving his family in Honolulu and his affairs in the hands of his friend Samuel M. Damon (1845-1924), son of the pioneer preacher Samuel C. Damon.[51]

Alexander Young sold most of his stake in the Pepeekeo Sugar Company to pay for constructing a stately hotel in Honolulu. Completed in 1903, it was the unofficial residence for visiting sugar planters transacting business with nearby sugar agencies. The Alexander Young Hotel became a landmark that served several generations until it was levelled in the early 1970s. (Hawai'i State Archives)

PEPEEKEO SUGAR COMPANY (39)

By 1890, Samuel M. Damon had incorporated Afong's plantation as Pepeekeo Sugar Company and retained 27 percent of the shares for Afong, with Hackfield & Company holding most of the rest, along with the plantation's agency contract. In 1893 Hackfield sold the agency agreement to Theo H. Davies and Afong's shares were sold to Davies' associate Alexander Young (1832-1910).[52] In 1904 C. Brewer & Company purchased controlling shares from Young and took over the agency agreement.[53]

The plantation had been profitable under Afong. Much to his credit, the first pioneering vacuum pan used in the sugar-making process was introduced at Ka'upakuea mill in 1861.[56] Afong also led the way in providing amenities and good housing for his workers and their families. C. Brewer & Company, Ltd. perpetuated this by improving the housing and providing a model hospital that became a standard for other plantations. Production was 400 tons in 1867[54], increased to 500 tons in 1872[55], and to 1,259 tons in 1880.[7]

The lands, however, were acidic and required liming for neutralization. Longtime manager (1905-1936) James Webster and C. Brewer & Company, Ltd. met this challenge in a very unusual way. In 1914 over 20,000 tons of O'ahu's Wai'anae Coast coral sands were taken by the O.R.& L. railroad to the Honolulu docks, then via the Inter-Island Steam Navigation Company to the Hilo docks, and onward with the Hawai'i Consolidated Railway Company to Pepe'ekeo. There the sand was bagged and hauled into the fields by mules to be spread. This remarkable effort turned the acidic soil into a hospitable host for sugarcane and the machinery used to cultivate it.[57]

Pepeekeo's mill was located at the shore to make use of fluming to transport the harvested cane. For many years before 1935 the hydraulic head of mountain ground water drove a hydroelectric plant that supplied all of the mill's needs and also supplied power for housing. Until 1913 product was shipped from a landing near the mill.[1] From 1913 until 1946 sugar went by railroad to the Hilo docks. After the 1946 tsunami, all shipments went by truck.

In 1946 production rose to 25,055 tons[11] when C. Brewer merged Pepeekeo's fields with the neighboring Honomu Sugar Company. Almost two decades later, in 1962, C. Brewer & Company, Ltd. further increased the acreage by merging Hakalau Plantation into the surviving Pepeekeo Sugar Company, and reaped the economies of scale.[36] In 1973, C. Brewer & Company, Ltd. merged Pepeekeo Sugar Company into Mauna Kea Sugar Company, and the original name was no longer used.[36]

ONOMEA SUGAR COMPANY (40)

Before 1867, S.L. Austin & Company established the Onomea Sugar Company on 3,000 acres about eight miles north of Hilo.[58] Production progressed from 500 tons of sugar reported for 1867, to 6,800 tons reported for 1890.[16] The first commercially produced fertilizer used on Hawai'i cane farms was introduced at Onomea in 1879.[56] Cultivated acreage was increased by about 1,000 acres in 1888, when C. Brewer & Company, Ltd. added the neighboring Papaikou Sugar Company and took over the Pāpa'ikou mill.[59]

By 1895 production had increased to 5,907 tons,[60] after C. Brewer & Company, Ltd. acquired Paukaa Sugar Company in 1894.[61] For the next 70 years there were no further mergers, and, beginning in 1924, annual production stabilized between 20,000 and 30,000 tons.[1] During this time Onomea Sugar Company was blessed with two outstanding managers. William Goodale, from 1884 to 1898, followed by John Moir (1859-1933) from 1899 to 1932.[62] Goodale experimented with various varieties of cane until he found those that grew best on the wet fields at different elevations. Moir, who had served as overseer under Goodale for six years, was credited with doubling the yield per acre and for improving conditions for employees and their families.

In the 1920s Onomea was a model of efficiency which would command admiration today. Of all the Hilo Coast plantations, it most thoroughly exploited the hydraulic head of the mountain ground water. Until 1933 a 125-kw hydroelectric plant ran on mountain ground water that supplied the plantation's auxiliary power and electrical needs.[63] But Onomea went one step further; water wheels were used as direct drives to run machinery in the machine shop, elevators, and cane carriers.[64] Product shipping followed a typical pattern:

until 1913 from a landing near the mill, until 1946 to Hilo via the railroad, and after that by truck. In 1965 C. Brewer & Company, Ltd. merged Onomea Sugar Company lands with those of neighboring Hilo Sugar Company to form Mauna Kea Sugar Company. The name and identity of Onomea Sugar Company then disappeared into history.

Intrigued by its past, in 1992 the author visited the site to see what remained. Decaying buildings and some machinery were visible, but getting too close was hazardous. The mill at the foot of a bluff several hundred feet high was obscured by jungle that had grown up around it. Upper portions of the factory remained, along with rusting cane transport machinery and a large banyan tree growing through it. No evidence of the storage or transport flumes survived, although an elevated crane used to lift the cane from the storage flume (and probably from trucks when trucks replaced fluming after World War II) was hidden by trees and weeds.

PAUKAA SUGAR COMPANY (41)

By 1867 the S.L. Austin & Company had established Paukaa Sugar Company on 9,000 acres owned by Judge S. L. Austin (1825-1896), and located a half mile north of Hilo.[58] In 1880 his son Johnathan, destined to become Minister of Foreign Affairs from 1888 to 1890 under King Kalākaua, managed the plantation.[7] In 1884 C. Brewer & Company, Ltd. merged Paukaa Sugar Company lands with those of Onomea Sugar Company and the former name was no longer used.[61]

HITCHCOCK & COMPANY / PAPAIKOU SUGAR COMPANY (42 & 43)

In 1876, E.G. Hitchcock & Company established a plantation at Pāpaʻikou, on 11,000 acres five miles north of Hilo.[7] Hitchcock was a son of Harvey Hitchcock (1800-1855), who arrived in Hawaiʻi in 1832 with the fifth company of missionaries.[65] The plantation got off to a rough start when the mill burned down, and had to be replaced before the first crop was ground in 1877.[7] Production reached 800 tons of sugar in 1880 and was projected to increase to over 1,000 tons.[7] In 1886 the plantation's name was changed to Papaikou Sugar Company. Two years later, in 1888, C. Brewer & Company, Ltd. merged its lands with its northern neighbor, Onomea Sugar Company, and the Papaikou name was no longer used.[61]

AMAUULU PLANTATION / SPENCER'S PLANTATION (44)

The colorful Hilo merchant and investor Capt. Thomas Spencer (1812-1884) purchased Amauulu Plantation from Aiko, its Chinese proprietor, in 1867.[66] The business consisted of a mill and 4,000 acres one mile north of Hilo. Production was reported to be 500 tons of sugar in 1872[55], and in 1880.[7] This amount was doubled under Aiko's management.[54] But in 1884 this small plantation's lands were added to those of Hilo Sugar Company, and Amauula Plantation Company no longer existed.[67]

HILO SUGAR COMPANY / WAINAKU PLANTATION (45 & 46)

In 1880 Claus Spreckels and William Irwin formed a partnership to buy land and start plantations.[68] The wet slopes of Mauna Kea and the uplands outside of Hilo town captured their interest. By 1884 they had bought a number of small parcels and incorporated the Hilo Sugar Company. The lands of Wainaku Plantation were included along with those that had belonged to Captain Spencer. The new plantation grew to 4,800 acres of owned and leased land, and the mill served many small-parcel, independent farmers in and around Hilo and Wainaku. In its first year of production, 1887, the yield was 3,500 tons of sugar.

The abandoned Hilo Sugar Company mill building at Alakea Point in 1990. Vines and jungle overtook the remains at the shore overlooking Hilo Bay. (W. H. Dorrance)

From the beginning, Hilo Sugar Company was blessed with strong management. First was John Scott (1848-1925), hired away from the Hilea Sugar Plantation in the Kaʻū District of the Big Island in 1884. He built up the new operation and and managed it for 35 years. An innovator, Scott invented a juice strainer that became widely used throughout the Islands.[70]

Many small parcels of cane were grown close to Hilo and workers shopped in the town. The plantation never had a store, so its manager had great influence on the development of Hilo. In 1890 Scott organized the Hilo Electric Company and for several years managed two hydroelectric plants that the plantation relied on. He also ran the Hawaiian Telephone Company, was president of the Hilo Library, and a church trustee.

In addition, Scott influenced events throughout the Islands because of his longtime friendship with shipping pioneer William Matson (1848-1917). Hilo Sugar Company supplied cargo for Matson's budding freight enterprise, and Scott invested in several of vessels, helped Matson secure cargo contracts, and raised funds to increase the fleet.[71]

C. Brewer & Company, Ltd. acquired the W.G. Irwin & Company agency in 1910 and, with it, the agency for Hilo Sugar Company.[72] Gradually C. Brewer acquired control. After the 1923 harvest, land from the Hawai'i Mill Company was added. Production at the mill on the shore at 'Āle'ale'a Point rose to 23,105 tons in 1925.[11] Harvests were flumed down from eight miles up on the slopes of Mauna Kea. The cane moved continuously through the mill because its tandem crushers were arranged on lower and lower levels. Maximum production was 28,423 tons in 1939[1], under Alexander Fraser (1877-1940), who managed the plantation from 1902 until his death almost four decades later.[69]

Truck hauling replaced flumes and mechanical harvesting replaced the back-breaking work of hand-cutting cane. With the return of veterans from World War II, Hilo's residential area expanded. The cane lands in Hilo were sold off, and in 1965 C. Brewer & Co. combined the remaining fields with its northern neighbor, Onomea Sugar Company, to form Mauna Kea Sugar Company. The Hilo Sugar Company mill ground its last crop in 1976.[66]

The building at 'Āle'ale'a Point in the northern Hilo suburb of Wainaku was one of very few abandoned mills that survived until 1996. The internal machinery had been removed and many of the auxiliary buildings leveled, but a substantial concrete flume that crossed Highway 19 remained. After 1996 C. Brewer & Company, Ltd. moved its headquarters here from Honolulu.

MAUNA KEA SUGAR COMPANY (47)

In 1972, Mauna Kea Sugar Company and the new United Cane Planters' Cooperative, representing almost 400 independent farmers, formed a nonprofit corporation, the Hilo Coast Processing Company (HCPC), to harvest and grind sugarcane on shares. A year later, in 1973, C. Brewer & Company, Ltd. merged Pepeekeo Sugar Company with Mauna Kea Sugar Company, thus combining under one corporate name what had once been five separate plantations: Honomu Sugar Company, Hakalau Sugar Company, Pepeekeo Sugar Company, Onomea Sugar Company, and Hilo Sugar Company.[36] For a time the three mills at Pepe'ekeo, Pāpa'ikou, and Wainaku were operated by HCPC, but by 1979 only the large, improved mill at Pepe'ekeo survived.[66]

Even with these consolidations, sugar operations in the wet Hilo Coast area were unprofitable. The number of independent farms dwindled to 22. In 1992 C. Brewer & Co. announced that Hilo Coast Processing Company, and its now-named Mauna Kea Agribusiness Company (formerly Mauna Kea Sugar Company), would shut down after grinding the 1994 harvest. More than 450 jobs were affected. After a run of over 150 years, sugarcane permanently left the Hilo area.[73]

WAIAKEA MILL COMPANY (48)

In 1878 Hilo businessmen C.E. Richardson, W.H. Shipman and others leased thousands of acres of undeveloped land in the ahupuaʻa of Waiākea on Hilo's south and southwest borders.[66] Alexander Young, manager and co-owner of Honolulu Iron Works, had operated a machine shop and foundry in Hilo for several years. He convinced fellow co-owner Theo H. Davies that the land was good for raising sugar. Davies persuaded Richardson and others to plant the cane in return for putting up a modern mill. Young and Davies built the mill in 1878, and Waiakea Mill Company was in business.[74]

The planters combined their operations as Waiakea Plantation Company and by 1880 had 350 acres under cultivation.[7] It produced 4,400 tons of sugar in 1890, with 2,240 acres under cultivation serviced by a 36-inch narrow gauge railroad.[16]

While Waiakea Mill Company continued to produce sugar, ownership of the fields shifted. Starting in the mid-1890s, the government sold off small parcels to homesteaders. After 1918 much of the plantation's acreage was made up of individually owned plots leased to the mill. The mill's operators realized that eventually their growth would be stunted as the town of Hilo expanded. Today, it is difficult to distinguish where the city stopped and Waiakea Plantation began.

The mill was located a mile inland at the shore of a large fishpond connected to Hilo Bay by Wailoa River. Product was transported on barges that passed from the pond out through locks and down the river to ships anchored in Hilo Bay. Another unusual feature of the mill was that, beginning in 1930, the bagasse was piped directly to a neighboring factory, Hawaiian Cane Products Company (Canec), where it was made into wallboard. The process had been invented and patented by long-time Waiakea Mill Company manager (1925-1938) William Williams, and attracted the attention of Big Island businessmen who built the plant.[66]

Maximum production by Waiakea Mill Company was 17,939 tons of sugar in 1940.[11] After World War II the plantation gave up much of its land as Hilo town continued to grow. Hauling harvests to the mill with trucks proved unsatisfactory, and the rocky terrain did not lend itself to mechanized harvesting. These difficulties led to Theo H. Davies shutting down the mill after the 1947 harvest. A resort hotel developed by C. Brewer & Company, Ltd. replaced the mill, and much of the mill yard and Canec plant became a spacious community park bordering the former fishpond.[75]

OLAA SUGAR COMPANY / SECOND PUNA SUGAR COMPANY (49)

The rocky, acidic Puna District south of Hilo had a much smaller number of plantations. In the 1890s the land was peppered with small homesteads, some devoted to coffee growing. After Hawaiʻi was annexed to the United States, Benjamin Dillingham saw a sugar-growing opportunity in Puna. Along with investors that included Lorrin Thurston and James Castle, he incorporated Olaa Sugar Company to exploit the land.[76] At the time, Dillingham was building the Hilo Railroad Company (after reorganization, the Hawaiian Consolidated Railway, Ltd.) and considered the new plantation a source of revenue for the railroad. By 1905 Olaa Sugar Company had a modern mill, and 7,676 acres under cultivation serviced by the only standard gauge plantation railway in Hawai'i.[1]

Production increased when Olaa Sugar Company began milling Puna Sugar Company's harvests in and around Kapoho. But Olaa Sugar Company waxed and waned during the first 20 years of its life, paying dividends only twice in all that time.[77] The land was rocky, sticky, acidic, and difficult to clear and cultivate. Not every acre received adequate rainfall, growth was stunted, and irrigation water was lacking. An infestation of leaf hoppers in 1916-1917 ruined 10,000 tons of sugar from the 1918 crop.[78] In later years mechanical harvesting was limited because field equipment rusted and eroded too rapidly under the difficult conditions.

Shops in nearby Kea'au ('Ōla'a) served the mill camps and homesteaders who supplied harvests to the 'Ōla'a mill. When it shut down in 1982, many small businesses were devastated. Highway 11 leading to Kīlauea Volcano bypassed the town and further accentuated the demise of its prosperity. (W. H. Dorrance; 1992)

In the 1930s, cultivated acreage stabilized at slightly over 15,000 acres. The fields extended up to 23 miles from the mill. Harvests were delivered via the Glenwood branch of Hawaiian Consolidated Railway, which ran from 'Ōla'a toward Kīlauea Volcano, and stopped seven miles short of it at the village of Glenwood. Harvests from the Pāhoa region were delivered by the Kapoho branch of tracks that extended 17 miles southwest of the mill. Flumes and the plantation's railroad took care of about half of each harvest, while the Hawaiian Consolidated Railway hauled the rest, and also transported product to the Hilo docks.[1]

In 1935 the plantation housed 5,648 workers and dependents in 1,086 company-supplied houses distributed among over 15 camps or villages. In addition, some 230 homesteaders lived and grew cane on family plots.[1] Maximum production of the combined 'Ōla'a and Puna/Kapoho enterprises was 52,011 tons of sugar in 1937.[1]

The tsunami of 1946 struck a serious blow when it caused the Hilo railroad to shut down. Then the 1955 volcanic eruption covered thousands of acres in the Kapoho Division and isolated it. Despite all, the plantation company, renamed Puna Sugar Company in 1960 at the urging of landowner Herbert Shipman (1892-1976), struggled on. William Bomke (1904-1999) was assistant manager from 1958-1965, and then manager from 1965-1969.[79]

By 1982, the 'Ōla'a mill generated over 40 million kilowatt hours of electric power that was sold to Hawai'i Electric Light Company.[80] The end of sugar operations came when its owners, Amfac, Inc. closed the Puna Sugar Company in the same year. But the mill's generating capability was perpetuated and increased. Oil was burned in the furnaces instead of the former mixture of bagasse and oil, and fulfilled a dire need for electrical energy.

FIRST PUNA SUGAR COMPANY (50)

The same people who incorporated Olaa Sugar Company also founded the first Puna Sugar Company in 1900. By 1905 its harvests were being ground at the Olaa mill. To all intents and purposes, Puna Sugar Company operated as a division of Olaa Sugar Company. The merger was made official in 1936, when the latter company purchased the assets of the former at auction.[81] However, the 1955 lava flow removed any possibility of harvesting cane again on the former Puna Sugar Company lands.

Sugar farming in both the Hilo and Puna Districts came to a close after more than a century and a half. The Hilo Coast plantations were too wet, muddy, sticky and gulch-ridden. Rains often prevented burning the fields before a harvest, increasing the amount of trash at the mill.

Puna cane fields were drier but had an abundance of rocks and boulders, and sticky, acidic soil that lacked sufficient water. The wide dispersal of suitable land made transportation of harvests unduly expensive. Shortly before Puna Sugar Company was shut down, leadership at Amfac, Inc. indicated that they would never have started a plantation in the district given the knowledge and understanding available to the modern industry.[79] An era unlikely to be repeated passed for the Big Island, and it will take years for Hilo to recover.

SUGAR IN THE KAʻŪ AND KONA DISTRICTS

The history of sugar in the remote Kaʻū District was based on a continual combining of plantations as mill and harvest transportation improvements made possible the realization of the economies of scale. In the end, in 1996, all Kaʻū lands were farmed by one corporation, Kau Agribusiness Company, Inc.

Kaʻū is the southernmost district in the Hawaiian archipelago, and its neighbor, South Kona, is only slightly less isolated. Divided up by ancient lava flows and subject to droughts, the lands seemed uninviting for cultivation. Nevertheless, sugar farming came to Kaʻū before the catastrophic Mauna Loa eruption of 1868, survived that event, and lived on to include the last sugar farm on the Big Island. The Kaʻū District was relatively inaccessible in the nineteenth century, but drew some of the shrewdest entrepreneurs in the Kingdom.

NAALEHU PLANTATION (54)

Following the eruption, lava flow, and mud slide of 1868, Alexander Hutchinson (died 1877) moved to Nāʻālehu in the Kaʻū District. He had been an engineer at the Honolulu Iron Works, and entered the sugar business with John Costa. In 1870 they established the Naalehu Sugar Company on leased land, and Costa erected a mill.[82] However, the men soon had a falling out. In 1872 Costa sold his partnership to Charles R. Bishop (1822-1915), Honolulu banker and husband of heir to the throne Bernice Pauahi Bishop. In 1877 Hutchinson added to Naalehu Sugar Company's lands by acquiring neighboring Waiohinu Plantation, organized in 1875 by John Nott & Company.[83]

Under Hutchinson's management the acreage of Nāʻālehu continued to increase. But keeping field workers was a constant problem in remote Kaʻū. Planters held onto laborers as best they could with three- to five-year contracts. This kept workers under bondage, and the sheriff tracked down deserters and

Honuʻapo Harbor and the remains of the dock in 1991. This is the rugged shore where Alexander Hutchinson met his untimely death in 1879. The harbor was permanently shut down in 1942 because of the Japanese submarine threat to inter-island shipping during War World II. (W. H. Dorrance)

returned them to the plantations. The practice led to a dramatic event: in 1879 two deserters were returned to Nāʻālehu by inter-island steamer. Hutchinson met the steamer off Honuʻapo landing and took the pair on board a large rowboat. But the boat capsized near the rugged shore; Hutchinson hit his head on a coral outcropping, and died from injuries a few days later.[84]

HUTCHINSON SUGAR COMPANY (55)

In 1880 Claus Spreckels and William Irwin purchased Naalehu Sugar Company from the estate of Alexander Hutchinson. Four years later they incorporated as Hutchinson Sugar Company. In 1889 they increased its land holdings by acquiring nearby Hilea Sugar Company.[85] Production in 1889 was 1,200 tons of sugar[7], and 5,000 tons in 1890.[16] By this time, the plantation was solidly established and totally owned by United States citizens.

Production grew to 14,534 tons in 1930, eventually reaching a level of about 30,000 tons that was maintained for the rest of the plantation's life.[1] Harvests were brought to the mill's railroad by a system of flumes that reached as far as six miles up Mauna Loa's slopes. Flume water was collected in holding reservoirs fed by water tunnels dug 3,000 feet to 8,000 feet into the mountain, some nine miles above the reservoirs. The fields were situated above the mill on a series of ledges hundreds of square acres in size.[1] The last of several mills was located at Honuʻapo (near Nāʻālehu), less than a mile from where sugar was shipped until the onset of World War II.[86]

Hutchinson Sugar Company operated Honuʻapo landing until it was closed in 1942, after which product was trucked 60 miles to the port of Hilo. From 1930 until 1942 the landing also served Hawaiian Agricultural Company's mill in Pāhala[87] via a narrow gauge railroad. In 1971 owners C. Brewer & Company merged Hutchinson Sugar Company into Hawaiian Agricultural Company to form Kaʻu Sugar Company, Inc., and the Hutchinson and Hawaiian Agricultural Company names passed out of existence.[88]

In 1992 the author inspected the remains of the Hutchinson mill at Honuʻapo. The workers' houses had been removed so that the mill building sat in isolated splendor, obscured from the highway by a canopy of kiawe trees, banyan trees, vines and miscellaneous weeds. It was an eerie scene that generated questions and feelings of nostalgia. Nothing is now left of the mill, and little survives at Honuʻapo landing to remind the viewer of the warehouse, railroad, derricks, and wharf that dominated the landscape between 1878 and 1942.

HILEA SUGAR COMPANY (56)

The Hīlea plantation was established in 1870 by a group of investors, including Charles Spencer, Alexander Hutchinson and William Irwin, on 3,000 cultivated acres situated five miles northeast of Nāʻālehu.[89] By 1880 the Hīlea mill was producing 1,200 tons of sugar annually. Managed by Capt. O.B. Spencer, the proprietor was C.N. Spencer & Company.[7] In 1889 the plantation and mill were acquired by the Hutchinson Sugar Company and the Hilea company name was no longer used.[90]

HONUAPO PLANTATION (57)

The short-lived Honuapo Plantation was started in 1879 by Dr. Richard Oliver on 3,600 acres of cultivated land. In 1880 a distinguishing feature of this venture was the presence of 10,000 to 20,000 goats.[91] By 1885 the plantation was no longer producing sugar.[92] It is probable that the lands were leased or sold to independent planters, Hutchinson Sugar Company, and Hawaiian Agricultural Company.

HAWAIIAN AGRICULTURAL COMPANY (58)

In 1876 a high-powered group of investors met to organize the Hawaiian Agricultural Company. They included the wealthy banker Charles Bishop, John Dominis (1832-1891), and Peter Jones, Jr. (1837-1922).[93] Dominis was governor of Oʻahu and husband of heiress to the throne Lydia Liliʻuokalani.[94] Jones was a partner and later president of C. Brewer & Company, Ltd. They controlled over 50,000 acres of leased and purchased land in and around Pāhala, Kaʻū. By 1880 the plantation's steam-driven mill was the most modern and largest in the Islands.[7] Production increased to 3,000 tons of sugar in 1890, with 2,175 acres under cultivation.[16]

Early in the plantation's life, a fraction of its harvests were grown by independent planters and ground in the plantation's mill on shares. Until 1928 all harvests were flumed to the mill. Over the next eight years, mule and horse-drawn carts began to replace fluming as a transport method. Then, in 1936, trucks began to replace carts, and eventually the miles of flumes were abandoned.[1] Flume maintenance was expensive and the water

A Corliss steam engine placed as a monument opposite the Kau Agribusiness Company's offices in Pāhala. These reliable steam engines served every Hawaiʻi mill for over 50 years. (W. H. Dorrance)

The abandoned Pahala Plantation Theater in 1992. TVs and VCRs have made inroads in remote Ka'ū as the old ways are replaced with the new. The nearby plantation store suffered a similar fate when a mini-market opened in 1990. (W. H. Dorrance)

had to be transported from mountain-side tunnels some two to five miles above the flume-head reservoirs.

From 1916 to 1937 James Campsie was the plantation's manager. He also started the highly successful Pahala Stock Farm subsidiary on otherwise idle land.[1] Many a field overseer was proud to make his rounds on a Pahala-bred horse. Campsie's attitudes toward work were revealed in a conversation he had with a fellow Scotsman and manager of Kohala Sugar Company, George Watt. They were discussing the fact that public schools turned out graduates who disdained plantation work at a time when American-born workers were in short supply. Said Campsie, "Public education beyond the fourth grade is not only a waste, it is a menace. We spend to educate them and they will destroy us."[96]

When Campsie died in 1937, Hawaiian Agricultural Company hired William Cushnie as its promising new manager. Seven years later, however, in December of 1944 Cushnie's life came to a tragic end. During a period of prolonged drought he was fighting a large cane fire, got trapped, and could not be rescued.[95]

The plantation's production stabilized at about 45,000 tons, then increased in 1972, when the acreage of Hutchinson Sugar Company was added by merger.[36] The combined plantations produced 50,149 tons in

1990 from 12,800 acres under cultivation.[2] Yet, under economic pressure, sugar farming operations were shut down in 1996. Much of the former cane fields have been cleared and planted in macadamia trees, which require seven years to mature, and great patience in a region where droughts are frequent.

KAU SUGAR COMPANY / KAU AGRIBUSINESS COMPANY (59 & 60)

In 1972, the name of Hawaiian Agricultural Company was changed to Kau Sugar Company, Inc., and in 1986 to Kau Agribusiness Company.[36] After plantations on the Hāmākua Coast and in North Hilo were closed, the future of sugarcane in Ka'ū was tenuous. It seemed unlikely that this sole Big Island survivor could support the port of Hilo's bulk sugar facility with a production of only 50,000 to 60,000 tons of sugar per year. In fact, changing economics had the final word, and in 1996 the plantation's sugar farming ceased.

KONA SUGAR COMPANY / KONA DEVLOPMENT COMPANY (61 & 62)

The first record of the Kona Sugar Company, headquartered in the North Kona District at Kailua-Kona, was from 1891.[97] The plantation operated in the fields on the ocean-side plateau south of the town, and extended into the South Kona District. Production by the mill in Kailua-Kona started at 285 tons of sugar in 1900, and four years later rose to 895 tons.[98] But by this time the plantation was failing, and it shut down after the 1904 harvest.

The plantation's railroad ran 11 miles south of Kailua-Kona, roughly parallel to the coastline. In 1908, visionary James Castle stepped in and incorporated the Kona Development Company, which activated the former company's mill and plantation. At the same time, he formed the West Hawaii Railway Company to operate the narrow gauge railroad. Castle put the planting in the hands of independent homesteaders and contractors, with his railroad hauling their harvests to the company's mill to be ground in shares.[99] He hoped to attract Caucasian farmers and bring in what he described as "a better class of immigrants."[100] Over the next 18 years his enterprise reported harvests with a maximum production of 4,219 tons of sugar in 1921. Then, after the 1926 harvest, the entire plantation was shut down.[101] The railroad was sold to Japanese investors and the mill shipped to the Philippines.[100]

BIG ISLAND MUSEUMS

No single museum represents the widespread sugar operations that existed on the island of Hawai'i. The Railroad Museum in Laupāhoehoe describes the Hilo train line that served the North Hilo and Hāmākua plantations, and offers some of the sugar industry's history on the Hāmākua Coast. Lyman Museum in Hilo describes plantation life in and around Hilo. On the opposite side of the Big Island, the Kona Historical Society Museum in Kalukalu, Kona, offers a summary of sugar history on the Kona Coast.

The story of sugar plantations on the Big Island was tied to the the Reciprocity Treaty of 1876. Following this landmark agreement, sugar farming survived for 120 years because of the ingenuity of owners and managers. Their accomplishments were all the more impressive in a tough, competitive environment where prices were kept perilously low by foreign and mainland sugar producers and sugar substitutes. The owners met these challenges by continuously updating factory technology, building roads, replacing flumes and railroads with trucks, mechanizing the cycle of planting, fertilizing and harvesting, and combining plantations to minimize overhead. All of this contributed to reaping the economies of scale. In the end, Kohala Sugar Company farmed all Kohala District lands, Hamakua Sugar Company farmed all Hamakua District and some North Hilo District lands, Hilo Coast Processing Company milled most of the cane grown on North Hilo District lands, and Kau Agribusiness Company farmed all Ka'ū District lands. No more cost-saving combining of operations could be done.

For over a century, entrepreneurs built fortunes by growing sugarcane on the island. Their story is one of powerful interests and the political peculiarities of the Hawaiian kingdom. Missionaries and their descendants played a strong role, along with legions of workers, both native-born and immigrants. If fortunes were made by the powerful, it was clever on-site management of resources and the the efforts of nameless laborers that made it all possible.

Lahaina Plantation
(Robert Van Dyke)

CHAPTER 8

INDEPENDENT FARMERS AND INDEPENDENT SUGARMILLS (1876-1996)

When I joined Theo H. Davies & Co. in 1946, they represented two mills on the Big Island that took in harvests supplied by independent growers. The Waiākea Mill was entirely dependent on cane from homestead lands. The Laupāhoehoe plantation, then owned by the Davies family but represented by Theo H. Davies & Co., had a minority of its cane—only about a third—that came from independent or "adherent" farmers. Early in the century, when the Territory opened up this land to homesteaders, it was believed that small growers could cultivate cane and share in the prosperity. However, as technology advanced and fertilizers were developed, mechanical planting and harvesting replaced work by hand, and small plot farmers fell behind. They couldn't afford the expense of modernizing.

Cooperation developed. The mill, having greater financial resources, would supply the fertilizer and do the plowing, planting, and harvesting, using new machinery, and the small-plot farmer would hoe the weeds and spread the fertilizer. From the proceeds received for sugar produced by the farmer's plot, the mill subtracted the costs of milling cane, fertilizer supplied, and other work.

The Department of Agriculture called annual meetings to determine a fair split of production costs between the mill and the grower. As a result, the mill's share of the proceeds for grinding, transporting, warehousing, and marketing the grower's sugar might be 45 percent, and the grower's share might be 55 percent. The grower could also contract with the mill to do his share of the work. The cost to the mill would be further subtracted from the proceeds due the grower from the sale of his sugar.

As time went on, more and more growers contracted with the mill to do their share of the work. The grower might have a full-time job, or no access to mechanical harvesting equipment and be forced to do expensive hand cutting. Or the fact that his attention was required only eight months out of two years might not provide enough sustained effort. All these were contributing factors.

This cooperative arrangement was operating smoothly at Laupahoehoe Sugar Company's plantation when I joined Theo H. Davies & Co. However, a law had removed the ban on corporations purchasing homesteaders' plots. As more and more growers stopped working their fields and no replacements were found, the mill purchased the land. What started out as an effort to encourage small-plot farmers ended up as corporate farming because of the need for large-scale operations if profits were to be made. The homesteaders departed for more lucrative pursuits when they gained the legal right to sell their land.

It would be wrong to assume that homestead land was inferior to what the corporations owned. At Laupāhoehoe both were equally good, and the homestead lands were closest to the mill, which minimized the cost of hauling. Very few houses were built on these lands while they were used for planting cane.

The situation was different at the Davies-owned Waiakea Plantation mill. Homestead lands remained in the hands of their original owners or descendants until the plantation and mill were shut down in 1947. In the beginning the homesteaders did a large share of the planting, cultivating, and harvesting work. However, when very expensive field machinery began to be used, the mill did most of the work, leaving only the weeding to homesteaders. In the end, even this was done by the mill. When it was shut down, the mill's employees were cultivating and harvesting the cane, and homesteaders were charged against their sale proceeds. They received more that way than if they had done the work themselves.

While it didn't amount to much, we had a few remaining independent farmers at Laupāhoehoe. We called them "pali planters," because they planted on steep slopes that were impossible to reach using the mill's cultivating and harvesting machinery. They accounted for less than a hundred acres.

Before my time, the Davies company employed cultivation contractors on several of Hamakua Mill Company's fields. The company did the initial planting and cultivating, and the contractors did the fertilizing and weed control. While this minimized expenses, fields cultivated by independent growers tended to yield less than those maintained by the company.

⊕ ⊕ ⊕

BEFORE THE GREAT Mahele of 1848 and the Kuleana Act of 1850, Hawai'i was a fiefdom with temporary land usage allocated by the monarchs.[1] There was no mechanism for homesteading. Following the Mahele, a long-time resident could purchase title to his land and add to it by purchasing from neighbors, chiefs, the crown or the government. Providing an investor had sufficient funds, credibility, and/or political connections, he could build a substantial estate.

In the immediate post-Mahele years, planters with large landholdings had to build their plantations during a time when workers were scarce. They had enough problems to solve without trying to encourage small-plot holders to grow sugarcane. While some Native Hawaiians cultivated cane in well-settled areas, usually it was a casual arrangement. The cane was ground at a nearby mill and the proceeds of the sale were shared. Certain rich lands were known for growing small plots of cane; the Kōloa District on Kaua'i; the North Shore on O'ahu; the Lahaina, Wailuku and Hāna Districts on Maui; the North Kohala, South Hilo, and Ka'ū Districts on the island of Hawai'i. However, the effort died out as small-plot owners, mostly Native Hawaiians, sold out or let their land lie fallow.

The perspective of the large plantations changed in the years following the Reciprocity Treaty. Retaining the services of indentured workers once their contracts expired became a problem. Mostly Chinese immigrants at the time, they migrated to Honolulu and set up shopkeeping, or returned to China rather than staying on as plantation laborers. During this same period, business interests in Queensland, Australia, were developing the concept of a central sugar factory milling the crops of surrounding independent farmers as a way to attract and hold cane growers.[2] Planters in Hawaiʻi saw a similar kind of homesteading as a method of holding on to sugarcane farmers, and the Kingdom felt it could attract immigrants at a time when Hawaiʻi's population was sparse.

The legislature passed the Homestead Act of 1884, which made available some 12,000 acres of government land to be purchased at no more than 20 acres per claim. Over 527 claims were consummated by 1895.[3] The short-lived Republic of Hawaiʻi perpetuated homesteading with the more liberal (larger parcels) Land Act of 1895. By 1911, 2,402 claims had been processed and 92,224 acres of public lands distributed to claimants.[4] However, the most productive of these lands were eventually leased or sold to the large planters, and the government's homesteading efforts were a failure.[5]

The Organic Act of 1900 established laws governing the Territory that were consistent with the laws of the United States. Bondage by labor contracts was forbidden, and the cozy relationship between the large planters and the Hawaiʻi government weakened. A new homesteading campaign was undertaken that included plantations giving up land to homesteaders. By 1915, there were 2,926 new homesteads taken by small farmers.[6] These parcels were mostly occupied by farmers dedicated to cultivating sugarcane. By 1923, the educational establishment was encouraging students to become independent sugarcane farmers by homesteading or as tenant farmers. A public school textbook devoted one of its 15 chapters on the Hawaiʻi sugar industry to "the small planter." The chapter closed with a paragraph that carefully qualified the place occupied by an independent cane farmer.

"One may have the craving to own a farm of his own and he may do so through the homesteading method. Another, however, who wants an outdoor life and a part in a big and important industry may care less about the actual ownership of a piece of land and will gladly identify himself with the big business of producing cane sugar, as an employee of a corporation or as a contractor working with a corporation. Each must see that his success and prosperity depends on cooperation."[7]

Table 9 shows how the number of independent and tenant farmers declined over the years at a rate consistent with the declining number of plantations. Between 1915 and 1952 the total went down by almost half, from 2,926 to 1,501.[8] It took only 19 years, 1952 to 1971, to halve the number again from 1,501 to 715.[9] In nine more years, in 1980, the number was more than halved from 715 to 318.[10] By 1992 the total had decreased to a mere 22 farmers who still held small plots.[11]

TABLE 9 | SMALL-PLOT, INDEPENDENT SUGARCANE FARMERS

YEAR	FARMING HOMESTEADS & ADHERENT PLANTERS	HCPC COOPERATIVES	TOTAL
1915	2,296	0	2,926
1949	>2,000	0	>2,000
1952	1,501	0	1,501
1971	715	0	715
1974	unk.	450	(1)unk.
1977	193	312	505
1980	15	303	318
1985	13	112	125
1990	unk.	40	unk.
1992	unk.	22	unk.

Note: (1) Hilo Coast Processing Company (HCPC), a cooperative, was organized in 1971.
Sources: Beechert; HSPA., *Sugar in Hawai'i*, 1949; HSPA., *Hawaiian Sugar Manual*, 1972, 1897, 1991; Heinz, HSPA, 1987; Holderness, et al., U. of Hawai'i, 1979; Holderness, et. al., U. of Hawai'i, 1982; *Honolulu Advertiser*, Aug 1, 1992; Kahane, et. al., Legislative Reference Bureau Report No. 9, 1987; Philips.

In 1971 C. Brewer & Company organized the Hilo Coast Processing Company, a cooperative with ownership allocated among Brewer's Mauna Kea Sugar Company and 450 small-plot, independent planters.[12] As the trends shown in Table 9 indicate, in 1985 half, or 112, of a total of 125 processed their cane at the HCPC mill.[13] By 1985, all of them were on the island of Hawai'i.

Under the Agricultural Adjustment Act passed by Congress in the 1930s, the independent farmer was protected by the Department of Agriculture. The department held yearly hearings in the Islands, attended by growers and mill representatives, at which data was presented and used to determine a fair distribution of costs between the growers and the mill. Income from selling the sugar was then distributed in proportion to the division of costs. This system worked satisfactorily for over 50 years, until the last of the independent farmers ceased operations.

Despite everything, prospects for small farmers were poor from the start. Disadvantages arose because of expensive technological improvements. A small operator could not afford the latest labor-saving machinery and remained dependent on hand labor, usually provided by his own family. The "adherent" small farmers were sometimes left behind when the plantation operator made cultivating and crop transportation changes. For example, from 1940 to 1961, Hilo Sugar Company reduced the amount of crop flumed to its mill by over 90 percent by using trucks to haul the harvest.[14] Small farmers located at the fringes of the plantation incurred a disproportionate increase in costs because trucks hauled their supplies upward and crops downward the greatest distance to the mill.

There was also the problem of generation-to-generation restlessness. A farm built and nurtured by a father with dawn-to-dusk work no longer attracted such devotion from a son. The son saw better prospects in Honolulu or in college. As on the mainland, it was difficult to keep them "down on the farm."

The author interviewed an elderly resident about his experiences. Alex, of Japanese descent, was born on a tenant farm in the Hilo district worked by his father, who had immigrated to Hawai'i from Hiroshima Prefecture in the 1920s. His mother came later as a "picture bride," and the couple raised eight children in a three-bedroom plantation house. In the 1930s Alex lived on a small-plot cane farm of about ten acres. He and the other children constantly worked in the fields when not in school—hoeing, weeding, killing rodents, fertilizing, and stripping stalks during harvesting. His day began at public school miles away, followed by walking to a separate Japanese school, where he spent several hours drilling in the language and customs of the old country. Then there was another walk home to work in the fields. As he described it: wet work half the time, and dirty work all of the time. Many of his schoolmates did the same.

When the Hilo Coast Processing Company was shut down in 1994, the era of small-plot, independent sugarcane farmers ended. The long period of their contributions to Hawai'i's economy and culture will be difficult to replace.

INDEPENDENT SUGARMILLS

Capital was scarce in Hawai'i during the days of the monarchy. Foreign investors were reluctant to risk doing business in the small and turbulent kingdom, and little excess capital was locally generated. The outlook was changed by the Reciprocity Treaty of 1876 and many entrepreneurs exploited the situation.

Several cooperative ventures were launched. "If you plant the cane, I'll put up the mill" was a typical proposal. Here on Table 10 these are referred to as "independent sugarmills." Between 1876 and 1900, 13 of them were distributed among the islands of Kaua'i, O'ahu, Maui, and Hawai'i.

TABLE 10 | **NUMBER OF INDEPENDENT SUGARMILLS 1874-1996**

YEAR	NUMBER	YEAR	NUMBER
1874	1	1900-1925	2
1878	4	1925-1943	1
1880	8	1944-1973	0
1885	10	1974-1994	1
1890	6	1996	0

Sources: Gilmore, 1935-1948; Kohala Sugar Company, 1863-1963; Morgan, 1993 interview; Thrum, 1875-1940, *Honolulu Advertiser.*

By 1876 the concept of one partner planting the cane and another putting up a mill was well established. In 1870 H.P. Baldwin and S.T. Alexander had entered into an agreement with Robert Hind by which he built and operated a mill to grind the crops from their newly established plantation.[15] In fact, this kind of agreement went back to the very first milling enterprise in the islands: the Chinese sugarmaker's 1802 mill on Lāna'i.

Table 11 lists the post-Reciprocity Treaty independent mills which were originally not part of a plantation, along with their dates of operation.

TABLE 11 | **INDEPENDENT SUGARMILLS 1878-1994**

NAME OF MILL	LOCATION	FIRST DATE*	LAST DATE*
Union Mill Company#	Kohala, Hawai'i	1874	1896
Laupahoehoe Mill#	Laupāhoehoe, Hawai'i	1876	1884
Star Mill Company#	Kohala, Hawai'i	1878	1883
Hamakua Mill Company#	Hāmākua, Hawai'i	1878	1900
Paalaa Mill	Waialua, O'ahu	1879	1880
Waiakea Mill Company	Hilo, Hawai'i	1879	1947
Paauhau Mill#	Hāmākua, Hawai'i	1880	1885
Kekaha Mill Company#	Kekaha, Kaua'i	1882	1897
Hanamaulu Mill	Hanamā'ulu, Maui	1882	1898
Kipahulu Mill#	Hāna, Maui	1882	1886
Huelo Mill Company	Huelo, Maui	1882	1891
Waimea Sugar Mill#	Waimea, Kaua'i	1884	1896
Hilo Portuguese Sugar Company	Hilo, Hawai'i	1896	1901
Kukaiau Mill Company#	Hāmākua, Hawai'i	1902	1913
Kaiwiki Milling Co.#	Hilo, Hawai'i	1917	1924
Wailea Milling Company	Hakalau, Hawai'i	1921	1943
Crescent City Milling	Hilo, Hawai'i	1925	1925
Hilo Coast Processing Company	Pepe'ekeo, Hawai'i	1974	1994

Notes: * "First Date" and "Last Date" are the first and last years these mills were listed in the sources.
These mills were acquired and operated by a plantation in subsequent years.
Sources: Gilmore, *Hawai'i Sugar Manual*, 1947-1948; Kohala Sugar Company, 1863-1963; Morgan, 1993 interview; Thrum, *Hawaiian Almanac and Annual*, 1875-1939.

Most independent mills were eventually combined with the lands they served to form a single sugar-producing enterprise. For example, Theo H. Davies financed the Hāmākua mill that was later incorporated into Hamakua Plantation Company.[16] The Kekaha, Kaua'i mill also ended up being incorporated into Kekaha Sugar Company when it was organized in 1898.[17]

One mill established to service small farmers exclusively was Waimea Mill Company, located at Hakalau on the north Hilo coast. This plucky cooperative enterprise operated from 1921 until shutdown in the war year of 1943.[18] It served 60 small farmers in addition to grinding crops grown on 550 acres bordering the mill. Production peaked at 6,004 tons of sugar in 1931 for

1,296 acres under cultivation, an average of about 21 acres per farm. Many were located miles from the mill at the 1,500- to 2,000-foot elevation on the slopes of Mauna Kea.[19]

Typically, the farmer and his family lived and worked on his land. The gulch-ridden terrain did not allow the use of a railroad. Twelve miles of permanent flumes and four miles of portable flumes using mountain water transported harvests to the low-level mill. The abundant Hilo rainfall meant that none of the fields required irrigation. When the mill closed, the island of Hawai'i had no independent mill for the next 31 years. Farmers who stayed in business took their harvests to the Hakalau Plantation Company to be ground for a share of the sugar, or made arrangements with other nearby mills.

In 1962 C. Brewer & Company, Ltd. merged Hakalau Sugar Company into Pepeekeo Sugar Company, and in 1973 merged Pepeeko Sugar Company into Mauna Kea Sugar Company. Finally in 1974, C. Brewer & Company, Ltd. organized the cooperative Hilo Coast Processing Company to grind Mauna Kea Sugar Company's crops, as well as those of 450 small farmers on the Hilo Coast. Thus the island regained an independent mill, since HCPC cultivated no land.

In 1992, C. Brewer & Company, Ltd. announced that the HCPC mill would be shut down after the 1994 harvest.[20] The number of independent farmers had dwindled to 22. An exceptionally wet harvest season and years of Mauna Kea Sugar Company losses contributed to the demise. The Hilo District lost an employer and taxpayer that will be difficult to replace. The time of the independent sugarmill had passed in Hawai'i.

The exhausting labor of cutting cane was required on sugar plantations year-round, and for 10 to 12 hours a day under the hot sun. (Lyman House Memorial Museum)

CHAPTER 9

THE PLANTATION WORKERS

When Captain Cook came to Hawai'i, he estimated the Native Hawaiian population to be about 300,000. By the mid-1800s, the Hawaiian population was down to around 50,000. That's a tremendous death rate and it was due to imported diseases. It's no wonder that the sugar plantations of those times were desperate for workers. There just weren't enough Hawaiians to supply the needs of the planters.

The Hamakua Sugar Company found that Native Hawaiians were excellent employees. A Native Hawaiian held the job of harvesting supervisor on its plantation, and that's one of the most demanding jobs there is. He did an excellent job. The plantation had a number of other Native Hawaiian employees—some were supervisors—and they all did a good job. Many Chinese workers were imported before annexation. In my grandfather's opinion, the Chinese were also excellent workers. Those that stayed in Hawai'i prospered to the extent that around 1945, people of Chinese descent were the most affluent segment of the population.

After annexation, a U.S. exclusion act forbade further importation of Chinese, so the planters turned to Japan. This required a change in Japan's laws because, until then, emigration by its citizens to any country was forbidden. Efforts by Hawai'i planters and the government changed this. The Kingdom of Hawai'i enjoyed the distinction of being the first foreign land to which Japanese citizens were allowed to emigrate.

The Japanese government was very concerned that the potential workers be reliable and of good character, so they investigated their backgrounds. Each male immigrant arrived with a document called a "koseki tohon." It described his ancestry and was considered by him to be sacred. Many Japanese preserved the document in a small shrine within their homes. The koseki tohon played an interesting role in Hāmākua Coast plantations.

In 1948, when we converted to an insured retirement plan for our workers, the insurance company needed their birth dates. That was no problem for employees born in the Territory, but those born in Japan lacked birth certificates. However, they did have the koseki tohon, giving their family history, including their date of birth, all in Japanese. Of course, they didn't want to entrust this sacred family document to insurance agents. We worked out an agreeable compromise. An office supervisor who understood Japanese visited the employee's house to read the *koseki tohan*, or the worker brought it to the plantation office. Our employee would determine the worker's date of birth and we would certify its accuracy for the insurance company.

Filipinos came after the Japanese, and they were also industrious workers but retained certain characteristics acquired in the old country. When I first joined Davies, an older manager described the *patrone* system to me—in the Philippines a worker gave his allegiance to a local employer in return for protection, care and problem-solving. When the day's work was done, it was not unusual for this older manager to find men lined up outside his house seeking advice, an advance in pay, or help in solving some domestic problem. They looked upon him as their *patrone*.

This concept had a great deal to do with the direction the union took during the 1946 industry-wide strike. The union tried to break the bond between the workers and management. "Those guys are your enemy. We are your friends," went the propaganda of the International Longshoremen's and Warehousemen's Union. It appeared to me that the union's primary focus was on breaking the trust we had with our employees, not necessarily to reach a particular settlement on wages. The strike was settled on terms we were willing to grant before the strike was called, and the union knew it. The ILWU wanted to break the bond with management and substitute a bond to the union.

Over the years I saw the union's attitude toward management change. The ILWU representatives began to realize that management had the good of the organization—including its employees—uppermost in mind, and developed a spirit of constructive cooperation. By the time I owned the plantation, I never had any trouble with the union's representatives. We had our differences, but I respected them and they respected me.

Plantation camp housing, at least that built since 1900, has been unfairly disparaged. When I first joined the Davies company, we had some camp housing that went back to the turn of the century. The houses had electricity, sewerage, and running water, and the inhabitants were quite happy. They particularly enjoyed the social life in the camp communities. Employees built their own churches according to their religious beliefs.

Sugar prices held fairly firm during the Depression years, but unemployment was high in Honolulu. The sugar industry was determined to help out by hiring many of the unemployed, but housing had to be built for them. Kaiwiki Sugar Company, owned by Theo H. Davies & Co., built two villages in the 1930s. As was customary throughout the Territory by then, the new communities came complete with gyms, ballparks, and recreation facilities, including community meeting halls. Every house had running water, sewerage, and electricity, and these well-maintained Hāmākua Coast villages are occupied to this day.

Hawai'i sugar employees have long been the highest-paid agricultural workers in the world. An old Japanese worker told me that long before the strike of 1946, wages were high enough that men routinely saved one-half of their salary every month. Bonuses were also paid, based on the New York price for sugar, and "What's the price of sugar today?" became a commonplace question among the workers. Japanese employees created the tanomoshi (rotating credit system) with their savings. At the time, no bank would loan money to a Japanese, so the pooled savings in the tanomoshi were often loaned to budding entrepreneurs. The ILWU ended the perquisite system when it sued to have workers paid one-half the value of the perquisites, in addition to time-and-a-half for overtime. The industry converted to all-cash wages, including suitably increased hourly rates, and did away with the perquisite system entirely to avoid complexities brought on by the union's demand.

By 1947, every plantation had its own clinic with nurses and at least one doctor. The industry was concerned that the medical support be the best, so the HSPA retained a highly respected physician, Dr. Nils Larsen (1890-1964), to oversee plantation medical practices. Every plantation doctor filed periodic reports with him on the status of workers' health. He was influential in hiring competent doctors, and plantations provided the best medical service, as shown in one remarkable episode.

The HSPA hired a prominent mainland consultant to visit every plantation hospital and report on improvements or changes to be made. The result was somewhat unexpected but received with great satisfaction. "The Hawai'i plantation medical system is the best we have ever encountered," went the report. "Don't change it. Those served by plantation practitioners rank (in health) with the upper ten percentile of affluent mainland Americans. If anything, the system should be extended to the general public."

When I combined all of Davies' Hamakua plantations into one large operation, I replaced individual clinics with one large clinic in Honoka'a that served both the plantation population and the general public. This clinic, still operating, employed four doctors, including one surgeon. They were encouraged to treat patients from the general public and, for each such case, were paid a commission in addition to their regular plantation salary. The patient paid the company and the company paid the staff doctor. It was a point of personal satisfaction that the clinic's administrator, a very competent lady, happened to be the daughter of a Kūka'iau Ranch cowboy. When an outside specialist or hospital was needed, she got one at a favorable rate.

We also paid promptly, whereas most hospitals usually delayed payment because of more time-consuming billing procedures. Other plantations throughout the Islands did away with their clinics and relied on outside services. Theo H. Davies & Co. never abandoned the plantation hospital concept, and, when I bought the plantation, I continued the hospital because of its admirable record.

⊕ ⊕ ⊕

THE SUGAR INDUSTRY was built on the muscle and sweat of thousands of hard-working laborers. Until the Reciprocity Treaty of 1876, these anonymous men were mostly Native Hawaiians. A 1872 census of plantations revealed that 79 percent of the 3,786 employees were Native

Hawaiians.[1] They probably provided their own housing on a kuleana (small land holding), or lived near the beach with no expense to the plantation. Hawaiians were accustomed to subsistence living. A man would construct his house wherever the management wanted if given grass for the thatched roof, and bamboo and wood for a frame. Housing was not a major operating cost.

In the mid-1860s, young J.M. Lydgate moved with his parents to Onomea on the Big Island, where his father became manager of Judge S.L. Austin's plantation, which later became Onomea Sugar Company. In his memoirs, Lydgate described the workers' living quarters as small grass-house villages built by their inhabitants and close to the mill. When new, the houses were delightfully clean, cool, fragrant and well-ventilated, but not very durable. There can be no doubt that the workers were Hawaiian, because Lydgate remembered one native, a D. Kamai, who made his living supplying the inhabitants with poi under contract to the plantation. The poi was delivered throughout the villages once a week by pack train in 50-pound bundles wrapped in ti leaves.[2]

This agreeable arrangement between plantation management and Native Hawaiians could not endure into the post-Reciprocity Treaty era, much as both parties might have desired it. Hawaiians were dying off from imported diseases and not reproducing in large enough numbers to make up for losses. The small kingdom was in danger of disappearing from a lack of subjects, much to the despair of Kings Kamehameha III, IV, V, Lunalilo, and Kalākaua.

As shown in Table 12, in 1853 the total population was a mere 73,137 and the trend was downward.[3] At the same time, prospects for selling Hawai'i-made sugar and the numbers of plantations increased as California was settled. Competition among planters for labor rose at the same time that the native population was in sharp decline.

TABLE 12 | **POPULATION AND NUMBER OF PLANTATIONS 1853-1878**

YEAR	TOTAL POPULATION	NUMBER OF PLANTATIONS
1853	73,137	5 (1857)
1860	69,800	10
1866	62,959	29 (1867)
1872	56,897	32
1878	57,578	80

Sources: Table 1; Thrum 1876; Nordyke.

Both the Kingdom and the planters were concerned about the situation. The only answer was imported labor. In 1850 the Royal Hawaiian Agricultural Society convened in part to address the issue. The Chief Justice of the Superior Court, Judge William L. Lee (1821-1857), a planter himself, drafted legislation to make imported contract labor legal.[4] The "Act for the Government of Masters and Servants" was passed, and planters soon exploited it.

The first imported laborers were some 500 Chinese from Amoy Province in 1852. They contracted for five years of labor in return for their transportation, housing, food, clothing and pay of $3.00 per month.[5] Despite an initial period of turmoil caused in part by the language barrier, these Chinese were valuable employees. Few, if any, women were among them, and they lived in rudimentary barracks or bunkhouses that cost little to construct and maintain. The terms of their contracts held them to their assigned plantation under penalty of law for desertion or refusal to work.

The labor problem seemed to be solved. Unfortunately, the market for sugar had collapsed after California was admitted to the Union in 1850. Under the U.S. Tariff Act of 1846, a 30-percent ad valorem tax applied to sugar imports, and was now levied against Hawaiian product exported to California. As a result, numerous enterprises in Hawai'i went bankrupt and importation of labor ceased. But, when the Civil War broke out in 1861, this was a windfall for Hawai'i's sugar producers. Labor recruiters were sent to Hong Kong and other Chinese port cities. In 1864 the Kingdom established a Bureau of Immigration to control the new flow of workers and put an official stamp on the effort.[7]

In 1865 Chinese immigration to Hawai'i was renewed. It continued for over three decades, until prevented by United States exclusion laws after annexation in 1898. By 1897, 56,700 Chinese had arrived in Hawai'i. Of these, some 8,000 came from California.[8] This time they proved to be a mixed blessing. Once convinced of the merits of cooperating with management and their labor contracts, they were excellent workers. On the other hand, they preferred to control their destinies as independent small farmers, or migrated to the towns to become shopkeepers or day laborers. Some deserted their assigned plantations before their contracts expired. Sheriffs were kept busy capturing them and bringing them before magistrates, who were frequently also planters. When the Chinese cooperated, they were excellent workers; but, when they didn't, they were headaches for management.

R.R. Hind wrote of an early attempt to outwit potentially fractious Chinese employees by means of a technique that became commonplace. In the early 1880s the first shipload of Chinese arrived in Kohala on the Big Island. Mr. C. Chapin, manager of Kohala Sugar Company, was determined to control his quota of 90 men. Each arrival was told to stand before the camera, on a platform which happened to be a scale, while Chapin took a photograph. He was immensely pleased by his cleverness—getting a record of weight as well as a picture—until he discovered that he'd failed to change plates after each exposure, and had photographed all the men, one after another, on a single plate.[9]

Planters observed that the Oriental was an excellent worker, so why not try the Japanese? The Kingdom arranged with independent contractors to do the recruiting for contract laborers. In 1868, when this began, rural Japan was suffering a depression and work in faraway Hawai'i was an appealing prospect. An initial shipment of some 200 indentured Japanese came that same year, followed by a 17-year hiatus caused by political difficulties and a recession in sugar.[10] In 1884, after King Kalākaua's successful 1881 world tour, during which he established amicable relations with the Emperor of Japan, immigration of indentured workers resumed. By 1897, on the eve of annexation, 68,279 Japanese had emigrated to Hawai'i.[11] When treated with respect, they were reliable and excellent workers.

Japanese labor camp, Wainaku, Hawai'i, 1890.
(Bishop Museum)

In the North Atlantic, the Portuguese island of Madeira had a long history of sugar production. Cane was cultivated there and exported to Europe as early as 1433, and continued into the nineteenth century.[12] Dr. William Hillebrand (1821-1886), former member of King Kamehameha V's privy council, visited Madeira in 1877 and noted that its agriculture flourished in a climate similar to Hawai'i's. This resulted in a new wave of immigration that began the following year. Between 1878 and 1886 some 17,500 Portuguese arrived in Hawai'i, and came intermittently until 1913.[13] Because they brought their families, planters were forced to upgrade employee housing and offer the humane necessities of life. One- or two-room thatched huts no longer sufficed. The Portuguese were more expensive to support, but more than made up for this in industriousness and productivity.

All ethnicities of workers often refused to renew their contracts, or returned to their homelands, and replacements were continuously needed. Modern machinery introduced in the 1850s and 1860s—steam engines to drive the grinders and centrifugal separators to speed up sugar production—created discrepancies between mill capacities and lands being served. As shown in Table 13, the difference was restored by increasing the acreage under cultivation. This translated into an increased demand for field labor.

As the plantations grew in size, they distributed laborers to strategically located villages called "camps." Each had assigned fields and was presided over by a foreman. Comparable to mainland farms of the time, none of these early camps had electricity, running water, kitchens, sewerage, or indoor toilets. Community baths were the norm, and living conditions were primitive, but far better than where the immigrants had come from. Northern Europeans and South Sea islanders were hired between 1878 and 1885[14], but they didn't work out. The Europeans were critical of the living and working conditions, and the cultural change was too much for the islanders. It was up to the Chinese, Japanese, Portuguese, and a dwindling number of Native Hawaiians to carry the Hawai'i sugar industry into the twentieth century.

Assuming that roughly 50 percent of the population was male, Table 13 shows that on the eve of annexation fully 40 percent or more worked on the plantations, with disproportionate numbers of Japanese, Chinese, and Portuguese.

TABLE 13 | **POPULATION GROUPS AMONG SUGAR EMPLOYEES IN 1896**

ETHNIC ORIGIN	ETHNIC POPULATION	PERCENT OF TOTAL	NUMBER OF SUGAR WORKERS	PERCENT OF TOTAL
Japanese	24,407	22.3%	12,893	52.9%
Chinese	21,616	19.7	6,289	29.1
Portuguese	15,191	13.7	2,268	14.9
Hawaiian	39,494	36.1	1,615	4.1
Other	8,912	8.2	83	5.4
Totals	109,620	100%	23,548*	21.0%

*Note: The maximum number of workers was 56,600 in 1927, 18 percent of the total population.
Sources: Lind; Nordyke.

Annexation was anticipated by the planters with mixed emotions. Some, like Isenberg and Spreckels (German citizens), and Davies (a British national), had supported the monarchy and resisted annexation. Others, who were more numerous, pressed for annexation by the United States. Arguments in favor of it included ending the threat of American import tariffs being applied to Hawaiian sugar. Those opposed to annexation pointed to mainland laws that would end the Masters and Servants Act, and prohibit importation of Chinese labor. In 1898 the annexationists won out and the Republic of Hawai'i became part of the United States.

Following the Organic Act of 1900, which officially established annexation and ended labor contracts, workers saw themselves as being freed. In the next year, 22 strikes by Japanese and others occurred at one plantation or another.[15] They demanded better housing and higher pay. Agitators went to work in Honolulu and spread strike news to the plantation workers. The planters responded in 1907 by ending Japanese importation and beginning to bring in Filipinos.

At the turn of the century, housing was substandard on many plantations. Instead of encouraging a feeling of community, camps resembled a haphazard arrangement of shacks used by migrant laborers throughout America. They lacked parks, churches, and other social amenities. None of the houses or barracks had suitable kitchen facilities or even running water.

In 1895 the Hawaiian Sugar Planters' Association had succeeded the Planters' Labor and Supply Company as industry leader and spokesman. HSPA committees studied workers' complaints and recommended solutions. Improvements to camp housing and increased social benefits topped the list of suggestions. Standard plantation-worker house designs were prepared by the HSPA and distributed industry-wide.[16]

Plantation camp housing, 1925. (Hawaiian Sugar Planters' Association, 1926)

Rarely has anyone spoken in defense of the plantations on this issue. In 1910, for example, of 52 plantations (Table 13), revenues from sugar and molasses exports amounted to $42,625,069—an average of about $820,000 per plantation.[17] Assuming a reasonable profit of 10 percent for each, an average of $82,000 was available for investments, and some of the expense of building camps was tax deductible. Nevertheless, this was not a large sum for constructing perhaps five up-to-date camps or villages. Modern communities are built over a period of years, using funds taxed from landowners and residents. Paved and lighted roads, potable water distribution systems, and sewerage cost far more than what was available from plantation profits. Camp inhabitants paid no taxes or rent. Full-service, contemporary-style communities simply could not be built from the proceeds of sugar sales at the year-to-year market prices. Plantation owners have been unfairly criticized by those who insisted on comparing plantation camps with long established, mainland communities built by taxpayers and from the proceeds of state and federal taxes. The Hawai'i planters tried very hard to improve the situation.

Between 1920 and 1925, millions were spent on repair, remodeling and construction of new housing. Single-family units had at least two bedrooms, with a wash house, baths, and privies nearby. However, only rarely was there running water or sewers, and streets were not paved or lighted. Yet, it was widely acknowledged that such amenities were needed and that the camps must be further improved. By 1925 the industry was pleased with the progress, mildly boasted of it, and labor was appeased, if not content.

Another cycle of camp improvements started in 1930. Running water, sewers, attached baths, and larger houses became standard. The HSPA kept statistics on the developments, the better to spur more efforts and reassure outsiders. Some newer plantations like ʻEwa on Oʻahu concentrated camp living by grouping their workers in houses near the mill, and transporting them to and from the fields on the plantation's railroad. This centralized life in a community, and made it less costly than providing theaters, recreation fields, gymnasiums, day-care centers, and medical dispensaries or hospitals for each camp. On the remote Hāmākua Coast of Hawaiʻi, the Davies plantations distributed these amenities throughout their various camps. However, employment figures for the industry began to decline in 1927, a trend that was never reversed. By the late 1930s, mechanical loading of harvested cane, which required less field workers, was introduced, and some camp houses were vacated for good.

In a remarkably candid HSPA report of progress made by 1938, it was indicated that 67 percent of plantation houses still failed to meet the new standards.[18] In the camps, however, a community spirit was evident. Plantation living had begun to generate a certain sense of pride.

Plantation worker's house of pre-1930s design. In 1996 it was still in use at the mill camp of the Waialua Sugar Company. (W. H. Dorrance)

The Hawaiian Commercial & Sugar Company operation in central Maui provided many examples of life at the time. In 1938 this plantation, Hawaiʻi's largest, housed 7,973 employees and dependents in 1,545 company-owned houses in 30 camps distributed over 35,000 acres. Its hospital had a staff of ten, including three physicians. Two power plants supplied electricity to the entire plantation. For groceries and supplies there were Kahului Store and Puʻunēnē Store in Kahului, and three branch stores in Spreckelsville, Kīhei, and the Camp 5 Store in Puʻunēnē.[19] In addition, there were ten churches, four public schools, three Japanese language schools, and three movie theaters. The largest camps had recreation parks. All houses were supplied with electricity generated at the mill.[20] Until about 1940, Maui High School was located at Hāmākua Poko, and students in the large camps near the Kahului Railroad

Company tracks rode back and forth on the trains. Management was highly organized and efficient, and this also meant maintaining the health and welfare of the plantations' large, diverse mixture of inhabitants. Until union labor contracts took effect after World War II, all employees who earned $100 a month or less received free medical treatment. This was an industry-wide practice. A day-care center was provided for working mothers, and two nurses and a dietician made regular visits to individual houses in the camps.

This plantation included all the features to be found in one or more of the other plantations in the Islands. The management of field labor was allocated to divisions of about 3,000 cultivated acres.[21] In effect, each division overseer, or luna, operated a mini-plantation. The figure below shows a typical hierarchy from this period.[22]

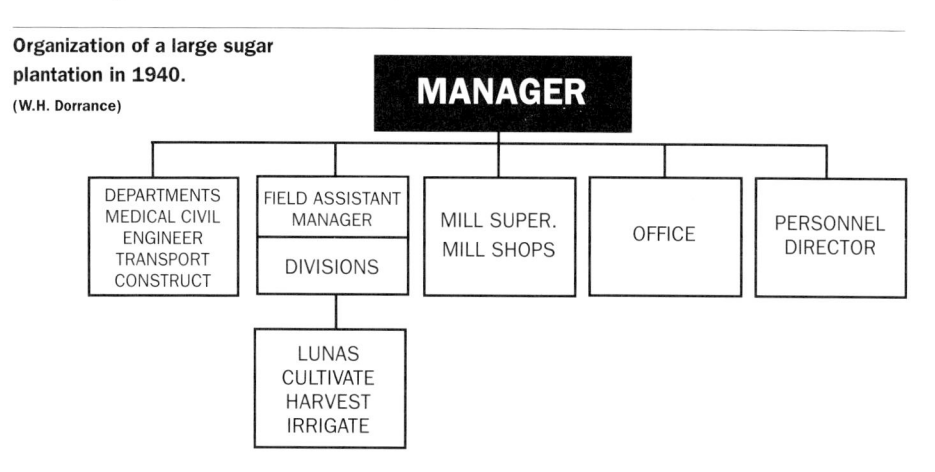

Organization of a large sugar plantation in 1940.
(W.H. Dorrance)

```
                        MANAGER
    ┌──────────┬──────────┬──────────┬──────────┐
DEPARTMENTS  FIELD       MILL SUPER.  OFFICE   PERSONNEL
MEDICAL CIVIL ASSISTANT  MILL SHOPS            DIRECTOR
ENGINEER     MANAGER
TRANSPORT    ─────────
CONSTRUCT    DIVISIONS
                 │
              LUNAS
              CULTIVATE
              HARVEST
              IRRIGATE
```

Throughout the industry, a work-contract system was used. A field employee belonged to a work gang under contract, or worked as an independent contractor assigned to fields by the division luna and his subordinates. This was in accordance with a cultivation and harvesting schedule coordinated with production at the mill. Depending on the cycle, a work gang might be assigned to weeding, irrigating, fertilizing, or cane-cutting. A contractor's salary depended on the yield of the fields he tended. The mill whistle was heard throughout the plantation, and regulated the work day from wake-up at 4:30 a.m. to end of work (pau hana) at 4:30 p.m.

Camp life was perpetuated through World War II, although the number of workers continued to decrease year by year. From 1941 to 1944 Hawai'i remained under martial law and sugar was declared an essential commodity. Workers were frozen at their jobs, pay was not increased, and union organizing was forbidden. Despite this, many plantation workers entered the armed services. Mechanical harvesting took up the slack. But returning veterans were not about to accept pre-war conditions of employment.

When martial law was lifted in 1944, the unions renewed their organizing efforts and focused on plantation field workers. By 1946, the International Longshoremen's and Warehousemen's Union had strength throughout the Islands.

It called a strike for higher pay, better working conditions, fringe benefits, and an end to the patriarchal treatment of sugar workers and their families. After weeks of work stoppage, a compromise settlement was reached that heralded the end of the plantation lifestyle.[23] The development of modern community housing, and the reduced number of workers needed due to mechanization led to the inevitable abandonment of most plantation camps.

After the settlement of 1946, the pay and benefits of sugar workers continued to increase and the number of camps steadily decreased as they found housing in nearby, modern communities. The plantations accommodated the wage increases by increasing overall productivity and reducing the work force. It was during this period that Hawai'i's sugar workers became the highest-paid agricultural workers in the world. Table 14 gives the number of plantation workers, wages, and fringe benefits from 1876 to 1990.

TABLE 14 | **AVERAGE DAILY WAGES 1876-1990**

YEAR	NUMBER OF WORKERS	DAILY WAGES	DAILY BENEFITS
1876	3,786 (1874)	$0.49	n/a
1900	36,057	0.76	n/a
1925	48,473	1.71	n/a
1950	15,935	8.30	n/a
1975	7,800	37.34	$15.81
1990	4,453	76.82	43.07

*Note: Until 1946 no benefits were paid, since housing was provided and all employees earning less than $100 per month, and their dependents, received free medical care. Beginning in 1946, labor contracts gradually removed all "free" benefits and substituted payments. By 1975 payments were made for all previously furnished free benefits.
Sources: Beechert; HSPA, *Story of Sugar* 1926; HSPA, *Sugar Manual* 1991; Schmitt; Hughes.

For every camp that remained, numerous others were bulldozed away. In 1989 the large Mana camp of the Kekaha Sugar Company on Kaua'i was levelled.[24] Some of the plantation houses, along with others from the mill camp of Waimea Sugar Company, were moved to the south shore and restored for use as a resort owned by the Faye family and called "Kikiaola."[25] Contrasted with this is the disappearance of all traces of the substantial Maui Agricultural Company camp near the still-operating Pā'ia mill. In 1992 the author visited the site and found sugarcane growing where once there had been a thriving community with a plantation hospital.

While in recent years Hamakua Sugar Company workers and retirees occupied some 500 company-owned houses, few continued to live in traditional camp housing. The highest-paid moved to modern residences in nearby communities. Only certain retirees and the lowest-paid workers still live in plantation housing. Yet, some old-style communities do survive. In 1999, on O'ahu, the former Waialua Plantation Company "mill camp" could still be found behind the remains of the mill, largely occupied by Filipino workers and retirees.

Honolulu Iron Works
(Bishop Museum)

CHAPTER 10

FACTORS, THEN AGENCIES

In Hawai'i, Theo H. Davies & Co., Ltd. also played a strong role outside the sugar industry. It conducted wholesale merchandising, had insurance and shipping agencies, and sold jewelry, lumber and heavy equipment. In addition, Davies supplied numerous island stores with groceries, dry goods, and hardware, and maintained offices in New York and San Francisco to get favorable terms from the manufacturers of these goods and products. Davies established the Piggly Wiggly chain in Hawai'i, and only Amfac, of the other agencies, engaged in similar ventures. Merchandising was a big share of its business when I joined the company, but this aspect dried up when large supermarkets came to the Islands.

Theo H. Davies got into sugar farming indirectly. When purchases were made on behalf of a plantation and payment was past due, the Davies company took over the plantation and ran it until the debt was paid off. Then the plantation was returned to its owners. For decades this was a sideline and merchandising remained the significant activity at Davies.

Things changed when the company and the Englishman Alexander Young acquired control of Honolulu Iron Works, preeminent in manufacturing sugarmill machinery and making good money. Davies himself visited likely sites for mills, and became convinced that the Kohala, Hāmākua, and Hilo Districts on the Big Island of Hawai'i were promising locations. He invested in Niulii Mill and Union Mill in Kohala, Hamakua Mill, Kaiwiki Plantation, Laupahoehoe Plantation, and Waiakea Mill near Hilo.

The old Davies building in Honolulu was a good example of the company's original focus on merchandising. Eight acres of storage space were kept under one roof in a building that occupied an entire city block. The upper stories were built before mechanical finger lifts, and all cartons were stacked by hand, so ceilings were low. Around 1918 every one of the Big Five agencies was planning to put up a new building in downtown Honolulu. Informally they agreed to use the same style of architecture, deciding that uniformity would make the business district a more attractive place. Theo H. Davies & Co.. erected the first building according to the understanding. However, a year or so went by before the next was constructed, and during that time the other four agencies decided to change the style. The Davies building stood alone with a unique orange stone facade.

It was obsolete by the time I joined, and warehousing was moved out near the airport. The heavy concrete construction and low ceilings on the upper floors made them unsuitable for conversion into office space. One entrance on the corner of Merchant and Bishop Streets opened into a large foyer; a smaller entrance was mid-block on Bishop Street. Two elevators went to the upper floors, and there were several freight elevators on the Queen Street side. Special chutes also led from upper floors to street-level loading docks. It was a convenient structure for the company's operations in the 1920s and 1930s but became pretty old-fashioned. The new building, on the same lot as today's Davies Pacific Center building, replaced a livery stable. My office overlooked an inner courtyard with plants, a pool, and fountains. It was a peaceful vista in the middle of busy downtown Honolulu.

F.A. Schaefer & Co. was a small family-owned agency not numbered among the Big Five. For decades it owned and represented Honokaa Sugar Company. Theo H. Davies Co. bought the Schaefer agency in 1951 to acquire the Honokaa plantation, and I once asked Fred Schaefer III why his family sold out. He replied that his father was convinced the time had come when a small, independent plantation could no longer stand the expenses of mechanization and still be profitable.

⊕ ⊕ ⊕

IN THE EARLY 1800s, Oʻahu residents began trading in ship's provisions with Don Francisco De Paula Marin, Stephen Reynolds, and William French. There being no coin of the realm, "bills of exchange" were introduced. These were accepted by Hawaiʻi merchants in payment for ship's provisions, and were backed up with a claim on a share of the proceeds from the sale of cargoes. The bill could be exchanged in Boston, for example, for cash or for a shipment of goods to be sent to Hawaiʻi.

Whaling ships began visiting Hawaiʻi in the 1820s and for 15 years the provisioning of whalers dominated trade. Foodstuffs, water, rope, salt, and other necessities were exchanged with a whaler for a bill claiming a share of the proceeds from sale of the oil. Only the most trustworthy and dependable ship's captains and traders survived.

Advancing funds in return for a claim on goods, such as a warehouse receipt, is known as "factoring." In that sense, the early Honolulu merchants who were engaged in the ship-provisioning trade were factors. In 1835 the Honolulu mercantile firm of Ladd & Company became the first sugar factor when it advanced supplies to the Koloa Plantation in return for a claim on the proceeds of the sale of sugar produced. A promising new industry had been born.

A New England supplier was more inclined to trust an established ship-provisioning merchant in Honolulu rather than some little-known plantation in a remote location on one of the islands. Honolulu merchants acted on behalf of these plantations. On a commission basis, they purchased supplies for the plantations and sold the sugar they produced. Much advancing of funds and supplies on credit, or factoring, was involved. The factors charged interest on the value of funds, goods, and supplies they advanced. When the services, including writing insurance and scheduling shipping, went beyond factoring, these multi-service merchants were more properly referred to as "agencies."

The sugar industry suffered several recessions during the last half of the nineteenth century, and many plantations incurred insurmountable debts to their agencies. The debt was frequently discharged in exchange for a share of ownership in the plantation. Alternatively, the agency might underwrite the sale of plantation stock to retire debt, and end up purchasing all or a portion of the issue. In one way or another, by the turn of the twentieth century the agencies owned several plantations outright and large shares in most of the rest.

The principal agencies that dominated this activity came to be known as the "Big Five." By the end of 1910 they were C. Brewer & Company, Ltd., Theo H. Davies & Co., Ltd., H. Hackfield & Company, Castle & Cooke, and Alexander & Baldwin. All have grown beyond representing Hawai'i sugar and are integrated wholly or partly into major corporations. Their history is an integral segment of the history of Hawaiian sugar.

C. BREWER & COMPANY, LTD.

James Hunnewell (1794-1869), a Massachusetts seafaring man, came to Honolulu for the third time in 1826 to establish a mercantile business.[1] Based on what he'd seen during previous visits, he brought a shipload of goods to trade. His business prospered, and in 1828 he took on Henry Peirce (1808-1885) as a clerk-employee. In 1830 Hunnewell went back to Boston, turning the business over to Peirce. He bought out Hunnewell's share in 1833, and in 1836 entered into a partnership with Capt. Charles Brewer (1804-1885), calling the firm Peirce & Brewer[1]. In 1842, when Peirce also returned to Boston, it became C. Brewer & Company with Boston money behind it.

In 1845 Captain Brewer moved to Boston and left the business in the hands of new partners J.F. Marshall (1819-1891) and Francis Johnson, who brought their own mercantile business into the firm.[1] Captain Brewer's nephew, Charles Brewer, II, had come to the Islands in 1845 and founded a business. In 1858 he accepted a job with C. Brewer & Company, and a year later acquired sole ownership of Haliimaile Plantation on Maui and served as its agent.[2] By 1863, C. Brewer & Company was also agent for Kualoa Plantation on O'ahu, and 'Ulupalakua, Hana, and Wailuku Plantations on Maui. By 1879 the company had added the Onomea and Princeville plantations to its agency list, and was involved in developing the Hawaiian Agricultural Company and Honomu Sugar Company plantations.[3]

In 1880, when funds were short, Charles Bishop, owner of Hawai'i's only bank at the time, became a silent partner.[4] Several new agency contracts were negotiated in the wake of this scarcely concealed development. In 1883 C. Brewer & Company incorporated, and shares were soon publicly traded.[5] By 1909, the plantations represented by the company were producing 26 percent of Hawai'i's sugar.

William G. Irwin & Company was an agency competitor, and in 1910 represented eight plantations on Kaua'i, O'ahu, Maui, and Hawai'i, with ownership stakes in several of them. Following a chance conversation over lunch between Irwin and Brewer executive George Carter, a merger of the two agencies was negotiated, with an exchange of cash and stock. C. Brewer & Company, Ltd. was the survivor.[7]

From 1923 until World War II, C. Brewer & Company, Ltd. shipped the sugar produced by its two Ka'ū plantations direct from Honu'apo landing to San Francisco, which also put the company in the shipping business for nearly two decades.[8]

C. Brewer had outstanding partners and executives from the start. Henry Peirce eventually served as United States Minister to the Kingdom from 1861 to 1878; H.A. Carter (1837-1891), a one-time partner, was the Kingdom's representative in Washington D. C. from 1883 to 1891[1]; Peter Jones, President of C. Brewer from 1883 to 1899, made the company grow during uncertain times and served as the Kingdom's Minister of Finance in 1892; Charles Cooke, Sr. (1849-1909) scion of the prominent family, had an early start in Castle & Cooke, then was elected president of C. Brewer & Company in 1899, and held that position until 1909.[12] More recent leaders included Philip Spalding, president from 1940 to 1951; his successor, Boyd McNaughton; and current chairman J.W. Buyers, who gambled that C. Brewer & Company, Ltd. could generate sufficient profits to pay for taking the company private when sugar prices were uncertain. Strong leaders have kept C. Brewer & Company, Ltd. in the forefront of Hawai'i-based industries since James Hunnewell landed in 1826 to start a trading enterprise.

In 1969, led by Eastern investor Howard Butcher, International Utilities Corporation began buying shares of C. Brewer stock, and by 1978 owned all of it.[9] In 1986 management, led by J.W. Buyers, acquired control and the company became a private corporation.[10] At the end of 1991 it owned Mauna Kea Agribusiness Company and Kau Agribusiness Company on Hawai'i, Olokele Sugar Company on Kaua'i, and produced 18 percent of Hawai'i's sugar that year.[11] However, by the end of 1996, C. Brewer & Company, Ltd. was out of the sugar business. In somewhat typical fashion for Hawai'i, the former agency survived in somewhat altered form when the plantations did not.

THEO H. DAVIES & CO., LTD.

In 1845 Robert Janion arrived in Honolulu with a consignment of goods from Starkey, Janion & Company of Liverpool.[13] In 1850 the partnership was dissolved, with Janion continuing the business under his name.[14] He hired young William Green as a clerk, who was made a partner when Janion returned to England.[15] In 1857 Theophilus Harris Davies, age 23, arrived in Honolulu as a clerk for Janion, Green & Company. In 1862 he also returned to England, only to be persuaded by Janion to go back to Honolulu in 1867 and salvage the faltering firm. Davies did so after buying out Janion's interest. Theo H. Davies & Co. was established in 1870 with Liverpool money behind it.[16]

Davies began buying interest in the sugar business, starting with ownership of two plantations on the island of Hawai'i.[17] By 1879, the company was agent for the Laupahoehoe Plantation, the Hamakua Plantation, Hamakua Mill, Waiakea Mill, Union Mill & Plantation, Niulii Mill & Plantation, and Kaalaea Plantation, and charged a two-percent commission on purchases and sales. Davies also personally owned shares in the mills and plantations.[18] Later he added Olowalu Plantation, McBryde Sugar Company, Pepeekeo Sugar Company, and Honokaa Plantation to his agency list.

In 1894 the business was incorporated, with Davies (and later on his family), in possession of controlling shares.[19] The sale of wholesale merchandise, insurance, and the shipping agency and investment in the Honolulu Iron Works contributed greatly to profits. While Davies remained a power in sugar with plantations along the Hāmākua Coast, after incorporation among the "Big Five" it never rose above fifth place in total earnings. In 1940, for example, profits were less than half of those of the fourth-ranked agency, C. Brewer & Company, Ltd.[20]

Nevertheless, Theo H. Davies & Co., Ltd. never lost its determination to prosper in Hawaiian sugar. In 1951 the small F.A. Schaefer agency was bought to get control of its Honokaa Sugar Company. Paauhau Sugar Company, acquired from C. Brewer & Company, Ltd. in 1972, was merged into Honokaa Sugar Company.[21] The Hong Kong conglomerate of Jardine Matheson & Company acquired Theo H. Davies & Co., Ltd. in 1973.[9] In 1979 Honokaa Sugar Company and Laupahoehoe Sugar Company were merged to form the 35,000-acre Davies Hamakua Sugar Company. It was the last survivor of what had been seven separate Hāmākua Coast plantations. In 1984 Davies executive Francis S. Morgan purchased the plantation from Jardine, Matheson & Company, and Theo H. Davies & Co., Ltd. departed from the Hawai'i sugar industry.

H. HACKFIELD & COMPANY/AMFAC, INC.

In 1849 Capt. Heinrich Hackfield (1815-1887), his wife and brother-in-law J.C. Pfluger arrived in Honolulu from Bremen, Germany, with a shipload of goods to trade.[1] By 1853 H. Hackfield & Company was established in a Fort Street building in downtown Honolulu, with Pfluger as partner. In 1857

Dr. Robert Wood was in financial straits and in danger of losing his East Maui and Kōloa, Kaua'i plantations. Hackfield offered to help in return for becoming agent for the plantations, and thus entered the sugar business.[22] In 1861 Hackfield returned to Germany, leaving Pfluger in charge. That same year the accounts of Lihue Plantation, Pioneer Mill, and Grove Farm were added to Hackfield's agency list.[23]

After Captain Hackfield returned to Germany, investment funds began to flow from Bremen to the Honolulu firm. By 1879, H. Hackfield & Company was financing 18 plantations in Hawai'i, and, by 1880, it backed one-third of all plantations in the Islands.[24] In 1881 Paul Isenberg, H.F. Hackfield, and H.F. Glade arrived from Bremen to become active partners in the firm. In 1897 the partnership was dissolved and a corporation, H. Hackfield & Company, Ltd., was organized from the assets, with the former partners holding controlling shares.[25] The corporation then owned all of Lihue Plantation Company, Kekaha Sugar Company, and Koloa Sugar Company.

All the principals were German nationals, and, when the United States entered World War I, their ownership claims were expropriated by the United States Enemy Alien Property Custodian. A new corporation, American Factors, Ltd., took over the assets of the former Hackfield concern and continued operations as before.[26] By 1940, American Factors was the third most profitable agency among the Big Five, and a major wholesaler in competition with Theo H. Davies & Co., Ltd.[20] In 1967 the corporation's name was shortened to Amfac, and the Amfac Center office complex at the corner of Bishop Street and S. Nimitz Highway at Honolulu's waterfront was dedicated.[9]

Amfac Tower and Dillingham Transportation Building are in the foreground of this photograph taken from the Aloha Tower at the waterfront. The two buildings illustrate the architectural style of the second and third generation of agency buildings in downtown Honolulu. (W. H. Dorrance, 1987)

By 1983, the majority of Amfac's business was on the mainland and the corporate headquarters moved to San Francisco.[9] A Chicago investment group began to buy up Amfac stock and gained control in 1988. Today the company's interests in Hawai'i carry on under the name Amfac/JMB-Hawai'i. In 1991 their subsidiaries, O'ahu Sugar Company, Lihue Plantation Company, Kekaha Sugar Company, and Pioneer Mill Company, produced 25 percent of Hawai'i's sugar.[11] O'ahu Sugar Company went out of business in 1995, Pioneer Mill was shut down in 1999, and Lihue Plantation Company is operated with Kekaha Sugar Company under common management.

CASTLE & COOKE

In 1837 Samuel Castle and Amos Cooke were sent from Boston to Hawai'i by the American Board of Commissioners of Foreign Missions to be its fiscal agents and clerks.[27] In 1851 they were cleared by the board to start their own business, providing they continued to act as agents for the missions. The co-partnership Castle & Cooke was formed and soon acted as commission merchants for mainland suppliers.[28]

In 1858 Amos Cooke invested personally in Haiku Sugar Company, started on land owned by missionary Richard Armstrong. In 1862 Castle & Cooke underwrote missionary Elias Bond's Kohala Sugar Company venture, and took an ownership position. Finally, in 1872, believing that Haiku Sugar Company was paying too much in transaction commissions, Castle & Cooke acted as the agency for the plantation.[29] It was the firm's first agency assignment, and they charged a three percent commission on transactions when other agencies were charging five percent. Soon after, Castle & Cooke represented three more plantations and incorporated as Castle & Cooke, Inc. in 1894.[30]

By 1898 Castle & Cooke's mercantile business was overshadowed by the work it did as an agency. The retail operation, mostly hardware sales, was bought by Benjamin Dillingham.[31] Castle & Cooke continued to add to its agency list and acquired stock in several plantations. By 1940 it was the most profitable of the Big Five agencies and the preeminent Hawai'i-based corporation.[20]

In 1948 Castle & Cooke entered into a new agricultural enterprise by organizing its subsidiary, the Royal Hawaiian Macadamia Nut Company.[32] This first attempt at diversification was successful enough that in 1961 a second venture was taken on. Since 1933 Castle & Cooke had controlled management of the Dole Pineapple Company, and now became the owners.[9] By 1970 Castle & Cooke was the largest of the Big Five corporations. Land-rich, it attracted the attention of financier David Murdock, who began to buy its stock. In 1985 he acquired controlling interest, merged Castle & Cooke with his Flexi-Van Corporation, and changed the name to Dole Food Company.[9]

In 1991, Dole Food Company's subsidiary, Waialua Sugar Company, produced eight percent of Hawai'i's sugar.[11] However, the plantation was

Castle & Cooke's corporate headquarters on "agency row" in downtown Honolulu. This building was designed by C.W. Dickey and occupied in 1919. (Hawaiian Sugar Planters' Association)

unprofitable in subsequent years, and the Dole company shut it down in October 1996. After almost a century and a half, this business descendant of Castle & Cooke is no longer in the Hawai'i sugar business.

ALEXANDER & BALDWIN, INC.

Alexander & Baldwin was the last of the Big Five agencies to be organized, and the first whose origins had been in sugar. In the 1860s missionary sons Samuel Alexander and Henry Baldwin acquired land on Maui, then in 1869 started a plantation in Makawao with two other men.[33] Three years later, in 1872, Alexander & Baldwin formed the partnership that led to today's corporation of the same name.[34] From 1871 to 1892 Castle & Cooke was their agent and financed many of their efforts, including the construction of the pioneering Hāmākua ditch in 1874.[35]

In 1892 Castle & Cooke was in financial straits, and Alexander & Baldwin was encouraged to make other agency arrangements. Sugar sales to the refineries in San Francisco were a prime concern, so Alexander & Baldwin sent Joseph Cooke (1870-1918) to act as their general agent.[36] His office in San Francisco became Alexander & Baldwin's first agency business. In 1897 Cooke returned to Honolulu and established Alexander & Baldwin's office with the first clients being Paia Plantation Company and Haiku Sugar Company.[37] Cooke's experience served him well, as he eventually became Alexander & Baldwin's president from 1911 to 1918.[12]

In 1898 Alexander & Baldwin purchased control of Claus Spreckels' Hawaiian Commercial & Sugar Company, a large operation. By 1900, the agency was representing seven plantations and Alexander & Baldwin, Inc. was chartered with the two former partners retaining a controlling interest.[38] As a matter of policy, agency representation was limited to plantations no further away than Maui on the grounds that producers on the island of Hawai'i "were too far away" to be properly served. This conservative policy resulted in giving up the agency of South Hilo's Olaa Sugar Company shortly after it was founded, despite having invested in its founding stock.[39] By 1940, Alexander & Baldwin represented five (consolidated) plantations and reported profits that made it second to Castle & Cooke among the Big Five agencies.[20]

In 1964 a consent decree was negotiated with the U.S. Department of Justice that required a change of ownership of Matson Navigation Company. Majority owner Alexander & Baldwin purchased all shares owned by Castle & Cooke, C. Brewer & Company, Ltd., and Amfac, and by 1969, Alexander & Baldwin owned 100 percent of the shipping company.[9]

Alexander & Baldwin established vertical integration of its sugar operations in 1993 by purchasing all shares in the California & Hawaiian Sugar Company's refineries in Crockett, California, and 'Aiea, Hawai'i.[40] This

Alexander & Baldwin headquarters, designed by C.W. Dickey and completed in 1926. Sandwiched between Amfac and Castle & Cooke on Bishop Street, the building was a short three blocks from the Alexander Young Hotel. All the Big Five agencies were clustered within one block of each other. (George Mellen, Bishop Museum)

meant the company controlled its Hawai'i sugar operations from plantation to refining to marketing. The arrangement lasted until 1998, when Alexander & Baldwin sold most of its interest in the C & H refinery.

AGENCIES IN THE TWENTIETH CENTURY

After 1900, Honolulu-based agencies employed attorneys, technical experts, chemists, insurance agents, accountants, and engineers who supplied guidance and services to plantation clients. Tax reporting, account auditing, uniform bookkeeping systems, land title searches, shipping schedules, and insuring plantation operations were agency responsibilities.[41] Its employees managed the administration of the Hawaiian Sugar Planters' Association and served on the board of the California & Hawaiian Sugar Refining Corporation. An individual plantation might suffer a year, or years, of losses, but each year its agency would still profit. Whether or not the client-plantation was profitable, agency commissions were taken and interest on outstanding amounts was assessed. If a struggling plantation couldn't settle its debt to an agency, often the agency took over management until the operation was profitable, turned it back, and took partial or total ownership in payment.

Table 15 shows how the agencies fared during a 50-year period in the twentieth century, and how production and acreage controlled by each agency changed during that period.

Hawaiian Sugar Planters' Association, 'Aiea, Hawai'i. (W.H. Dorrance)

TABLE 15 | **SUGAR PRODUCTION CONTROLLED BY AGENCIES**

AGENCY	1936 TONS OF SUGAR PRODUCED	ACRES IN SUGAR	1986 TONS OF SUGAR PRODUCED	ACRES IN SUGAR
American Factors	297,979 (31%) (10 plantations)	70,650	0	0
Amfac, Inc.	0	0	283,570 (27%) (4 plantations)	44,921
C. Brewer & Co., Ltd.	226,514 (23%) (13 plantations)	8,688	195,830 (19%) (3 plantations)	9,170
Alexander & Baldwin, Inc.	200,223 (21%) (5 plantations)	38,528	283,716 (27%) (2 plantations)	48,269
Castle & Cooke	132,629 (14%) (3 plantations)	28,185	0	0
Dole Food Co.	0	0	72,485 (7%) (1 plantation)	11,832
Theo H. Davies & Co., Ltd.	72,279 (8%) (4 plantations)	28,793	0	0
Hamakua Sugar (Former Davies Hamakua Sugar)	0	0	171,651 (17%) (1 plantation)	34,688
Co-ops & Independents	39,168 (4%) (3 plantations & coops.)	11,597	35,233 (4%) (1 plantation & coop.)	5,301
Totals	968,783	246,441	1,042,452	184,181

Sources: Gilmore, *Hawai'i Sugar Manual* 1935-1936; HSPA, *Hawaiian Sugar Manual* 1987; Morgan; Thrum, *Hawaiian Annual*, 1937.

The above figures clearly show that plantations were consolidated, production efficiency increased, and total acreage in sugar reduced during the 50-year period covered. One Big Five agency, Theo H. Davies & Co., Ltd., left the agency business in 1984, when its last remaining plantation, Davies Hamakua Sugar, was sold to Francis S. Morgan.

SMALL AGENCIES

Over the years numerous small agencies went in and out of business. Many were associated with prominent businessmen and entrepreneurs of the day. The Big Five captured the lion's share and few of the small agencies survived for more than several years. In chronological order they included: Walker, Allen & Company; C. Afong; G.W. Macfarlane & Co.; F.A. Schaefer & Co.; J.T. Waterhouse; E. Hoffschlaeger & Co.; J. McColgan;

J.S. Walker; Wong, Leong & Co.; Wilder & Co.; H.A. Widemann; M.S. Grinbaum & Co.; C. Bolte; S.M. Damon; James B. Castle; J.F. Morgan; C.O. Berger; F. Hustace; Gear, Lansing & Co.; W.H. Pain; J.M. Dowsett; Hind, Rolf & Co.; Waterhouse & Co.(later Waterhouse Trust Co.); McChesney & Sons; Wong Kwai; Dillingham Co.; C.J. Hutchins; Bishop & Co. (later Bishop Trust Co., Ltd.); Hawaiian Development Co.; Fred L. Waldron, Ltd.; Jos. Herrscher; Pacific Development Co., Ltd.; and Kaeleku Plantation Co., Ltd..[42] F.A. Schaefer & Co. was the last of these small agencies to leave the scene when it was acquired by Theo H. Davies & Co., Ltd. in 1951.

MISSIONARY FAMILY PARTICIPATION

Members and descendants of four missionary families played prominent roles in the agency system. They entered relatively late but soon made their presence felt in a major way. These included Gerrit Judd, Amos Cooke, Samuel Castle, Dwight Baldwin, and William Alexander. Doctor Judd, along with his son Charles and son-in-law Samuel Wilder, founded and operated the short-lived Kualoa Plantation. Charles Judd's son-in-law Francis Swanzy worked for and eventually became Managing Director of Theo H. Davies & Co., Ltd. John Morgan, Swanzy's son-in-law, was a financial manager for the same company. John Morgan's son Francis S. Morgan devoted his career to managing the Davies plantation operations before buying the company's surviving plantation and operating it as Hamakua Sugar Company. David Morgan, son of Francis Morgan, was managing the plantation when it shut down, completing six generations of Judds, Judd descendants, and in-laws engaged in Hawai'i's sugar industry.

The Cooke descendants showed a propensity for agency management. Joseph Cooke presided over Alexander & Baldwin from 1870 to 1910, and his son, Joseph Platt Cooke, Jr. (1896-1953) presided from 1946 to 1947. Charles M. Cooke was president of C. Brewer & Company, Ltd. from 1899 to 1909. The patriarch, Amos Starr Cooke, was co-founder of Castle and Cooke and an active partner in the agency until his death in 1871.

The Alexander & Baldwin family descendants preferred to stay closer to plantation management. Samuel T. Alexander managed Haiku and Paia Plantations for a time, and his son Frank managed the McBryde Sugar Company plantation. The Baldwin family produced seven plantation managers extending two generations beyond the founding patriarch and missionary son Henry Perrine Baldwin. At one time or another, a Baldwin managed the Hawaiian Commercial & Sugar Company, Maui Agricultural Company, Kahuku Plantation Company, Hawaiian Sugar Company, and McBryde Sugar Company plantations.

The Castle family's presence was less widespread but still prominent. James Castle, son of Castle & Cooke co-founder Samuel Castle, founded

Kahuku Plantation Company and Koolau Agriculture Company, and served as a partner and later as director of Castle & Cooke, and then of Alexander & Baldwin.[43]

Every agency has moved beyond Hawai'i sugar production, and the concept of independent sugar agencies no longer applies. The former agencies are now conglomerates, some of which happen to own sugar plantations. Such are their investments that only three of the originals, Theo H. Davies & Co., Ltd., C. Brewer & Company, Ltd., and Alexander & Baldwin, Inc. maintain corporate offices in Honolulu. All would survive if sugar production ceased in the Islands. Sugar is far from being "king" in modern Hawai'i.

Pepeekeo Mill, village and plantation, Hawai'i, 1933.
(Baker/Van-Dyke Collection)

CHAPTER 11

COOPERATION IN THE INDUSTRY

One lasting memory from working over 50 years in the sugar industry is of cooperation between management and workers. This developed because the plantations weren't competing with each other in the marketplace. Selling was done for all of us by the California and Hawaiian Sugar Company cooperative. The remoteness of Hawai'i from other producers and the industry's success in using cooperative efforts to solve common problems contributed to the positive atmosphere.

My first exposure to this cooperative spirit was through the Hawaiian Sugar Planters' Association. Immediately after I joined Theo H. Davies & Co. in 1946, I was appointed its representative to the HSPA Industrial Relations Committee and served there for over 40 years. During this time I had to know the status of labor relations on every plantation. Discussions were conducted about labor problems that members were experiencing, and the rest of us would listen, comment, and make constructive suggestions. Frequently these were based on successful solutions used by other members.

One cooperative event had great impact on the financial survival of the Davies Honoka'a and Hāmākua plantations. During negotiation of a three-year contract with the ILWU, an immediate wage increase was proposed with specific increases in subsequent years for every plantation with an ILWU labor force. The contract's terms were unacceptable to us and we sought a special accommodation, which was unusual but granted for "distress cases."

During the three previous years the Hāmākua Coast had suffered a terrible drought. In fact, the first was the worst since 1898 and each of the following two years had been worse yet. Harvests at the Honoka'a and Hāmākua plantations were less than 50 percent of normal. We were losing money and our survival hung in the balance. For the new contract, we proposed, in our case only, that the term cover five years without wage increases in the first year; that over a five-year period wages rise to the level covered in the three-year contract. The request was referred to as the "H & H problem" during the negotiations, and it's a tribute to the spirit of cooperation between management and labor that this concession was included when the contract was ratified.

Through the years I became more and more involved in HSPA oversight and management. In 1975 I served as president, in 1980 as vice president, and as chairman (formerly called "president") in 1986, 1987, 1988, 1991 and 1992. I was on its board of directors continuously after being named group vice president for agriculture by Theo H. Davies & Co. This service was without compensation and consistent with voluntary participation by all members of the HSPA. Members of various committees served gladly because it was a mark of respect and competence to be asked to participate.

My grandfather was active in the formation of the HSPA and served as its first president in 1895-1896. In subsequent years he served two more terms. Sharing his experience as leader of the HSPA has been one of my most satisfying life accomplishments.

I believe that the sugar industry could not have survived in Hawai'i without the spirit of industry-wide cooperation fostered by the HSPA, and exemplified by the many problems solved by its technicians. As a common practice, they visited every plantation to describe recent developments at the agricultural experiment station, and give their observations of progress at other plantations. The HSPA propagated the latest technical advances throughout the industry. It also served as the industry's agent for importing labor, most recently from the Philippines after World War II. I was Davies' labor relations executive when the last contingent of Filipinos arrived in 1946. In an earlier parallel, my grandfather was president of the HSPA when importation of Korean workers began.

Until 1997, the HSPA had a vice president in Washington, D.C. to represent the industry's interests when sugar-related legislation was pending. The last HSPA Washington vice president, John Roney, was exceptionally knowledgeable and effective.

The Association of Hawaiian Sugar Technologists is another example of industry-wide cooperation. The HSPA Experiment Station and every plantation sent representatives to the annual meeting hosted by the technologists. Talks were given on the latest developments, followed by a healthy give-and-take discussion, where a plantation soil chemist might learn of progress with fertilizers from an HSPA technician.

Industry-wide cooperation led to the California & Hawai'i Sugar Company refinery in Crockett, California, becoming a cooperative owned by the Hawai'i plantations and agencies. The refinery had operated as a company owned by the plantations until this conversion. The company paid for the raw sugar when delivered, and recovered costs and profits by selling the refined sugar. All went well until 1920, when the refinery had a large inventory of paid-for raw sugar along with an inventory of unsold refined product, and sugar prices collapsed. The refinery could not recover the cost of its inventory and was in serious financial trouble. The plantations and agencies formed a new cooperative, took over the refinery, and made sure the problem never would occur again, because the plantations were paid after their raw sugar had been processed and sold, not before.

The Hawaiian Sugar Transport Company was established to operate two bulk sugar transport vessels. Matson had been doing this with container ships, and it was expensive. The sugar plantations had to pay for the extra travel and cargo handling costs because both sugar and containers were carried together. A shipment sequence went like this: a Matson transport arrived at Honolulu from the mainland and off-loaded all containers. The vessel then made a side trip to neighbor islands to load bulk sugar into its empty holds, and returned to Honolulu to load empty containers on top of the bulk sugar for return to the mainland. The vessel stopped at Seattle or Oakland to off-load the empty containers then finally went to the Crockett refinery to unload the sugar before returning to Seattle or Oakland to repeat the cycle. As a result, Matson's billing to the planters included the costs for the extra travelling, work, and time consumed during these side trips, in addition to the cost of transporting the sugar from Hawai'i to the refinery. We made some calculations and found we could save by operating our own transports. The Hawaiian Sugar Transport Company's bulk carriers took island sugar directly to the Crockett refinery, and the C & H cooperative did the scheduling for us. For years this was a profitable enterprise because our transports were two of a very few U.S.-owned bulk carriers. The company moved other bulk cargo when not transporting sugar—for example, a government-subsidized shipment of U.S.-grown grain to Israel, which according to law had to move in U.S. bottoms.

I incorporated many improvements in my plantation's operations and shared them with others. For example, Hamakua Sugar mixed its own fertilizer rather than purchasing a mixed variety. We saved about $1 million per year by running our own fertilizer mixing plant, and I made known these savings to others. However, the other Hawai'i plantations didn't always follow my lead because their situations greatly differed from mine. I was fighting for survival, so I put profits into improving my operation. By now the other plantations were owned by corporations, and they used profits to pay out dividends, or they were too small to profit from my innovations. However, the Hawai'i sugar industry in general benefited greatly from the principle of sharing and cooperating.

✦ ✦ ✦

IN 1848 NUMEROUS trappers, prospectors and cattle grazers inhabited Oregon and California when each became a Territory of the United States. A strong market developed for sugar and was accelerated by the 1849 California gold rush. East Coast refineries were four to five months away by sailing ship but Honolulu could be reached in only 20 days. Numerous Hawai'i-based entrepreneurs responded by starting sugar plantations to supply the growing market, and their common geographical isolation fostered a spirit of cooperation.

ROYAL HAWAIIAN AGRICULTURAL SOCIETY

In April of 1850 a meeting was held in Honolulu to form an organization for the promotion of agriculture in Hawai'i. The result was the Royal Hawaiian

Agricultural Society, presided over for the next five years by lawyer-planter Judge William Lee (1821-1857). A committee of a few planters with first-hand experience, including Stephen Reynolds, R.W. Wood, and W.L. Lee, described their goals in a paper read at one of the Society's first sessions: "For years past the agricultural interests of these islands have been insignificant and their pursuit unprofitable. With an uncertain and distant market—with little or no encouragement of facilities given to foreign tillers of the soil, without proper knowledge of the soil, or sufficient capital to experiment upon its capabilities, most of the agricultural enterprises have languished or utterly failed."

With respect to sugar, the committee went on to say: "It is a fact worthy of remark that as your committee believe, without a single exception, all of the sugar plantations that have been commenced at these islands have been so commenced by persons possessing neither experience in the business they were undertaking, nor the requisite capital and knowledge of the soil, to carry it through to a successful result."

The committee closed its report by urging that the newly formed Society encourage the importation of foreign labor.[1] Judge Lee read the draft of legislation he proposed to further the importation of contract labor. The Kingdom's legislature passed the proposed law without incident, and in 1852 some 500 Chinese indentured laborers were the first to come to Hawai'i.[2]

For five years the Society met, published proceedings and awarded prizes for quality in crop production. One year Doctor Wood's Koloa Plantation took first prize in sugar and George Wilfong took second prize.[3] A spirited competition was fostered by the Society.

TABLE 16 | **HAWAI'I SUGAR EXPORTS 1850-1856**

YEAR	TONS OF SUGAR EXPORTED
1850	375
1851	11
1852	365
1853	315
1854	290
1855	145
1856	277

Source: Kuykendall, *Hawaiian Kingdom 1778-1854*.

In 1850 California was admitted to the Union, and United States import tariffs began to be levied on sugar sent from Hawai'i. This contributed to an enthusiasm for cooperation to solve common problems. Where before Hawai'i's producers had netted eight to nine cents a pound for their sugar, overnight this was reduced to six to seven cents per pound, an insurmountable reduction at a time when heavy investments in land and machinery were being made.[4] In subsequent years, importation of labor stopped, several planters failed, including pioneer Linton Torbert, and by 1857 the number of operating plantations had decreased to five.[5]

Under the circumstances, support for the Society dwindled. It continued to exist without regular meetings or useful proceedings until 1865, when it was merged into the short-lived (1864-1869) Planters' Society formed by the Kingdom.[6] Nevertheless, the Royal Hawaiian Agricultural Society established the precedent for cooperation by planters in solving problems that continued to the end of the twentieth century.

THE PLANTERS' LABOR AND SUPPLY COMPANY

By 1882 the planters had enjoyed six years of prosperity following the Reciprocity Treaty of 1876. United States imports of Philippine and Cuban sugar paid an ad valorem tax of up to 30 percent, while Hawaiian sugar entered duty-free. The increasing number of imported contract laborers supported the steady growth of Hawai'i's sugar industry. However, this positive atmosphere had an unstable side.

The Reciprocity Treaty was due for review in 1884, and the United States populace was being stirred into righteous indignation by the assumption that Hawai'i planters profited at the expense of "slave labor." Newspapers, the *San Francisco Chronicle* among them, printed "exposes" containing lurid descriptions of how plantation laborers were treated. These stories had great weight in a nation still healing from a bloody war fought "to free the slaves."[7]

The Hawai'i sugar agencies called for a Planters Convention to be held in March 1882. While the name of the resulting The Planters' Labor and Supply Company suggested a preoccupation with labor, the invitation from Castle & Cooke, Bishop & Co., H. Hackfield & Co., C. Brewer & Company, Ltd., Theo H. Davies & Co., Ltd., F.A. Schaefer & Co., and E.P. Adams left no doubt as to the motivations of the organizers: "It must be evident to you and others who own property in this Kingdom, that the most energetic and united action is now required to protect it. Prudence and forethought require that there be no delay. We are threatened by a serious check, if not great disaster, to our prosperity under the reciprocity treaty....A powerful opposition to its continuance is manifested throughout the United States, so far as it is possible to judge from the newspapers. The means in this opposition are of the boldest and most unscrupulous character. Newspapers in the United States which have much influence, accept as true the charges against the planting interest of maintaining a species of human bondage, and defrauding the United States Government (press accusations that Hawai'i interests purchased cheap Asian sugar to sell on the mainland, thus cheating on tariff payments), while the original sources of these charges are forgotten..."

The invitation ended with the observation: "What is needed then at this critical period is a prompt and full gathering of all who are interested in these subjects that we may confer together and take such united measures as may bring mutual prosperity..."

The call met with an unprecedented response among the rugged individualists to whom it was addressed. The attendance list read like a "Who's Who in Hawai'i Sugar." Fifty-five powerful plantation owners and agency executives came to the organizing sessions on March 20, 1882. Almost without exception, every responsible planter and agency executive in the Islands was there.

The charter for incorporation of The Planters' Labor and Supply Company was drawn up, and stock subscribed to by attendees with shares allotted "in accordance with the tonnage of sugar produced..." A Board of Trustees was elected, officers were appointed, and it was resolved that a periodical, to be known as *The Planters' Monthly* should be published. Committees on Labor, Cultivation, Machinery, Legislation, Reciprocity, Transportation, Manufacture of Sugar, and the Executive were established and assignments made to each.[8]

Table 17 lists the presidents of the company from its first formal meeting until it was dissolved in 1895 in favor of the Hawaiian Sugar Planters' Association. For the span of time covered, it would be difficult to compile a list of more influential persons.

TABLE 17 | PRESIdents of The Planters' LABOR & SUPPLY COMPANY

PRESIDENT	YEARS OF TENURE
Z.S. Spalding	1882-1884
Johnathan Austin	1884-1885
S.B. Dole	1885-1886
H.P. Baldwin	1886-1889
Alexander Young	1889-1892
W.G. Irwin	1892-1894
F.A. Schaefer	1894-1895

Sanford Dole (1844-1926) served the Kingdom as an elected legislator in 1884, was appointed to the Supreme Court for six years in 1886, and led the movement that overthrew the monarchy. He was also the only president of the short-lived Republic of Hawai'i (1893-1898). After annexation, he was appointed Governor of the Territory of Hawai'i by President McKinley.[9]

The terms of the Reciprocity Treaty remained in effect. Labor importation increased and technical improvements of benefit to all members were described in *The Planters' Monthly*. During this time there was a growing appreciation of scientific farming. Experiments in cane varieties, fertilization, and field and mill mechanization were carried out by individual plantations and reported in *The Planters' Monthly*. The most important contribution the company made was to provide the body and substance for its successor.

HAWAIIAN SUGAR PLANTERS' ASSOCIATION

In 1895 Hawai'i was a republic whose leaders looked for annexation by the United States. In that year, to put the status of The Planters' Labor &

Supply Company more in line with the requirements of U.S. law, the company was disincorporated and the Hawaiian Sugar Planters' Association formed. The objectives and purposes were the same. By-laws were adopted that provided for:... 1) the improvement of the sugar industry, the support of an experimental station and laboratory, the maintenance of a sufficient supply of labor, and the development of agriculture in general; 2) membership was open to companies and individuals directly interested in sugar plantations or mills, new memberships were to receive approval of the Board of Trustees; and 3) the business of the Association would be conducted by a Board of Trustees elected by the membership at the annual meeting.[10]

Also in 1895, following consultation with mainland scientists, the Experiment Station and laboratory were established under the direction of Dr. Walter Maxwell, formerly of the Louisiana Sugar Experimental Station.

Immediately following annexation in 1898, the Association established an office in Washington, D.C. to monitor legislative actions that impacted the sugar industry. Many years later, in 1978, the Association was incorporated with no change in objectives. Some indication of the change in interests is suggested by the titles of the 1994 standing committees: Accounting, Energy, Environmental Standards, Experiment Station Advisory, Industrial Relations, Insurance, Land and Water, Legal Advisory, Legislative, Public Relations, Raw Sugar Technical, Retirement Plans and Tax.[11] The HSPA's representative and staff in Washington were maintained until the office closed in 1996.

HAWAI'I AGRICULTURE RESEARCH CENTER

In 1995 the HSPA was disbanded and the Experiment Station became The Hawai'i Agriculture Research Center (HARC), reflecting the diminished status of the sugar industry and the turn to a broader focus. Currently programs at the Center's Experiment Station include the development of new sugarcane varieties, fertilizers, and improvement in insect, disease, weed, and rat control. Because of these programs Hawai'i's plantations enjoy the greatest yields per acre in the world, and the Experiment

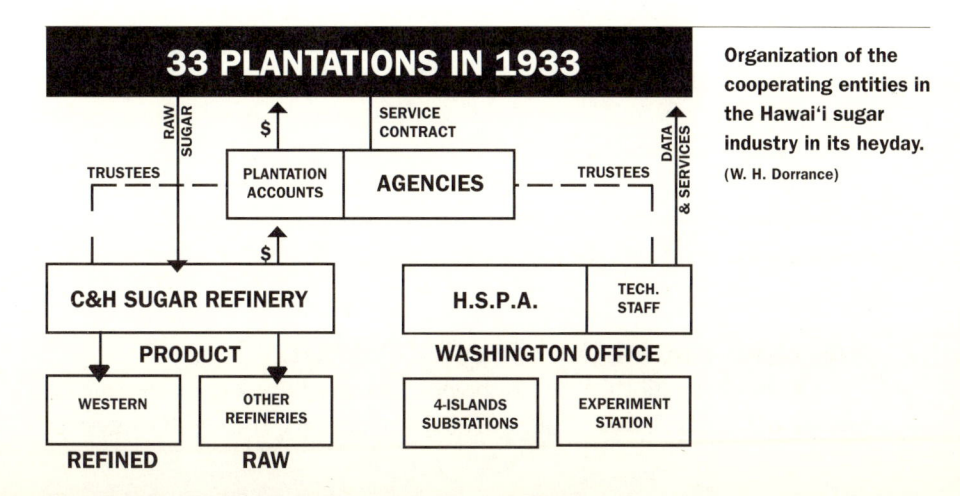

Organization of the cooperating entities in the Hawai'i sugar industry in its heyday.
(W. H. Dorrance)

Station enjoys the reputation of being among the foremost agriculture research organizations.

CALIFORNIA & HAWAIIAN SUGAR COMPANY

The marketing of sugar was changed in a fundamental way after the refining of raw sugar was perfected during the nineteenth century. Housewives, bakers, and confectioners were willing to pay a premium for refined sugar instead of using cheaper, but less desirable, raw sugar. The focus of marketing shifted from the producers to the refineries, which struck hard bargains with the planters in order to increase their profits. A plantation was at the mercy of the few refineries, since adding on-site refineries was impractical because importing refined sugar was prohibited by United States law.

Before the turn of the century Hawai'i plantations shipped product to the California Sugar Refining Company in San Francisco, or to East Coast refineries. Neither arrangement was satisfactory but Hawai'i's plantations had no alternatives. They were at the mercy of the monopolistic refineries. After annexation in 1898, planters moved to break the hold of the refineries. Col. Z.S. Spalding, of the Makee plantation on Kaua'i, Castle & Cooke, C. Brewer & Company, and Alexander & Baldwin financed the purchase of the Starr flour mill in Crockett, California.[12] The mill was converted to sugar refining and operated as the California Beet Sugar and Refinery Company. By 1899, beet sugar refining was dropped and processing was confined to Hawaiian sugar. However, the capacity was inadequate to process all Hawai'i-grown sugar, and The Western Sugar Refining Company (successor to Spreckels' California Sugar Refinery Company), and the eastern American Sugar Refining Company (The "Sugar Trust"), took the rest. It was a first step in breaking the refining monopoly.

In 1905 the 33 independent plantations not part of the Spreckels' interests formed a corporation, Sugar Factors Company, Inc. It purchased the California Refinery Company from the agencies, upgraded its machinery, and began operating as the California & Hawai'i Sugar Refining Company.[13] A drastic drop in sugar prices after World War I forced the corporation into bankruptcy. The refinery was reorganized as a cooperative, with most of the Hawai'i plantations being members. In 1947 the rest of the Hawai'i plantations became members, with the shares held in trust by the agencies.[14] In 1993 Alexander & Baldwin purchased C & H shares held by others, and became sole owners of the refinery until it was sold in 1998.

Today all Hawai'i-produced sugar is refined and marketed through the C & H company to its network of western state distributors. The plantations pool their product and receive the same price from C & H, which is adjusted for the quality of sugar supplied.

HAWAIIAN SUGAR TRANSPORT COMPANY

From 1905 until 1973 the Matson Navigation Company vessels transported raw sugar to the Crockett, California, refinery and returned with cargoes of goods for Hawai'i. The turnaround times were inefficient and charges were high, so the plantations terminated the service. The Hawaiian Sugar Transport Company (HSTC), a cooperative, was formed in 1973 and purchased one bulk transport, the *Mokupahu*, and leased a second, the *Sugar Islander*.[15] C & H scheduled the voyages of the two vessels and otherwise managed the company's operations. In 1996, with the reduction in the number of plantations, one vessel was retained and the other returned to the owners.

THE CHANGE TO SHIPPING BULK SUGAR

During the mid-1800s, Hawai'i-produced sugar was shipped in 125-pound kegs.[16] A healthy trade in barrel components was developed by Honolulu merchants who imported the makings. Each plantation employed a cooper to assemble the kegs. However, kegs were awkward and by 1890 bags began to replace them as shipping containers.[17] Until bag-making was mechanized, plantation wives made them and earned 15 to 25 cents apiece. Yet some plantations used 100-pound bags, while others used a measurement of 125 pounds. A study showed that the industry could save over $200,000 a year if all the plantations would settle on a 100-pound bag.[18] However, standardization came slowly and shipment in bags of various weights continued for over 80 years.

By 1942, bulk shipment was seen to be less costly, and the port of Kahului on Maui became the first to convert to this method.[19] In 1949 the same form of transport began in Hilo, then at Nawiliwili, Kaua'i in 1950, Honolulu in 1955, and Kawaihae in 1959.[20] By 1973 bulk transport ships were specially constructed, with a capacity that exceeded all previous dry haul vessels by a wide margin.[21] As a result, fewer ships and fewer voyages were required. Today all Hawaiian sugar is shipped in bulk.

TABLE 18 | EVOLUTION OF FACTORS LEADING TO COOPERATIVE SHIPPING

YEAR	VESSEL TYPE	TONS EXPORTED	TYPICAL SHIP CAPACITY	MINIMUM CONTAINERS	VOYAGES
1885	sail	85,675	800 tons	kegs	07
1925	steam	780,000	10,000 tons	bags	78
1975	steam	1,107,199	31,000 tons	none-bulk	37

Sources: Emmet; HSPA, Sugar Manual 1987; Lydgate; *The Planters' Monthly*, Oct. 1899; Simonds; Sullivan; Simpich.

The history of sugar production in Hawai'i demonstrated that private industry could cooperate without government intervention while still preserving competition. This is Hawai'i's heritage—along with the remarkable, peaceful racial mixture of its workers—and sugar production made it possible. ❧

Niulii Plantation,
Kohala, Hawai‘i, 1933
(Baker, Van-Dyke Collection)

CHAPTER 12

SUGAR-RELATED INDUSTRIES

In the mid-1930s, I took my first trip on the Hilo railroad, north to Pa'auilo and back again. After I joined Theo H. Davies & Co. in 1946, the railroad was still operating. It ended at the Pa'auilo mill, and the turntable used to rotate the locomotive was there until the plantation closed down. Locomotives could also turn around two-thirds of the way from Hilo at Laupāhoehoe where there was a wye (a Y-shaped section) in the tracks. The line ran along the same route as today's highway. Spurs connected the main track to the sugarmills. The North Hilo and Hāmākua Coast mills were always built close to the ocean because downhill fluming was used to transport harvests for grinding.

Locating mills near the shore had other advantages. The hydraulic head of mountain water drove turbines that generated electricity to operate the mill and, if large enough, to supply the camps, as well. Before the railroad was completed in 1913, sugar product was shipped on vessels anchored offshore, and the mill's location minimized the distance it had to move to be loaded aboard ship. However, fluming and gravity transport largely dictated the shore locations of the mills. At the same time, the railroad's shoreline location worked against its survival. The tracks crossed several gulches and gullies near the coast, and trestles were built. The tsunami of 1946 wiped out some of them and weakened the foundations of others. The track that crossed the front of Hilo bay was uprooted, and general destruction was so widespread that the railroad shut down.

Plantation supplies were hauled north from Hilo and sugar product was hauled south to the Hilo docks. When the railroad closed, every little plantation store and enterprise north of Hilo benefited. Shopping for Hilo residents became inconvenient and business picked up in the small stores.

The government road to Hilo was narrow and twisting, and ran along the coastline. The many bridges over streams in the gulches were single-file bottlenecks. It took half a day to drive south from Pa'auilo to Hilo, while the train covered the distance in about an hour. The tsunami disaster put pressure on the Territory to build a new road. In the meantime, for about four years the Hāmākua Coast plantations turned back the clock and shipped sugar from Kukuihaele and molasses from the Honoka'a landing. The small plantation stores prospered and residents made out as best as they could.

My great-granduncle Samuel Wilder organized the company that built the railroad for the Big Island's North Kohala plantations. He also founded the Wilder Steamship Company, an inter-island business that for many years was the principal means of travelling to Hilo. In the 1930s our family used one of the vessels that succeeded the original Wilder line, the Haleakala. These small steamers had comfortable staterooms and it was an overnight trip.

A typical voyage to Hilo from Honolulu went like this: depart at 4:00 p.m. and, before nightfall, anchor off Moloka'i, where a lifeboat was lowered to take persons and/or cargo ashore. Up anchor for a short trip to Lahaina, Maui, and anchor offshore where the lifeboat routine was repeated. Up anchor and depart for Hilo, arriving the next morning at 8:00 a.m.

Honolulu Iron Works made most of Hawai'i's sugarmill machinery. It was owned by Theo H. Davies when I joined them, and I owned a share of the Works through my Davies company holdings. But, for a short time, I had a more direct connection. On the Big Island, Honolulu Iron Works owned a similar, smaller foundry and metal-working operation called the Hilo Iron Works. It made and repaired machinery for local sugarmills and Davies' mills on the Hāmākua Coast.

When Theo H. Davies sold the whole iron works business, we bought the machinery that the Hilo operation had used to repair parts for the mills. This portion of the business was decreasing as the number of mills was reduced, and they were going to shut down, anyway. We installed the machinery in our Hāmākua machine shop and from then on did our own mill repairs. It saved us a lot of money.

We built the new Haina factory in such a way that the switch to refining raw sugar could be made easily when the time came. I negotiated terms with the Great Northern Railroad for shipment of refined sugar from Seattle to Chicago, where there were firms for beet sugar packaging and marketing. This innovation could not be pursued immediately because first we had to complete a long-term contract to ship our product to C & H. We would have pursued this option if the plantation had survived.

Another sugar-related industry we tried to enter was the construction material business. A German company, Bison-Barre, had perfected a process that produced very hard wallboard from bagasse. We shipped several containers of bagasse to this firm, and they made two prefabricated houses from it. When these were erected at two locations on O'ahu, they proved to be quite sturdy and satisfactory. Although the material passed an aging test and had been certified, the insurance companies refused to acknowledge the material until it had been subjected to 20 years of exposure to the weather. We moved on to other innovations.

The feedlot and slaughterhouse business appeared to offer opportunities. Competing with mainland beef on the local market seemed possible because we would save on shipping expenses and could produce molasses-based feed. We experimented with growing corn to mix in with the feed, a promising technique that involved planting the stalks between the rows of cane. In addition, we built a machine to harvest the corn before the cane grew so high that it closed in and *covered the corn. But the plantation shut down before we could reap the full benefits of this experiment.*

I believe that the long-term survival of Hawai'i's sugar industry depends on such innovations, for example the production of furfural and ethanol from bagasse, and acrylic acid from molasses.

⊕ ⊕ ⊕

CLOSE STUDY OF Hawai'i exports for the years 1875-1920 reveals why the sugar industry determined industrial developments during that time. As shown in Table 19, after the Reciprocity Treaty of 1876, and until pineapple shipments grew to compete, eighty-five percent or more of Hawai'i's exports consisted of sugar. During these years the visitor industry and military activities contributed little to the economy. Sugar was king and brought in the money to finance new industries.

TABLE 19 | **HAWAI'I SUGAR EXPORTS AND CONCURRENT EVENTS**

YEAR	SUGAR EXPORTS AS PERCENT OF TOTAL	CONCURRENT EVENT
1875	59.8	Before Reciprocity Treaty
1880	87.6	Post-Treaty prosperity
1890	91.7	Sugar dominated commerce
1893	93.1	Monarchy deposed
1915	85.3	Pineapple made inroads
1929	58.0	Pineapple's peak

Sources: Kuykendall, *Hawaiian Kingdom* 1874-1839; Thrum, *Hawaiian Annual* 1916, 1921, 1931; U.S. House Representatives Hearings Pursuant H. R. 236, 1946.

To put the matter in perspective, by 1991 the value of sugar produced was 37.7 percent of the total agricultural crop, and agriculture was third behind the visitor industry and military presence in contributions to the economy.[1] Sugar remained significant but macadamia nut and pineapple production had made appreciable inroads, and money to finance new enterprises went elswhere.

During the prosperous years between 1880 and 1900, an average of five to six percent of the amount that exports exceeded imports was invested in the stock of sugar plantations.[2] The rest was available for investment in industries that depended on sugar production. It is not surprising to find that many island entrepreneurs who owned and/or controlled the plantations also invested in these related ventures.

INTER-ISLAND SHIPPING

Before 1883, voyages between the islands depended on a fleet of small schooners, many owned by individual plantations and crewed mostly by Native Hawaiians. There were also a few small steamers, the largest being the

Kilauea, an old, unreliable ship owned by the government. While a steamer might complete the Honolulu to Hilo voyage in a day and a half, the schooners took as long as six days, depending on prevailing winds and the captain's skill.

By 1883 the combined plantations on Kaua'i, Maui, and Hawai'i were producing over 20,000 tons of sugar yearly. Many relied on these small vessels, which carried only 75 to 100 tons, to deliver product to Honolulu. Something had to be done to increase inter-island shipping capacity or growth would be stunted. In 1883 Samuel Wilder and others, including William Irwin and Samuel Damon, organized the Wilder Steamship Company, Ltd. The *Likelike* was its first company vessel. Wilder had purchased it from the Kingdom in 1879 after supervising its construction in San Francisco.[3] That same year Capt. Thomas R. Foster, whose wife Mary (1844-1930) bequeathed the botanical Foster Gardens to the City of Honolulu,[4] also got involved. With others, including G.N. Wilcox, Foster organized the Inter-Island Steam Navigation Company using three of his own steamers.[5] The Wilder firm serviced ports on Maui and the windward coast of Hawai'i, and the Inter-Island Company serviced Kaua'i ports, and those in Kona and Ka'ū on the Big Island.[6]

By 1899, the Wilder company was operating eight steamers, Inter-Island had eleven, and Waimanalo Sugar Plantation and R.R. Hind of Kohala operated one each.[7] Sugar and inter-island travel supported this fleet of coastal steamers,

The Inter-Island Navigation Company ship *Mauna Kea*, 1908.
(Baker Collection-Bishop Museum)

as well as some 20 independently-owned schooners. The Wilder company charged $4.00 per ton of cargo transported from Hilo to Honolulu.[8]

Plantations used these small vessels to move sugar to Hilo, Kahului, or Honolulu for transshipment to mainland refineries and to bring back supplies. In certain places (Hanalei, Kaua'i, Waimānalo on O'ahu, Kā'anapali on Maui, and at Honu'apo, Hawai'i), plantations had a well-constructed pier for transferring cargo to lighters or whale boats. Although service anywhere had to be suspended in poor weather.

The four-masted schooner *Muriel* discharging cargo at the old Honoipu cable system. In the 1880s and 1890s this vessel and its sister ship transported Hawi Mill sugar directly to the refinery in San Francisco.
(R.R. Hind/Bishop Museum)

In some locations the situation was more primitive. A plantation's landing on the Hāmākua Coast frequently consisted of a rocky ledge at the foot of a cliff washed by waves during rough weather. Approaching such a landing taxed the abilities of the very competent Hawaiian seamen to the limit. Some plantations had no landing at all, and an ingenious wire and trolley system was devised to transfer cargo to and from the ship. The trolley's cable was anchored on top of a cliff hundreds of feet above sea level, and attached to a permanent buoy beyond the ship. One enduring vision of bygone days was the ship's purser riding the cable-supported trolley to shore in order to check cargo, followed by the transfer of cargo to the heaving and pitching ship.[9]

All traces of most of these primitive landings have vanished. In some locations it is difficult to imagine that such a landing ever existed. Table 20 lists many of the ports and landings no longer in use for inter-island shipping.[10]

In 1905 the Wilder company was merged into the Inter-Island Steam Navigation Company, and the latter survived as the principal inter-island shipping firm.[11] It curtailed its operations as railroads were built, but continued to service North Hilo and Hāmākua Coast plantations until 1942.

TABLE 20 — SUMMARY OF COASTAL VESSEL LANDINGS, HARBORS, AND PORTS, MOST NO LONGER IN USE

KAUAʻI	MAUI	HAWAIʻI	
Hanalei	Kahului	Kukuihaele	
Kāhili	Huelo	Honokaʻa	
Anahola	Hāna	Pāʻauhau	
Kapaʻa	Kīpahulu	Kohealele	
Ahukini	Mākena	ʻOʻōkala	
Nāwiliwili	Māʻalaea	Laupāhoehoe	
Poʻipū	Lahaina	Paʻauilo	
Hanapēpē	Kāʻanapali	Hakalau	
Waimea			

OʻAHU	KOHALA, HI	KaʻŪ, HI	KONA, HI
Haleʻiwa	Kawaihae	Honuʻapo	Nāpōʻopoʻo
Lāʻie	Honomū	Punaluʻu	
Heʻeia	Pepeʻekeo		
Waimānalo	Māhukona		
Waiʻanae	Onomea		
	Honoipu		
	Kūkaʻiau		
	Kohala		

Sources: Bowser; Gilmore; Hind; Nelson.

In January 1942 a Japanese submarine sank the Hilo-bound U.S. Army transport *General Royal T. Frank*, and, as a precaution, many harbors and landings were closed. After World War II barges and inter-island airlines replaced the plucky little steamers and a picturesque era ended.

Common Carrier Railroads

In the late 1870s a few visionaries, Samuel G. Wilder chief among them, saw that common carrier railroads could be useful in moving sugar to market. Transferring sugar from a primitive landing to an offshore vessel was an expensive operation and sometimes delayed by poor weather. George Wilfong managed an independent plantation near Honokaʻa at the time, and told Wilder he paid the operators of the nearby landing $2.50 per ton to have sugar transferred to vessels offshore.[12] Wilder decided a common carrier railroad could deliver the sugar to the main port like Hilo at a lower cost, no matter what the weather was.

In July of 1878, Wilder was appointed to the King's cabinet as Minister of the Interior.[13] A month later King Kalākaua signed into law "An Act To Promote The Construction of Railways" which provided for eminent domain to create rights-of-way. The race was on to exploit the opportunity.[14]

Two years later, in July of 1880, over the signature of the Minister of the Interior, the Kingdom awarded a charter of incorporation to the Hawaiian Railroad Company, which was majority-owned and controlled by Wilder.[15] The charter granted exclusive rights to build a railroad on the island of Hawai'i between a South Kohala port and North Kohala plantations.

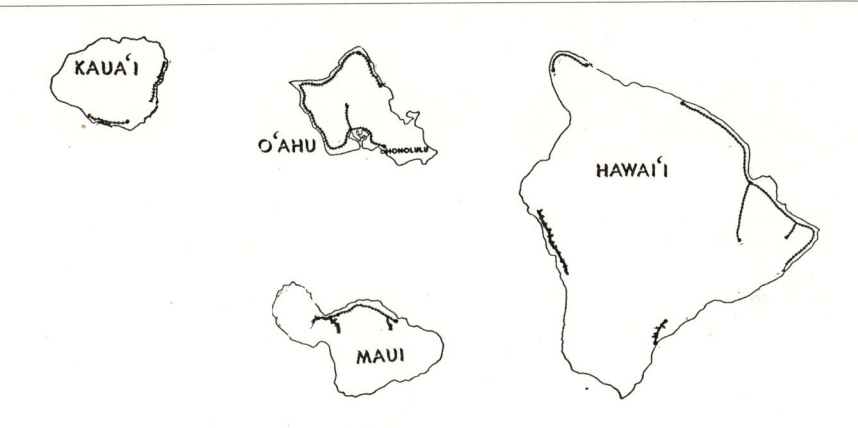

Common carrier railroads on four Hawaiian islands. Not to scale. (W. H. Dorrance)

Wilder wasn't through yet. The 1878 act was deficient in one important way: it overlooked payments of subsidies by the Kingdom for railroad construction. A month after the charter was issued, King Kalākaua signed an amendment that corrected that omission. In August of 1880, Wilder resigned as Minister of the Interior when the King appointed a new cabinet[16], and was now free to pursue his business plans.

In 1883 Wilder petitioned the Kingdom to change the wording of his corporation's charter so that he also had exclusive rights to develop a railroad north from Hilo to Waipi'o Valley. The Secretary of the King's Privy Council, Wilder's brother-in-law and former business partner[17] Col. Charles Hastings Judd, instructed the current Minister of the Interior to grant Wilder's request.[18]

Over the years, common carrier railroads were built on all four of the major sugar islands. Table 21 lists them and their years of operation. Only the Hilo railroad was standard gauge; the rest had narrow-gauge tracks typical for the plantations.

TABLE 21 | **COMMON CARRIER RAILROADS AND YEARS OF OPERATION**

KAUAʻI RAILROADS	START DATE	END DATE
Kauai Railway Company	1906	1933
Koloa/Lihue Connection	1930	1957
Ahukini Terminal & Railway Company	1920	1934
OʻAHU RAILROADS		
Oahu Railway & Land Co.	1886	1947
Koolau Railway Company	1905	1931
MAUI RAILROADS		
Kahului Railroad Co.	1879	1966
HAWAIʻI RAILROADS		
Hawaiian Railroad Co.	1881	1896
Hawaiʻi Railway Company	1896	1937
Mahukona Terminals, Ltd.	1937	1951
Hilo Railroad Company*	1899	1916
Hawaiian Consolidated Ry.	1916	1946
West Hawaiʻi Railway Co.	1906	1926
Honuapo Landing Railway	1930	1942

Note: In 1916 the Hilo Railroad Company was reorganized as The Hawaiian Consolidated Railway Company and lasted through 1946.
Sources: Conde & Best; Hungerford; Kau Sugar Company; Kelly, Nakamura, and Barrere; Kuykendall, *Hawaiian Kingdom 1854-1993*; McBryde Sugar Company; Nellist, 1925.

Capt. Thomas H. Hobron started his railroad on Maui in 1878 and by 1881 had incorporated it as the Kahului & Wailuku Railroad Company.[19] Initially it ran between the town of Wailuku and the port of Kahului. In a few years Hobron extended the line east to Pāʻia, then sold out to Samuel G. Wilder in 1884. Wilder died in 1888 and the business, then called the Kahului Railroad Company, was sold to Hawaiian Commercial & Sugar Company after it was acquired by Alexander & Baldwin. The last train was dispatched in May 1966.[20] The Kahului Railroad Company enjoyed the distinction of being the last common carrier railroad to transport commercial cargo in Hawaiʻi.

Samuel Wilder built his North Kohala railroad over the rugged land from the southwest landing at Māhukona to the northeast Kohala plantations. It was completed in 1882 and began generating revenue at the rate of $2.50 per ton hauled.[21] After Wilder's death in 1888, four plantations in the Kohala District purchased the railroad and incorporated it in 1897 as the Hawaiʻi Railway Company.[22] Four decades later, in 1937, all the Kohala plantations were absorbed into Kohala Sugar Company. The railroad was reincorporated and operated as the Mahukona Terminals, Ltd. until its demise in 1945.[23] Māhukona Harbor was closed during World War II, truck hauling started, and the little railroad never recaptured the lost business. Wilder's dream of connecting Kohala and Hāmākua with his railroad never came to pass.

The exploits of Benjamin Dillingham in building the Oahu Railway & Land Company (O.R.& L.) were described in connection with the development of Ewa Plantation Company, Oahu Sugar Company, Waialua Plantation Company, and Kahuku Plantation Company. After enjoying profitable years hauling military cargo during World War II, the railroad surrendered to trucking and most of the track went out of business in 1947.[24]

Dillingham and his associates also started the standard gauge Hilo Railroad Company in 1899 to service plantations throughout the Hāmākua, North Hilo, South Hilo, and Puna Districts. It was built out 35 miles north of Hilo through some of the most rugged and beautiful country in Hawai'i. Branches of the railroad ran several miles south into the Puna District, and northwest toward Kīlauea volcano. By 1916 it was struggling financially and taken over by mainland investors who reincorporated it as The Hawai'i Consolidated Railway. Four decades later, in 1946, the famous tsunami struck its mortal blow to trains in the Hilo area. With the exception of the Puna branch which hauled harvests to 'Ōla'a for one more year, the railroad ceased operations.[27]

Inter-island steamer docked at Kahului Wharf and being serviced by a Kahului Railroad Company locomotive, 1910. (Ray Jerome Baker/Bishop Museum)

On O'ahu, James Castle's Koolau Railway Company connected with the O.R.& L. terminus at Kahuku and ran down the northeast side of the island to Kahana Bay. Described in connection with the Kahuku Plantation Company, it was seldom a moneymaker, was absorbed into the plantation company in 1931, and soon after shut down as a common carrier. Castle dreamed of restarting the moribund Kona Sugar Company mill on Hawai'i and operating it as a cooperative with homestead farmers cultivating sugarcane in South Kona. The former plantation railroad would serve as a common carrier running from the mill eleven miles into the Ka'ū District.[25] With this plan in mind, Castle and associates organized the West Hawai'i Railway Company in 1906 and operated it until 1916. Then it was taken over by Japanese investors who ran it for a decade and closed it down in 1926.[26] The route led to lands that lacked water and were unlikely for successful sugarcane cultivation.

Common carrier railroads came late to Kaua'i. After the Railway Act was passed, H.M. Von Holt, son of successful Honolulu merchant Herman Von Holt (1830-1867), obtained a royal patent for a railway on the southern coast of Kaua'i. For years nothing further was done. Then the McBryde Sugar Company wanted to avoid the cost of maintaining a railroad to the harbor at 'Ele'ele, and had an opportunity to join forces with Von Holt. The Kauai Railway Company was incorporated in 1906, with Von Holt as a minor shareholder. In exchange for majority interest, the McBryde company contributed land, tracks as far as Kōloa, and a wharf and warehouse at 'Ele'ele Harbor.[28]

In 1909 the Kauai Railway Company extended its business to the Hawaiian Sugar Company, to Kauai Fruit and Land Company in 1910, and Koloa Sugar Company in 1912, in addition to serving McBryde Sugar Company.[29] In 1909 the 'Ele'ele Harbor was renamed "Port Allen" in honor of Samuel Allen, a successful Honolulu merchant whose widow contributed to financing the port.[30] The railroad continued on until 1933, when the tracks were apportioned out to the individual plantations. Today all that remains is a length of track embedded in the wharf at Port Allen.[31]

On the southeast part of the island, in 1919 the U.S. Army Corps of Engineers built a breakwater and improved the harbor at Nāwiliwili. Their participation came with the condition that the plantations connect their railroads to form a continuous line from the east to the west coast of the island, undoubtedly to facilitate defense. The McBryde, Kōloa, Grove Farm, and Līhu'e plantations cooperated, and by 1930 it was possible to run a train from Port Allen to Lihue plantation.[32] The last stretch of this line was terminated when Lihue Plantation Company shut down its plantation railroad in 1957.

Initiated by Lihue Plantation Company, Ahukini Terminal and Railway Company was incorporated in 1920 as a common carrier to connect Lihue Plantation Company, Hawaiian Canneries Company, Makee Plantation Company, and Anahola with the terminal and wharf at Ahukini Harbor. After the Makee plantation was purchased by Lihue Plantation in 1933, and the cannery turned to trucking, the plantation absorbed the railroad, which ran until shutdown in 1957.[33]

Last of the common carriers to enter the picture was the short Honuapo Landing Railway that served the Hutchinson Plantation Company and Hawaiian Agricultural Company in the Ka'ū District. In 1930 the Hawaiian Agricultural Company closed its port facilities at Punalu'u, and began railroading its product to Honu'apo, where it was moved by the Hutchinson Sugar Company railroad branch to Honu'apo Landing. This one-half mile length of track thus became a "common carrier." The railroad operated until 1942, when the port of Honuʻapo was closed because of the Japanese submarine menace, and never reopened.[34]

The colorful Hawaiian common carrier railroads displaced many of the coastal steamers and, in turn, were displaced by motor trucks. Little remains of the workhorse trains that served Hawaiʻi's businesses and residents so well for over 70 years.

FOUNDRIES AND MACHINING WORKS

In the mid-1800s, the machinery works and foundries for casting, forging, and machining the heavy metal parts for sugarmills and locomotives were largely confined to Europe. A three-roller mill weighed several tons and parts were machined on large lathes not found in the United States.[35] Mirilees, Tait, and Watson of Glasgow, Scotland, supplied machinery to the Islands; John Fowler & Sons of Leeds, and Ransome & Rapier of Ipswich, both in England, supplied locomotives and rolling stock; the German firms Hohenzollern and Krauss also supplied locomotives.

The Glasgow firm was especially aggressive. Its junior partner, Watson, visited Hawaiʻi and signed up prospects on the spot.[36] Plantation owners found it hard to resist his offer of credit on lenient terms. For years they preferred machinery made in Great Britain to that from the United States.[37] Europeans had a long tradition of manufacturing equipment for sugarcane farmers in Australia, the South Pacific, and the Caribbean. However, when the American Henry Peirce returned to Boston in 1849, he took an order for a mill for Lihue Plantation. It was manufactured in a New England works and shipped to Kauaʻi in 1850, accompanied by skilled mechanic David M. Weston. He erected the mill, stayed on in Hawaiʻi, and in 1852 started a small machine shop and flour mill in Honolulu. Soon Weston had his hands full with the repair and manufacture of sugarmill parts, and abandoned the business of milling flour. In 1853 he started what became the Honolulu Iron Works (HIW).[38]

A few years earlier, in 1851, Weston helped his own cause by inventing a way to use the centrifuge to separate sugar and molasses during the sugar-making process. This took several weeks using traditional methods, but only minutes with a centrifuge. Weston's apparatus was an instant success, generated business for his works, and today the concept is used in sugar manufacturing throughout the world.[39]

The Iron Works prospered and, needing capital to grow, incorporated in 1876. Theo H. Davies' associate, Alexander Young, and relatives of Davies' business associates, Janion and Green, purchased shares.[40] Davies had bought control of the Works in 1868 and exchanged his equity for controlling shares. This transaction led to a long run of profit-making for his company. Alexander Young came over from Hilo to manage the Works, and, when he retired in 1896, the Davies company purchased his stock.[41]

The Honolulu Iron Works developed the capability to cast and machine large parts previously ordered in Europe or America. Anything not manufactured, like locomotives and steam plows, was ordered from John Fowler & Co., H.K. Porter Locomotive Works, or Lima Locomotive Works, all of which the Works represented as agent. For decades the number of sugarmills kept increasing and older mills needed repairs and replacements, and this generated constant business for Honolulu Iron Works.

Roll crusher at HC&S Company Mill, Puʻunēnē, Maui, Hawaiʻi, 1974.
(John C. Wright/Bishop Museum)

In 1890, former Davies associate George Macfarlane started Union Iron Works and competed for plantation business using machinery imported from Scotland. Manager Alexander Young met this threat by selling some of his HIW shares to Castle & Cooke and H. Hackfield & Company, thus assuring the business of plantations controlled by those agencies.[42] The ploy drove Union Iron Works from the field within two years (HIW bought the company out), and was so successful that additional HIW shares were later sold to C. Brewer & Company, W.G. Irwin & Company, F.A. Schaefer & Company, Benjamin F. Dillingham, Waterhouse family members, and the Wilder family.[43] By the turn of the century HIW employed over 500 workers and generated hundreds of thousands of dollars of profits for Theo H. Davies & Co., Ltd.

Kaka'ako factory of the Honolulu Iron Works, 1930. (Bishop Museum)

In 1899 HIW built a large new foundry and machine shop in the Kaka'ako section of Honolulu.[44] It considered this a gamble, and hedged by expanding sales into Louisiana, the Philippines, Formosa, Mexico, Cuba, Puerto Rico, Santo Domingo, and Jamaica. But Honolulu Iron Works survived the risk of expansion and became Hawai'i's first international entrepreneur. Its motto proudly proclaimed, "The Sun never sets on HIW."[45]

In 1924 the company reported having built 45 sugarmills, one refinery (in 'Aiea, O'ahu, replaced by a more modern refinery in 1993, and shut down in 1996), and modernizing 52 mills, some for the second time. A curious fact of world-wide sugar production was that HIW manufactued its largest mill for Cuba, which was three times the size of any made for a Hawai'i plantation.[45]

Beginning in 1925, Honolulu Iron Works earned steady profits that did not waver when the number of mills shrank as plantations consolidated. The New York office of HIW generated world-wide business whenever the opportunity arose. Hilo Iron Works was acquired by Theo H. Davies & Co., Ltd. and C. Brewer & Company, Ltd., and defense work during World War II created temporary prosperity, but the company's heyday had passed. Ownership in HIW became widely dispersed, and in 1963 Theo H. Davies & Co. Ltd. sold its shares.[47] In 1966 Ward Foods, Inc., a conglomerate, acquired 93 percent of the stock.[48] The Kaka'ako plant was levelled in the late 1980s and the site occupied by commercial and retail development. No evidence remains of what was once Hawai'i's largest international enterprise.

BY-PRODUCTS OF SUGAR

From the Royal Hawaiian Agricultural Society in the 1850s to the present, the Hawai'i sugar industry sought by-products and alternative crops that could make the industry less dependent on sugar prices. Bagasse was considered, particularly since about 1.9 tons of it were produced for each ton of raw sugar.

In 1925 a group of Hilo businessmen incorporated Hawaiian Cellulose, Ltd. to convert bagasse into wallboard. William Williams, manager of Waiakea Mill Company, had invented a process and been granted a U.S. patent. Hawaiian Cellulose, Ltd. was sold to a new corporation, Hawaiian Cane Products, Ltd., and shares were purchased by a consortium, including Alexander & Baldwin, American Factors, Castle & Cooke, C. Brewer & Company, Ltd., Theo H. Davies & Co., Ltd. and Walter Dillingham (1875-1963). The purpose of this was fundraising, as well as ensuring a steady supply of bagasse. Johns-Manville Corporation agreed to market the product, and the Territorial Legislature helped out by making the enterprise tax-exempt for five years.[49]

A factory was erected close to the Waiākea mill. Bagasse produced at the mill was blown through a large pipe to the wallboard plant, and the mill's boilers were converted to burning fuel oil instead of the bagasse. Hilo Sugar Company and Olaa Sugar Company also converted to oil and shipped their bagasse to the wallboard factory via the Hawaiian Consolidated Railway.[50] The product, called "Canec," prospered until the depression year of 1933, when the plant closed for lack of sales. Following a 1933 reorganization, the plant reopened and operated intermittently, plagued with fires and labor unrest, until 1948, when it was sold to Flintcoat Company. The Canec plant continued to suffer from fires, sales indifference, and threats to the renewal of the land lease until 1966, when it was shut down. C. Brewer & Company had purchased the land in 1965 and eventually built its Waiākea hotel complex on the site.[51] A valiant try to develop a by-product had ended in frustration.

The HSPA developed and patented a process for producing a heavy paper out of bagasse. This dark cardboard was suitable for shipping containers. However, no market was found where the product could compete with locally produced cardboard. Because of the dark shade of the cardboard, the HSPA was also unsuccessful in licensing the process in sparsely forested areas of the world where sugarcane was cultivated.

Another "indirect" by-product has already been covered: the history of how McBryde Sugar Company, Lihue Plantation Company, Hawaiian Commercial & Sugar Company, and Waialua Agricultural Company generated electricity that was sold to surrounding communities before 1940. Since then, the generating capacity increased until in 1990 about 10 percent of Hawai'i's electricity was supplied by sugar plantations.[52] Both Hamakua Sugar and Hilo Coast Processing installed new high-pressure boilers and topping cycle turbines to burn more of the trash-mixed bagasse. Of the 12 sugar mills active in 1991, all but Kau Agribusiness Company's mill sold excess power to the utilities.[53] Hawai'i provided a model for generating power from a renewable fuel source because of the sugar industry.

Other by-products developed over the years included the pioneering effort by Paia Plantation in 1917 to produce ethanol from bagasse, a feedlot and beef processing effort by Hamakua Sugar Company that ended when that plantation was shut down, and an additional attempt to manufacture wallboard from bagasse, technically successful but unmarketable because of requirements made by insurance companies.

Almost every subsidiary industry that prospered because of sugar farming has disappeared from the scene, most without leaving a trace. Electric power is the one by-product of sugar production that endures. It continues to contribute to Hawai'i's economy by reducing the amount of imported fuel.

Sugarmill, Oʻahu, Hawaiʻi
(Robert Van Dyke)

CHAPTER 13

SUGAR AND SCIENCE

Hawai'i's sugar farmers led the world in field technology. Their secret was science, the HSPA's research, and management's application of the results. The industry could not have survived without the contributions of the HSPA's technicians to developments in both the factory and the field.

Consider the advantage enjoyed with two-year crops, and in the case of Hāmākua's upper fields, three-year crops. Hawai'i plantations produced the highest yields per acre in the world, even when averaged for annual yield. The proper variety of cane was necessary to do this. It had to mature in two or three years with high sucrose content and match the weather conditions and soil. The HSPA's Experiment Station crossed and tested thousands of varieties of cane until just the right ones were found for Hawai'i's different field conditions. Even after finding a superior variety of cane, the HSPA continued the search for improvements. Hamakua Sugar always took the most improved variety available at planting time, usually replacing the previous one.

Whenever a new pest or disease appeared—and there was always a new one—the HSPA got right on the problem and, with their help, the industry countered the threat. There's a story connected as to why the HSPA suggested that the Bufo Marinus, or cane toad, be imported to Hawai'i. The popular notion was that it fed on insects that ate the cane. It did, and farmers were grateful, but the cane cutters were most appreciative. Before the toad came, Hawai'i was infested with centipedes, a curse to field workers. The cane toads just about cleared out the centipedes.

There was an HSPA substation on every sugar-growing island, and new varieties of cane especially suited to that island's conditions were distributed. Every plantation participated by testing out the new varieties. HSPA personnel visited the plantations to observe progress, give welcome advice, then sold seedlings for planting whatever new variety of cane had been selected. Periodically we took samplings from the leaves and leaf sheaths, and sent them to the Hilo laboratory. There, the levels of nutrients were tested and that determined the proper mixture of fertilizer to use. Almost every area on the island needed a different mixture.

The HSPA also helped to develop ripeners to apply to the cane and increase the sugar content. Ripeners took advantage of sugarcane's natural survival mechanism. In the wild, when plants came under stress, such as during drought, they converted the stalk's pulp to sucrose to regenerate the plant when conditions improved. We put the cane under stress with ripeners to increase the sucrose content before harvest. The same principle worked on irrigated plantations by withholding water, but not in places such as Hāmākua, which had high levels of rainfall. We used an airplane to apply the ripener, essentially a diluted weed killer, Polado; sprayed six to twenty weeks before harvest, depending on the variety of cane and elevation of the field.

Hamakua Sugar Company developed methods to produce furfural and ethanol from bagasse, and a feedstock for making a biodegradable plastic from molasses. Had our research been carried to production, sales of these by-products would have exceeded sales of the sugar produced. We didn't get the time to install pilot plants to demonstrate the feasibility of these processes before the plantation was shut down.

Shortly after World War II, we applied science in another way by installing a radio transmitter to communicate with workers and trucks in the field. Hamakua Sugar Company covered more than 35,000 acres spread out over 30 miles of coastline, and a radio kept track of operations. It especially helped when we cut personnel to a minimum. A radio license was necessary to operate and ours was awarded to "The Hawaiian Communication Company at Hāmākua," a subsidiary of Hamakua Sugar Company. It was always amusing to listen in on the chatter among workers. And, when there was trouble in the fields, we heard about it right away.

⊕ ⊕ ⊕

IN THE EARLY nineteenth century, the Kingdom of Hawai'i struggled to find a profitable export to replace the sandalwood trade. For the remainder of that century, sugarcane farming was the answer. Entrepreneurs came and went as the search for profits took planters to remote corners of the archipelago to raise sugarcane. Import tariffs, insect infestations, cane diseases, droughts, labor shortages, and the actions of monopolists were all met with ingenuity. Hawai'i sugar farmers became the most efficient in the world because of their application of science. Mechanization of field work, efficient use of the work force, and computer-controlled and automated mills were contributing factors. Two requirements for success were: high crop yields per cultivated acre with high sucrose content of harvested cane, and high extraction of sucrose from the harvests. Profits came from satisfying these requirements at the lowest possible cost.

HIGH CROP YIELDS PER ACRE

In the early nineteenth century, indigenous Hawaiian sugarcane was there for the taking. George Wilfong wrote about fields of native cane in Kohala and milling cane in Hāna.[1] While the raw material came cheap, the fields yielded no more than one ton of sugar per acre. Planting this cane did little to improve the yields, and, by the mid-1800s, the industry was struggling to remain profitable.

Lahaina-based missionary Dwight Baldwin reported that in 1854 the whaling ship *George Washington* dropped anchor on a return voyage from Tahiti.

Capt. Pardon Edwards brought samples of two varieties of sugarcane which he intended to deliver to Kaua'i planter Charles Titcomb (died 1833).[2] This delivery was the precursor of a revolution in the scientific development of improved sugarcane varieties in Hawai'i.

Titcomb never got the samples. United States Consul Chase planted them in his garden, where both varieties, "Tahiti" and "Cuban" flourished. Their lush growth attracted the attention of other planters, and within a few years cuttings were being widely planted. At first the Cuban strain was preferred, but the Tahitian variety eventually took over and came to be called "Lahaina cane."[3]

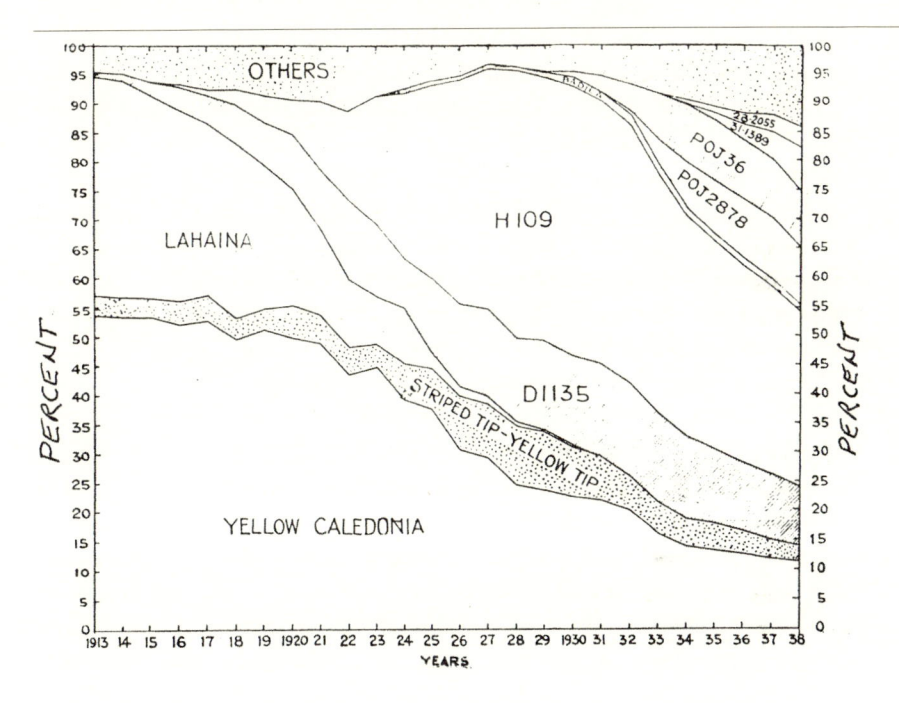

Varieties of sugarcane planted in Hawai'i fields between 1913 and 1938, in percentage of total planted area. By 1999 these varieties had been replaced by newer hybrids.
(Gilmore 1939)

The choice proved to have a lasting effect. Lahaina cane was better because of its rapid growth, deep rooting (more efficient drawing of nutrients from the soil), hard rind (discouraging rodents), richness of juice (yields per acre more than doubled), and firm fiber (the bagasse made good fuel). In the last half of the nineteenth century Lahaina cane predominated throughout the Hawai'i plantations. Success with it encouraged planters to try other varieties from the cane-growing world. Between 1854, and 1903 when the Territory imposed an import quarantine, 25 types of sugarcane were brought in.[4] Four were widely planted, including the long-surviving Yellow Caledonia imported from Queensland, Australia, by manager John Scott of Hilo Sugar Company.[5] It was grown on the Hilo Coast for over 70 years because of its suitability to wet regions.

During the first decade of the twentieth century, Lahaina cane began to succumb to root-rot disease. The industry was threatened with extinction, but applied science came to the rescue. In 1895 the newly formed Hawaiian Sugar Planters' Association initiated its Experiment Station and began hiring staff, beginning with the experienced Dr. Walter Maxwell. He hired chemist Charles F. Eckert, who started breeding sugarcane, using native and imported varieties. One seedling, coded simply "H-109" to keep track of it, was tried in 1907 by manager George Renton of Ewa Plantation. This variety proved to be outstanding.[6] The Experiment Station had found a successor to Lahaina cane and the industry lived on.

H-109 yielded higher tonnage per acre than previous varieties and demonstrated the value of cane-breeding. The program was expanded to find varieties best suited for each plantation's particular weather and geography. Some grew better in irrigated lands having days of sunshine, while others thrived in more cloudy regions with high rainfall. Varieties that grew best at sea level differed from those that flourished at altitudes of 1,000 to 2,000 feet. Different types required different applications of fertilizer. Some varieties leafed quickly and discouraged the growth of weeds. Some were more impervious to insects or diseases, or better suited to fluming, or were easier to grind. The possibilities for tailored breeding were endless, and the Experiment Station bred hundreds of thousands of combinations.

In 1923 the embargo of imported canes was lifted to provide more breeding candidates.[7] In 1928 the concern that imported canes might bring with them unwanted insects and diseases was met by establishing a quarantine station on Moloka'i.[8] By 1938 regional stations were established on all four sugar islands for testing the new varieties of cane. As shown in Table 22, the regional stations were situated in a number of cane-growing environments.

TABLE 22 | **1939 LOCATION OF REGIONAL EXPERIMENT STATIONS**

STATION-PLANTATION	ELEVATION	YEAR ESTABLISHED
Waipio-Oahu Sugar Company	50 feet	1911
Kailua-near Waimanalo	50 feet	1926
Ewa-Ewa Plantation Company	20 feet	1938
Helemano-Waialua Ag. Company	700 feet	1938
Hilo (shore)-Hilo Sugar Co.	350 feet	1930
Hilo (high)-Hilo Sugar Co.	1,000 feet	1931
Hamakua-Hamakua Mill Co.	1,250 feet	1931
Hamakua-Hamakua Mill Co.	2,000 feet	1933
Hawai'i Seed Nursery-Hamakua	700 feet	1935

STATION-PLANTATION	ELEVATION	YEAR ESTABLISHED
Kohala-Kohala Sugar Co.	900 feet	1932
Maui-H. C. & S., Ltd.	100 feet	1938
Kauai-Lihue Pltn. Co.	350 feet	1930
Kauai Seed Nursery-McBryde	600 feet	1935

Minor amounts of the elements calcium, phosphorous, potassium, and other metals, called "nutrients," had to be in the soil for cane growth to occur in a reasonable time. During the last years of the nineteenth century, harvests carried off the nutrients, no natural process replaced them, and crops became stunted. Chemical analysis determined the depletion and a proper mixture of fertilizers was applied. This marked the birth of the fertilizer industry in Hawai'i. A study of fertilizers used during the 1938 season revealed that Doctor Maxwell's analyses were farseeing; island-to-island the fertilizer compositions agreed with the nutrient requirements suggested by the data in Table 23.[10]

TABLE 23 | NUTRIENTS IN THE SOIL OF THE HAWAIIAN ISLANDS

ISLAND	LIME %	POTASH %	PHOS. ACID %	NITROGEN %
O'ahu	.380	.342	.207	.176
Kaua'i	.418	.309	.187	.227
Maui	.396	.357	.270	.388
Hawai'i	.185	.346	.513	.540

*Note: Lime contains calcium; Potash contains potassium; and Phosphoric Acid contains phosphorus.
Source: *The Planter's Monthly*, February 1899.

In Hawai'i the application of fertilizer was raised to a high level of efficiency. Samples of the young leaves and sheaths were taken during the early months of growth to test for nutrients, and fertilizer was tailored to any deficiency.

In 1900 a pest came to O'ahu with seedlings of imported cane. By 1905 the leafhopper (*Parkinsiella sacharicida*) had moved to the island of Hawai'i and decimated a crop of the Hawaiian Agricultural Company in the Ka'ū District. The fields blackened, withered, and died under the attack, but the Experiment Station rose to the occasion.[11]

In 1903 two entomologists, R.C. Perkins and A. Koebele, were sent to the Australian cane fields to search for the leafhopper's natural enemy. With great difficulty they succeeded in locating the parasite that kept the Australian pests under control, and brought samples back to Hawai'i.[12] The parasite was a very small insect that deposited its eggs within the hopper and the resulting larvae devoured the host. When introduced into the Hawai'i fields, the parasite eliminated the leafhopper menace in a surprisingly short time.

The cane borer (*Rhabdocnemis obscura*) was brought under control in 1910 by the Tachinid Fly, found by Frederick Muir of the Experiment Station after several years of searching the jungles, swamps and forests of the South Pacific islands and New Guinea.[13] In 1912 the root-destroying Anomala Beetle was brought under control by its natural enemy, a small wasp found in the Philippines. Introduced to Hawai'i in 1916, it brought the beetle under control within two years.[14]

One of the most exciting counter-insect introductions was the cane toad Bufo Marinus. This hardy, voracious creature was introduced into Hawai'i in 1932, and promptly reproduced with astonishing vigor. The ubiquitous toad provided a generous share of Hawai'i's road-kill, and fed on every insect it encountered, including centipedes, scorpions, termites, moths, leaf and grasshoppers, grubs, slugs, beetles, and cockroaches.[15] The toad was the enemy of all insect pests and a boon to many a gardener.

In 1985 a search was underway to find the enemy of the lacebug causing damage to cane at Pioneer Mill Company on Maui. The search went to Central and South America, where the lacebug originated.[16] The technique of introducing natural enemies to sugarcane insect-pests continued as Hawai'i's sugar producers led the world in biological control of pests, without the use of insecticides.

Plant diseases were another matter. Viruses, bacteria, fungi, and systemic diseases attacked the leaves, stalks and roots of cane and were spread by mixing healthy and diseased cuttings during planting, and by the accidental use of contaminated soil. The most effective control was to replace susceptible cane with resistant varieties developed by the Experiment Station.[17]

When the industry started in the nineteenth century, there was room for all and the first planters located their farms on the wet or windward sides of the islands. Thousands of otherwise fertile acres elsewhere were ignored because of lack of water. When all the wet lands were occupied, the planters began to eye the potentially profitable dry acres. Irrigation was an answer, and beginning in 1876 on Maui, when Samuel Alexander and Henry Baldwin completed their Hāmākua Ditch, the race was on to claim and irrigate the dry lands.

In 1905, in addition to water delivered by wells, over 100 million gallons were collected daily and distributed to the fields of eight plantations on the islands of Kaua'i, O'ahu, and Maui.[19] The Hāmākua Ditch, originally intended to supply mill and flume water, was completed in 1907 and provided irrigation for some 15 miles of coastal fields on the island of Hawai'i. O'ahu's most remarkable engineering project, involving a tunnel through the Ko'olau mountains constructed by the Waiahole Ditch Company, a subsidiary of Oahu Sugar Company, was completed on 1916. In its systems of tunnels, about 30 million gallons of water were developed daily from the Kahana, Waikāne and Waiāhole Valleys on the windward side of the mountains. Water was delivered via a system of ditches, tunnels, siphons, and large pipes.[20] Table 24 lists a few of the major artesian well and tunnel projects completed by 1905.[18]

TABLE 24 | IRRIGATION TUNNELS AND WELLS IN 1905

PLANTATION	SYSTEM	DATE COMPLETED	DAILY FLOW MILLIONS OF GALS.
Pioneer Mill Co.	Tunnel	1904	11
Pioneer Mill Co.	45 Artesian Wells	1904	35
Kohala Sugar Co.	Tunnel	1903	7
Kihei Plantation	Tunnel & Ditches	1902	27.5
Ewa Plantation	48 Artesian Wells	1903	69.75
Oahu Sugar Co.	68 Artesian Wells	1903	63.5
Kahuku Plant.	25 Artesian Wells	1903	41.2
Waialua Agri. Co.	Wells & Reservoir	1903	unk.
McBryde Sugar Co.	Tunnel & 38 Wells	1903	20
Kekaha Sugar Co.	26 Wells	1898	18

Source: Thrum, *Hawaiian Almanac*, 1905.

Growth rates of cane varieties were studied to determine when water was most needed, and the irrigation flow metered accordingly.[21] Distribution costs were minimized by adopting drip irrigation.[22] This system required fewer workmen and less water, an innovation that did much to preserve the industry in Hawai'i.

The 1932 crop yielded 1,026,615 tons of raw sugar, the second of what became a long run of annual million-ton crops. The average yield per acre was 7.35 tons. Non-irrigated acres, about 45 percent of the total harvested, yielded 5.39 tons, as compared with 9.0 tons in irrigated fields.[23] The advantage was clear, and by 1991 over 60 percent of the fields were irrigated and produced an average of 10.7 tons per acre.[24]

Most of the sugar islands were denuded of their forests during the sandalwood harvesting that preceded large-scale sugar farming. Rain water washed rapidly over land lacking cover, carried away soil, and gouged out gullies and ravines in the process. The industry, led by HSPA Experiment Station scientists, initiated a reforestation program to restore the watershed. A botany and forestry department was established within the Experiment Station in 1919, and a nursery started in upper Mānoa Valley for the growing of young trees. Plantations were supplied with seedlings, and seeding by low-flying aircraft was begun in the early 1920s. By 1926, over one million trees had been planted throughout the Islands, many saplings coming from the HSPA nursery. The state owes much of its forested beauty to this reforestation effort.

HIGH EXTRACTION OF SUCROSE

The most widely used method of extracting sugar from cane involved running the stalks through rollers or grinders to squeeze out the juice. This method was used for centuries by Chinese and Indian sugarmakers, and Hawai'i sugar farmers used it exclusively during the early years. The juices were collected and then subjected to purification, distillation, crystallization, and separations to make sugar.

The primitive water- and animal-powered three-roller mills of the 1850s rarely extracted more than 50 percent of the sugar. The bagasse emerged wet and had to be spread out to dry before it could be burned. Wet bagasse was a distinct disadvantage when steam engines were introduced to power the mills. The solution was to use more grinders to press out more of the cane juice, and recover more sugar in the process. Table 25 describes the growth in the number of rollers.[25]

TABLE 25 | EVOLUTION OF HAWAI'I SUGARMILLS

YEAR	NUMBER OF ROLLERS	EXTRACTION EFFICIENCY %	PLANTATION
pre-1876	3	.50 to .75	all
1884	5	.85 to .90	Waiakea Mill Co.
1890	6	.88	Wailuku Sugar
1895	9	.90 to .93	Ewa Plantation
1907	12	.96	Oahu Sugar Co.
by 1935	18	.98+	Ewa Plantation

Source: Gilmore, Sugar Manual 1938-1939; *The Planters Monthly*, 1905.

By 1935, Ewa Plantation Company was achieving an extraction rate of over 98 percent and producing dry bagasse for boiler fuel. Many innovations contributed to this kind of improvement. Particular credit went to Alexander Young, who introduced water into the processing stream before it entered the last grinders for "maceration," or diffusion extraction under pressure.[26] As more grinders were added to the train, maceration juices from the first grinders were fed into the second set and the repetition continued to the end of the train.

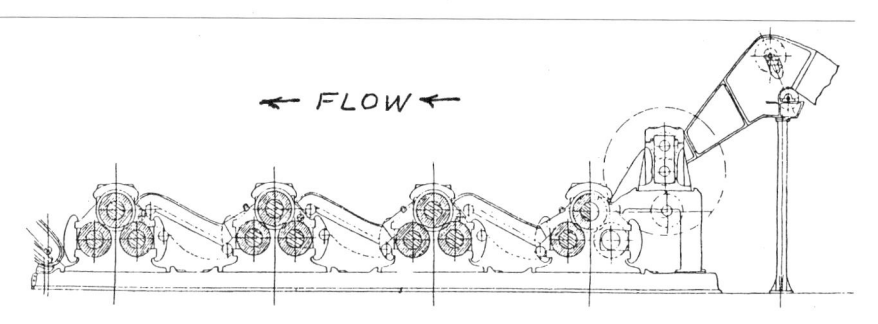

Typical 14-roller sugarmill configuration. (*Planters' Monthly*)

In 1913, P.A. Messchaert of Oahu Sugar Company invented circumferential grooves in the rollers that made space for cane juice to flow.[27] A year later, William Searby invented a machine that shredded the cane feeding into the mill and made a more even blanket entering the grinders.[28] Engineers continued to make on-site improvements that resulted in Hawai'i's mills being equal to the best in the world. Nor was the rest of the manufacturing process neglected. The juices produced by the grinders had to be clarified, filtered, evaporated, crystallized, and separated from the molasses. Revolving screens, multiple-effect evaporators (using hot vapor from the first evaporator to provide heat to boil off the vapor in the second evaporator, etc.), and Weston's centrifugal separator all improved processing efficiency. By the end of the twentieth century, an 82 to 90 percent recovery rate was expected. ("Recovery" refers to the overall process of making crystallized sugar. "Extraction" refers only to extracting sucrose from the cane stalks.)

The diffusion method of extracting sugar involved immersing stalks in a bath of hot water to dissolve the sugar. Removing the water followed a procedure like that in a grinding mill, and diffusion was a highly efficient method that extracted 99 percent of the sugar. However, it could be highly energy-intensive because heat was used to dry the wet pulp before burning it. The diffusion process was improved by adding efficient grinders to press the water out of the pulp so it could be burned. By 1970 Pioneer Mill Company, Hawaiian Commercial & Sugar Company's Pā'ia mill, and Puna Sugar Company had installed modern diffusion plants.[29]

MINIMIZING PRODUCTION COSTS

Before 1880 harvests were brought to the mill by bullock and mule carts. Every plantation had a substantial paddock and teams of animals for hauling. Housing, feed, pasturage and the manpower to maintain them were all expensive. Claus Spreckels made an advancement in 1882, when he installed a narrow gauge railroad on his Maui plantation.[30] The cost savings were considerable, and soon other methods were sought to replace the expensive and cumbersome animal-drawn carts. Many Hilo Coast and Hāmākua Coast plantations were divided by gulches and planted on slopes too steep to be serviced by railroads. They developed flume systems and cable trolleys to replace hauling by carts. Eventually motor trucks and tournahaulers replaced the railroads, and cable trolleys and flumes also reduced manpower and expenses. Table 26 describes the cost reductions made in harvest transport over the years.

TABLE 26 | COST REDUCTION

YEAR	FROM	TO	FACTOR	PLANTATION
1882	bullocks	railroad	.39	H.C. & S. Maui
1904	bullocks	cable trolleys	.685	Kukaiau, Hawai'i
1904	railroads	flumes	.877	25-plantation avg.
1938	railroads	trucks	.75	Kilauea, Kaua'i

Source: Conde; *The Planters' Monthly* 1882 and 1904.

Not every plantation produced results agreeing with those on Table 26. In 1929, for example, Wailea Milling Company had no plantation railroad and reported flume transport costing $1.43 per ton, compared with $.64 per ton by rail.[31] Fluming costs varied with the length of flumes.[32] Nevertheless, in this case both costs were far below what was charged by both common carrier railroads on the island at the time ($2.50 per ton).

If harvesting cane brings to mind machete-wielding workers chopping stalks while others carry 125-pound bundles up a loading ramp, those sights disappeared from the scene long ago. Mechanical loading of cane began in the 1920s and, by World War II, had completely replaced hand loading. In 1958 the last hand harvesting was done on the wet Hilo Coast.[32] The steady decline of field workers had begun more than three decades earlier, after the mid-1920s, owing to the modernization of cultivating and harvesting tasks. In 1923 the first mechanical loading of a complete harvest, using a self-propelled machine, was done at Kahuku Plantation Company.[33] This labor-saving concept was eventually adopted by every plantation where access permitted its use, and manager William Goodale of Waialua Agricultural Company first used it in 1920.[34]

For years plantations had experimented with a variety of harvesting machines. One was so complicated a manager remarked, "You have to have a doctorate from M.I.T. to run this contraption!"[35] Such a machine would never have survived the rugged conditions in Hawai'i cane fields. Fortunately, the answer to the problem was more direct. In 1937 Ewa Plantation tried harvesting with one of its grab loaders.[36] Conveniently, the cane stalks broke off at a socket just above the roots. Large "push-rakes" mounted on Caterpillar tractors accomplished much the same as the grabs. The ranks of human cane cutters shrank as plantation after plantation converted to mechanical harvesting from 1937 to the beginning of World War II. This breakthrough was one of the last true revolutions in labor force reduction.

Hamakua Plantation designed and manufactured a long cane harvester that cut the stalks and deposited them in windows suitable for grab loading by the cane-haul truck. This type of harvester was used in wet fields, and push-rake harvesting was used in dry fields. But the grab or push-rake picked up considerable trash, dirt, and discarded metal parts. Almost 35 percent of the weight was unwanted junk which had been avoided by hand harvesting. Mills were swamped with this soil and trash, and production was frequently stopped or slowed to a crawl. Metal tools, remnants of discarded appliances and cars, rail car links, and anything a careless workman might lose or discard went to the mill. Shredders and rollers were damaged and superintendents looked desperately for a solution.[37]

Eventually powerful magnets were used to remove metal trash. Each plantation built its own "cane washer" that the harvest passed through before entering the mill. Features of successful cane washers were circulated via the HSPA Committee on Labor Saving Devices, and by 1945 the problem was

Grab loading in 1991. (W.H. Dorrance)

under control. Conversion to mechanical harvesting had been accelerated by the scarcity of labor during World War II, so that the cane-cutting machete became an artifact of the past.[38]

Improvements in operating efficiency led to labor reduction and increased tons of sugar produced per worker. In principle, pay increases were offset by increased sugar produced per employee, as shown in Table 27. However, on one plantation the number of workers declined 54 percent between 1933 and 1943. While this decreased operating expenses, during that same period employee pay increased by 65 percent.[39] Nevertheless, the Hawai'i sugar industry increased worker productivity to a level envied throughout the cane-growing world. Yet, the number of workers has diminished to the point where the labor force is no longer a political factor in the state. Table 27 also helps explain why many sugar camps have been bulldozed away and why the "plantation lifestyle" drew to a close.

TABLE 27 | GROWTH IN SUGAR WORKER PRODUCTIVITY

YEAR	NUMBER OF EMPLOYEES	TONS OF SUGAR PER EMPLOYEE
1915	45,654	14.3
1925	48,473	16.1
1935	46,720	21.1
1945	20,806	39.5
1965	10,346	117.7

Sources: HSPA, *Story of Sugar* 1925; HSPA, *Sugar Manual* 1992; Schmitt.

Cane cleaning plant installed by Wailuku Sugar Company in 1941. (Wailuku Sugar Company)

COMMUNICATION

When the only means of getting a message to Honolulu from the Hilo Coast was by a schooner that could take a week, a plantation manager operated with considerable freedom. In his independent way he could commit to expenditures beyond the plantation's means. In those days profit-making, if any, was in his hands and he was treated with tremendous respect by the agencies.

This changed around the turn of the century. Marconi had invented the wireless telegraph, and in 1899 Mr. F.J. Gross contracted with him to link the Hawaiian Islands to the United States.[40] After much experimentation and public skepticism, in 1905 an inter-island network was completed, with stations at Nāwiliwili Point on Kauaʻi, Barbers Point on Oʻahu, Lahaina on Maui, and Puakō on the island of Hawaiʻi.[41] Gross had organized his wireless company on a shoestring, and from 1900 to 1905 the sugar agencies stepped in to provide financing and keep it going.[42] Prompt communication between agency and manager was now possible, and control of operations shifted toward Honolulu. The era of the independent manager-operator had passed.

The survival of Hawai'i's sugar industry can be explained by the sound application of science and engineering. All the plantations entered into a cooperative effort, exemplified by the Hawaiian Sugar Planter's Association's research and development program. This resulted in perfecting a plantation system that led the sugar-producing world in efficiency while paying its employees the highest wages of agricultural workers in any country. 🌺

Oahu Sugar Co.'s mill, O'ahu, Hawai'i. (Robert Van Dyke)

CHAPTER 14

COMPETITION AND PRICE SUPPORTS

Government programs to stabilize the price of sugar have been around almost as long as the industry itself. This is because the sugar business is extremely capital-intensive and requires an expensive mill close to the cane fields. Cut cane must be processed within eight hours of harvesting, so prolonged transportation time to supply distant factories isn't possible. Because of basic expenses and the need for trained workers in the mills, cane farmers also cannot shift from crop to crop depending on price, like farmers of most other crops. Governments realized that without some form of price stability, planters and investors would be reluctant to get into the sugar business. The answer was government price supports.

About 70 percent of world sugar production is consumed in the country that makes it. Every government has some mechanism to stabilize the revenue of sugar farmers and processors. Of the remaining sugar, approximately 20 percent is exported under bilateral agreements which also stabilize the price. This leaves only about 10 percent of total production to be disposed of on the world sugar market. Only a small segment of the demand side looks to this market to satisfy its requirements. Minor changes in the supply due to weather conditions (or in demand due to changes in the standard of living), are reflected in this limited world market, and can easily overwhelm it, resulting in either excessively low or high figures. Frequently the world price is well below the costs of the lowest-cost producer, and at other times it has risen inordinately. Because they reflect such a small percentage of the total market, these fluctuations have relatively little impact on the overall picture.

Since the Great Depression, the United States has had a sugar program to stabilize the income of its farmers and processors. Originally the Sugar Act worked very well and provided for fair prices to both the producers and the consumers. Under this act, foreign suppliers had U.S. quotas and protected them by fulfilling the quantities as called for. However, when the Sugar Act expired in 1974, there were no more quota obligations to protect, and foreign suppliers refused to export sugar to the U.S. unless it paid the high world price. This drove up the domestic price.

The high price and its expected long-term continuation triggered a tremendous expansion in world production, including a major increase in Florida. It also gave impetus to the development of liquid high-fructose corn syrup (HFCS), used in the soft-drink industry. The price difference was sufficient that soft-drink bottlers switched from sugar to high-fructose corn sweeteners. This caused a reduction in the total demand for sugar in the U.S., affecting the domestic price.

Only a year later, in 1975, the combination of increased supply and reduced demand caused a precipitous drop in the price of sugar. As a result, the domestic industry was in serious trouble, and Congress reinstated a sugar price-support program, incorporating it as part of the Farm Act. The domestic price of sugar was controlled by regulating the amount of foreign imports to maintain an appropriate domestic supply. Because no subsidies were involved, this resulted in a program at no direct cost to the American taxpayer. The government charged a fee for every ton of sugar produced by a domestic operation and therefore made money on the program.

At first foreign imports were controlled by establishing a quota; however, volume quotas were illegal, and replaced with tariff quotas. This meant a very high tariff was applied when imported sugar reached a stipulated level, which had the same effect of controlling import volume. When the Farm Act expired, Congress reestablished a program under a separate Sugar Act.

The latest challenge facing domestic sugar producers is the North American Free Trade Agreement (NAFTA). As originally drafted, this agreement would have destroyed domestic sugar producers by allowing duty-free importation of Mexican sugar without quotas. It is a strong probability that the Mexicans will increase corn production so that their soft drink bottlers also switch to high-fructose corn syrup. This would free up a large portion of the three million tons of sugar per year that Mexico produces to be shipped into the United States market, close to 35 percent of domestic U.S. production. The duty-free importation of such a large tonnage of sugar would drive the U.S. market price down to far below production costs, killing off domestic producers.

But domestic sugar producers were alert to this threat, and worked hard for a solution to insure the survival of their industry. At this point, mainland beet and cane sugar representatives and the HSPA's Washington-based vice president, Jack Roney, demonstrated their value. A modification of the NAFTA agreement was worked out that gives our sugar producers at least 15 years of protection while they devise a more lasting solution. Import quotas were replaced by a sliding scale of tariffs. In the first six years, Mexico can ship 25,000 metric tons of sugar into the United States, duty free. Any sugar over that amount will be subject to a sizable tariff. So far, no excess sugar has been imported. As time goes on, this tariff is adjusted downward so that after fifteen years there will be no restrictions on importing Mexican sugar.

Hawai'i's sugar executives must be prepared with little warning to travel to Washington, D.C., to meet with members of Congress and their staffs. I always met first with each of the four delegates from Hawai'i in order to bring them up to date on the industry's situation, answer their questions, and get the names of other Congressional members I should meet. Our delegates always informed me of upcoming hearings and proposed legislation that would affect us. These visits, along with competent representation by Jack Roney and others, helped the sugar industry to hold off many potential legislative disasters.

HAWAI'I'S SUGAR IN THE MARKETPLACE

From the beginning, California and the mainland United States were the principal markets for Hawai'i sugar. Occasional attempts to establish markets in Australia and Canada were short-lived. California is much closer, and commerce and sentiments favored shipping between Hawai'i and the West Coast of America.

COMPETITION 1837-1876

Hawai'i was a latecomer to sugar production. By 1837, when Koloa Plantation exported its first two tons of raw sugar, the industry had been established in the West Indies and South America for more than a century. Cuba produced over 100,000 tons annually and production was increasing.[1] By 1850, world production of cane sugar approached one million tons, and the French and Germans were also producing beet sugar.[2] North American sugar consumption depended on imports. Louisiana sugar supplied the eastern United States, but not nearly enough, and Cuba and other Caribbean Basin islands made up most of the balance. However, the growing populations of Oregon and California were at least five months away from Cuba by sailing ship. Hawai'i was only ten to twenty days distant, and its plantation owners seized the new markets.

California was annexed by the United States in 1848 and the 30 percent ad valorem tax on imported sugar was applied.[3] Shortly thereafter, in about 1852, merchant ships operating between the West Coast and the Orient began to flood the San Francisco market with inexpensive Chinese and Philippine sugar.[4] This combination of events caused a severe reduction of sugar prices and a recession in Hawai'i. By 1857 its number of plantations had been reduced to five.[5]

Prospects improved in 1861, when the Civil War broke out. The Union Navy blockaded Confederate ports and the Louisiana plantations were cut off from the northern refineries. For four years Hawai'i sugar enjoyed a prosperous period as it helped satisfy the United States demand. Many plantations weathered the post-Civil War recession and survived to compete in the western market. Nevertheless, U.S. import tariffs limited profits and discouraged modernizing the mills at a time when the world was enjoying an industrial revolution.

Table 28 compares sugar production between Hawai'i and its international competitors between 1850 to 1875. Competition drove Hawai'i sugar from almost any market it attempted to enter. Only the California market offered the advantage of competitive shipping costs. Unfortunately, after 1848, exporting to California required the payment of the onerous tariff.

TABLE 28 | **SUGAR PRODUCTION, SUGAR PRICES, AND TARIFFS, 1850-1875**

	1850	1862	1875
World Cane-tons	1,035,000	1,322,000	1,763,000
World Beet-tons	165,000	495,000	1,322,000
Cuba-tons	352,000	551,000	738,000
Louisiana-tons	126,000	42,000	77,000
Hawai'i-tons	280	848	11,154
Sugar-cents/lb.	6.85	7.16	5.43
U.S. Tariff-cts./lb.	2.06	2.15	1.63

Notes: All figures are five-year averages/one ton=2,000 pounds
Sources: Galloway; HSPA, *Story of Sugar* 1926; Jarves; Kuykendall, *Hawaiian Kingdom* 1778-1854; Kuykendall, *Hawaiian Kingdom* 1854-1874; Sullivan.

The data in Table 28 show the depression of Louisiana sugar during the 1861-1865 war, and the growth of the Hawai'i industry during it and afterwards. Cuba was well established in the United States market and used slave labor until 1880. There was little hope that Hawai'i sugar could penetrate markets served by Cuban producers.

The growth of the beet sugar industry was more ominous to the long-term future of cane sugar producers. Technology for producing sugar from sugar beets was developed in France and Germany in the late eighteenth and early nineteenth centuries.[6] Sugar beets grow in the temperate zone, their leafy tops make good forage and fertilizer, and the sucrose produced is identical to that from cane. France and Germany subsidized beet sugar producers by paying bounties because of their beneficial effects.[7] European beet sugar underpriced cane sugar in any market it entered, and became a major factor during this period. If Hawai'i were to continue to compete in the United States, something had to be done to remove the burdensome tariff on imported sugar.

COMPETITION 1876-1898

King Kalākaua was determined to keep his realm from reverting to a subsistence economy by furthering the advancement of agriculture. His government concentrated on obtaining duty-free entrance of Hawai'i sugar into the United States. On August 15, 1876, the "Treaty of Reciprocity between the United States of America and the Hawaiian Islands" was ratified by the United States Senate and signed by President Grant.[8] It was to be in effect for seven years, with right of cancellation upon notice in the eighth year. Under the terms of the treaty, sugar (among many commodities) was to enter either country free of import duties. Overnight Hawai'i sugar received a generous increase in profits and the race was on to exploit this.

By 1884 the number of plantations increased to its maximum of eighty. Afterwards the number declined with consolidations because it had been proven that only large operations were profitable. Railroads began to be installed, extending the reach of a plantation's mill. European beet sugar production drove prices down, and beet sugar production gained a foothold on the U.S. mainland. The years between 1890 to 1895 were particularly difficult for the Hawai'i industry. In 1890 Congress passed the McKinley Tariff Act, which became operative in April 1891. It removed all tariffs on imported sugar no matter what the source, and required a two-cents-per-pound bounty paid to domestic sugar producers.[9] This eliminated the advantage Hawai'i had enjoyed over other foreign producers. Sugar prices decreased, and it was only by absorbing losses that the fittest survived until the act was repealed in 1894. The lesson was not lost on those who sought annexation to the United States.

In 1893 the monarchy was overthrown and the Republic of Hawai'i formed by a faction determined to gain annexation to the United States.[10] Commissioners, including Charles Cooke of C. Brewer & Company in one group, were sent to Washington to lobby for annexation.[11] After turning down one offer by the new Republic, in 1898 Congress acted and Hawai'i became a Territory of the United States.

Table 29 summarizes the position of Hawai'i sugar in the world market from 1876 to annexation in 1898. By then beet sugar had passed cane sugar in world tonnage and showed signs of exterminating competition. The technology was firmly established in the United States, and sugar beet acreage was growing in the Midwestern farm belt. Cuban production was hurt by the insurrection that started in 1868, and as a result, Louisiana sugar enjoyed a post-Civil War recovery. Hawai'i's capacity increased, despite the decrease in sugar prices. Nevertheless, from the late 1880s about 70 percent of United States sugar consumption continued to be imported from Europe and Cuba, with European beet sugar producers supplying the lion's share.[12]

TABLE 29 | **WORLD AND HAWAI'I SUGAR PRODUCTION, 1876-1898**

	1876	1887	1898
World Cane Sugar-tons	1,873,000	2,259,000	2,755,000
World Beet Sugar-tons	1,322,000	2,865,000	5,690,000
Cuban Sugar-tons	666,000	705,000	556,000
Louisiana Sugar-tons	80,000	126,000	407,000
Hawai'i Sugar-tons	11,572	85,709	200,667
Hawai'i Plantations	37	75	54
Indep. Hawai'i Mills	3	8	4
Sugar Price-cents/lb.	5.24	4.97	3.47

Notes: All figures are five-year averages/one ton=2,000 pounds
Sources: Galloway; HSPA, *Story of Sugar* 1926, Jarves; Thrum, *Hawaiian Almanac* 1874-1898.

Hawaiʻi's producers knew they needed to modernize but lacked the capital to do it. Foreign capital was shy about investing in a small kingdom and its successor republic. When Hawaiʻi became part of the United States, the resources of mainland capitalists were tapped and the producers entered an era of growth.

COMPETITION 1898-2000

The United States had always imported sugar to keep up with demand. Domestic producers never satisfied the market created by an increasing per capita consumption, as well as an ever-increasing population. Until 1934 an uneasy truce existed between Hawaiʻi producers and mainland beet and cane sugar producers. Yet, there was room for all, and sugar prices were protected by U.S. import tariffs. The western states were supplied by Hawaiʻi sugar refined and marketed by the cooperative, California & Hawaiʻi Sugar Company and Western Sugar Refinery. The main concern of domestic cane-sugar producers, both on the mainland and in Hawaiʻi, was to protect market share from the inroads of beet sugar producers.

The truce between sugar producers broke down with the passage of the Jones-Costigan Sugar Control Act of 1934. The United States substituted import quotas for tariffs in order to support prices. Mainland beet producers in 22 states seized the chance to "freeze out Hawaiian cane" by successfully lobbying to put Hawaiʻi producers in the same category as foreign producers.[13] Hawaiʻi competed with Cuba for a share of the residual foreign producer quota rather than sharing a quota with the mainland producers. As a consequence, Hawaiʻi had to reduce its cultivated acreage by 10 percent. Then the Sugar Act of 1937 removed the inequity, and placed Hawaiʻi among the other domestic producers.[14] Each year the Secretary of Agriculture assigned production quotas to each "producing area."

Prices stabilized and Hawaiʻi's producers took profits year to year under the quota system. The number of plantations was reduced as consolidations continued for the sake of efficiency. Various sugar acts, with the exception of the period between 1974 and 1981, provided price supports and stabilization of the number of domestic producers.

About 1970 a serious threat to both beet and cane sugar producers emerged.[15] High-fructose corn syrup (HFCS) production began to capture the high-volume soft-drink market at the expense of sugar. HFCS enjoyed a 10 to 20 percent price advantage over sugar and the savings for soft-drink manufacturers were hard to ignore. About the same time, non-caloric sweeteners (saccharine and aspartame) entered the competition. Sugar retained a market share because no cost-effective way to crystallize HFCS was found. Table 30 compares sugar and sweetener production in 1925 and 1985.

TABLE 30 | SUGAR PRODUCTION 1925 AND 1985

	1925	1985
Total U.S. Cane Sugar-tons	1,806,896	3,033,000
Total U.S. Beet Sugar-tons	1,091,087	3,000,000
High-Fructose Corn Syrup-tons	0	8,100,000
Louisiana Sugar-tons	88,480	532,000
Hawai'i sugar-tons	692,804	1,042,542
Mexican Cane Sugar-tons	185,049	3,848,750
N.Y. Sugar Price-cents/lb.	4.33	20.39
U.S. Tariff on Sugar-cents/lb.	1.256	none-quotas

Note: All figures are absolute; no averaging/one ton=2,000 pounds
Sources: HSPA, *Story of Sugar* 1926; HSPA, *Sugar Manual* 1986; Thurston.

By 1985 HFCS had driven sugar from the soft-drink market and exceeded the combined tonnage of cane and beet sugar by a wide margin.[16] The growth of Mexican sugar signalled a threat to domestic producers if import quotas were abandoned. In 1991 United States domestic producers of cane sugar included Florida, with 1.81 million tons; Louisiana, with 0.76 million tons; Hawai'i, with 0.72 million tons; Texas, with .07 million tons; and Puerto Rico, with a smaller amount. Sugar beets were harvested in 14 states, with Minnesota, Idaho, California, and North Dakota being the leaders.[17]

Knowledgeable observers believe that the life of the Hawai'i sugar industry is possible only with goverment support.[18] When the record of sugar price supports is examined, it is difficult to fault this view. With few exceptions, the industry has enjoyed over a hundred years of legislative protection in one form or another. Other countries support their production in similar ways, as do bilateral trade agreements, so that 90 percent of the world's sugar production is supported in a variety of ways.

TREATIES AND LEGISLATION

From 1789 until the federal income tax was established in 1913, the United States depended on import duties and customs revenues to finance the government. During this time, import tariffs were adjusted periodically as shortfalls or surpluses developed.[19] In the last half of the nineteenth century, up to a 30 percent ad valorem tax was applied to imported sugar. Until 1876 Hawai'i sugar exporters paid this tax on every pound exported to the United States.

California not being part of the U.S. until 1848 encouraged Hawai'i producers to ship to the West Coast import-free, and helped establish long-term market relationships that survived after California became a Territory. Then Hawai'i producers had to pay the import tax and suffered accordingly. The Kingdom vigorously negotiated with the United States to remove the burdensome tariffs, and, after years of lobbying, Congress ratified the

Reciprocity Treaty in 1876.[20] Since sugar made up almost 60 percent of the value of Hawai'i exports at the time, and was sure to grow, all the islands profited from the treaty. When it was renewed in 1887, the United States was given the right to establish a naval station at Pearl Harbor.[21] At this point, international politics entered into the Hawai'i sugar equation, never to be removed.

The McKinley Tariff Act, in effect between 1891 to 1894, devastated the Hawai'i sugar industry by cancelling the price advantage enjoyed under the Reciprocity Treaty. All tariffs were removed on imports and a two-cents-per-pound bounty paid to domestic sugar producers. The New York sugar price dropped from an average 4.68 cents per pound in 1890 to a low of 2.76 cents per pound in 1892.[22] At least four prominent Hawai'i plantations closed down, and pressures grew on the monarchy to seek annexation to preserve the industry. In 1893, the Hawaiian monarchy was overthrown and replaced with a constitutional republic.[23] The advantages of the Reciprocity Treaty were restored the following year in 1894 when the McKinley Tariff Act was repealed.

Following annexation in 1898, U.S. tariffs on sugar imports became a weapon in international affairs and the target of powerful domestic interests. After Cuba's independence was declared in 1901, eastern sugar interests invested heavily in Cuban plantations. They lobbied strongly, and in 1903 won an important concession when the tariff on Cuban sugar was reduced to 80 percent of what was applied to foreign sugar imports.[24] Then, in 1913, the Internal Revenue Service and income taxes were established, and the government no longer depended so heavily on tariffs for funds. The manipulation of tariffs became an instrument to protect domestic sugar producers, including Hawai'i, and to reward or penalize foreign producers.

When the United States entered World War I in 1917, the price of sugar was fixed by the Sugar Equalization Board of the U.S. Food Administration at 7.28 cents per pound.[25] This price held until 1919, when controls were removed and the domestic market governed by tariffs was restored. A constituency of domestic consumers developed that was opposed to import tariffs. By 1933, something had to be done to appease this powerful lobby. At the same time, the sugar industry proclaimed it was unlikely to survive if the tariffs were lifted. Foreign sugar, subsidized by bounties and slavelike labor, would drive domestic producers into bankruptcy. A compromise was sought.

The Jones-Costigan Bill amending the Agricultural Adjustment Act of 1933 established the basic concept that was perpetuated until 1974.[26] After provisions of this legislation were carried out by the Sugar Act of 1937, all domestic sugar was allocated an annual production quota determined each year by the Secretary of Agriculture.[27] Since domestic production was short of demand, foreign producer import quotas were also established annually by the Secretary. Domestic sugar prices were kept at a viable level year to year by quota allocations and the "law of supply and demand." Consumers got their sugar at a reasonable price and producers were assured of a stable market.

The costs of administering the sugar acts and making compliance payments were covered with a tax on refined sugar. "Conditional payments" of a fraction of one cent per pound were made to beet and cane sugar producers who complied with standards on wages, and employment. Hawai'i producers easily met the these standards. When the United States entered World War II in 1941, all quotas on sugar production were suspended for the duration and the price fixed at 3.74 cents per pound by the Office of Price Administration. This was not enough to cover production costs, so the Commodity Credit Corporation made "support payments" of 0.20 cents per pound in 1944, and 0.55 cents per pound in 1945.[28] The provisions of the Sugar Act were reinstated at the war's end.

The 1940 Sugar Act changed the quota allocations from percentages to fixed tonnages and otherwise retained the features of the 1937 act.[29] Opposition to import quotas grew, but the sugar industry could point to years of price stability under the act and a domestic production capability that survived. Finally, in 1974, the import quota opponents won out and the Sugar Act was defeated. Eight years of chaos for domestic sugar producers ensued.[30] Annual average prices varied wildly between 11.11 cents and 29.43 cents a pound. No industry could long survive in such an unstable environment, and the Agriculture and Food Act of 1981 (commonly called the "U. S. Farm Act") stabilized the situation. Eventually extended in 1985 and 1990, the Farm Act set price supports for domestic sugar. Import quotas were to be used to maintain at least the "market stabilization price" as determined by the Secretary of Agriculture. To protect sugar producers from unstable price reductions, the Commodity Credit Corporation would loan funds at a predetermined rate secured by the borrower's sugar. The initial rate was 17 cents per pound of sugar collateral, later increased to 18 cents.[31]

Under the Farm Act supports, Hawai'i sugar producers managed to have marginally profitable years. Plantations reduced costs by improving productivity, mechanizing to the greatest extent, and taking low-yielding lands out of cultivation. Many factors, including the pressures of urban sprawl, inordinate debt service, expiration of land leases, and low market prices led to the final reduction of Hawai'i plantations.

The history of sugar in the Islands had many examples of fending off the encroachments of foreign producers and domestic alternative sweeteners. The Hawai'i interests were represented in Washington from 1898 until 1996 by an officer of the HSPA. In 1997, along with other threats, he dealt with the tariff and quota-free importation of Mexican sugar. Today Mexico consumes almost all of the sugar it produces and exports next to nothing.[32] However, if the Mexican soft-drink industry converts to HFCS, Mexican sugar will be free to enter the U.S. marketplace unless the industry is protected by the provisions of NAFTA. Up to three million tons of Mexican sugar could enter the United States. But provisions were adopted that protect domestic sugar production with a 15-year quota system applied to Mexican sugar.

Cutting Sugar Cane, Hawaiian Islands. (Robert Van Dyke)

CHAPTER 15

SUGAR'S FUTURE IN HAWAI'I
(2000)

Sugar farming can survive in Hawai'i depending on price supports by the U.S. government and/or innovations by Hawai'i sugar farmers. For example, technology exists for on-site refining of the raw sugar produced at our mills. Such refined sugar will be as marketable as the sugar produced by the C & H refinery at Crockett, California, and cost less to produce. Refining at the mill saves money because of the consolidation of production processes.

Generating electricity by burning the bagasse is a proven technology, and there are possibilities for manufacturing high value by-products from low-value molasses. Chemical feedstocks can be extracted from bagasse. Forward-looking management, such as that at Gay & Robinson can survive and make money in sugarcane farming for a long, long time.

⊕ ⊕ ⊕

THE LAST DECADE of the twentieth century was important to anyone forecasting the future of Hawai'i's cane farmers. The sequence of events began in August of 1992, when C. Brewer & Company announced that the Hilo Coast Processing Company (HCPC) and Mauna Kea Sugar Company would close down following the 1994 harvest.[1] Barring unforeseeable circumstances, sugarcane will never again be cultivated in the wet South Hilo District. The reasons for this went back decades: after World War II, when mechanical harvesting replaced field workers and trucks replaced fluming, Hilo processors incurred costs 50 percent higher than their Hāmākua neighbors because of the mechanically harvested, untrimmed, wet, and dirty cane delivered to the mill.

The next jarring announcement came two weeks later, when Hamakua Sugar Company declared bankruptcy. A series of hearings resulted in the decision to close down following the harvesting of cane still in the fields.[2] The debt service incurred proved to be more than the company could bear when sugar prices declined.[3]

In September of 1992, Amfac/JMB-Hawai'i had announced a reorganization of Kekaha Sugar Company and Lihue Plantation Company.[4] Top management was streamlined and other personnel changes were made to cut costs. Along with an agreement between Lihue Plantation Company and Kaua'i Electric Company announced the following month regarding payments for electricity supplied by the plantation, this action strengthened the chances for its long-term survival.[5] Also in September, the HSPA announced a 14 percent cut in the number of employees because of reduced support.[6] Then Hurricane Iniki struck Kaua'i and destroyed up to 30 percent of the unharvested cane.[7]

In October of this fateful year, Kau Agribusiness Company announced a 10 percent reduction of employees.[8] This signaled that the end was near for the last plantation on the island of Hawai'i. In fact, it continued a little longer, but Kau Agribusiness harvested its last crop in 1996, and the mill was shut down.

In 1993 events seemed to take a turn for the better. In February, C & H Sugar Company announced it would replace its antiquated 'Aiea refinery with automated machinery to produce liquid sugar better suited to the needs of Hawai'i-based industrial users.[9] This proved to be a short-lived reprieve when the new refinery was shut down in 1996 after Hawai'i's soft-drink bottlers converted to HFCS.

Also in February of 1993, two key executives responded to the challenge to either convert to different crops or close down. James Andrasick, C. Brewer & Company officer and chairman of the Hawaiian Sugar Planters' Association, and John Couch, chairman of California & Hawaiian Sugar Company, declared: "It's a mistake to assume that sugar is not economically viable or that it has no role to play in Hawai'i's future…in the year 2000…sugar cane will still be producing 500,000 tons or more of raw sugar a year…."[10]

More good news followed. In March of 1993, Alexander & Baldwin, Inc. announced it was buying the interests of the other sugar producers in the cooperative C & H Sugar Company; a purchase completed in July of that year.[11] With this move, Alexander & Baldwin re-created the vertical integration first established by Claus Spreckels in 1881, when he incorporated his Oceanic Steamship Company to connect his Hawai'i plantations with his San Francisco refinery.[12] Alexander & Baldwin owns Matson Navigation Company and, with the operations of the sugar transports being managed by the shipping company, the re-creation would be complete.

Alexander & Baldwin is the largest Hawai'i sugar producer, and these changes signalled their determination to continue in the business for years to come. However, the consolidation had the curious effect of putting Alexander & Baldwin on the opposing side of sugar price supports. They preferred for import quotas to be increased in order to lower costs at their C & H refinery—and, if anything, the other Hawai'i producers wanted reduced quotas. In 1998 Alexander & Baldwin got back on the same side of the issue with the others when it sold its controlling interest in the C & H refinery.[13]

In early 1999 Amfac/JMB-Hawai'i announced it would close down its Pioneer Mill operations late in the summer.[14] This small, marginal plantation had been on the edge for years. But encouraging news for the industry in general came from another direction: in August 1999, manager Alan Kennett of Gay & Robinson announced their intention to add refining to their mill, and enter a niche market for specialty sugar when their contract to supply C & H expired in 2000.[15] Alexander & Baldwin followed suit with manager G. Stephen Holaday of H.C. & S. announcing a budget of several million dollars to modernize the Puʻunēnē mill to reduce operating costs, and produce specialty sugars. Plans for developing particle board from bagasse, discovering alternative uses for molasses, and conducting experiments to find a variety of cane suitable for one-year green harvesting were approved. The new cane would eliminate burning the fields before harvesting and be suitable for four to five years of ratoons.[16]

However, production for the 60-year period from 1932 through 1991 should be considered before turning to a projection of the future. Which plantations thrived and which showed mediocre results? Table 31 compares the tons of sugar produced per harvested acre in 1932 with the record for 1991.

TABLE 31 — GROWTH IN TONS OF SUGAR PER ACRE (TSA)

OWNER AND PLANTATION	ISLAND	TSA 1932	TSA 1991	PERCENT CHANGE
A & B Hawaiʻi, Inc.				
H.C.& S. Co.	Maui	10.69	2.35	+16%
McBryde Sugar	Kauaʻi	7.55	7.39	-2%
Amfac/JMB-Hawaiʻi				
Kekaha Sugar	Kauaʻi	8.40	11.36	+35%
Lihue Plantation	Kauaʻi	7.18	7.05	-2%
Oʻahu Sugar	Oʻahu	12.04	13.53	+12%
Pioneer Mill	Maui	9.30	12.87	+38%
C. Brewer & Co.				
Kau Agribusiness	Hawaiʻi	7.04	11.62	+65%
Mauna Kea Sugar	Hawaiʻi	5.83*	8.60	+48%
Olokele Sugar	Kauaʻi	10.53*	12.60	+20%
Dole Food Company				
Waialua Agri.	Oʻahu	10.46	10.60	+1%
Hamakua Sugar Co.				
Hamakua Sugar	Hawaiʻi	5.23*	10.38	+98%
Gay & Robinson				
Gay & Robinson	Kauaʻi	8.55	14.39	+68%
Average for all:		7.36	10.69	+45%

*Note: 1932 data used for Pepeekeo Sugar Company; Hawaiian Sugar Company and Hutchinson Sugar Plantation Company; and Honokaa Sugar Company, which were succeeded by Mauna Kea Sugar Company, Olokele Sugar Company, and Hamakua Sugar Company, respectively.

Data on Table 31 suggests some surprising conclusions.

First: despite 60 years of trying, McBryde Sugar Company and Lihue Plantation Company on Kaua'i and Waialua Sugar Company on O'ahu were unable to increase the tons of sugar per acre (TSA) yielded by their fields. This was particularly disturbing for the first two plantations, which had far below average yields. Either they were candidates for large improvements with new varieties of cane and improved agricultural practices, or were not likely to survive. (Indeed, by 1996 McBryde Sugar Company and Waialua Sugar Company had been closed down, and Lihue Plantation was marginally profitable.)

Second: As one example, O'ahu Sugar Company showed what could be done with irrigation water. O'ahu Sugar's TSA was high in both 1932 and 1991. (The plantation was closed down in 1995 because Amfac/JMB-Hawai'i was unable to renew land leases on favorable terms.)

Third: The smallest operations—Gay & Robinson, Olokele Sugar, and Pioneer Mill—showed improvement in TSA and had above-average yields each year. "Bigger is better" was not necessarily true when it came to TSA. (Pioneer Mill's small size eventually led to its closing in 1999.)

Fourth: The increase in TSA shown by Hamakua Sugar Company exemplified what was achievable through ever-improving field technology. (The high expense of debt service led to bankruptcy in 1992.)

With respect to the future of Hawaiian sugar, domestic policy and trade agreements can be conclusive. However, assuming that whatever policies and agreements are adopted will protect domestic sugar producers, Hawai'i will produce sugar into the indefinite future for four reasons:

1. You can make money producing sugar in Hawai'i.
2. Sugar helps Hawai'i move closer to energy self-sufficiency.
3. Sugarcane bolsters Hawai'i's tourist industry.
4. A satisfactory substitute crop is hard to find.

YOU CAN MAKE MONEY PRODUCING SUGAR IN HAWAI'I

The United States must continue to import sugar to satisfy its voracious appetite. Domestic production falls short of demand. Beet sugar costs about the same per pound to produce as cane sugar. It is possible that government protection will change to the extent that domestic beet and cane producers are driven under by price reductions. However, beet sugar producers are allied with cane sugar producers, and the operations of both affect the economies of 32 states.[17]

Alexander & Baldwin has shown that Hawaiian sugar is profitable if the organization is well run. In 1987 they reported healthy profits on their sugar operations in a year when the majority reported losses, and did it despite the low figures of McBryde Sugar Company.[18] McBryde's land was being planted in coffee and macadamia nuts, with sugar cultivation reduced year to year. By 1991, there were 7,015 acres in cane, 4,850 in coffee, and 580 in macadamia trees.[19] In

1987 McBryde sold 18.2 million kwh to Kaua'i Electric Company, representing 6.6 percent of the island's total sales, but these disappeared in 1996, when McBryde was shut down.[20]

A 1987 position paper prepared under the direction of Dr. Don Heinz, Director of the HSPA's Experiment Station, stated unequivocally, "...Hawaiian sugar is and will continue to be an important economic force for years to come...."[21] The evidence supports this bold statement.

SUGAR HELPS HAWAI'I BECOME ENERGY SELF-SUFFICIENT

In 1994, 10 percent of Hawai'i's electricity was generated by the sugarmills burning bagasses. As long as Hawai'i grinds cane, the state will have a supply of electricity. Ethanol has been manufactured in Hawai'i from molasses, and is a proven technology. In the past it was treated as a curiosity because the production cost per gallon exceeded that for gasoline. But this situation is changing, and there will be an economic incentive to switch first to "gasahol" (10 percent ethanol and 90 percent gasoline), and later to 100 percent ethanol. Hawai'i is a likely state to first make this switch because of its insular geography. What's required is awareness in both the state government and the public. This will come when gasoline costs about $2.50 a gallon at the pump.

SUGARCANE BOLSTERS HAWAI'I'S VISITOR INDUSTRY

Survey the scene on Maui from the heights near Makawao. Imagine how it would change if the pleasant green and weedless fields were replaced with scrub, ragged mesquite, and patches of trash dumped by the careless. Would you return to look upon such a scene? I think not.

It is impossible to reconstuct the beauty of Kaua'i without including the lush green fields of cane. And one needs only to visit Kahuku and Waialua on O'ahu, and North Hilo, Hāmākua and Puna on the Big Island to see the contrast that develops when sugarcane leaves a community.

Hawai'i's mystique, which helps to draw the inquisitive visitor, includes sugarcane in the past and the present. What a new visitor anticipates may no longer be there but what remains of the industry is sufficient to satisfy. Sugarcane, for the visitor, is part of Hawai'i's heritage. In recognition of this, for years Amfac/JMB-Hawai'i tolerated indifferent profits from Pioneer Mill, which borders Amfac's Ka-'anapali development and provides a pleasant green background with a resurrected cane haul railroad for scenic excursions. As its former chairman Henry Walker said, "Sugar has value as a ground cover if nothing else."[22] However, Pioneer Mill is more than ground cover. In the words of Dr. Thomas Hitch, "Sugarcane is an economic asset just standing in the field and waving in the breeze."[23]

A SATISFACTORY SUBSTITUTE CROP IS HARD TO FIND

The Kingdom of Hawai'i began a search for crops when the Royal Agricultural Society was formed in 1850. There has been no more persistent myth than that something better than sugar exists for Hawai'i's 250,000 tillable acres. Millions have been spent by the Kingdom, Territory, state and federal governments, universities, planters, and the HSPA in search of that perfect crop. Consider an important economic fact: Hawai'i is 2,300 miles from the closest continental market, and Matson Navigation Company's rate for bulk transport of commodities from Honolulu to San Francisco is about $58.80 per ton.[24] To put this in perspective, that amount is more than mainland farmers pay to transport their crops to the market, and the shipping cost just gets the Hawai'i crop to the starting point.

Since 1971, Hawai'i's sugar plantations have given up more than 120,000 acres. Only a small fraction has been successfully planted in another profitable crop. In 1987 there was a total of 34,200 acres in coffee, macadamia nuts, papaya, bananas, and guava.[25] That's about as much as the export market could absorb at the premium prices Hawai'i producers must charge to show a profit after expenses, including shipping costs.

There's another myth to deal with: Why not grow all our own produce here in Hawai'i? Surely that would occupy the acreage. Not so. Take potatoes, for example. With the growing number of fast-food outlets selling french fries, surely Hawai'i consumes an impossible number of potatoes. Not so. The possibility has been studied several times. A study completed in 1984 found that 2,000 acres of potatoes would be adequate for 1985 consumption.[26] Quadruple that amount and you still fall far short of the 155,000 acres planted in cane in 1991. Sugarcane farming fits Hawai'i's circumstances better than any alternative crop because of regulatory protection and the marvelous economies achieved by Hawai'i's sugar producers.

SUMMING UP—THE FUTURE OF SUGAR IN HAWAI'I

There can be no doubt that the Hawai'i sugar industry is in a weakened state. Any one of a number of events could finish it off: removal of price supports and import barriers, diseases or insect damage resulting in one year or more of crop failures; a last round of demands for increased wages and benefits. The industry has also approached the limits of substituting machinery for workers.

Assuming such catastrophic events are avoided, an estimate was made of the tons of sugar likely to be produced in the year 2000. This estimate is subjective and takes into account the author's judgment as to the number of acres in cultivation. The possibility that one plantation, say, Kekaha Sugar Company, might give up land to neighboring Gay & Robinson is factored in.

TABLE 32 | **ESTIMATED SUGAR PRODUCTION IN HAWAI'I IN 2000**

OWNER/PLANTATION	1991 ACRES	1991 TONS	PROB. GIVE-UP*	PROB. EXIST*	PROBABLE* 2000 CROP
Alexander & Baldwin					
H.C.& S. Co.	35,857	214,122	0	1.0	214,122
Amfac/JMB-Hawai'i					
Kekaha Sugar	8,294	40,770	0.1	0.9	36,693
Lihue Plantation	11,220	49,133	0.5	0.5	24,566
Gay & Robinson					
Olokele lands	4,716	29,042	0	1.0	29,042
Original lands	2,747	19,047	0	1.0	19,047
Totals	69,482	377,977			323,470 tons

*Note: Probability of existence (in year 2000)=1-probability that acreage was given up (by year 2000). Probable crop (in year 2000)=year 1991 crop times probability of existence (in year 2000). Gay & Robinson purchased Olokele Sugar Company's mill and harvesting equipment in 1993.

In 1900, 289,544 tons of sugar were produced; in 1901, 360,033 tons of sugar were produced. In Table 32 the estimated 323,470 tons falls between the 289,544 tons produced in 1900 and the 360,038 tons produced in 1901. Sugar was king in 1901, but today the income from such an output is far overshadowed by the income from the combined sales of other crops, the military, and the visitor industry.

The Hawai'i sugar industry can survive for a long time and grow, helped by refining raw sugar at the mill and/or by production of ethanol motor fuel and other by-products. Whether or not it actually survives depends on public support and farsighted management by the industry, state and federal governments, and the labor unions. The Hawai'i sugar industry will continue if the citizens of the state want it to survive.

Wai'anae, O'ahu, Hawai'i
(Hawai'i State Archives)

APPENDIX A | MONARCHS AND MISSIONARIES

MONARCHS

Monarch	Born	Died	Reign From	To
Kamehameha I	1758?	1819	1795	1819
Kamehameha II	1797	1824	1819	1824
Kamehameha III	1813	1854	1824	1854
Kamehameha IV	1834	1863	1855	1863
Kamehameha V	1830	1872	1863	1872
William C. Lunalilo	1832	1874	1873	1874
David Kalākaua	1836	1891	1874	1891
Lili'uokalani	1838	1917	1891	1893

The Republic of Hawai'i was formed on July 4, 1894 and Hawai'i was annexed to the United States on July 7, 1898. Territorial government began on June 14, 1900, with Sanford Ballard Dole as the first governor. March 18, 1959, President Dwight D. Eisenhower signed the enabling act making Hawai'i the 50th state to be admitted to the United States.

MISSIONARIES

The American Board of Commissioners for Foreign Missions sent 12 companies of Congregationalist missionaries to Hawai'i between 1820 and 1848. The majority stayed and settled in Hawai'i and many of them and their descendants played key roles in O'ahu's history down to the present.

First Company: Arrived March 21, 1820
Rev. and Mrs. Hiram Bingham, Rev. and Mrs. Asa Thurston, Dr. and Mrs. Thomas Holman, Mr. and Mrs. Samuel Whitney, Mr. and Mrs. Samuel Ruggles, Mr. and Mrs. Elisha Loomis, Mr. and Mrs. Daniel Chamberlain and five children. Native Hawaiians John Honolii, Thomas Hopu, William Kenui, and George Kaumuali'i, prince of Kauai, sailed with the company.

Second Company: Arrived April 27, 1823
Rev. and Mrs. Artemas Bishop, Mr. and Mrs. Abraham Bratchley, Mr. and Mrs. James Ely, Mr. and Mrs. Joseph Goodrich, Rev. and Mrs. William Richards, Rev. and Mrs. Charles S. Stewart, Miss Betsey Stockton, Mr. Stephen Popohe, Mr. William Kamooua, Mr. Richard Kalaialu, Mr. Kupelii.

Third Company: Arrived March 30, 1828
Rev. and Mrs. Lorrin Andrews, Rev. and Mrs. Ephriam W. Clark, Rev. and Mrs. Johnathon S. Green, Rev. and Mrs. Peter J. Gulick, Dr. and Mrs. Gerritt P. Judd, Miss Maria Ogden, Miss Maria Patten, Miss Delia Stone,

Miss Mary Ward, Mr. and Mrs. Stephen Shepard, Mr. Henry Tahiti, Mr. Tyler Mills, and Mr. Phelps.

Fourth Company: Arrived June 7, 1831
Rev. and Mrs. Dwight Baldwin, Rev. and Mrs. Sheldon Dibble, Mr. and Mrs. Andrew Johnstone, and Rev. and Mrs. Rueben Tinker.

Fifth Company: Arrived May 17, 1832
Rev. and Mrs. William P. Alexander, Rev. and Mrs. Richard Armstrong, Dr. and Mrs. Alonzo Chapin, Rev. and Mrs. John S. Emerson, Rev. and Mrs. Cochran Forbes, Rev. and Mrs. David B. Lyman, Rev. and Mrs. Lorenzo Lyons, Mr. Edmund H. Rogers, Rev. and Mrs. Harvey Hitchcock, Rev. and Mrs. Ephraim Spaulding.

Sixth Company: Arrived May 1, 1833
Rev. and Mrs. John Diell, Rev. and Mrs. Benjamin W. Parker, Rev. and Mrs. Lowell Smith.

Seventh Company: Arrived June 6, 1835
Miss Lydia Brown, Rev. and Mrs. Titus Coan, Mr. and Mrs. Henry Dimond, Mr. and Mrs. Edwin O. Hall, and Miss Elizabeth M. Hitchcock.

Eighth Company: Arrived April 9, 1837
Dr. and Mrs. Seth L. Andrews, Mr. and Mrs. Edward Bailey, Rev. and Mrs. Isaac Bliss, Mr. and Mrs. Samuel N. Castle, Mr. and Mrs. Amos S. Cooke, Rev. and Mrs. Mark Ives, Mr. and Mrs. Edward Johnson, Mr. and Mrs. Horton O. Knapp, Dr. and Mrs. Thomas Lafon, Mr. and Mrs. Edwin Locke, Mr. and Mrs. Charles McDonald, Mr. and Mrs. Bethuel Munn, Miss Marcia M. Smith, Miss Lucia G. Smith, Mr. and Mrs. William S. Van Duzee, and Mr. and Mrs. Abner Wilcox.

Ninth Company: Arrived May 21, 1841
Rev. and Mrs. Elias Bond, Rev. and Mrs. Daniel Dole, Rev. and Mrs. John D. Paris, and Mr. and Mrs. William H. Rice.

Tenth Company: Arrived September 21, 1842
Rev. and Mrs. George B. Rowell and Dr. and Mrs. James W. Smith.

Eleventh Company: Arrived July 14, 1844
Rev. and Mrs. Claudius B. Andrews, Rev. and Mrs. Timothy D. Hunt, Rev. John F. Pogue, Miss Maria K. Whitney, and Rev. and Mrs. Eliphalet Whittlesey.

Twelfth Company: Arrived February 26, 1848
Rev. Samuel G. Dwight, and Rev. and Mrs. Henry Kinney.

Not every missionary came from Boston. Some served elsewhere before arriving in Hawai'i. These included:

From New York: Arrived in 1842, Rev. and Mrs. Samuel C. Damon;

From Tahiti: Arrived on February 4, 1822, Rev. William Ellis;

From Oregon: Arrived on September 21, 1843, Rev. and Mrs. Asa R. Smith; arrived on May 11, 1849, Dr. and Mrs. Charles H. Wetmore; arrived on October 20, 1854, Rev. and Mrs. William C. Shipman; arrived on March 31, 1855, Rev. and Mrs. William O. Baldwin and Mr. and Mrs. William A. Spooner, on March 31, 1855; Rev. and Mrs. Anderson Forbes arrived in 1868; Rev. and Mrs. Cyrus T. Mills arrived in 1860; Rev. and Mrs. S.E. Bishop arrived in 1862; Rev. and Mrs. William DeWitt Alexander arrived in 1865; Rev. and Mrs. O.P. Emerson arrived in 1889; and Rev. and Mrs. John Leadingham arrived in 1894.

⊕ ⊕ ⊕

My great-great-grandfather, Dr. Gerrit P. Judd, arrived in Hawai'i in 1828 as a medical doctor attached to the third company of missionaries. While it was his original intent to train for the ministry, to save time he came as a medical man and not to preach the gospel.

Doctor Judd had just finished medical school when he learned of the search for a physician to accompany a mission to the Sandwich Islands. He was intrigued, saw an opportunity to do good, and applied to the Board of Missions. He passed the interview but was told that before he was hired they must also interview his wife, to be certain she was right for the circumstances. This surprised him. At the time he didn't even have a girlfriend, much less a wife. He commiserated with a friend about the situation. There wasn't much time to lose because the mission was due to leave within weeks. His friend told him he knew of a good family in upstate New York who had an unmarried daughter (actually, a niece) who was interested in the mission and might be a candidate for Doctor Judd. A visit was arranged and Judd got on his horse and rode to visit the family.

The meeting was a success. Miss Laura Fish agreed to marry Doctor Judd, and she was interviewed and found to meet all specifications. They were soon man and wife. The family that had raised her received a letter on the eve of her departure with the mission. This letter was passed down in the family to my mother, and I read it myself. In it the young woman was effusive in praise to her family for the protective care and consideration she had experienced in their custody. She thanked them for her upbringing (her parents had died when she was very young), and regretted that they would never see each other again. Yet, she expressed enthusiasm for the adventure to come and was happy to be part of it.

The sentence that I particularly remember was the last: "...and I really think I'm going to like my young doctor." And so she did. Doctor and Mrs. Judd raised nine children who were all born in Hawai'i.

APPENDIX B | SUGAR PRICES

For years there was no statistic more closely followed by Hawaii's sugar men than the "New York price," that is, what was paid for raw sugar containing 96 percent sucrose delivered on the dock at New York. Until C & H became a cooperative in 1921, this index helped determine what was paid for the product sold by each plantation. "What's the price of sugar today?" was as good a way to greet a co-worker as asking, "How are you?"

TABLE B.1 | **FIVE-YEAR AVERAGE NEW YORK DOMESTIC SUGAR PRICES**

YEARS	SUGAR CENTS/LB.	YEARS	SUGAR CENTS/LB.	YEARS	SUGAR CENTS/LB.
1840-44	2.0	1895-99	3.13	1945-49	5.19
1845-49	4.42	1900-04	3.84	1950-54	6.13
1850-59*	6.95	1905-09	3.96	1955-59	6.16
1862-63*	9.25	1910-14	4.01	1960-64	6.83
1863-69*	10.00	1915-19	6.16	1965-69	7.26
1872*	6.00	1920-24	6.94	1970-74	13.09
1875-79	6.00	1925-29	4.28	1975-79	15.17
1880-84	5.89	1930-34	3.17	1980-84	20.64
1885-89	4.70	1935-39	3.24	1985-89	21.57
1890-94	3.35	1940-44	3.47	1990-94	21.95

*Note: Prices for continuous five-year interval not available.
Sources: HSPA: HSPA, Sugar Manual 1965-95; Jarves; Sullivan; Thrum, Hawaiian Annual 1900-1929; Thurston.

Sugar was exported to California tariff-free until it became a U.S. Territory in 1848; then, until the Reciprocity Treaty of 1876 took effect, Hawaii producers paid an ad valorem import tariff on all sugar imported into the United States. This tariff made the period from 1848 to 1876 difficult for Hawaii sugar farmers, but the Reciprocity Treaty removed it.

In 1907 the C & H sugar refining corporation was formed. From then until 1921, C & H Hawaii's plantations were paid according to a formula tied to the New York price. In 1914, for example, the amount paid by C & H was the New York price less one-quarter of a cent per pound for sugar delivered in San Francisco, the difference accounting for freight costs between New York and San Francisco. During this period, the New York price determined the plantation's raw sugar income.

In 1922 the C & H corporation converted to an agricultural cooperative, and, until 1993, the plantations were paid based on the price received by C & H for its refined sugar product. In several years the competing production of beet sugar and high-fructose corn syrup drove the prices C & H paid to the plantations lower than New York prices. This situation prevailed during the troubled years of Hamakua Sugar Company.

All outside shares of C & H were purchased in 1993 by Alexander & Baldwin, which became the corporation's sole owner. The plantations then received a price equal to the New York price less (in 1996) $25.00 per ton (0.125 cents per pound). In 1998, Alexander & Baldwin sold controlling shares of C & H, putting them back on the side of advocates for sugar price supports.

⊕ ⊕ ⊕

During the life of Hamakua Sugar Company and its predecessor, the C & H refinery operated as an agricultural cooperative owned by the Hawai'i plantations. The price paid to Hawai'i's producers was equal to the price received by C & H for its refined sugar less refining, shipping, administrative, and marketing costs. During this time, the price paid by C & H did not necessarily track the so-called "New York" price of raw sugar because mainland beet sugar and high-fructose corn syrup sales adversely affected the prices paid for C & H-produced sugar. At best, the New York price indicated approximately what C & H should be paying the plantations.

APPENDIX C | HOW SUGAR IS MANUFACTURED

The methods for extracting sucrose from sugar beets and sugarcane differ in several respects. Refined sugar results directly from the beet sugar processing, whereas the raw sugar produced by Hawai'i's mills must be sent to a refinery for processing. Raw sugar from cane is extracted by grinding mills, and from beets by slicing them into small portions and immersing them in hot water, where the sucrose diffuses. Although cane sugar can also be extracted by the diffusion process, the majority of Hawai'i sugar factories employ and have employed the grinding process described here.

Harvested cane is currently delivered to the mill in trucks or tournahaulers (step 1 on the flow-sheet of Figure C.1). While cane can stand in the mill yard for a few hours awaiting processing, it must be processed within eight hours after harvesting before spoiling (fermenting). Since all Hawai'i cane is mechanically harvested, the delivered cane contains dirt, rocks, trash, and scrap metal. The cane is floated across a vat to remove rocks, placed on a conveyor that passes by a powerful magnet to remove metal, and then through a cane washer to remove soil and trash. The cane stalks then enter the processing stream and encounter rotary knives and shredders that prepare a uniform blanket as feed to the grinding mills (step 2).

FIGURE C.1 Steps involved in making raw sugar in a conventional grinding mill.

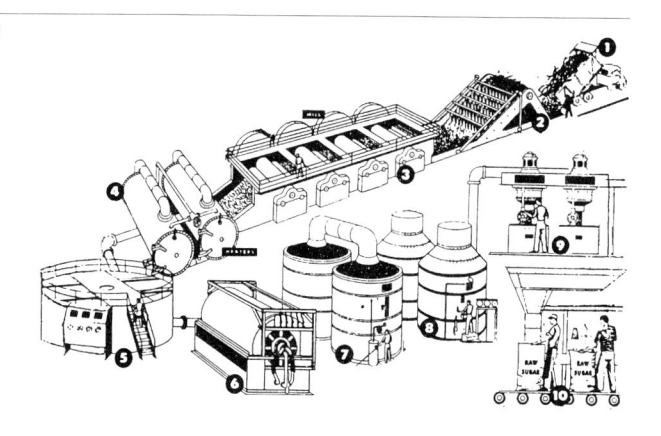

The mill consists of a tandem array of groups of three or five grooved rollers that squeeze out the juice with pressure being applied by the upper rollers. From three to six such groups may make up the stream (step 3). Water ("macerating water") or cane juice is applied to the cane entering the second and succeeding groups of grinders to assist the sugar extraction. The juice drains to collection pans under the processing stream and is sent to the clarification step. The fibrous material exiting the mill is bagasse, and is sent to a bagasse house and burned in the factory's boilers.

The next stage consists of clarification, evaporation, boiling, and centrifuging. Clarification begins when the juices are heated and precipitating agents, including milk of lime, are added to the juice as it is passed to a clarification tank (steps 4 and 5). Many of the impurities precipitate out in these tanks. The settlings or "mud" are vacuum-filtered to recover juices that are returned to the stream (step 6). The clarified juice goes on to the evaporators.

In the evaporators the juices are heated under vacuum to evaporate the water (step 7). Water in a vacuum can be boiled at lower temperatures and thus avoids damaging the sugar. The evaporators are a series of interconnected vessels and, depending on their number, are called triple, quadruple, and quintuple effect evaporators. As the juice passes from one vessel to the next, the hot vapor from the first vessel provides the heat for the second vessel, thus economizing on steam. The juice enters the first evaporator containing perhaps 14 percent sugar and exits the last evaporator containing about 56 percent sugar.

Next, boiling is done in "vacuum pans" that are essentially single-effect evaporators (step 8). The juice-thickening process proceeds in the pan and, under careful control of temperature and vacuum, a supersaturated solution is created and sugar crystals are introduced that cause additional sugar crystals to form and multiply. This is done automatically in modern factories. It used to be that the wisdom and skill of the sugar boiler came into play at this point. He would periodically withdraw small samples to examine them under a microscope. When he observed that tiny crystals had grown to the proper size, he "made a strike," that is, emptied the pan. The resulting mixture of sugar crystals and molasses, called "massecuite," is cooled while being stirred with paddles.

The cooled massecuite is delivered to the centrifugal machines, where the sugar crystals are separated from the molasses. The mixture is spun at high rpm within a three-to-six-foot diameter perforated basket (step 9). The molasses and any washings go out through the perforations and the sugar crystals, golden brown in color and 93 to 97 percent sucrose, drop onto a conveyor that takes them to bulk storage (step 10). The molasses contains some sugar and is recycled back to a vacuum pan to repeat the process. This repetition sometimes occurs twice. For example, the South Africans use the crystals produced by the second (B) and third (C) strikes as the crystals introduced in the first (A) strike of this process. Since the sequence produces increasingly lean (of sugar content) molasses, two types of centrifugals are used, one for high-grade and the other for low-grade molasses. The raw sugar produced by Hawai'i's mills is shipped in bulk to the refinery.

The grinding mills are driven by Corliss steam engines or turbines. Giant flywheels and reducing gears are used with the engines, and reducing gears are used with the turbines in order to connect them with the grinders at lower revolutions. Steam to run the apparatus, pumps, juice heaters, conveyors, and electrical generators is produced in boilers heated by burning bagasse, sometimes trash, and sometimes oil. The electricity generated supplies the mill and any excess is sold to the local electric utilities by all but one of Hawai'i's grinding sugarmills.

Until the refinery shut down in 1996, some of the raw sugar was refined at the C & H refinery at 'Aiea, O'ahu, for sale to Hawai'i-based consumers. Two kinds of refined sugar were produced: crystallized, bagged sugar and liquid sugar. However, the vast majority of the raw sugar was, and now all of it is, shipped to the C & H refinery at Crockett, California, or to other mainland refineries when the Crockett refinery capacity is exceeded. The economies of scale favor the much larger Crockett refinery's product in the Hawai'i market.

The refining process repeats many of the post-clarification steps described above and adds a color-removing step using ion exchange, bone char filtering, or other impurity-removing processes.

Visitors to O'ahu have a rare opportunity to inspect mill machinery at close hand. The Kahuku Plantation Company sugarmill in northern O'ahu was shut down in November 1971. A concerned group of citizens initiated its preservation and the construction of a shopping center around it. Much of the mill remains intact. The machinery was cleaned up and painted, and placards were placed to explain the function of each piece.

⊕ ⊕ ⊕

We used the latest available technology when we rebuilt our Haina mill. A topping turbine was incorporated to generate electricity to be sold to the local utility. Our extra-large boiler produced very high pressure steam that could be used to generate electricity before the steam exiting the turbine was used to run the mill and supply heat to the boiling house. The increased capacity allowed us to sign a contract with the local utility to supply firm power at a higher payment rate than was paid for dump power.

The improved boiling house concepts used by the South Africans to produce higher quality sugar were also incorporated. I included an accommodation so refining could be easily added when the time came for it. But our exclusive C & H contract had over a decade to run when we had to shut down.

I have been asked why Hawai'i producers never refined their sugar at the factories in the first place. Doing so would have saved on refined sugar production costs and improved the competitive sales position versus beet sugar prices. The answer is simple. For decades the mainland refineries were successful in getting a law passed that forbade the importation of refined sugar into the United States. By the time this law was negated, bulk shipping of the raw sugar was standard, the planters had invested in a two-ship bulk sugar transport company, and were tied down with a long-term contract with the C & H refinery. Contracts with C & H run from 15 to 20 years.

GLOSSARY

Abbreviations

C & H	California & Hawaiian Sugar Company (Crockett, refinery)
HARC	Hawaii Agriculture Research Center (successor to HSPA)
H.C.& S.	Hawaiian Commercial & Sugar Company
HCPC	Hilo Coast Processing Company
HFCS	High-Fructose Corn Syrup
HIW	Honolulu Iron Works
HSPA	Hawaiian Sugar Planters' Association
HSTC	Hawaiian Sugar Transport Company
ILWU	International Longshoremen's and Warehousemen's Union
NAFTA	North American Free Trade Agreement
O.R.& L.	Oahu Railway & Land Company
Sc.D.	Doctor of Science, an academic graduate degree.
(WHD)	William Henry Dorrance
(FSM)	Francis Swanzy Morgan

Hawaiian Words and Phrases

Ahupua‘a	Land division
Aloha	Love, greetings, affection
Ali‘i	Royalty: chiefs, high and low
Hāpai kō	Lifting sugarcane; i.e. loading it onto a cane hauler
Kama‘āina	Born of the land
Kuleana	Small parcel of land
Luna	Field supervisor, foreman, or boss
Mahele	Dividing up of the land
Pau hana	End of work day

Words Often Used in the Sugar Industry

Bagasse	Residue remaining after sugarcane has been milled.
Massecuite	Dense mass of sugar crystals within mother liquor obtained by evaporation.
Molasses	Mother liquor within massecuite.
Ratoons	Second and succeeding crops of cane grown from roots of previous growth.
Sucrose	Commonly known as sugar.

CHAPTER NOTES

Chapter 1 | AN OVERVIEW OF SUGAR IN HAWAI'I

1. Hawaiian Sugar Planters' Association, *Hawaiian Sugar Manual 1995*, Hawaiian Sugar Planters' Association, 'Aiea, Hawai'i, 1995, p. 11.
2. Hass, H. B., "Sugar," The World Book Encyclopedia Volume 16, Field Enterprises Educational Corporation, Chicago, 1960, p. 770.
3. Galloway, J. H., *The Sugar Cane Industry*, Cambridge University Press, Cambridge, U.K., 1989, pp. 31-119.
4. Cushing, Robert L., "The Beginnings of Sugar Production in Hawai'i," *The Hawaiian Journal of History*, Vol. XIX, 1985, p. 18.
5. Cook, James, *A Voyage to the Pacific Ocean-in His Majesty's Ships the Resolution and Discovery; in the years 1776, 1777, 1778, 1779, and 1780*, Vol. II, G. Nicol and T, Cadell, 1784 pp. 192, 193, and 244. See also Cushing, op. cit.
6. Barratt, Glynn, *The Russian Discovery of Hawaii*, Editions Limited, Honolulu, 1987, p. 138.
7. Wilfong, George W., "Sugar Plantations in the Early Days in the Hawaiian Islands," *The Planters' Monthly*, Honolulu, December 1882, p. 228.
8. Damon, Ethel M., "Father Bond of Kohala," *The Friend*, Honolulu, 1927, p. 52.
9. Baldwin, Henry P., "Sugar and Hawaii," *The Mid-Pacific*, August 1928 (reprint), p. 133.
10. Thrum, Thos. G., *Hawaiian Almanac and Annual*, Black & Auld, printer, 1876.
11. *The Friend*, Honolulu, August 9, 1862, p. 58.
12. Jarves, James Jackson, *History of the Hawaiian Islands*, Henry M. Whitney, Pub., 1872, p. 205.
13. Whitney, Caspar, "Hawaiian Sugar Industry," *The Planters' Monthly*, Honolulu, August 1899, pp. 367-368.
14. Hawaiian Sugar Planters' Association, *Hawaiian Sugar Manual 1991*, 'Aiea, Hawaii, 1991.
15. Thrum, Thos. G., Hawaiian Annual: *All About Hawaii*, Black & Auld, Printer, Honolulu, 1901.
16. Smith, Kit, "Isle business leader Malcolm MacNaughton dies," *Honolulu Advertiser,* December 31, 1992, p. A2.
17. Department of Geography, *Atlas of Hawaii,* University of Hawai'i Press, Honolulu, 1983, p. 107.
18. Nellist, George F., "The Story of Hawaii and Its Builders," *Honolulu Star-Bulletin*, Inc., Honolulu, 1925, p. 45.

Chapter 2 | SUGAR IN HAWAI'I BEFORE RECIPROCITY

1. Thrum, *Hawaiian Almanac*, 1875, p. 39.
2. Jarves, *History of the Hawaiian Islands*, p. 205.
3. Judd, Gerrit P., *The Friend*, Feb. 1867, Enclosure No. 3.
4. Kuykendall, Ralph S., *The Hawaiian Kingdom 1778-1854*, Vol. 1, University Press of Hawai'i, Honolulu, 1938, pp. 327-328.

5. Thrum, pp. 84-85. See also, Cushing, "The Beginnings of Sugar Production in Hawaii," pp. 19-24.
6. Gast, Ross H., *Don Francisco de Paula Marin; a Biography*, University Press of Hawai'i, Honolulu, 1973, pp. 136-145.
7. ibid., p. 228.
8. Kuykendall, *Hawaiian Kingdom 1778-1854*, p. 172. See also, Cushing, pp. 29-30.
9. Ii, John Papa, *Fragments of Hawaiian History*, Bishop Museum Press, Honolulu, 1959, p. 145.
10. ibid., p. 147.
11. Kuykendall, *Hawaiian Kingdom 1778-1854*, p. 173. See Pauline N. King, (Editor), *Journal of Stephen Reynolds* Volume 1 1823-1829, Ku Paa Incorporated, Honolulu, and The Peabody Museum of Salem, Salem, Massachussetts, 1989, pp. 177, 189, 245, 254, 295, 261 and 267 for brief accounts of the Mānoa mill operations under Reynolds' and French's stewardship.
12. Char, Wai-Jane, "Three Chinese Stores in Honolulu," *The Hawaiian Journal of History*, Volume VIII, 1974, p. 14.
13. Thrum, 1875, p. 35.
14. *Polynesian*, May 29, 1841.
15. Char, pp. 16-19. See also, Silva, Alvin K. (Ed.), "Wailuku Sugar Company 1862 November 1962 Centennial," Wailuku Sugar Company, Wailuku, Maui, 1962, pp. 9-10.
16. Day, A. Grove, *History Makers of Hawaii*, Mutual Publishing of Honolulu, Honolulu, 1984, p. 46.
17. Alexander, Arthur C., *Koloa Plantation 1835-1935*, Kauai Historical Society, Līhu'e, Kaua'i, 1937, pp. 5-6.
18. Char, p. 15.
19. Kai, Peggy, "Chinese Settlers in the Village of Hilo Before 1852," *The Hawaiian Journal of History*, Volume VIII, 1974, pp. 44, 54. See also, Damon, *Father Bond*, pp. 72, 73.
20. ibid., p. 56.
21. ibid., p. 58.
22. Lydgate, J.M., *Hawaiian Annual*, 1918, pp. 74-76. See also, Isabella L. Bird, *Six Months in the Sandwich Islands*, Charles E. Tuttle Company, Rutland Vermont, seventh edition, pp. 74-78, for a graphic description of sugar making in the 1870s on the Hilo Coast.
23. Kuykendall, *Hawaiian Kingdom 1778-1854*, p. 199-202.
24. Char, p. 34.
25. ibid., p. 33.
26. Wilfong, *The Planters' Monthly*, p. 148.
27. ibid.
28. Baldwin, Henry P., "Sugar and Hawaii," *Mid Pacific* (reprint), August, 1928, p. 137.
29. Sullivan, Josephine, *A History of C. Brewer & Company 1826-1926*, Walton Advertising & Printing Company, Boston, 1926, pp. 111-112.
30. Wilfong, *The Planters' Monthly*, p. 227.
31. Char, p. 14.

32. Cushing, "The Beginning of Sugar Production," p. 22.
33. Gilman, Gorman D., "Streets of Honolulu in the Early Forties," *Hawaiian Annual,* Thrum, Honolulu, 1904, pp. 74, 79. Gorham D. Gilman (1821-1909) was a member of a New England seafaring family who worked his way to Hawai'i in 1841 as a seaman. He stayed on for several years working in the sugar industry including as manager of Koloa Plantation for several months in 1848. He then spent some 12 years in the islands as a merchant and shipping agent before returning to Massachusetts about 1860. See, for example, Alfons L. Korn, *The Victorian Visitors,* The University of Hawai'i Press, Honolulu, 1958, n.10, pp. 314-315. Upon his return to Massachusetts Gilman became a prolific contributor of Hawai'i-based articles to Boston and New York newspapers. For a time he was president of the Hawaii Club of Boston and served as the Kingdom's consul there for a time. See, Kuykendall, *Hawaiian Kingdom 1778-1854,* p. 633. A later member of this family, Joseph Atherton Gilman (1891-1983), became Hawai'i's first All-American football player when named to Walter Camp's 1915 team while attending Harvard University.
34. Kuykendall, *Hawaiian Kingdom 1778-1854,* p. 329.
35. Beechert, Edward D., *Working in Hawaii A Labor History,* University of Hawai'i Press, Honolulu, 1985, p. 63.
36. Sterling, Elspeth P., and Catherine C. Summers, *Sites of Oahu,* Bishop Museum Press, Honolulu, 1978, p. 179.
37. Judd.
38. Nellist, *Hawaii and Its Builders,* 1925, p.187.
39. ibid.

Chapter 3 | SUGAR ON KAUA'I (1876-2000)

1. Hawaiian Sugar Planters' Association, *Hawaiian Sugar Manual 1991,* HSPA, 'Aiea, Hawai'i, 1991.
2. Kuykendall, *Hawaiian Kingdom 1778-1854,* pp. 49-51.
3. Alexander, *Koloa Plantation,* pp. 1-24.
4. ibid.
5. ibid., pp. 45-70.
6. ibid., pp. 48-49. By 1884 the manager's salary was $3,000 per annum and by 1912 it was $5,000 per annum. ibid., pp. 86, 147.
7. Alexander, *Koloa Plantation,* p. 48.
8. Wilfong, *The Planters' Monthly,* 1882, pp. 312-313.
9. ibid., p. 245. See also, Krauss, Bob and William P. Alexander, *Grove Farm Plantation The Biography of a Hawaiian Sugar Plantation,* Pacific Books, Palo Alto, California, second edition, 1984, p. 367.
10. Day, *History Makers,* p. 104. See also, Damon, Ethel M., *Koamalu A Story of Pioneers on Kauai and of What They Built in that Island Garden,* Vol. 1, Privately Printed, Star-Bulletin Press, Honolulu, 1931, pp. 367, 408 et.seq.
11. Hawaiian Sugar Planters' Association, *Hawaiian Sugar Manual 1965,* HSPA, 'Aiea, Hawai'i, 1965, p. 9.

12. Nellist, *Hawaii and its Builders*, 1925, pp. 125-129.
13. Simonds, William A., *Kamaaina-A Century in Hawaii*, American Factors, Ltd. Honolulu, 1949, pp. 45-46.
14. Damon, *Koamalu*, Vol. 2, p. 744.
15. Day, *History Makers*, p. 127.
16. Damon, *Koamalu*, Vol. 2, pp. 912-920. See also, A.B. Gilmore, *The Hawaii Sugar Manual*, New Orleans, 1936, p. 175. L.A. Faye pointed out to co-author [WHD] that Kekaha Sugar Company pioneered the installation of hydroelectric power in 1907 with an installation at the head of Waiawa Valley. Notes in co-author's possession.
17. Plasch, Bruce S., *Hawaiian Sugar Industry and Sugarcane Lands Outlook, Issues, and Options*, Decision Analysts Hawaii, Inc., Honolulu, April 1989, p. 11-4.
18. Smith, Jared G., *Plantation Sketches*, The Advertiser Press, Honolulu, 1924, pp. 13-14.
19. Day, *History Makers*, p. 132.
20. Damon, *Koamalu*, Vol. 1, p. 347.
21. Sullivan, *History of C. Brewer*, p. 149.
22. Gast, *Marin: A Biography*, p. 1.
23. Krauss and Alexander, *Grove Farm*, pp. 75-76.
24. Nellist, *Hawaii and its Builders*, pp. 365-367.
25. Thrum, Thomas G., "James Makee," *Hawaiian Annual 1927*, Honolulu, 1926, p. 27. Also, ibid., pp. 155-157.
26. ibid.
27. HSPA, *Sugar Manual 1965*, p. 9.
28. Simpich, Frederick, Jr., *Dynasty in the Pacific*, McGraw-Hill Book Co., New York, 1974, p. 81. L.A. Faye stated to the co-author (WHD) that the combination was probably encouraged when the Kaelia mill was destroyed by fire. Faye also stated that the mill machinery was salvaged and installed in the Līhuʻe mill. Curiously, it is believed that Līhuʻe's other mill-train was salvaged from the old Hanamāʻulu mill. Notes in co-author's possession.
29. Damon, *Koamalu*, Vol. 1, p. 357. See also, "Recent Deaths," *Paradise of the Pacific*, October, 1903, p. 11.
30. *Pacific Commercial Advertiser*, October 8, 1881, p. 1.
31. HSPA, *Sugar Manual 1965*, p. 9.
32. Stone, Scott C. S., *C. Brewer and Company, Ltd. Growing Cane Since 1826*, Island Heritage Pub., ʻAiea, Hawaiʻi, 1991, p. 153.
33. Kuykendall, Ralph S., *The Hawaiian Kingdom Volume III 1874-1893 The Kalakaua Dynasty*, University of Hawaiʻi Press, Honolulu, 1967, p. 501.
34. Day, *History Makers*, p. 114.
35. Dean, Arthur L., *Alexander & Baldwin and the Predecessor Partnerships*, Alexander & Baldwin, Ltd., Honolulu, 1950, pp. 31-34.
36. Day, *History Makers*, pp. 2, 8.
37. Gilmore, *Hawaii Sugar Manual, 1936*, pp. 157-158.
38. Schmitt, Robert and Doak C. Cox, "Hawaiian Time," *The Hawaiian Journal of History*, Vol. 26, 1992, pp. 219-220.
39. Smith, *Plantation Sketches*, p. 34.
40. ibid., p. 29.
41. Dean, *Alexander & Baldwin*, pp. 215-219.

42. Yamauchi, Hiroshi and Win Bui, *Drip Irrigation and the Survival of the Hawaiian Sugar Industry*, University of Hawai'i College of Agriculture and Human Resources, Honolulu, March, 1990, p. 6.
43. Obit., "Donald J. Martin of the sugar industry," *Honolulu Advertiser*, June 26, 1991, p. D 2.
44. Nellist, *Hawaii and its Builders*, 1925, pp. 143-145. See also, Eric A. Knudsen and Gurre P. Noble, *Kanuka of Kauai,* Tongg Publishing Company, Honolulu, 1944.
45. Simpich, *Dynasty*, pp. 81-83.
46. Smith, *Plantation Sketches*, p. 5.
47. ibid., p. 2. L.A. Faye described his family's long participation in the Hawaiian sugar industry to the co-author (WHD). Notes in co-author's possession.
48. McBryde Sugar Co., Ltd., *Story of McBryde Sugar Co., Ltd.*, McBryde Sugar Co., 1940 (limited edition).
49. Gilmore, *Hawaii Sugar Manual, 1936*, p. 178.
50. Conrow, Joan, "Hanging On and Hoping," *Hawaii Investor*, August 1992, pp. 20-25.
51. Damon, Koamalu, Vol. 1 and Vol. 2. See also, Edward Joesting, *Kauai The Separate Kingdom*, University of Hawai'i Press and Kauai Museum Association, Limited, Līhu'e, Kaua'i, 1984.

Chapter 4 | SUGAR ON O'AHU (1876-1996)

1. HSPA, *Sugar Manual, 1990*.
2. Day, *History Makers*, p. 50.
3. ibid.
4. Bowser, George, *An Account of the Sugar Plantations and the Principal Stock Ranches on the Hawaiian Islands*, George Bowser & Company, Honolulu, 1880, pp. 408-409.
5. Nellist, *Story of Hawaii*, 1925, pp. 115-116.
6. Bowser, *An Account*, pp. 407-408.
7. Day, *History Makers*, pp. 29-30.
8. HSPA data. See, also: Gilmore, A.B., *Hawaiian Sugar Manual 1938-39*, A.B. Gilmore New Orleans, 1939, p. 139.
9. Conde and Best, *Sugar Trains*, p. 356.
10. Gilmore, *Hawaiian Sugar Manual 1938-39*, p. 135.
11. Conde and Best, *Sugar Trains*, p. 358.
12. The Estate of James Campbell, *James Campbell, Esq.*, Honolulu, 1978, p. 23.
13. Yardley, Paul T., *Millstones and Milestones: The Career of B.F. Dillingham in Hawaii, 1844-1918*, University Press of Hawai'i, Honolulu, 1981.
14. Taylor, Frank J., Earl M. Welty and David W. Eyre, *From Land and Sea The Story of Castle and Cooke in Hawaii*, Chronicle Books, San Francisco, 1976, Ch. 7.
15. ibid.
16. HSPA data. See, also: ibid.
17. Taylor, Welty and Eyre, *From Land and Sea*, p. 261.
18. McClellan, Geo. B., *A Hand Book on the Sugar Industry of the Hawaiian Islands*, The Hawaiian Gazette Company, Ltd., Honolulu, 1899, p. 21.

19. Smith, *Plantation Sketches*, p. 141.
20. HSPA data. See, also: Gilmore, *Hawaiian Sugar Manual 1938-39*, p. 120.
21. Nellist, *Story of Hawaii, 1925*, pp. 85-87.
22. Thrum, Thos. G., *Hawaiian Almanac and Annual*, 1909-1924. See also, James B. Castle. "The Will of James B. Castle," August 19, 1912.
23. Taylor, Welty and Eyre, *From Land and Sea*, Ch. 7.
24. HSPA data. See, also: Gilmore, *Hawaiian Sugar Manual 1938-39*, p. 130.
25. HSPA data. See, also: HSPA, *Sugar Manual, 1990*.
26. Smith, *Plantation Sketches*, p. 146.
27. ibid., p. 151.
28. Gilmore, *Hawaiian Sugar Manual 1935-36*, pp. 63-64.
29. Wadsworth, H. A., "A Historical Summary of Irrigation in Hawaii," *Hawaiian Sugar Manual 1935-36*, A.B. Gilmore, New Orleans, 1936, p. 24.
30. HSPA data. See, also: HSPA, *Sugar Manual, 1990*.
31. Conde and Best, *Sugar Trains*, p. 327.
32. Gilmore, *Hawaiian Sugar Manual 1938-39*, p. 117.
33. Smith, *Plantation Sketches*, p. 733. James Gibb managed the Honolulu Plantation Company plantation from 1910 to 1923. See Thrum, *Hawaiian Almanac and Annual*, 1910-1924.
34. *Honolulu Star-Bulletin*, December 23, 1946, p. 1 et seq.

Chapter 5 | SUGAR ON MOLOKAʻI & LĀNAʻI (1878-1901)

1. Baldwin, Charles W., *Geography of the Hawaiian Islands*, American Book Company, New York, revised edition 1924, p. 106.
2. Thrum, *Hawaiian Almanac* 1891, p. 54. See also: Bowser, *An Account of the Sugar Plantations*, p. 411.
3. ibid., 1885, p. 68. See also: Bowser, *An Account of the Sugar Plantations*, p. 410.
4. Hackler, Rhoda E.A., *R.W. Meyer Sugar Mill, Its History and Restoration*, Molokaʻi Museum and Cultural Center, 1990. See also: Bowser, *An Account of the Sugar Plantations*, p. 410.
5. *Historic Hawaiʻi*, "Meyer Sugar Mill Plans Expansion," March 1991, p. 13.
6. McClellan, *A Hand Book*, p. 46.
7. Thrum, *Hawaiian Annual*, 1900, p. 49.
8. Alexander, *Koloa Plantation*, p. 109.
9. Sullivan, *History of C. Brewer & Company*, p. 163.
10. McBryde Sugar Co., Ltd., *Story of McBryde Sugar*, p. 23.
11. Sullivan, *History of C. Brewer & Company*, p. 163.
12. Conde and Best, *Sugar Trains*, p. 274.
13. Alexander, *Koloa Plantation*, p. 109.
14. McClellan, *A Hand Book*, p. 46.
15. Adler, Jacob, and Gwynn Barrett (Eds.), *The Diaries of Walter Murray Gibson 1886, 1887*, The University Press of Hawaiʻi, Honolulu, 1973, pp. vii.-xvii.
16. McClellan, *A Hand Book*, p. 46.
17. Conde and Best, *Sugar Trains*, p. 206.
18. HSPA data. See, also: Thrum, *Hawaiian Annual*, 1903, p. 41.
19. McBryde Sugar Co., Ltd., *Story of McBryde Sugar*, p. 40.
20. Thrum, *Hawaiian Annual*, 1900, p. 50.

Chapter 6 | SUGAR ON MAUI (1876-2000)

1. Gilmore, *Sugar Manual 1935-36*, p. 4.
2. HSPA, *Sugar Manual*, 1991.
3. Kuykendall, *Hawaiian Kingdom 1778-1854*, p. 125. See also: Alexander, *Koloa Plantation*, p. 57.
4. HSPA, *Sugar Manual 1965*, p. 9.
5. Dean, *Alexander & Baldwin*, pp. 27-28. See also: Sullivan, *A History*, p. 149.
6. Wilfong, *The Planters' Monthly*, October 1882, pp. 148-149.
7. HSPA data. See, also: Thrum, *Hawaiian Annual* 1891, p. 58
8. Conde and Best, *Sugar Trains*, p. 241.
9. HSPA data. See, also: Gilmore, *Sugar Manual 1938-39*, p. 180.
10. Nellist, *Hawaii and Its Builders*, 1925, pp. 155, 157.
11. Jarves, *History*, p. 205. See, also, Thrum, "James Makee," p. 33.
12. Taylor, Welty, and Eyre, *From Land and Sea*, Ch. 5.
13. ibid.
14. Jarves, *History*, p. 205.
15. Bowser, *An Account*, pp. 429-430.
16. Dean, *Alexander & Baldwin*, pp. 98-100.
17. The Estate of James Campbell, *James Campbell*.
18. Judd, *The Friend*, Enclosure 3.
19. Baldwin, Arthur D., *A Memoir of Henry Perrine Baldwin 1842 to 1911*, privately printed, 1915, p. 27.
20. Jarves, *History*, p. 205.
21. HSPA data. See, also: Gilmore, *Sugar Manual 1938-39*, p. 189.
22. HSPA data. See, also: H.S.P.A., *Sugar Manual 1991*. Robert Vorfeld, manager of Pioneer Mill from 1979 to 1987, told co-author (WHD) that production by Pioneer Mill ran between 50,000 tons and 55,000 tons of sugar in the 1970s through the early 1980s. Notes in co-author's possession.
23. Simonds, *Kamaaina*, p. 81.
24. Thrum, *Hawaiian Annual*, 1933, p. 155.
25. Silva, *Wailuku Sugar Company*, p. 12.
26. Baldwin, *Henry Perrine Baldwin*, p. 27.
27. Thrum, "James Makee," pp. 35-38. See, also, Bowser, *An Account*, p. 426.
28. Silva, *Wailuku Sugar Company*, p. 24.
29. ibid., p. 12.
30. Judd, *The Friend*, Enclosure 3.
31. Silva, *Wailuku Sugar Company*, p. 17.
32. HSPA data. See, also: Bowser, *An Account*, pp. 425-426.
33. Silva, *Wailuku Sugar Company*, p. 23.
34. Thrum, *Hawaiian Annual*, 1891, p. 60.
35. Silva, *Wailuku Sugar Company*, p. 24.
36. HSPA data. See, also: Gilmore, *Sugar Manual 1938-39*, pp. 191-192.
37. HSPA data. See, also: HSPA, *Sugar Manual 1987*, p. 5.
38. Bowser, *An Account*, pp. 430-431.
39. ibid.
40. Dean, *Alexander & Baldwin*, p. 30.
41. Bowser, *An Account*, pp. 428-429.

42. Thrum, *Hawaiian Annual,* 1891, p. 60.
43. HSPA data. See, also: Thrum, *Hawaiian Annual,* 1921, p. 151.
44. Dean, *Alexander & Baldwin,* p. 14.
45. ibid., p. 15.
46. Hind, R. Renton (Ed.), *John Hind of Hawi (1858-1933) His Memoirs,* Manaoag, Pangasinan, Philippines, 1951, p. 7.
47. Baldwin, *Henry Perrine Baldwin,* pp. 32-35.
48. Dean, *Alexander & Baldwin,* p. 18.
49. ibid., p. 22.
50. Adler, Jacob, *Claus Spreckels The Sugar King of Hawaii,* Mutual Publishing Paperback Series, Honolulu, 1966, pp. 21-23.
51. ibid., p. 71.
52. Thrum, *Hawaiian Annual,* 1891, p. 58.
53. Adler, *Claus Spreckels,* pp. 45-47, 73-76.
54. ibid., p. 84. See, also, Dean, *Alexander & Baldwin,* pp. 64-67.
55. ibid., Dean, pp. 62, 98.
56. Baldwin, *Henry Perrine Baldwin,* pp. 80-81.
57. Edson, Hubert, *Sugar From Scarcity to Surplus,* Chemical Publishing Company, Inc., New York, 1958, pp. 64-65. Edson's career in the sugar industry spanned 62 years starting in 1888. He served as a sugar chemist, mill-constructor, manager, and consultant, successively, in such diverse locations as Cuba, Puerto Rico, Haiti, Dominican Republic, Louisiana, and Florida along with the year 1894 spent on Maui. He was uniquely qualified to compare management and operations throughout the sugar world.
58. Sullivan, *A History,* p. 165.
59. Dean, *Alexander & Baldwin,* pp. 98-102
60. ibid.
61. Day, *History Makers,* p. 31.
62. HSPA data. See, also: Gilmore, *Sugar Manual 1938-39,* p. 182. Numerous mills were abandoned when plantations were combined or machinery became hopelessly outdated. William Baldwin, Manager, Personnel and Industrial Relations, H.C.& S., gave co-author [WHD] a list of abandoned Maui mills that was prepared in January 1955 by Mrs. Roy Savage. The listing is:

MILL	BUILT	ABANDONED
Olowalu	1881	1931
Waikapu (Cornwell)	1864	1895 (1)
Waihee (Lewers)	1863	1895 (1)
Old Wailuku No. 2	1880	1905
Spreckelsville	1878	1902
Hamakuapoko (Haiku)	1880	1906
Haiku Sugar	1861	1884
Kaluanui	1849 (1)	1886
Paliule (Hind)	1870	1880
Paholei	1851	1881
Ulupalakua	1856	1883
Hana (Kaeleku)	1864	1945
Kipahulu	1880 (1)	1925 (1)
Huelo then Maui (1)	1880s (1)	1904 (1)

Notes: (1) Correct dates provided by Robert H. Hughes. Waikapu and Waihee consolidated into Old Waluku No. 2 in 1895. Huelo mill operated about ten years when Maui Sugar Company mill erected in Huelo area about 1890 and commonly referred to as "Huelo." Letter, Robert H. Hughes, 9 January, 1995.

63. Dean, *Alexander & Baldwin*, pp. 209-210.
64. HSPA data. See, also: HSPA, *Sugar Manual*, 1991.
65. Hawaiian Sugar Planters' Association, *Story of Sugar in Hawaii,* Hawaiian Sugar Planters' Association, Honolulu, 1962, p. 66. See also: Smith, *Plantation Sketches*, p. 65.
66. Rho, Marguerite, "Alexander & Baldwin Sugar Museum," *Historic Hawai'i,* October 1988, pp. 4-7.

CHAPTER 8 | SUGAR ON THE ISLAND OF HAWAI'I (1876-1996)

1. HSPA data. See, also: Sugar production numbers and description of several plantations in the years 1905 through 1939 in A.B. Gilmore, *The Hawaii Sugar Manual 1939*, A.B. Gilmore, New Orleans, Louisiana, 1939, pp. 4 and 196-242. Production numbers for the years 1890 through 1940 are given in Thomas G. Thrum *Hawaiian Annual*, T.G. Thrum, Honolulu, annually 1890 through 1940. See also, Hall, "Luna's Log."
2. HSPA data. See, also: HSPA, *Sugar Manual 1991.*
3. Damon, *Father Bond*, pp. 182-184.
4. Taylor, Welty, and Frye, *From Land and Sea*, Ch. 5. See also, Hall, "Luna's Log."
5. ibid.
6. Wilfong, "Sugar Plantations..." pp. 227-228.
7. Production, acreage, managers, proprietors, and agencies for several plantations in 1880 are listed in George Bowser, *An Account of the Sugar Plantations and the Principal Stock Ranches on the Hawaiian Islands*, George Bowser & Company, Honolulu, 1880, pp. 411-425. See Hedemann, *A Scottish-Hawaiian Story*, for a description of the Purvis family in Hawai'i and pp. 146, 147 the Schaefer agency connection.
8. ibid.
9. Conde, J.C., *Narrow Gauge in a Kingdom The Hawaiian Railroad Company 1878-1897*, Railhead Publications, Felton, California, 1985, Ch. 2.
10. Hansen, Arthur R., *Kohala Sugar Company 1863-1963,* Kohala Sugar Company, Kohala, Hawai'i, 1963.
11. HSPA data. See, also: Gilmore, A.B., *Hawaii Sugar Manual 1948*, A.B. Gilmore, New Orleans, Louisiana, 1948, p. 11.
12. Conde, *Narrow Gauge*, Epilogue.
13. Taylor et. al., *From Land and Sea*, p. 262.
14. Hansen, *Kohala Sugar*. See also, Hall, "Luna's Log."
15. Hind, *Hind*, p. 50.
16. Production and acreage numbers taken from Thrum, *Hawaiian Annual,* 1891, pp. 58-60.
17. Hind, *Hind*, pp. 16-18.
18. Hansen, *Kohala Sugar.*
19. ibid. See also, Hind, *Hind,* p. 53.
20. Hind, *Hind*, pp. 38-45.

21. HSPA data. See, also: Thrum, *Hawaiian Annual,* 1903, p. 41. See also, Hall, "Luna's Log."
22. Hansen, *Kohala Sugar.* See also, Hind, *Hind,* pp. 25-26.
23. Hind, *Hind,* pp. 47-50.
24. HSPA data. See, also: Thrum, *Hawaiian Annual,* see years 1901 through 1904.
25. Hind, *Hind,* pp. 28-32. See also, Hall, "Luna's Log."
26. Schaeffer, Frederick A., III, *Endless Journey Generation to Generation,* Olomana Press, Kailua, Hawaiʻi, 1996, p 36. For more, see Nellist, *Story of Hawaii,* 1925, p. 179.
27. Nellist, *Story of Hawaii,* pp. 848-849.
28. Day, *History Makers,* p. 122.
29. Conde and Best, *Sugar Trains,* p. 43.
30. ibid., p. 44.
31. Hoyt, Edwin P., *Davies The Inside Story of a British-American Family in the Pacific and Its Business Enterprises,* Topgallant Publishing Company, Ltd., Honolulu, 1983, p. 433.
32. ibid., pp. 79-80.
33. ibid., p. 171. See also, Conde and Best, *Sugar Trains,* p. 22.
34. Hoyt, *Davies,* p. 342.
35. HSPA, *Sugar Manual 1965,* p. 11.
36. Dates for the following Big Island plantation companies were found in the Hawaiian Sugar Planters' Association archives. Co-author (WHD) telecon with Librarian Anne Marsteller, October 21, 1992. Notes in co-author's possession.

> Lauapahoehoe Sugar Company
> Kaiwiki Sugar Company
> Hamakua Sugar Company
> Davies Hamakua Sugar
> Honomu Sugar Company
> Hakalau Sugar Company
> Pepeekeo Sugar Company
> Onomea Sugar Company
> Hilo Sugar Company
> Hawaiian Sugar Company
> Kau Agribusiness Company

37. Neil, Christopher, "Hamakua Sugar Files Bankruptcy," *Honolulu Advertiser,* August 15, 1992, p. A 1.
38. Tanahara, Kris and Hugh Clark, "Union Protests Hamakua Sugar Closing," *Honolulu Advertiser,* December 21, 1992, p. A 3.
39. HSPA, *Sugar Manual 1991.*
40. On October 26, 1992 co-author (WHD) and wife visited Hamakua Sugar Company headquarters at Paʻauilo, Hawaiʻi, where they interviewed Mr. Francis S. Morgan for several hours. Mr. Morgan elaborated on the problems of growing sugarcane on the Hāmākua Coast and on the Hawaiʻi sugar industry in general. Notes are in the co-author's possession.
41. Statement during television interview. Francis S. Morgan elaborated on the difficulties of surviving while making sugar on the Hāmākua Coast during his

August 3-4, 1993 interviews with co-author (WHD). Notes in co-author's (WHD) possession.
42. Hoyt, *Davies*, p. 120.
43. Thrum, *Hawaiian Annual*, see years 1891 through 1818.
44. Conde and Best, *Sugar Trains*, p. 55.
45. Hoyt, *Davies*, pp. 79-80, 89.
46. The problems of cultivating sugarcane on the North Hilo Coast are thoroughly discussed in a report prepared for the Hawai'i State Department of Agriculture. This report is: Holderness, James S., Gary R. Vieth, and Francis Scott, Jr., Economic Viability of Independent Sugarcane Farms on the Hilo Coast, University of Hawai'i, Hawai'i Institute of Tropical Agriculture and Human Resources, Honolulu, December, 1979. See pp. 3-9.
47. Thrum, *Hawaiian Annual*, see years 1928-1937.
48. *Honolulu Advertiser*, October 29, 1941.
49. Philip E. Spalding, no relation to Andrew T. Spalding, was president of C. Brewer & Company from 1940 to 1950. See, for example, Stone, *C. Brewer*.
50. Thrum, *Hawaiian Annual*, 1876, pp. 39-40. See also, Judd, *The Friend*, Enclosure 3.
51. Day, *History Makers*, p. 1.
52. Simpich, *Dynasty*, p. 48.
53. Sullivan, *History of C. Brewer*, p. 164.
54. Judd, *The Friend*, Enclosure 3.
55. Jarves, *History*, p. 205.
56. HSPA, *Sugar Manual 1965*, p. 9.
57. Smith, *Plantation Sketches*, p. 80.
58. Judd, *Friend*, Enclosure 3. See also, Bowser, *An Account*, pp. 416-417; and, Bird, *Six Months*, pp. 71-78.
59. Sullivan, *History of C. Brewer*, p. 149.
60. Thrum, *Hawaiian Annual*, 1901, p. 45.
61. Sullivan, *History of C. Brewer*, p. 149 et. seq.
62. Thrum, *Hawaiian Annual*, see years 1883 through 1933. Francis Morgan told the co-author (WHD) that Onomea plantation was known for its strikingly high flume trestles. Their existence created a unique job requirement: "flume carpenters." Onomea plantation was the last of the Hawai'i plantations to use human cane-cutters. Notes in co-author's possession.
63. Smith, *Plantation Sketches*, pp. 82-88.
64. ibid.
65. Day, *History Makers*, p. 52.
66. Kelly, Marian, Barry Nakamura, and Dorothy B. Berrere, *Hilo Bay: A Chronological History Land and Water Use in the Hilo Bay Area, Island of Hawaii*, Bernice P. Bishop Museum, Honolulu, March 1981, pp. 86-93, and 117-141.
67. Smith, Jared G., "Nothing in the World Like a Hawaii Mill," *Honolulu Advertiser*, May 8, 1932.
68. Kuykendall, *Hawaiian Kingdom 1874-1893*, p. 60.
69. Obit., "Fraser, 62, Dies in Hilo," *Honolulu Advertiser*, January 27, 1940.
70. HSPA, *Story of Sugar*, 1926, p. 65.

71. Obit., "Pioneer Builder of Hawaii, John A. Scott, Dead," *Honolulu Star-Bulletin*, November 13, 1925.
72. Adler, *Claus Spreckels*, pp. 102-103.
73. Neil, Christopher, "Hilo Mill to Close," *Honolulu Advertiser*, August 1, 1992, p. A 1.
74. Hoyt, *Davies*, p. 78.
75. Stone, *C. Brewer*, p. 160.
76. Conde and Best, *Sugar Trains*, p. 92.
77. Smith, *Plantation Sketches*, p. 96. The co-author (WHD) was told by Lindsay A. "Tony" Faye that his uncle Hans Peter Faye was president of American Factors, Inc. when the difficult decision was made to continue Olaa Sugar Company operations. Faye was president from 1950 to 1952. Tony Faye became the last H.S.P.A. trainee at Olaa Sugar Company and the first at Puna Sugar Company when the name changed in 1960. Notes in co-author's possession.
78. ibid., p. 100.
79. Simpich, *Dynasty*, pp. 92-93.
80. Kahane, Joyce, and Jean Kadooka Marfin, *The Sugar Industry in Hawaii An Action Plan*, State of Hawai'i Legislative Reference Bureau, Report No. 9, 1987, p. 46.
81. Conde and Best, *Sugar Trains*, p. 93.
82. Handy, E.S., Craghill, and Mary Kawena Pukui, *The Polynesian Family System in Ka'u, Hawaii*, Charles E. Tuttle Company, Rutland, Vermont, 1972, pp. 245-246.
83. Kau Sugar Company, Inc., Kau Sugar Company, Inc., Pāhala, Hawai'i, 1972, pp. 7-27.
84. ibid., p. 13.
85. ibid., p. 15.
86. ibid., p. 20.
87. ibid.
88. ibid., p. 28.
89. ibid., p. 8.
90. ibid., p. 15.
91. Bowser, *An Account*, p. 422.
92. Thrum, *Hawaiian Annual*, 1886, pp. 35-37.
93. Kau Sugar Company, Inc., *Kau Sugar Company*, p. 11.
94. Day, *History Makers*, pp. 36-37.
95. Hawaiian Sugar Planters' Association, *Proceedings of 65th Annual Meeting*, Honolulu, December 10, 1945, p. 143.
96. Fuchs, Lawrence H., *Hawaii Pono: A Social History*, Harcourt, Brace & World, New York, 1961, p. 263.
97. Thrum, *Hawaiian Annual*, 1891, p. 59.
98. Thrum, *Hawaiian Annual*, 1906, p. 40.
99. Conde and Best, *Sugar Trains*, p. 87. See also, Castle, "Will."
100. Nellist, *Story of Hawaii*, 1925, p. 87. ibid., Castle, "Will."
101. Thrum, *Hawaiian Annual*, see years 1905 through 1907.

CHAPTER 9 | INDEPENDENT FARMERS AND INDEPENDENT SUGARMILLS

1. Don Francisco de Paula Marin recorded several instances in his journal about land being taken from him. On February 16, 1812, for example, he recorded that an estate on Hawai'i was given to him by King Kamehameha I. On July 11, 1813 he recorded that the estate was taken from him. See Gast, Marin, pp. 204 and 208. Kamehameha II was similarly capricious. Marin recorded on October 7, 1821 and on September 23, 1823 that land was taken from him. See Gast, *Marin*, pp. 244 and 281.
2. Galloway, *Sugar Cane Industry*, pp. 228-233.
3. Lind, Andrew W., *An Island Community*, Greenwood Press, New York, 1968 (second edition, first edition 1938), p. 85.
4. ibid.
5. ibid., pp. 85-86.
6. Beechert, *Working in Hawaii*, p. 127.
7. University of Hawai'i Textbook Series, *The Story of Cane Sugar*, University of Hawai'i, Honolulu, 1928, p. 127.
8. Phillips, Perry F., *Diversified Agriculture in Hawaii*, University of Hawai'i Press, Honolulu, 1953, Table A5 lists 1,501 small planters of sugar in 1952.
9. Hawaiian Sugar Planters' Association, *Hawaiian Sugar Manual 1972*, HSPA, 'Aiea, Hawai'i, 1972.
10. Holderness, James S., Gary R. Vieth, Frank S. Scott, Jr., and Nicomedes Briones, *Cost of Producing and Processing Sugarcane Among Hawaii's Independent Cane Growers, With Comparisons to Plantation Growers*, College of Tropical Agriculture and Human Resources, University of Hawai'i, Research Extension Series 032, June 1982, p. 2 lists 318 independent growers in Hawai'i in 1980.
11. Neil, Christopher, "Hilo mill to close," *Honolulu Advertiser*, Aug. 1, 1992, p. 1.
12. Kahane et. al., *The Sugar Industry in Hawaii*, p. 24.
13. Hawaiian Sugar Planters' Association, *The Hawaiian Sugar Industry: Perspectives on Current Issues*, HSPA, 'Aiea, Hawai'i, February 1987, p. 5.
14. Hilo Sugar Company, Inc., 1961 Annual Report.
15. Dean, *Alexander & Baldwin*, Ltd., pp. 14-15.
16. op. cit., Hoyt, *Davies*, pp. 78-79, 171 et. seq.
17. op. cit., Simpich, *Dynasty*, p. 82 and Simonds, Kamaaina, pp. 45, 52.
18. op. cit., Thrum, *Hawaiian Almanac*, 1920-1944.
19. op. cit., Gilmore, *Sugar Manual 1936*, p. 260.
20. op. cit., Neil, "Hilo mill to close."

CHAPTER 10 | THE PLANTATION WORKERS

1. Beechert, *Working in Hawaii*, p. 60.
2. Lydgate, *Hawaiian Annual*, 1918, pp. 81-82.
3. Odo, Franklin, and Kazuko Sinoto, *A Pictorial History of the Japanese in Hawaii 1885-1924*, Bernice Pauahi Bishop Museum, Honolulu, 1985, pp. 18-19.
4. Kuykendall, *Hawaiian Kingdom 1778-1854*, p. 330.
5. Beechert, *Working in Hawaii*, p. 63.
6. Kuykendall, *Hawaiian Kingdom 1778-1854*, p. 324.

7. Kuykendall, *Hawaiian Kingdom 1854-1874*, p. 178-180.
8. Beechert, *Working in Hawaii*, p. 86.
9. Hind, *John Hind*, pp. 92-93.
10. Beechert, *Working in Hawaii*, pp. 65-67.
11. ibid., p. 86.
12. Galloway, *Sugar Cane Industry*, pp. 50-55.
13. Beechert, *Working in Hawaii*, p. 86.
14. ibid., pp. 132-133.
15. Odo and Sinoto, *Pictorial History*, p. 196.
16. Beechert, *Working in Hawaii*, p. 195.
17. Thrum, *Hawaiian Annual*, 1905, p. 31.
18. Vandercook, John W., *King Cane The Story of Sugar in Hawaii*, Harper & Brothers, New York, 1939, p. 84.
19. University of Hawai'i, *Stores and Storekeepers of Paia & Puunene, Maui*, Vol. 1, Ethnic Studies Oral History Project, University of Hawai'i, Mānoa, June 1880, p. xxiii.
20. Gilmore, *Hawaiian Sugar Manual 1939*, pp. 172-179.
21. ibid., p. 172.
22. Hawaiian Sugar Planters' Association, *Hawaiian Sugar Manual 1940*, HSPA, 'Aiea, Hawai'i, 1940.
23. Beechert, *Working in Hawaii*, pp. 329-330.
24. Smith, Lydia, "Remembering Mana An Historical Review," *Historic Hawai'i*, March 1990, pp. 4-6.
25. Clark, Jeff, "Rescuing the Past: Waimea Plantation Cottages," *Historic Hawai'i*, March 1990, pp. 7-9.

CHAPTER 11 | FACTORS, THEN AGENCIES

1. Dates and short biographies of persons first cited in this chapter can be found in A. Grove Day, *History Makers of Hawaii*, Mutual Publishing Co., Honolulu, 1984. Data concerning Charles Brewer, H.F.P. Carter, Heinrich Hackfeld, James Hunnewell, and J.F.B. Marshall are found on pages 14, 19, 47, 54, and 95, respectively.
2. Sullivan, *History*, pp. 111-112.
3. ibid., pp. 134, 144.
4. ibid., p. 145.
5. ibid., p. 147.
6. Thrum, *Hawaiian Annual*, 1909, pp. 183-186.
7. Sullivan, *History*, p. 170.
8. Stone, *C. Brewer*, p. 112.
9. Andrade, Ken, "The Big Five's clout continues to erode," *Honolulu Star-Bulletin*, Feb. 21, 1989, Section 3, p. 2.
10. ibid.
11. *Honolulu Advertiser*, Mar. 20, 1992, p. C5.
12. Taylor, et. al., *Land and Sea*, p. 265.
13. Smith, Jared G., *The Big Five*, Advertiser Publishing Company, Ltd., Honolulu, 1942, p. 5.
14. ibid.

15. ibid.
16. ibid.
17. Hoyt, *Davies*, p. 62. Other plantations represented or aided by Davies included Heeia Plantation Company, Pepeekeo Sugar Co., Olowalu Company, and McBryde Sugar Company.
18. ibid., p. 89.
19. Smith, *Big Five*, p. 6.
20. Hoyt, *Davies*, p. 358.
21. ibid., p. 369.
22. Smith, *Big Five*, p. 9.
23. ibid., pp. 9, 10.
24. ibid., pp. 11, 12.
25. Simpich, *Dynasty*, pp. 49, 50.
26. Smith, *Big Five*, p. 11.
27. ibid., p. 15.
28. ibid., pp. 15, 16.
29. ibid., pp. 17, 18.
30. Taylor, et. al., *Land and Sea*, p. 122.
31. Smith, Big Five, p. 21.
32. Taylor, et. al., *Land and Sea*, p. 224.
33. Smith, *Big Five*, p. 23.
34. Dean, *Alexander & Baldwin*, p. 15.
35. Smith, *Big Five*, p. 23, 24.
36. ibid.
37. Dean, *Alexander & Baldwin*, p. 58.
38. Smith, *Big Five*, p. 25.
39. Dean, *Alexander & Baldwin*, p. 82.
40. Smith, Kit, "A & B buys up sugar firm," *Honolulu Advertiser*, Mar. 2, 1993.
41. Gilmore, *Sugar Manual 1936*, p. 83.
42. Thrum, *Hawaiian Annual,* 1876-1940. See also: Kuykendall, *Hawaiian Kingdom 1854-1874*, pp. 145-146 for Walker, Allen & Company. This company went bankrupt in 1867 following a recession in sugar prices paid in San Francisco.
43. Nellist, *Hawaii and Its Builders*, pp. 85-86.

CHAPTER 12 | COOPERATION IN THE INDUSTRY

1. Agee, H.P. (compiler), "A Brief History of the Hawaiian Sugar Planters' Association," *Hawaii Sugar Manual 1935-36,* A.B. Gilmore, New Orleans, 1936 pp. 8-13.
2. Kuykendall, *Hawaiian Kingdom 1778-1854*, p. 330.
3. Wilfong, "Sugar Plantations in the Early Days," p. 151.
4. Sullivan, *C. Brewer*, p. 110.
5. Thrum, *Hawaiian Almanac*, 1875, p. 39.
6. Kuykendall, Ralph, S., *The Hawaiian Kingdom 1854-1874*, University of Hawai'i Press, Honolulu, 1953, p. 153.
7. See, for example, C., "The Norwegian What To Do With Him," *The Planters' Monthly*, 1882, pp. 124-126.

8. Agee, "Brief History," pp. 10-12.
9. Day, *History Makers*, p. 36.
10. ibid.
11. HSPA, *Sugar Manual*, 1991.
12. Dean, A. L., *Cooperation in the Sugar Industry of Hawaii*, American Council, Institute of Pacific Relations, New York, 1933, p. 18.
13. ibid., pp. 18-19.
14. ibid., p. 20.
15. Simpich, *Dynasty*, pp. 73-74.
16. Lydgate, *Hawaiian Annual*, 1918, pp. 74-76.
17. Simpich, *Dynasty*, p, 72.
18. Emmet, Boris, Ph.D., The California and Hawaiian Sugar Refining Corporation, Graduate School of Business, Stanford University, California, 1928, p. 6.
19. HSPA, *Sugar Manual 1965*, p. 11.
20. ibid., pp. 11-12.
21. Simpich, *Dynasty*, pp. 73-74.

CHAPTER 13 | SUGAR-RELATED INDUSTRIES

1. TenBruggencate, Jan, "State reports drop in value of crop sales," *Honolulu Advertiser*, Feb. 4, 1993, p. D4.
2. Thrum, *Hawaiian Annual*, 1894, pp. 40-41, 1898, p. 49, with Kuykendall, *Hawaiian Kingdom 1874-1893*, p. 83, and calculations by the author.
3. Kuykendall, *Hawaiian Kingdom 1874-1893*, p. 102.
4. Day, *History Makers*, p. 42.
5. Kuykendall, *Hawaiian Kingdom 1874-1893*, p. 102.
6. Simonds, *Kamaaina*, p. 81.
7. Thrum, *Hawaiian Annual*, 1900, p. 48.
8. Conde, J. C., *Narrow Gauge in a Kingdom*, Railhead Publications, Felton, California, 1985, p. 51.
9. Nelson, Richard, "Notes on Wire Landings Along Hamakua Coast on the Island of Hawaii," *The Hawaiian Journal of History*, vol. VIII, 1974, pp. 136-142.
10. Inspection by the author in 1991.
11. Simonds, *Kamaaina*, p. 81.
12. Conde, *Narrow Gauge*, p. 54.
13. Kuykendall, *Hawaiian Kingdom 1874-1893*, p. 204.
14. Conde, *Narrow Gauge*, pp. 18-19.
15. ibid., pp. 19-20
16. ibid., p. 21. See also, Kuykendall, *Hawaiian Kingdom 1874-1893*, pp. 213-214.
17. Nellist, *Story of Hawaii*, 1925, p. 113.
18. Conde, *Narrow Gauge*, p. 43.
19. Kuykendall, *Hawaiian Kingdom 1874-1893*, p. 99.
20. Best, Gerald M., *Railroads of Hawaii: Narrow and Standard Gauge Common Carriers*, Golden West Books, San Marino, California, 1978, p. 33.
21. Conde, *Narrow Gauge*, p. 50. In 1910 the rates for hauling sugar from the Hilo Coast and Hāmākua Coast plantations to the Hilo port via the Hilo Railroad Company were set by contract at $2.25 per ton the first five years, $2.00 per

ton the second ten years (i.e., until 1925), and $1.75 per ton the next five years (until 1930). Hauling supplies from Hilo to the plantations was more expensive at $3.36 per ton to $6.72 depending on the nature of supplies hauled. Curiously, the furthest plantation from Hilo, Hamakua Mill Company, received a 15 percent discount on the rates for merchandise and lumber hauled up from Hilo. Contract in co-author's (WHD) possession.
22. Conde, *Narrow Gauge*, p. 72.
23. ibid., p. 75.
24. Best, *Railroads of Hawaii*, p. 98.
25. Nellist, *Story of Hawaii 1925*, p. 37. See also, Castle, "Will".
26. Conde, *Narrow Gauge*, pp. 87-89.
27. Hungerford, John B., *Hawaiian Railroads*, Hungerford Press, Reseda, California, 1963, pp. 49-66.
28. McBryde Sugar Company, *McBryde Sugar*, pp. 31-34.
29. ibid., p. 34.
30. ibid., p. 33.
31. Inspection by the author, 1991.
32. Conde, *Narrow Gauge*, p. 159.
33. ibid., pp. 185-187.
34. Kau Sugar Company, *Kau Sugar Company*, p. 20.
35. The shortage of heavy machine tools and foundries plagued the U. S. Army during 1880-1900, when the Army was seeking to manufacture large steel cannons to rearm the nation's coastal defenses.
36. Kuykendall, *Hawaiian Kingdom 1874-1893*, pp. 73-74.
37. Hind, *Hind,* p. 3.
38. Kuykendall, *Hawaiian Kingdom 1778-1853*, p. 326.
39. HSPA, *Story of Sugar 1926*, p. 65.
40. Hoyt, *Davies*, p. 107.
41. ibid., p. 169.
42. ibid.
43. ibid., p. 190.
44. Honolulu Iron Works Company, *Some Sugar Factories Built and Equipped by the Honolulu Iron Works Company*, Honolulu Iron Works, Honolulu, 1924, p. 8.
45. ibid., p. 10.
46. ibid., pp. 66-69.
47. Hoyt, *Davies,* p. 406.
48. Honolulu Iron Works Company, 1965 Annual Report, p. 3.
49. Kelly, et. al., *Hilo Bay*, pp. 136-137.
50. Gilmore, *Sugar Manual 1939*, pp. 207, 241.
51. Kelly, et. al., *Hilo Bay*, pp. 138-141.
52. Kinoshita, Charles W., *Cogeneration in the Hawaiian Sugar Industry*, Hawaiian Institute of Energy Research, Honolulu, 1990, p. 3.
53. ibid., p.11.

CHAPTER 14 | SUGAR AND SCIENCE
1. Wilfong, "Sugar Plantations," pp. 149-151, 228.
2. Damon, *Koamalu*, p. 332.
3. Baldwin, D.D., "Lahaina Cane," reprint, *The Planters' Monthly*, 1882, pp. 42-43.

CHAPTER NOTES   233

4. Mangelsdorf, A.J. and C.G. Lennox, "Sugar Cane Breeding in Hawaii," *Gilmore's Hawaii Sugar Manual 1935-36*, A.B. Gilmore, New Orleans, 1936, p. 18.
5. *Honolulu Star-Bulletin*, "Hawaiian Sugar Plantation History, No. 10-Hilo Island of Hawaii," 4 May 1935.
6. HSPA, *Story of Sugar 1926*, p. 39.
7. Hawaiian Sugar Planters' Association, *Sugar in Hawaii*, Hawaiian Sugar Planters' Association, Honolulu, 1949, p. 91.
8. ibid.
9. *The Planters' Monthly*, Feb. 1899, p. 75.
10. Gilmore, *Hawaii Sugar Manual 1939*, pp. 112-242.
11. Vandercook, *King Cane*, pp. 135-136.
12. HSPA, *Story of Sugar 1926*, pp. 40-41.
13. ibid.
14. ibid.
15. Pemberton, C.E., "The Tropical American Toad Bufo Marinus in Hawaii," *Gilmore's Hawaii Sugar Manual 1935-36*, A.B. Gilmore, New Orleans, 1936, pp. 29-30.
16. Hawaiian Sugar Planters' Association, *Experiment Station Annual Report 1985*, Hawaiian Sugar Planters' Association, 'Aiea, Hawai'i, 1986, p. 1.
17. Martin, J.P., and C.W. Carpenter, "Sugar Cane Diseases in Hawaii," *Gilmore's Hawaii Sugar Manual 1935-36*, A.B. Gilmore, New Orleans, 1936, pp. 26-29.
18. Thrum, *Hawaiian Annual*, 1905, p. 164.
19. ibid.
20. Wadsworth, H.A., "A Historical Summary of Irrigation in Hawaii," *Gilmore's Hawaii Sugar Manual 1935-36*, A.B. Gilmore. New Orleans, 1936, pp. 63-64.
21. Das, U.H., "Rate of Cane and Sugar Formation in a Cane Crop," *Gilmore's Hawaii Sugar Manual 1935-36*, A.B. Gilmore, New Orleans, 1936, pp. 36-38.
22. Yamauchi and Bui, *Drip Irrigation*.
23. Dean, *Cooperation*, p. 12.
24. HSPA, *Sugar Manual 1991*.
25. Hedemann, C., "Evolution of the Sugar Mill in Hawaii," *The Planters' Monthly*, September 1902, pp. 425-430.
26. ibid., p. 426.
27. HSPA, *Story of Sugar 1926*, p. 65.
28. ibid., p. 66.
29. Simpich, *Dynasty*, p. 90.
30. Adler, *Claus Spreckels*, p. 75.
31. Wailea Milling Company, Ltd., *1929 Annual Report*, p. 14.
32. Told to co-author (WHD) by retired sugar worker.
33. Smith, *Plantation Sketches*, p. 141.
34. ibid.
35. Vandercook, *King Cane*, p. 109. The machine was the Falkiner Cane Harvester tested in 1938 at Grove Farm Plantation on Kaua'i and earlier used in Australia, Cuba, and Florida, See Gilmore's *Sugar Manual 1938-39*, p. 26.
36. HSPA, *Sugar Manual 1965*, p. 11.
37. Wallace, A.F. "The Cane Washing Problem Presented by Mechanical Harvesting," *Gilmore's Hawaii Sugar Manual 1938-39*, A.B. Gilmore, New Orleans, 1939, pp. 28-30.

38. Smith, Walter E., "War and Our Sugar Industry," *Hawaii,* August 17, 1944, pp. 8-9.
39. ibid.
40. Gross, F.J., "Wireless Telegraph in the Hawaiian Islands," *The Planters' Monthly,* January 1907, p. 25.
41. ibid., pp. 27-28.
42. ibid., p. 28.

CHAPTER 15 | COMPETITION AND PRICE SUPPORTS

1. Galloway, *Sugar Cane Industry,* p. 159.
2. ibid., pp. 130-133.
3. Kuykendall, *Hawaiian Kingdom 1778-1854,* p. 323.
4. ibid.
5. Thrum, *Hawaiian Annual,* 1875, p. 39.
6. Galloway, *Sugar Cane Industry,* p. 130-133.
7. ibid.
8. Kuykendall, *Hawaiian Kingdom 1874-1893,* p. 40.
9. ibid., p. 466.
10. ibid., pp. 603-605.
11. Sullivan, *C. Brewer,* p. 160.
12. Edson, *Sugar,* p. 20.
13. HSPA, *Sugar in Hawaii 1949,* p. 83.
14. ibid., p. 84.
15. Kahane et. al., *The Sugar Industry,* p. 11.
16. HSPA, *Sugar Manual 1987,* pp. 16-17.
17. Hawaiian Sugar Planters' Association, *Hawaiian Sugar Manual 1992,* Hawaiian Sugar Planters' Association, 'Aiea, Hawai'i, 1992.
18. Kahane et. al., *The Sugar Industry,* pp. 19, 59.
19. Sullivan, *C. Brewer,* pp. 110, 160. See also: Lind, *Island Community,* p. 165, and Lorrin A. Thurston (Editor), *A Directory of Hawaiian Sugar Plantations and Data Concerning Sugar and the Sugar Business,* Hawaiian Gazette, Honolulu, December 1914, p. 8.
20. Kuykendall, *Hawaiian Kingdom 1874-1893,* p. 40.
21. ibid., p. 397.
22. Thrum, *Hawaiian Annual,* 1905, p. 30.
23. Kuykendall, *Hawaiian Kingdom 1874-1893,* pp. 603-605.
24. Dean, *Alexander & Baldwin,* p. 135.
25. Hoyt, *Davies,* p. 231.
26. HSPA, *Sugar in Hawaii 1949,* p. 83-84.
27. ibid., p. 84.
28. Dean, *Alexander & Baldwin,* p. 190.
29. HSPA, *Sugar in Hawaii 1949,* p. 84-86.
30. HSPA, *Sugar Manual 1987,* p. 18.
31. HSPA, *Sugar Manual 1992.*
32. ibid.

CHAPTER 16 | SUGAR'S FUTURE IN HAWAI'I (2000)

1. Neil, "Hilo mill to close."
2. Neil, "Hamakua sugar."
3. ibid.
4. TenBruggencate, Jan, "Shake-up of Kauai sugar firms," *Honolulu Advertiser*, Wednesday, Sept. 2, 1992, p. C7.
5. TenBruggencate, Jan, "Kauai bagasse-power deal approved," *Honolulu Advertiser*, Oct. 30, 1992
6. Smith, Kit, "HSPA cutting back staff," *Honolulu Advertiser*, Wednesday Sept. 9, 1992, p. C1.
7. *Honolulu Advertiser*, "Kauai sugar loss may hit 20-30 percent," Saturday, Oct. 10, 1992, p. C1.
8. ibid.
9. Lynch, Russ, "C & H to shut Aiea plant," *Honolulu Star-Bulletin*, Monday, Feb. 22, 1993 p. C1.
10. Andrasick, James S., and John C. Couch, "Sugar cane still Hawaii's most important crop," *Honolulu Advertiser*, Feb. 2, 1993.
11. Smith, "A & B buys up."
12. Adler, *Spreckels*, p. 78.
13. Cho, Frank, "A & B sells 60% stake in Hawaiian Sugar," *Honolulu Advertiser*, December 26, 1998, p. B6.
14. Tanji, Edwin, "Pioneer Mill ending sugar operations," *Honolulu Advertiser*, March 3, 1999.
15. TenBruggencate, Jan, "Mill bets $5 million on Hawaiian sugar," *Honolulu Advertiser*, April 4, 1999.
16. Hooper, Susan, "Sugar company upgrading its factory," *Honolulu Advertiser*, August 6, 1999, p. B8. See, also: Edwin Tanji, "Company hopes to grow sugar without cane fires," *Honolulu Advertiser*, August 31, 1999, p. A1 et. seq.
17. HSPA, *Sugar Manual 1992*.
18. Plasch, *Hawaii's Sugar*, p. 3-4.
19. Conrow, "Hanging On," p. 24.
20. Plasch, *Hawaii's Sugar*, p. 12-3.
21. HSPA, *Perspectives-1987*, Introduction.
22. Daws, Gavin and George Cooper, *Land and Power in Hawaii*, Benchmark Books, Honolulu, 1985, p. 222.
23. HSPA, *Perspectives-1987*, p. 15.
24. June 1, 1993 telephone quote to co-author (WHD) by Matson representative. Quote was $2.94 per 100 pounds with a full container minimum.
25. Plasch, *Hawaii's Sugar*, p. 1-4.
26. Manrique, Luis A., *Feasibility of Potato Production in Hawaii*, College of Tropical Agriculture and Human Resources, University of Hawai'i, Research Series 026, January 1984, p.7.

BIBLIOGRAPHY

The locations of the documents cited in the bibliography are identified as follows:

[**BM**]: Bishop Museum Library, Honolulu.
[**FSMC**]: Private collection of co-author Francis S. Morgan.
[**HL**]: Hamilton Library, University of Hawai'i at Mānoa, Honolulu.
[**HSL**]: Hawai'i State Library, Honolulu.
[**HSPA**]: Library and archives of Hawaiian Sugar Planters' Association [now Hawaii Agriculture Research Center] 'Aiea, O'ahu.
[**LC**]: Library of Congress, Washington, D.C.
[**LM**]: Archives at Lyman House Memorial Museum, Hilo, Hawai'i.
[**WHDC**]: Private collection of co-author WHD.

Primary Source Material
Interviews and Conversations

Data gathered from experienced and sometimes retired long-time sugar workers provided insight into twentieth century plantation operations and life. Co-author WHD held discussions with field and mill workers, field supervisors, managers, executives, and peripheral workers and shopkeepers on all four of Hawai'i's sugar islands. Most significant were:

Anon. Discussion with two elderly retired Filipino sugar workers at the long shut-down Onomea Sugar Company mill yard on the Big Island. They answered many questions about the history and operations of the plantation that was closed down almost twenty years before. May 4, 1992. [WHDC]

Anon. Discussion held with elderly retired Japanese sugar worker still living in Kahuku, O'ahu. He described the life in the plantation community when the Kahuku Plantation Company was operating. June 3, 1993. [WHDC]

Baldwin, William, Manager, Personnel and Industrial Relations, Hawaiian Commercial and Sugar Company, Inc. (H.C.& S.), Pu'unēnē, Maui. At the plantation office at Pu'unēnē, Mr. Baldwin reviewed a manuscript draft and described the recent history of the H.C.& S. plantation and the involvement of the Matson Navigation Company in transporting raw sugar. June 18, 1993. [WHDC]

Demoruelle, Joseph and Sandy. Operators of the South Point Public Radio, and Naalehu Theater, discussions centered on what happens to a sugar plantation community when the local plantation is shut down. Discussions held May 4, 1992 at Nā'ālehu, Hawai'i. [WHDC]

Faye, Lindsay A. "Tony," Retired Manager, Kekaha Sugar Company. Discussions were wide-ranging and lengthy concerning the past and future prospects of the Hawai'i sugar industry. Mr. Faye described three generations of the Faye family involvement in sugar farming on the island of Kaua'i. July 29 and 30, 1993 at Ko-loa, Kaua'i, and Waimea, Kaua'i, respectively. [WHDC]

Kauwe, Joseph, elderly retired Native Hawaiian supervisor with Hutchinson Sugar Plantation in Nā'ālehu, Hawai'i. Mr. Kauwe described in colorful language what it was like to work on a Hawaiian sugar plantation. Nā'ālehu, Hawai'i, May 4, 1992. [WHDC]

Morgan, David, son of co-author Francis S. Morgan, and manager and executive, Hamakua Sugar Company, from 1983 to 1992. Mr. Morgan described plantation housing and the many technical problems the plantation faced during the years that he was employed by it. Hilo, Hawai'i, November 19, 1996. [WHDC]

Morgan, John, son of co-author Francis S. Morgan, and president of Kualoa Ranch, Oʻahu. Mr. Morgan described the history of Kualoa Ranch going back to the ill-fated and short-lived sugar operations initiated by his great-great-grandfather, Col. Charles Hastings Judd, over a century ago. Discussion at Kualoa Ranch, Oʻahu, October 7, 1992. [WHDC]

Poppinga, Hans, Engineer, H.C.& S. At the plantation office in Puʻunēnē, Mr. Poppinga supplied valuable historical data on the evolution of mill machinery, as well as a description of his employment on Kauaʻi plantations. June 18, 1993. [WHDC]

Reis, Allen, Crew Chief, Pump 3, McBryde Sugar Company, Hanapēpē, Kauaʻi. Mr. Reis conducted an inspection of Pump 3 in Hanapēpē Valley and described how the hydroelectric plant in Wainiha Valley on the other side of Waiʻaleʻale Mountain is controlled from the Pump 3 location. Hanapēpē, Kauaʻi, December 28, 1993. [WHDC]

Russell, James, Field Manager, Waialua Sugar Company, Inc., Waialua, Oʻahu. At the plantation offices, Mr. Russell described the recent reorganization of the plantation and the struggle to regain profitability. June 1993. [WHDC]

Takaki, Alex, former worker, Hilo Sugar Company. Mr. Takaki described his youth in Hilo, Hawaiʻi, where his father was an adherent planter for Hilo Sugar Company. Mr. Takaki worked in the fields as a child while growing up in a plantation community. Numerous discussions in Kailua, Oʻahu, in 1987 and subsequently. [WHDC]

Vorfeld, Robert, retired Manager, Pioneer Mill Company. Mr. Vorfeld was particularly helpful in describing Amfac/JMB's post-war operations and the problems of producing at Pioneer Mill. Discussions at Puʻunēnē, Maui, June 18, 1993. [WHDC]

Letters

Hughes, Robert H., former Vice President, C. Brewer & Company, Ltd., and Chairman, Hawaiian Sugar Planters' Association. Mr. Hughes reviewed the first draft, made a few corrections, and contributed several suggestions that were incorporated into the final draft. January 2, 1995. [WHDC]

Reppun, Dr. J. I. Frederick, M.D. (deceased). Dr. Reppun reviewed the first draft, made several helpful suggestions and, in numerous conversations held with WHD, told what it was like to practice medicine as a plantation physician on Laˉnaʻi and Molokaʻi. May 16, 1994 until March 1995. [WHDC]

Listing of Plantations in Hawaiʻi in 1883-1884 and After 1900

This listing was found within the HSPA archives. [HSPA]

Annual Sugar Production by Hawaiʻi's Plantations: [HSPA]

Found in the HSPA archives. Cited in notes as "HSPA data." This data was cross-checked with individual plantation manager's annual reports and found to be the same or within reasonable tolerance. Any difference was less than plus or minus 10 percent and was usually attributable to including, or not including, the minor amount of sugar produced from the harvests of adherent or independent farmers.

Corporation Annual Reports
[HSPA, FSMC, LM, or where indicated]

Plantation Manager's Annual Report of Operations appeared verbatim in the corporation annual reports. The manager's report includes sugar produced that year, weather, predictions for next crop year, purchases of machinery and equipment, labor problems, mill operations, and other factors affecting the plantation's productivity. Reports were located within the archives of Lyman House Memorial Museum and the HSPA.

Co-author WHD examined every 1933 corporation annual report for several reasons: first, 27 of 40 plantations were incorporated so that their annual reports could be located; second, the 1933 crop year was only the second of many years when the total sugar production exceeded one million tons; third, 1933 was the last crop year before production quotas were applied by the 1933 Jones-Costigan Act; and fourth, the 1933 crop year was one of the last years that hand harvesting predominated and plantation labor exceeded 45,000 workers.

Those corporation reports examined include [FSMC, except where otherwise indicated]:

KAUA'I
Hawaiian Sugar Company
Kekaha Sugar Company, Ltd.
Kilauea Sugar Plantation Company
Makee Sugar Company
McBryde Sugar Company, Ltd.
The Koloa Sugar Company
The Lihue Plantation Company

O'AHU
Ewa Plantation Company
Honolulu Plantation Company
Kahuku Plantation Company
Oahu Sugar Company
Waimanalo Sugar Company
Waialua Agricultural Company
Waianae Agricultural Company, Ltd.

MAUI
Hawaiian Commercial & Sugar Company, Ltd.
Maui Agricultural Company, Ltd.
Pioneer Mill Company
Wailuku Sugar Company

HAWAI'I
Hakalau Plantation Company
Hawaiian Agricultural Company
Hilo Sugar Company
Honokaa Sugar Company [LM]
Honomu Sugar Company
Hutchinson Sugar Plantation Company
Kohala Sugar Company [LM]
Olaa Sugar Company
Onomea Sugar Company
Paauhau Sugar Plantation Company
Pepeekeo Sugar Company

Reports for several other years are cited in the notes.

Hilo Sugar Company: [HSPA]
The Hilo Sugar Company was unique for co-author WHD because a friend's father had cultivated sugar for that plantation as an adherent farmer during his childhood. He shared

his experiences and observations with the writer. [WHDC] Because Hilo Sugar Company had made a transition from fluming of harvests to trucking of harvests to the mill during his time, corporate annual reports and manager's reports for Hilo Sugar Company were examined for the years 1911, 1925, 1932, 1937, 1938, 1939, and 1941, through and including 1965, when Hilo Sugar Company was combined with Onomea Sugar Company to form Mauna Kea Sugar Company. Records were located within HSPA archives. This period saw a vast reduction in numbers of field and mill workers, union organization of workers, conversion to mechanical harvesting and truck hauling, abandonment of an extensive fluming system, and the giving up of land to Hilo's urban growth after World War II. The picture given by these reports is a microcosm of Hawai'i's twentieth century sugar industry.

Lyman House Memorial Museum Archives: [LM]

Lyman Museum in Hilo preserves records of Kohala Sugar Company following its closing in 1975 and Hamakua Sugar Company's archives after the company declared bankruptcy in 1992. The Kohala Sugar Company records include data on operations from 1912 through 1975, Bond estate, Mahukona Terminal Company (1937-1952), and Maʻhukona Harbor. The Hamakua Sugar Company records go back to before Davies Hamakua Sugar Company was formed in 1979 and includes data for Honokaa, Pacific Mill, Hamakua Mill, Paauhau, Laupahoehoe, Kaiwiki, Ookala, and Kukaiau plantations that were eventually combined to make up Davies Hamakua Sugar Company.

Collection of Letters, Documents, Contracts, and Reports [HL]

Note: Examined by co-author WHD when located in the HSPA archives. This material was transferred to Hamilton Library, located on the campus of the University of Hawai'i at Maʻnoa, on October 3, 1996. It includes documents relating to the following plantations.

KAUA'I
Kekaha Sugar Company (1880-1946)
H.P. Faye & Co. (1886-1898)
Meier & Kruse (1886-1898)
Waimea Sugar Mill Company (1884-1946)
Lihue Plantation Company (1850-1968)
Makee Sugar Company (1877-1933)
McBryde Sugar Company (1899-1960)
Princeville Plantation Company (1862-1894)

O'AHU
Honolulu Plantation Company (1899-1940)
Oahu Sugar Company (1898-1940)

MAUI
Lahaina Agricultural Company (1871-1878)
Pioneer Mill Company (1863-1960)
Olowalu Company (1881-1933)

HAWAI'I
Davies Hamakua Sugar Company (1879-1959). This material relates to separate plantations that were later combined to form Davies Hamakua Sugar Company in 1979. These include:
Hamakua Mill Company (1878-1959)
Honokaa Sugar Company (1874-1959)
Kaiwiki Sugar Company (1909-1943)

Kukaiau Plantation Company (1884-1959)
Laupahoehoe Sugar Company (1884-1954)
Pacific Sugar Mill (1879-1928)
Paauhau Sugar Plantation (1906-1966)
Rickard Plantation (1887-1891)
Hawaiian Agricultural Company (1876-1945)
Hutchinson Sugar Plantation (1885-1951)

Mauna Kea Sugar Company was organized by C. Brewer & Co. in 1965 and incorporated the lands of the following plantations:
Hakalau Plantation Company (1878-1946)
Honomu Sugar Company (1880-1946)
Onomea Sugar Company (1886-1947)
Papaikou Sugar Company (1886-1888)
Pepeekeo Sugar Company (1880-1946)
Olaa Sugar Company (1900-1975)
Puna Sugar Company (1899-1908)

Data found within this collection relate to irrigation companies on Kaua'i, O'ahu and Hawai'i, plantation populations, plantation camps, railroad and ship transportation contracts and costs, plantation hospitals, doctors' salaries, labor contracts, labor pay schedules, labor importation quotas for plantations, purchases of horses and mules, purchases of cultivation equipment, plantation stores, complaints by managers and agency executives, cost savings studies, and miscellaneous data. Notable for their absence are data for several plantations owned and/or represented by Castle & Cooke.

Reports
U.S. House of Representatives, *Hearings Before The Subcommittee of the Committee On The Territories*, Seventy-Ninth Congress, Second Session, Pursuant H. Res. 236, U.S. Government Printing Office, Washington, D.C., 1946, (Concerning Statehood for Hawai'i). pp. 801-811 list membership of boards of directors of Hawai'i-based corporations in 1946. [LC]

Independent Growers and Adherent Planters
Letter, Sugar Factors Company, Limited to Pepeekeo Sugar Company and C. Brewer & Company, Ltd., December 16, 1937. Defines "independent growers" and "adherent planters" for purposes of distributing crop quotas and compliance payments under the 1937 Sugar Act. [HL]

Tolling Agreement, Laupahoehoe Sugar Company with Independent Growers. [LM]

Memorandum, Laupahoehoe Sugar Company to Independent Growers, "Estimated Returns for Your (Independent Grower's) 1977 Crop," including compliance payment, February 1, 1978. [LM]

Inter-island Shipping Charges
Letter, F.A. Schaefer & Co. to Interisland Steam Navigation Company, June 26, 1922, citing loading and shipping costs via Interisland's vessels. [HL]

Labor, Labor Contracts, and Compensation
Labor contract between McBryde Sugar Company and Ishido Shunjiro, December 26, 1899. [HSPA]

Memorandum, "Joint Venture Between Hawaiian Sugar Industry & Hawaiian Pineapple Industry Relative to Philipino [sic] Labor," May 20, 1955. Describes commitments due imported Philippine laborers under agreements from 1909 until 1955. [HSPA]

Rates of Pay per Diem, Laupahoehoe Sugar Company, 1936-1938. [HL]

Plantation Medical Practices
Report of the Physician in Charge Of Pepeekeo Hospital (serving Onomea Sugar Company, Pepeekeo Sugar Company, and Honomu Sugar Company plantations), January 22, 1934. This document describes the causes of nineteen deaths that occurred in the hospital during 1933 and the health of the plantation population served. [HSPA]

Procurement of Work Animals
Letter, Schuman Carriage Company, Ltd. to H.P. Faye, Manager, Kekaha Sugar Company, April 27, 1915, along with Faye's reply of May 1, 1915. Describes cost of mules. [HL]

Railroad Shipping Charges
Agreement, Hilo Railroad Company and Hamakua Mill Company, May 1910, setting freight charges between Pa'auilo and Hilo. [HL]

Sugar Act Compliance Payments
Letter, C. Brewer & Company, Ltd. to Manager, Pepeekeo Sugar Company, January 11, 1938. Describes compliance payment due under Sugar Act of 1937. [HL]

Memoirs, Biographies, and Primary Documents
All of these documents were cited one or more times in the chapter notes.

Baldwin, Arthur D., *A Memoir of Henry Perrine Baldwin 1842 to 1911*,
 Privately printed, 1915. [HSL]
Baldwin, D.D., "Lahaina Cane," reprint, *The Planters' Monthly*, 1882, pp. 42-43. [HSL]
Baldwin, Henry P., "Sugar and Hawaii," *The Mid-Pacific*, August 1928 (reprint). [HSL]
Bird, Isabella L., *Six Months in the Sandwich Islands*, Charles F. Tuttle Company, Inc.,
 Rutland, Vermont, 1974, (First edition, John Murray, London, 1890). [HSL]
C., "The Norwegian What To Do With Him," *The Planters' Monthly*, 1882, pp. 124-126. [HSL]
Castle, James B., "Will of James B. Castle," August 39 A.D. 1912. [LM]
De Varigny, Charles, *Fourteen Years in the Sandwich Islands 1855-1868*, The University Press
 of Hawai'i and The Hawaiian Historical Society, Honolulu, 1981. [HSL]
Edson, Hubert, *Sugar from Scarcity to Surplus*, Chemical Publishing Company, Inc., New
 York, 1958. [WHDC]
Gast, Ross H., *Don Francisco de Paula Marin; a Biography*, University Press of Hawai'i,
 Honolulu, 1973.
Gilman, Gorman D., "Streets of Honolulu in the Early Forties," *Hawaiian Annual*, Thrum,
 Honolulu, 1904. [HSL]
Hall, Jack, "A Luna's Log," 1927. [LM]
Hedemann, C., "Evolution of the Sugar Mill in Hawaii," *The Planters' Monthly*, September
 1902, pp. 425-430. [HSL]
Hind, R. Renton (Ed.), *John Hind of Hawi (1858-1933) His Memoirs*, Manaoag, Pangasinan,
 Philippines, 1951. [HSL]
Ii, John Papa, *Fragments of Hawaiian History*, Bishop Museum Press, Honolulu, 1959. [HSL]
King, Pauline N. (Editor), *Journal of Stephen Reynolds, Volume 1: 1823-1829*. Ku Paa
 Incorporated and The Peabody Museum of Salem, Salem, Massachusetts, 1989. [WHDC]
Lydgate, J.M., Hawaiian Annual, 1918, pp. 74-76. [HSL]

Nelson, Richard, "Notes on Wire Landings Along Hamakua Coast on the Island of Hawaii," *The Hawaiian Journal of History*, Vol. VIII, 1974, pp. 136-142. [HSL]
Wilcox, Elsie H., "Hanalei in History," *The Kauai Papers*, Kauai Historical Society, Līhue, Hawai'i, 1991, pp. 5-19. [WHDC]
Wilfong, George W., "Sugar Plantations in the Early Days in the Hawaiian Islands," *The Planters' Monthly*, Honolulu, December 1882. [HSL]
Young, Lucien, U.S. Navy, *The* Boston *in Hawaii*, Gibson Bros., Printers and Binders, Washington, D.C., 1898. [WHDC]

ADDITIONAL SOURCE MATERIAL

The following listing includes a mixture of primary and secondary source documents that were also cited in the chapter notes. Heavy reliance was placed on the Hawai'i State Library system and the archives of the Hawaiian Sugar Planters' Association. Photographs were located in the collections of the Hawai'i State Archives, Hawaiian Sugar Planters' Association, and Bishop Museum. The bibliography prepared by Susan M. Campbell, cited herein, is particularly useful.

Adler, Jacob, *Claus Spreckels The Sugar King of Hawaii*, Mutual Publishing Paperback Series, Honolulu, 1966. [HSL]
Adler, Jacob, and Gwynn Barrett (Eds.), *The Diaries of Walter Murray Gibson 1886, 1887*, The University Press of Hawai'i, Honolulu, 1973. [HSL]
Agee, H.P. (compiler), "A Brief History of the Hawaiian Sugar Planters' Association," Hawaii Sugar Manual-1935-36, A.B. Gilmore, New Orleans, 1936. [HSPA]
Alexander, Arthur C., *Koloa Plantation 1835-1935*, Kauai Historical Society, Līhu'e, Hawai'i, 1937. [HSL]
Andrade, Ken, "The Big Five's clout continues to erode," *Honolulu Star- Bulletin*, Feb. 21, 1989, Section 3, p. 2.
Andrasick, James S., and John C. Couch, "Sugar cane still Hawaii's most important crop," *Honolulu Advertiser*, Feb. 2, 1993. [HSL]
Baldwin, Charles W., *Geography of the Hawaiian Islands*, p.248, American Book Company, New York, revised edition 1924. [WHDC]
Barratt, Glynn, *The Russian Discovery of Hawaii*, Editions Limited, Honolulu, 1987. [HSL]
Beechert, Edward D., *Working in Hawaii A Labor History*, University of Hawai'i Press, Honolulu, 1985. [HSL]
Best, Gerald M., *Railroads of Hawaii: Narrow and Standard Gauge Common Carriers*, Golden West Books, San Marino, California, 1978. [HSL]
Bowser, George, *An Account of the Sugar Plantations and the Principal Stock Ranches on the Hawaiian Islands*, George Bowser & Company, Honolulu, 1880. [HSL]
Campbell, Susan M., Compiled and Annotated by, *Sugar in Hawaii: A Guide To Historical Resources*, The Humanities Program of the State Foundation on Culture and the Arts in Cooperation with The Hawaiian Historical Society, Honolulu, 1986 [HSL]
Char, Wai-Jane, "Three Chinese Stores in Honolulu," *The Hawaiian Journal of History*, Volume VIII, 1974. [HSL]
Clark, Jeff, "Rescuing the Past: Waimea Plantation Cottages," *Historic Hawai'i*, March 1990, pp. 7-9. [HSL]
Conde, Jesse C. and Gerald M. Best, *Sugar Trains; Narrow Gauge Rails of Hawaii*, Glenwood Pub., Felton, California, 1973. (out of print) [HSL]
Conde, J.C., *Narrow Gauge in a Kingdom The Hawaiian Railroad Company 1878-1897*, Railhead Publications, Felton, California, 1985. [HSL]
Conrow, Joan, "Hanging On and Hoping," *Hawaii Investor*, August 1992. [WHDC]
Cook, James, *A Voyage to the Pacific Ocean-in His Majesty's Ships the Resolution and Discovery; in the years 1776, 1777, 1778, 1779, and 1780*, Vol. II, G. Nicol and T. Cadell, 1784. [LM]

Cushing, Robert L., "The Beginnings of Sugar Production in Hawai'i," *The Hawaiian Journal of History*, Vol. XIX, 1985. [HSL]

Damon, Ethel M., "Father Bond of Kohala," *The Friend*, Honolulu, 1927. [HSL]

————, *Koamalu A Story of Pioneers on Kauai and of What They Built in That Island Garden*, 2 volumes, privately printed, Star-Bulletin Press, Honolulu, 1931. [HSL]

Das, U.H., "Rate of Cane and Sugar Formation in a Cane Crop," *Gilmore's Hawaii Sugar Manual*-1935-36, A.B. Gilmore, New Orleans, 1936, pp. 36-38. [HSPA]

Daws, Gavin and George Cooper, *Land and Power in Hawaii*, Benchmark Books, Honolulu, 1985. [HSL]

Day, A. Grove, *History Makers of Hawaii*, Mutual Publishing of Honolulu, Honolulu, 1984. [HSL]

Dean, Arthur L., *Cooperation in the Sugar Industry of Hawaii*, American Council, Institute of Pacific Relations, New York, 1933. [HSL]

————, *Alexander & Baldwin and the Predecessor Partnerships*, Alexander & Baldwin, Ltd., Honolulu, 1950. [HSL]

Department of Geography, *Atlas of Hawaii*, University of Hawai'i Press, Honolulu, 1983. [HSL]

Dye, Bob, "Lihue-The Lost Plantation," *Honolulu Magazine*, November 1986, pp. 88-89, 140-143. [HSL]

Emmet, Boris, Ph.D., *The California and Hawaiian Sugar...Refining Corporation*, Graduate School of Business, Stanford University, California, 1928. [HL]

The Estate of James Campbell, *James Campbell, Esq.*, Honolulu, 1978. [HSL]

The Friend, Honolulu, August 9, 1862, p. 58. [HSL]

Fuchs, Lawrence H., *Hawaii Pono: A Social History*, Harcourt, Brace & World, New York. [HSL]

Galloway, J.H., *The Sugar Cane Industry*, Cambridge University Press, Cambridge, U.K., 1989. [HSPA]

Gilmore, A.B., *Hawaii Sugar Manual*, New Orleans, 1936. [HSPA]

————, *Hawaiian Sugar Manual* 1938-39, A.B. Gilmore, New Orleans, 1939. [HSPA]

————, A.B., *Hawaiian Sugar Manual* 1948, A.B. Gilmore, New Orleans, 1948. [HSPA]

Gross, F.J., "Wireless Telegraph in the Hawaiian Islands," *Planters' Monthly*, January 1907. [HSL]

Hackler, Rhoda E.A., R.W. Meyer, *Sugar Mill, Its History and Restoration*, Molokai Museum and Cultural Center, 1990. [WHDC]

Handy, E.S., Craighill and Mary Kawena Pukui, *The Polynesian Family System in Kau Hawaii*, Charles E. Tuttle Company, Rutland, Vermont, 1972. [HSL]

Hansen, Arthur R., *Kohala Sugar Company 1863-1963*, Kohala Sugar Company, Kohala, Hawai'i, 1963. [LM]

Hass, H.B., "Sugar," *The World Book Encylopedia* Volume 16, Field Enterprises Educational Corporation, Chicago, 1960. [WHDC]

Hawaiian Sugar Planters' Association, *The Story of Sugar in Hawaii*,

Hawaiian Sugar Planters' Association, Honolulu, 1926. [HSPA]

————, Hawaiian Sugar Manual 1940, HSPA, 'Aiea, Hawai'i, 1940. [HSPA]

————, Proceedings of 65th Annual Meeting, Honolulu, December 10, 1945. [HSPA]

————, *Sugar in Hawaii*, Hawaiian Sugar Planters' Association, Honolulu, 1949. [HSPA]

————, *Hawaiian Sugar Manual 1965*, H.S.P.A., 'Aiea, Hawai'i, 1965. [HSPA]

————, *Hawaiian Sugar Manual 1972*, H.S.P.A., 'Aiea, Hawai'i, 1972. [HSPA]

————, *Experiment Station Annual Report 1985*, Hawaiian Sugar Planters' Association, 'Aiea, Hawai'i, 1986. [HSPA]

————, *Hawaiian Sugar Manual 1987*, Hawaiian Sugar Planters' Association, 'Aiea, Hawai'i, 1988. [HSPA]

————, *Hawaiian Sugar Manual 1991*, Aiea, Hawaii, 1991. [HSPA]

————, *The Hawaiian Sugar Industry: Perspectives on Current Issues*, H.S.P.A., 'Aiea, Hawai'i, February 1987. [HSPA]

————, *Hawaiian Sugar Manual 1992*, Hawaiian Sugar Planters' Association, 'Aiea, Hawai'i, 1993. [HSPA]

―――――, *Hawaiian Sugar Manual 1993-1994*, Hawaiian Sugar Planters' Association, ʻAiea, Hawaiʻi, 1994. [HSPA]

―――――, *Hawaiian Sugar Manual 1995*, Hawaiian Sugar Planters' Association, ʻAiea, Hawaiʻi, 1995. [HSPA]

―――――, *Hawaiian Sugar Planters' Association Annual Report 1995*, Hawaiian Sugar Planters' Association, ʻAiea, Hawaiʻi, 1996. [HSPA]

Hedemann, Nancy Oakley, *A Scottish-Hawaiian Story The Purvis Family in the Sandwich Islands*, Book Crafters, Virginia, 1994.[HSL]

Hilo Sugar Company, Inc., 1961 Annual Report. [HSPA]

Historic Hawaiʻi, "Meyer Sugar Mill Plans Expansion," March 1991, p. 13. [HSL]

Hitch, Thomas Kemper, *Islands In Transition; The Past, Present, and Future of Hawaii's Economy*, First Hawaiian Bank, distributed by University of Hawaiʻi Press, 1992. [HSL]

Holderness, James S., Gary R. Vieth, and Frank S. Scott, Jr., *Economic Viabilty of Independent Sugarcane Farms on the Hilo Coast*, University of Hawaiʻi, Hawaii Institute of Tropical Agriculture and Human Resources, Honolulu, December, 1979. [HSL]

Holderness, James S., Gary R. Vieth, Frank S. Scott, Jr., and Nicomedes Briones, *Cost of Producing and Processing Sugarcane Among Hawaii's Independent Cane Growers, With Comparisons to Plantation Growers*, College of Tropical Agriculture and Human Resources, University of Hawaiʻi, Research Extension Series 032, June 1982. [HSL]

Honolulu Iron Works Company, *Some Sugar Factories Built and Equipped by the Honolulu Iron Works Company*, Honolulu Iron Works, Honolulu, 1924. [HSL]

―――――, *1965 Annual Report*. [HSL]

Honolulu Advertiser, Obit., "Fraser, 62, Dies in Hilo," January 27, 1940. [HSPA]

―――――, Obit., "Donald J. Martin of the sugar industry," June 26, 1991, p. D2. [HSL]

―――――, Mar. 20, 1992, p. C5. [HSL]

―――――, "Kauai sugar loss may hit 20-30 percent," Saturday, Oct. 10, 1992, p. C1. [HSL]

Honolulu Star-Bulletin, Obit., "Pioneer Builder of Hawaii, John A. Scott, Dead," November 13, 1925. [HSPA]

―――――, "Hawaiian Sugar Plantation History, No. 10-Hilo Island of Hawaii," 4 May 1935. [HSL]

Hoverson, Martha (ed.), "Historic Koloa: A Guide," Friends of the Koloa School Community Library, Kōloa, Hawaiʻi, 1985.[WHDC]

Hoyt, Edwin P., *Davies The Inside Story of a British-American Family in the Pacific and Its Business Enterprises*, Topgallant Publishing Co., Ltd., Honolulu, 1983. [HSL]

Hungerford, John B., *Hawaiian Railroads*, Hungerford Press, Reseda, California, 1963. [HSL]

Jarves, James Jackson, *History of the Hawaiian Islands*, Henry M. Whitney, Pub., 1872. [HL]

Joesting, Edward, *Kauai The Separate Kingdom*, University of Hawaiʻi Press and Kauai Museum Association, Limited, 1984. [HSL]

Judd, Gerrit P., *The Friend*, Feb. 1867, Enclosure No. 3. [HSL]

Judd, Gerrit P., IV, *Hawaii's Friend A biography of Gerrit Parmale Judd* (1803-1873), University of Hawaiʻi Press, Honolulu, 1960. [HSL]

Kahane, Joyce D. and Jean Kadooka Mardfin, *The Sugar Industry in Hawaii An Action Plan*, State of Hawaiʻi Legislative Reference Bureau, Report No. 9, 1987. [WHDC]

Kai, Peggy, "Chinese Settlers in the Village of Hilo Before 1852," *The Hawaiian Journal of History*, Volume VIII, 1974. [HSL]

Kau Sugar Company, Inc., Kau Sugar Company, Inc., Pāhala, Hawaiʻi, 1972. [HSPA]

Kauai Historical Society, *The Kauai Papers*, The Kauai Historical Society, Līhuʻe, Hawaiʻi, 1991. [WHDC]

Kelly, Marian, Barry Nakamura, and Dorothy B. Barrere, *Hilo Bay: A Chronological History Land and Water Use in the Hilo Bay Area, Island of Hawaii*, Bernice P. Bishop Museum, Honolulu, March 1981. [BM]

Kinoshita, Charles M., *Cogeneration in the Hawaiian Sugar Industry*, Hawaii Institute of Energy Research, Honolulu, 1990. [HSL]

Korn, Alphonse L., *The Victorian Visitors*, The University of Hawai'i Press, Honolulu, 1958. [HSL]

Knudsen, Eric A. and Gurre P. Noble, *Kanuka of Kauai*, Tongg Publishing Company, Honolulu, 1944. [WHDC}

Krauss, Bob and William P. Alexander, *Grove Farm Plantation The Biography of a Hawaiian Sugar Plantation*, Pacific Books, Palo Alto, California, second edition, 1984. [HSL]

Kurisu, Yasushi *"Scotch," Sugar Town Hawaii's Plantation Days Remembered*, Watermark Publishing, Honolulu, 1995. [HSL]

Kuykendall, Ralph S., *The Hawaiian Kingdom Volume 1 1778-1854*, University Press of Hawai'i, Honolulu, 1938. [HSL]

———, *The Hawaiian Kingdom 1854-1874*, University of Hawai'i Press, Honolulu, 1953. [HSL]

———, *The Hawaiian Kingdom Volume III 1874-1893 The Kalakaua Dynasty*, University of Hawai'i Press, Honolulu, 1967. [HSL]

Lind, Andrew W., *An Island Community*, Greenwood Press, New York, 1968 (second edition, first edition 1938). [HSL]

Lynch, Russ, "C & H to shut Aiea plant," *Honolulu Star-Bulletin*, Monday, Feb. 22, 1993, p. C1. [HSL]

Maclennan, Carol A., "Foundations of Sugar's Power: Early Maui Plantations," *The Hawaiian Journal of History*, Volume 29, 1995, pp. 33-56. [HSL]

Mangelsdorf, A.J. and C.G. Lennox, "Sugar Cane Breeding in Hawaii," *Gilmore's Hawaii Sugar Manual-1935-36*, A.B. Gilmore, New Orleans, 1936, p. 18. [HSPA]

Manrique, Luis A., "Feasibility of Potato Production in Hawaii," College of Tropical Agriculture and Human Resources, University of Hawai'i, Research Series 026, January 1984.

Martin, J.P., and C.W. Carpenter, "Sugar Cane Diseases in Hawaii," *Gilmore's Hawaii Sugar Manual-1935-36*, A.B. Gilmore, New Orleans, 1936, pp. 26-29. [HSPA]

McBryde Sugar Co., Ltd., *Story of McBryde Sugar Co., Ltd.*, McBryde Sugar Co., 1940 (limited edition). [HSPA]

McClellan, Geo. B., *A Hand Book on the Sugar Industry of the Hawaiian Islands*, The Hawaiian Gazette Company, Ltd., Honolulu, 1899. [HL]

Neil, Christopher, "Hilo Mill To Close," *Honolulu Advertiser*, August 1, 1992, p. A1. [HSL]

———, "Hamakua Sugar files Bankruptcy," *Honolulu Advertiser*, August 15, 1992, p. A1. [HSL]

Nellist, George F., *The Story of Hawaii and Its Builders*, Honolulu Star-Bulletin, Inc., Honolulu, 1925. [HSL]

Odo, Franklin, and Kazuko Sinoto, *A Pictorial History of the Japanese in Hawaii 1885-1924*, Bernice Pauahi Bishop Museum, Honolulu, 1985. [WHDC]

Pemberton, C.E., "The Tropical American Toad Bufo Marinus in Hawaii," *Gilmore's Hawaii Sugar Manual-1935-36*, A.B. Gilmore, New Orleans, 1936, pp. 29-30. [HSPA]

Phillips, Perry F., *Diversified Agriculture in Hawaii*, University of Hawai'i Press, Honolulu, 1953, Table A5 lists 1501 small planters of sugar in 1952. Aug. 1, 1992, p. 1. [HSL]

Plasch, Bruce S., *Hawaii's Sugar Industry and Sugarcane Lands: Outlook, Issues and Options*, Decision Analysts Hawaii, Inc., Honolulu, April 1989. [WHDC]

Polynesian, May 29, 1841. [HSL]

Rho, Marguerite, "Alexander & Baldwin Sugar Museum," *Historic Hawai'i*, October 1988. [HSL]

Schmitt, Robert and Doak C. Cox, "Hawaiian Time," *The Hawaiian Journal of History*, Vol. 26, 1992. [HSL]

Schaefer, Frederick A., III, *Endless Journey Generation to Generation*, Olomana Press, Kailua, Hawai'i , 1996.[WHDC]

Silva, Alvin K. (Ed.), "Wailuku Sugar Company 1862 November 1962 Centennial," Wailuku Sugar Company, Wailuku, Maui, 1962. [HSPA]

Simonds, William A., *Kamaaina-A Century in Hawaii*, American Factors, Ltd., Honolulu, 1949. [HSL]

Simpich, Frederick, Jr., *Dynasty in the Pacific*, McGraw-Hill Book Co., New York, 1974. [HSL]

Smith, Jared G., *Plantation Sketches*, The Advertiser Press, Honolulu, 1924. [HSL]

————, "Nothing in that World Like a Hawaii Mill," *Honolulu Advertiser*, May 8, 1932. [HSPA]

————, *The Big Five*, Advertiser Publishing Company, Ltd., Honolulu, 1942. [HSL]

Smith, Kit, "HSPA cutting back staff," *Honolulu Advertiser*, Wednesday, Sept. 9, 1992, p. C1. [HSL]

————, "Isle business leader Malcolm MacNaughton dies," *Honolulu Advertiser*, December 31, 1992, p. A2. [HSL]

————, "A & B buys up sugar firm," *Honolulu Advertiser*, Mar. 2 1993. [HSL]

Smith, Lydia, "Remembering Mana An Historical Review," *Historic Hawai'i*, March 1990, pp. 4-6. [HSL]

Smith, Walter E., "War and Our Sugar Industry," *Hawaii*, August 17, 1944, pp. 8-9. [HSL]

Sterling, Elspeth P., and Catherine C. Summers, *Sites of Oahu*, Bishop Museum Press, Honolulu, 1978. [HSL]

Stone, Scott C.S., C. Brewer and Company, Ltd. *Growing Cane Since 1826*, Island Heritage Pub., 'Aiea, Hawai'i, 1991.

Sullivan, Josephine, *A History of C. Brewer & Company 1826-1926*, Walton Advertising & Printing Company, Boston, 1926. [HSL]

Takaki, Ronald, *Pau Hana Plantation Life and Labor in Hawaii 1835-1920*, University of Hawai'i Press, Honolulu, 1983. [HSL]

Tanahara, Kris and Hugh Clark, "Union Protests Hamakua Sugar Closing," *Honolulu Advertiser*, December 21, 1992, p. A3. [HSL]

Taylor, Frank J., Earl M. Welty, and David W. Eyre, *From Land and Sea The Story of Castle and Cooke in Hawaii*, Chronicle Books, San Francisco, 1976. [HSL]

TenBruggencate, Jan, "Shake-up of Kauai sugar firms," *Honolulu Advertiser*, Wednesday, Sept. 2, 1992. [HSL]

————, "Kauai bagasse-power deal approved," *Honolulu Advertiser*, Oct. 30, 1992. [HSL]

————, "State reports a drop in value of crop sales," *Honolulu Advertiser*, Feb. 4, 1993. p. D4. [HSL]

Thrum, Thos. G., *Hawaiian Almanac and Annual*, Black & Auld, printer, 1876. [HSL]

————., *Hawaiian Annual: All About Hawaii*, Black & Auld, Printer, Honolulu, 1901. [HSL]

————, *Hawaiian Almanac and Annual, 1909-1924*. [HSL]

————, "James Makee," *Hawaiian Annual 1927*, Honolulu, pp. 27-39. [HSL]

Thurston, Lorrin A. (Editor), *A Directory of Hawaiian Sugar Plantations and Data Concerning Sugar and the Sugar Business*, Hawaiian Gazette Co., Ltd., Honolulu, December, 1914. [HL]

University of Hawaii, *Stores and Storekeepers of Paia & Puunene, Maui Vol. 1*, Ethnic Studies Oral History Project, University of Hawai'i, Mānoa, June 1980. [HSL]

University of Hawaii Textbook Series, *The Story of Cane Sugar*, University of Hawai'i, Honolulu, 1928. [WHDC]

Vandercook, John W., *King Cane The Story of Sugar in Hawaii*, Harper & Brothers, New York, 1939. [HSL]

Wadsworth, H.A., "A Historical Summary of Irrigation in Hawaii," *Gilmore's Hawaii Sugar Manual-1935-36*, A.B. Gilmore. New Orleans, 1936, pp. 63-64. [HSPA]

Wailea Milling Company, Ltd., 1929 Annual Report. [HSPA]

Wallace, A.F. "The Cane Washing Problem Presented by Mechanical Harvesting," *Gilmore's Hawaii Sugar Manual-1938-39*, A.B. Gilmore, New Orleans, 1939, pp. 28-30. [HSPA]

Whitney, Caspar, "Hawaiian Sugar Industry," *The Planters' Monthly*, Honolulu, August 1899, pp. 367-368. [HSL]

Wilcox, Carol, *Sugar Water Hawaii's Plantation Ditches*, University of Hawai'i Press, Honolulu, 1996. [HSL]

Yamauchi, Hiroshi and Win Bui, *Drip Irrigation and the Survival of the Hawaiian Sugar Industry*, University of Hawai'i College of Agriculture and Human Resources, Honolulu, March 1990. [HSPA]

Yardley, Paul T., *Millstones and Milestones: The Career of B. F. Dillingham in Hawaii, 1844-1918*, University Press of Hawai'i, Honolulu, 1981. [HSL]

Newspapers, Annuals, and Manuals

The following were consulted, without citation, while writing this book.

Anon., *All About Hawaii-Thrum's Hawaiian Almanac & Standard Guide*, SB Printers, Inc., Honolulu, 1974. [WHDC]

Gilmore, Abner Banks, *Gilmore's Hawaii Sugar Manual, 1931-32, 1935-36, 1938-39, 1957*. [HSPA]s

Hawaiian Sugar Planters' Association, *The Hawaiian Planters' Monthly, 1895-1909*. [HSPA]

Hawaiian Sugar Planters' Association, *Hawaiian Sugar Manual*, Page 254, 1946-1995. [HSPA]

Honolulu Advertiser, 1985-1993. [HSL]

Honolulu Star-Bulletin, 1885-1993. [HSL]

Planters' Labor and Supply Company, *The Hawaiian Planters' Monthly, 1882-1895*. [HSPA]

Thrum, T.G., *Hawaiian Almanac and Annual, 1875-1891*. [HSL]

———, *Hawaiian Annual: All About Hawaii, 1892-1940*. [HSL]

INDEX

A

Aamano Plantation, 94
Adams, E.P., 32, 153
Afong, Chun, 99-100, 145
Agricultural Adjustment Act, 118, 196
Ahpong, 12, 18
Ahukini Terminal & Railway Company, 166, 168
Aiko, 17, 102
ʻAkaka Falls (Hawaiʻi), 99
Akanaliilii, T., 66
ʻĀleʻaleʻa Point (Hawaiʻi), 104
Alexander & Baldwin Plantation. *See* Alexander & Baldwin, Inc.
Alexander & Baldwin Sugar Museum, 73
Alexander & Baldwin, Inc. (A&B-Hawaiʻi, Inc.), 7, 23, 33, 36, 47, 61, 64, 67-69, 87, 137, 142-147, 156, 166, 172, 200-202, 205, 211
Alexander, Frank, 33
Alexander, James M., 61, 68
Alexander, Rev. William, 33, 146, 208-209
Alexander, Samuel, 33, 63-64, 67-68, 119, 142, 146, 180
ʻAmauulu (Hawaiʻi), 17
Amauulu Plantation (Spencer's Plantation), 83, 102
American Factors, Ltd. *See* Amfac/JMB-Hawaiʻi, Inc.
American Guano Company, 30
American Sugar Company, 36, 54-55, 57, 67
American Sugar Refining Company, 156
Amfac Sugar/West, 35
Amfac/JMB-Hawaiʻi, Inc., 7, 29, 35, 45-46, 49-50, 63-64, 67, 107, 135, 140-141, 143, 145, 172, 199-201, 203, 205
Andrasick, James, 200
Andrews, Lorrin, 207
Annexation, 23, 36, 55, 71, 105, 123, 127-129, 154, 156, 196
Apokaa Sugar Company, Ltd., 41, 46
Armstrong, Rev. Richard, 63, 141, 208
Artesian wells, 44-45, 47, 49, 53, 55, 60, 63, 181
Association of Hawaiian Sugar Technologies, 150
Atai, 12, 15-17, 19
Austin, Johnathan, 102, 154
Austin, Judge S.L., 102

B

Bailey Brothers, 60
Bailey, Rev. Edward, 65, 208
Bailey, William, 65
Bal & Adams, 60, 65
Bal, Eugene, 54
Baldwin Locomotive Works, 55
Baldwin, Arthur, 67-68
Baldwin, Benjamin D., 33
Baldwin, Douglas, 33
Baldwin, Dwight, 33, 63, 86, 146, 176, 208
Baldwin, Henry, 33, 59, 62-64, 67-71, 119, 142, 146, 154, 180
Barbers Point (Oʻahu), 186
Beecroft Plantation, 82, 89
Beet sugar, 156, 160, 191-195, 202
Bellows Army Air Field, 43
Bennett, George, 75
Berger, C.O., 146
Big Five, 7, 40, 42, 135-145. *See also names of specific companies.*
Bingham, Hiram, 207
Bishop & Company, 153
Bishop Estate, 47, 49
Bishop Trust Company, Ltd., 7, 146
Bishop, Bernice Pauahi, 108
Bishop, Charles R., 108, 110, 137
Bishop, Rev. Artemas, 3, 207
Bishop, Rev. S.E., 209
Bison-Barre, 160
Black, Martin, 76
Boki, High Chief, 12, 14-15
Bolte, C., 146
Bomke, William, 107
Bond, Rev. Elias, 85-86, 141, 208
Bratchley, Abraham, 207
Brewer Plantation (Haliʻimaile Plantation), 12, 18, 23, 66, 137
Brewer, Capt. Charles, 19, 137-138
Brewer, Charles II, 137
Brinsmade, Peter Allen, 26
Brown, Lydia, 208
Bruce, Robert, 76
Bryant, Mrs. H.R., 90
Bureau of Immigration, 127
Burnham, James
Buyers, J.W., 138

C

C & H (California & Hawaiian Sugar
    Company), 50, 149-150, 155,
    194, 210-211;
    refineries, 81, 143-144, 150, 155-156,
    160. 199-201, 208, 214;
    Sugar Refining Corporation, 144
C. Brewer & Company, Ltd., 7, 19, 23-24,
    28, 30, 32-35, 39, 43, 55, 61-62,
    65-67, 78-80, 93, 98-102, 104-105,
    109-110, 118, 121, 137-139, 143,
    145-147, 153, 156, 170-172, 193,
    199-201
C.N. Spencer & Company, 109
California Beet Sugar and Refinery
    Company, 156
California Sugar Refining Company, 156
California, 126-127, 143, 151-152, 191,
    195, 210. See also San Francisco.
Campbell Estate, 46
Campbell, James, 42, 44, 46, 63
Campbell, Thomas, 97
Campsie, James, 111
Cane toads, 175, 180
Canec, 172
Carter, George, 138
Carter, H.A., 138
Carysfort, 31
Castle & Cooke , 6-7, 42, 45-47, 49,
    63, 79, 85-87, 137-138, 141-143,
    145-147, 153, 156, 170, 172
Castle, James, 42, 45-47, 69, 71, 105, 112,
    146, 167
Castle, Samuel, 42, 45, 63, 85, 141, 146,
    208
Cattle ranching, 62, 76, 85, 151, 160
Center, D., 55, 62
Chalmers, John, 62
Chamberlain plantation, 42
Chamberlain, Daniel, 207
Chance, 27-28
Chapin, C., 127
Chapin, Dr. Alonzo, 208
Chinese: as contract labor, 4, 11, 20, 71,
    117, 123, 127, 129, 152;
    Chinese Exclusion Act, 123, 127, 129;
    first to mill sugar in Hawai'i, 13-14, 120;
    merchants, 15, 19, 99, 127;
    as sugar masters, 15-18, 99, 181
Civil War, U.S., 9-10, 12, 127, 191, 193
Clark, Rev. Ephriam W., 207
Coffee, 37, 99, 202

Commodity Credit Corporation, 197
Cook, Captain James, 2, 123
Cooke, Amos, 55, 63, 141, 146, 208
Cooke, Charles, 55, 138, 146, 193
Cooke, Joseph, 142, 146
Corn, 160-161
Corsair, 32
Costa, John, 108
Couch, John, 200
Crescent City Milling, 120
Cuba, 5, 153, 171, 191-193, 196
Cummings, John Adams, 43
Cushnie, William, 111

D

Damon, Samuel C., 99, 146, 162, 209
Damon, Samuel M., 71, 99-100
Davies Hamakua Sugar Company. See
    Hamakua Sugar Company
Davies, Theophilus H., 89, 93, 96-98, 105,
    115, 129, 135, 139. See also Theo H.
    Davies & Co., Ltd.
Department of Agriculture. See USDA
Dibble, Rev. Sheldon, 208
Dickey, C.W., 71
Diell, Rev. John, 208
Dillingham Company, 146
Dillingham, Benjamin Franklin., 23, 36,
    44-46, 49, 105, 141, 167, 170
Dillingham, Walter, 172
Dole Food Company, 141, 145, 201. See
    also Castle & Cooke; Dole Pineapple
    Company
Dole Pineapple Company, 141
Dole, Rev. Daniel, 208
Dole, Sanford B., 154, 207
Dominis, John, 110
Dowsett, J.I., 43
Dowsett, J.M., 146
Dunbar, James, 44

E

E. Hoffschlaeger & Company, 145
East Maui Plantation Company, 60-62
Eckhart, Charles F., 178
Ednie, Douglas, 76
Edson, Hubert, 70
Edwards, Capt. Pardon, 177
'Ele'ele Harbor, 168
Eleele Plantation, 25, 36-37
Ellis, Rev. William, 209
Ely, James, 207

Emerson, Rev. John S., 208
Emma, Queen, 20
EPA (Environmental Protection Agency), 80
Europeans:
    on plantations, 76, 92, 112, 129, 139-140
'Ewa (O'ahu), 40, 44-45, 51
Ewa Plantation Company, 41, 45-46, 49, 51, 55, 65, 131, 167, 178, 181-183
Experiment Stations, 155-156, 175, 178-179, 181

F

F.A. Schaefer & Co., Ltd., 7, 91-92, 136, 145-146, 153, 170
Fagan, Paul, 62
Farm Act, 190
Faye, H.P., 35-36
Filipinos:
    as plantation labor, 4, 11, 45, 124, 129, 133, 150
First Puna Sugar Company, 84, 107
Flexi-Van Corporation, 141
Flintcoat Company, 172
Forbes, Rev. Anderson, 208
Forbes, Rev. Cochran, 208
Ford Island, 49
Foster Gardens, 162
Foster, Capt. Thomas, 162
Foster, J.P., 71
Foster, Mary, 162
Fraser, Alexander, 104
Fred L. Waldron, Ltd., 146
French, William, 12, 15-17, 19, 136
Fricke, Robert, 44
Fulton Iron Works, 90

G

G.W. Macfarlane & Co., 145
Gay & Robinson, 7, 24-25, 32-35, 37, 199, 201-202, 204-205
Gay, Francis, 33
Gear, Lansing & Company, 146
General Royal T. Frank, 164
George Washington, 176
German immigrants, 139-140
Gibson, Walter Murray, 56
Gilman, Gorham D., 27
Glade, H.F., 140
Glenwood (Hawai'i), 107
Goats, 110

Goodale, William, 47, 101, 184
Goodrich, Joseph, 16, 26, 207
Gower, John L., 18
Great Depression, 124, 189
Great Mahele Land Act (1848), 9, 17, 41, 66, 116
Great Northern Railroad, 160
Green, Rev. Johnathon S., 207
Green, William, 138
Grinbaum & Company, 146
Gross, F.J., 186
Grove Farm Plantation, 25, 28, 30, 35, 140, 168;
    Homestead museum, 37
Grove Ranch Plantation, 60, 66, 68
Gulick, Rev. Peter J., 207

H

H. Hackfeld & Company, 28, 35, 63, 67, 99, 137, 139-141, 153, 170
H.C. & S. (Hawaiian Commercial & Sugar Company), 59, 61, 66, 68-70, 72, 131, 143, 146, 166, 172, 179, 183, 201, 205
H.P. Faye & Company, 25, 35
Hackfeld, Capt. Heinrich, 139-140
Haiku Fruit & Packaging Corp., 67
Haiku Plantation, 45, 59, 65, 67-68, 146
Haiku Sugar Company, 60, 62-63, 68, 71, 141-142
Haina (Hawai'i), 59
Haina Mill, 80, 160
Hakalau Plantation Company, 78, 83, 98, 101, 104, 121
Hakalau Sugar Company, 121
Hālawa (Hawai'i), 87
Halawa Mill & Plantation, 82, 86-87
Haleakala, 160
Hale'iwa (O'ahu), 164
Hali'imaile Plantation. *See* Brewer Plantation
Halstead & Gordon, 42
Halstead & Sons, 41-42, 47
Halstead, Robert, 42
Hāmākua Coast (Hawai'i), 77-79, 88, 90-98, 112-113, 123-124, 131, 135, 139, 149, 159-160, 163-164, 166-167, 183
Hamakua Ditch Company (Hawaiian Irrigation Company), 68, 77
Hāmākua Ditch, 69, 77, 80, 142, 180
Hamakua Mill Company, 75-76, 80, 82, 93-95, 116, 120, 135, 139, 178;

Hamakua Mill Company, independent mill, 120
Hamakua Plantation Company, 93, 120, 125, 139, 149, 175, 184
Hāmākua Poko (Maui), 70-71, 131
Hamakua Sugar Company, 80-82, 90, 92-97, 113, 123, 133, 145, 151, 172-173, 176, 199, 201-202, 210
Hamoa Plantation, 55
Hāna (Maui), 62, 67, 116, 164, 176
Hana Plantation Company, 55, 60, 62
Hanalei (Kauaʻi), 164
Hanamaulu Plantation, 25, 28-29; independent mill, 120
Hanapēpē (Kauaʻi), 34, 164
Harris, Charles Coffin, 41
Hart, Judge C.F., 88
Hasson, W.F., 57
Hawaiʻi (Big Island), 75-113, 116, 119, 135, 164, 166, 179
Hawaiʻi Agricultural Research Center (HARC), 155. *See also* Hawaiian Sugar Planter's Association
Hawaiʻi Consolidated Railway, 167
Hawaiʻi Electric Light Company, 107
Hawaiʻi Plantation Village, 46, 51
Hawaiʻi Railway Company, 166
Hawaiʻi Railway Society, 51
Hawaiian Agricultural Company, 84, 109-112, 137, 168
Hawaiian Cane Products, Ltd., 105, 172
Hawaiian Cellulose, Ltd., 172
Hawaiian Commercial Company, 68-69
Hawaiian Consolidated Railway Limited, 86, 94, 101, 106-107, 166, 172
Hawaiian Development Company, 146
Hawaiian Electric Company, 47
Hawaiian Irrigation Company. *See* Hamakua Ditch Company.
Hawaiian Railroad Company, 86, 88, 90, 165-166
Hawaiian Sugar Company, Inc., 25, 33-34, 65, 146, 168
Hawaiian Sugar Planters' Association (HSPA), 1, 5, 10, 50, 59, 78-79, 81, 95, 125, 130-131, 144, 149-150, 154-155, 175, 178, 184, 187, 199-200
Hawaiian Sugar Transport Company, 151, 156-157
Hawaiian Telephone Company, 103
Hawaiian Tramways Company, Ltd., 57
Hawi Mill & Plantation Company, 82, 86, 88, 90, 163

Heʻeia (Oʻahu), 164
Heeia Agricultural Company, 41, 43, 47
Heinz, Dr. Don, 203
Hellespont, 26
Henry, 20
Herrscher, Jos., 146
Heyselden, Frederick, 57
Hickam Air Field, 50
High-fructose corn syrup (HFCS), 189, 194-195, 197
Hilea Sugar Company, 84, 103, 109-110
Hillebrand, Dr. William, 128
Hilo (Hawaiʻi), 76, 78-79, 86, 91-94, 98, 100-105, 107, 109, 112-113, 116, 119-121, 135, 163-165, 167, 178, 183-184
Hilo Coast Processing Company (HCPC), 104, 113, 118-119, 121, 172; independent mill, 120, 199
Hilo Electric Company, 103
Hilo Iron Works, 160, 171
Hilo Portuguese Sugar Company, 120
Hilo Railroad Company, 106, 166-167
Hilo Sugar Company, 39, 75-76, 78, 83, 102-104, 118, 172, 178
Hind, Henry, 89
Hind, John, 67, 88, 90
Hind, Robert, 67, 87-90, 120, 127, 162
Hind, Rolf & Company, 146
Hitch, Dr. Thomas, 203
Hitchcock & Company, 83, 102. *See also* Papaikou Sugar Company.
Hitchcock, Elizabeth, 208
Hitchcock, Rev. Harvey, 102, 208
Hobron, Captain H.T., 66, 68, 71, 166
Hohensollern & Kraus, 169
Holaday, G. Stephen, 201
Holman, Dr. Thomas, 207
Homestead Act (1884), 117
Honokaʻa Landing (Hawaiʻi), 78-79, 91, 125, 164
Honokaʻa Sugar Company, 7, 77, 80, 82, 91-95, 136, 139; plantation, 78, 80, 93, 97, 139, 149
Honolii, John, 207
Honolulu (Oʻahu), 40, 49-50, 53, 85, 91, 117, 124, 129, 136, 140, 162-163, 169-170
Honolulu Iron Works, 29, 44, 105, 108, 135, 139, 160, 169-171
Honolulu Plantation Company, 39, 41, 50, 55

Honolulu Rapid Transit, 47
Honomu Sugar Company, 83, 98-99, 101, 104, 137
Honomū (Hawaiʻi), 164
Honuʻapo Landing (Hawaiʻi), 108, 138, 163-164, 168-169
Honuapo Landing Railway, 166, 168
Honuapo Plantation, 84, 110
Hooper, William, 26
Hopu, Thomas, 207
Horner, J.M., 96
Hossack, Sandy, 76
Howe, A.B., 62
Huelo Plantation, 60, 66;
   independent mill, 120
Hungtai Company, 12, 15, 19
Hunnewell, James, 137
Hurricane Iniki, 200
Hustace, F., 56, 146
Hutchins, C.J., 146
Hutchinson Sugar Company, 84, 109-111, 168;
   plantation, 168
Hutchinson, Alexander, 109
Hydroelectric power, 29, 36, 47, 92, 98, 101, 103, 159

I

ILWU (International Longshoreman's and Warehousemen's Union), 35, 124-125, 132, 149. *See also* Labor
Inter-Island Steam Navigation Company, 100, 162, 164
Irwin, William G., 43, 67, 93, 103, 109, 138, 154, 162, 170
Isenberg, Paul, 28-29, 129, 140

J

J. McColgan, 145
J.T. Waterhouse, 145, 170
Jackson, Henry Beecroft, 89, 93
Jackson, Frederick, 93
Janion, Green, & Company, 139, 169
Japanese:
   investors, 112, 168;
   language schools, 119, 131;
   picture brides, 119;
   as plantation labor, 4, 11, 31, 45, 71, 119, 123-125, 127-129;
   submarines, 164, 169
Jardine, Matheson & Co., 81, 139
Jarvis Island, 30

John Fowler & Sons, 169-170
John Nott & Company, 108
Johns-Manville Corporation, 172
Johnson, Francis, 137
Johnstone, Andrew, 208
Jones, Florence Wood, 20
Jones, Peter, 138
Jones, Peter, Jr., 110
Jones-Costigan Sugar Control Act, 194, 196
Judd, Col. Charles Hastings, 9, 19, 165
Judd, Dr. Gerrit P., 9, 21, 27, 62, 95, 146, 207, 209

K

Kaʻahumanu, Queen, 15, 18
Kaalaea Plantation, 139
Kaʻanapalı (Maui), 64, 163-164
Kaeleku Plantation Company, Ltd., 60, 62, 146
Kahuku (Oʻahu), 46-47, 167
Kahuku Plantation Company, 41-42, 46, 146-147, 167, 181, 184, 214
Kahuku Sugar Company, 49;
   mill, 51
Kahului & Wailuku Railroad Company, 166
Kahului (Maui), 157, 163-164, 166
Kahului Railroad Company, 132, 166-167
Kailua Plantation, 61, 71
Kaiwiki Sugar Company, 80, 83, 94-95, 97, 124;
   independent mill, 120;
   plantation, 75, 80-81, 135
Kalaialu, Richard, 207
Kalākaua, King David, 29, 31-32, 43-44, 56, 68, 85, 99, 102, 126, 128, 165, 192, 207
Kalama, Harriet, 41
Kalianui Plantation Company, 61, 71
Kamai, D., 126
Kamalo Sugar Company, 54, 56;
   plantation, 54
Kamamalu, Queen, 14
Kamehameha I, 14, 85, 207;
   conquest of the Hawaiian Islands, 3, 26
Kamehameha II, 14, 207
Kamehameha III, 9, 12, 14, 16, 26, 30, 41, 63, 126, 207;
   and Great Mahele, 11
Kamehameha IV, Alexander Liholiho, 20, 30, 126, 207

Kamehameha V, 30, 32, 43, 126, 128, 207
Kamooua, William, 207
Kāneʻohe Ranch, 42
Kaneʻohe Sugar Plantation Company, 41-42
Kapoho (Hawaiʻi), 106-107
Kaʻū (Hawaiʻi), 103, 108-112, 116, 138, 162, 164, 167-168
Kau Agribusiness Company, 84, 108, 112-113, 138, 173, 200-201
Kau Sugar Company, Inc., 84, 109, 112
Kauaʻi Electric Company, 36, 200, 202
Kauai Fruit & Land Company, 168
Kauaʻi Museum, 37
Kauaʻi Railway Company, 36, 166, 168
Kauaʻi, 7, 12, 16, 23-37, 116, 119, 133, 157, 164, 166, 168, 179, 200
Kauikeaouli, Prince Albert, 30
Kaumakani (Kauaʻi), 34
Kaumualiʻi, George, 26, 207
Kaʻupakuea Mill & Plantation, 83, 99-100
Kawaihae (Hawaiʻi), 79, 86, 94, 157, 164
Kekaha Mill Company, 25, 28, 35;
 independent mill, 120
Kekaha Sugar Company, Inc., 25, 29, 35-37, 120, 133, 140-141, 181, 199, 201, 204-205
Kekuanaoʻa, High Chief Mataio, 15
Kennett, Alan, 201
Kenui, William, 207
Kihei Plantation, 71, 181
Kihei Sugar Company, 61, 70
Kikīaola resort, 133
Kīlauea (Kauaʻi), 22, 24, 32, 44
Kilauea Sugar Company, 25, 32, 183
Kīlauea Volcano, 106-107, 167
Kilauea, 162
Kipahulu Sugar Company, 60, 67;
 independent mill, 120;
 plantation, 55
Knudsen, Valdemar, 35
Koebele, A., 179
Kohala (Hawaiʻi), 17, 84-90, 113, 116, 127, 135, 160, 164-166, 176
Kohala Ditch Company, 88
Kohala Landing, 86
Kohala Sugar Company, 3, 25, 28, 45, 82, 84-90, 111, 113, 127, 141, 166, 179, 181;
 plantation, 16
Kolekole Canyon (Hawaiʻi), 99
Kōloa (Kauaʻi), 26, 28, 30, 35-37, 56, 61, 116, 140, 168

Koloa Agricultural Company, 36
Kōloa Museum, 37
Koloa Sugar Company, 26, 28, 35, 140, 168;
 plantation, 28, 30, 56, 61, 136, 150, 168, 191
Kōloa/Līhuʻe Connection, 166
Kona (Hawaiʻi), 108-113, 162
Kona Development Company, 84, 112
Kona Historical Society Museum, 113
Kona Sugar Company, 84, 112, 167
Koʻolau Agriculture Company, 41, 46-47, 146
Koolau Railway Company, 166-167
Koreans, as plantation labor, 11, 150
Kuakini, Governor, 17-18
Kualoa Ranch, 9, 75;
 sugar plantation, 10-12, 21, 39, 137, 146
Kukaiau Plantation Company, 82, 94, 96, 183;
 independent mill, 120
Kukaiau Mill Company, 96, 120
Kūkaʻiau Ranch, 76, 125
Kukuihaele Landing (Hawaiʻi), 78-79, 91-92, 93-94, 159, 164
Kula Plantation Company, 61, 71
Kuleana Act (1850), 116
Kupelii, 207

L

Labor, 4, 11, 20-21, 51, 59, 70-71, 75, 101, 107-108, 113, 127, 149, 152, 154, 172, 176,
 Labor, cont., 183, 196, 200;
 contracts, 117, 126, 132;
 deserters, 108, 127;
 legislation, 127;
 medical care, 75, 125, 132-133;
 strikes, 76, 124, 133;
 plantation housing, 124, 126-127, 128, 130-131, 133;
 recruitment, 127;
 wages, 124, 127, 132-133, 185, 187, 204. *See also* ILWU (International Longshoreman's and Warehousemen's Union); *See also individual ethnic groups.*
Ladd & Company, 26, 136
Ladd, William, 26
Lahaina (Maui), 18, 63, 85, 116, 164, 177-178, 186

Lahaina Sugar Company, 63
Lahaina, Ka'anapali & Pacific Railroad, 64
Lā'ie (O'ahu), 164
Laie Plantation, 41-42, 47
Lāna'i, 53-54, 56-57
Langsdorf, Georg H., 2
Larsen, Dr. Nils, 125
Laupahoehoe Point (Hawai'i), 77, 112, 159, 164
Laupahoehoe Sugar Company, 76, 80, 83, 92, 94-95, 97, 139;
    independent mill, 120;
    plantation, 115, 135, 139
Lee, Judge William L., 126, 152
Liberty ships, 78, 94
Lidgate & Campbell, 83, 97
Lidgate, William, 97
Lihue Plantation Company, 25, 28-30, 140-141, 168-169, 172, 179, 200-202, 205
Lihue Sugar Company, 37
Likelike, 162
Lili'uokalani, Queen Lydia, 30, 32, 43, 110, 207
Lima Locomotive Works, 170
Lingrin, (first name unknown), 62
Lisianskii, Captain Iurii F., 2
Loomis, Elisha, 207
Louisiana, 5, 12, 155, 171, 191-193, 195
Louisiana Sugar Experimental Station, 155
Lunalilo, King William, 92, 126, 207
Lydgate, Rev. John M., 17, 126
Lyman Museum, 113
Lyman, Rev. David B., 208
Lyons, Rev. Lorenzo, 208

M

Macadamia nuts, 37, 66, 141, 161, 202
Macfarlane, George, 170
Macfie, R.A., 32
Mahele. *See* Great Mahele Land Act
Māhukona (Hawai'i), 86, 90, 164, 166
Mahukona Terminals, Ltd., 166
Maine, 31
Mākaha Resort, 44
Makahaula Plantation, 99
Makawao (Maui), 18, 61, 66
Makawao Plantation Company, 61, 71
Makaweli (Kaua'i), 33-34
Makee Plantation. *See* Ulupalakua Plantation
Makee Sugar Company, 25, 31-32, 65

Makee, Captain James, 19, 31, 62, 64
Malo, David, 18
Mana plantation camp, 133
Manalua Gulch, 97
Mānoa Valley:
    nursery, 181;
    plantation, 15
Marin, Don Francisco De Paula, 12, 14, 30, 136
Marshall, J.F., 137
Martin, Donald J., 35
Masters and Servants Act, 127, 129.
    See also Labor
Matson Navigation Company, 78, 94, 104, 143, 151, 156, 200, 204
Matson, William, 104
Maui Agricultural Company, 59, 61, 63, 71-73, 133, 146
Maui, 59-73, 116, 119, 131, 140, 157, 164, 166, 179
Mauna Kea (Hawai'i), 77, 81, 90-91, 103-104, 121
Mauna Kea Agribusiness Company, 104, 138. *See also* Mauna Kea Sugar Company
Mauna Kea Sugar Company, 84, 101-102, 104, 118, 121, 199, 201. *See also* Mauna Kea Agribusiness Company
Mauna Kea, 162
Mauna Loa (Hawai'i), 81, 108-109
Maunalei Sugar Company, 54, 57
Maxwell, Dr. Walter, 178
Maxwell, Walter, 155
McBryde Sugar Company, 23, 25-26, 30, 33, 36-37, 55, 57, 139, 146, 168, 172, 179, 181, 201-203
McBryde, John Duncan, 36
McChesny & Sons, 146
McCorriston, D., 54
McKeague, John, 43
McKinley Tariff Act, 193, 196
McLane, Patrick, 55, 67
Medeiros, Alfred, 75
Meier & Kruse, 25, 35
Melchers & Co., 91
Menzies, Archibald, 1
Messchaert, P.A., 182
Messers, Siemson & Marsdon, 91
Mexico, 171, 190, 195, 197
Meyer Sugar Mill, 56
Meyer, R.W., 54-55
Military, 161;
    martial law, 132

Mills, J.R., 82, 91
Mills, Tyler, 208
Mirlees, Tate & Watson, 85, 169
Missionaries, 9, 28-29, 33, 37, 42, 46, 55-57, 65, 70, 85, 102, 113, 141-142, 146-147, 176, 207-209
Moanui Plantation, 54
Moir, John, 101
Mokupahu, 157
Moler, R. D., 29
Moloka'i Museum and Cultural Center, 56
Moloka'i Ranch, 55
Moloka'i, 36, 53-56, 178
Morgan, David, 146
Morgan, Francis Swanzy, 95-96, 139, 145-146
Morgan, John F., 146
Morgan, Lt. Van R., 27
Mormons, 42, 56
Mott-Smith, Dr. John, 85
Murdock, David, 141
Muriel, 163

N

Nā'ālehu (Hawai'i), 108-109
Naalehu Plantation, 84, 108-109
Naalehu Sugar Compay, 109
NAFTA (North American Free Trade Agreement), 190, 197
Native Hawaiians, 1, 47, 123, 161;
    arrival, 2;
    foreign diseases, 123, 126;
    independent farmers, 116;
    and missionaries, 207;
    as plantation labor, 4, 9, 20, 26, 51, 85, 125-126, 129;
    plantation owners, 66
Nāwiliwili (Kaua'i), 157, 164, 168, 186
Ni'ihau, 32
Niulii Mill & Plantation Company, 82, 86-88, 135, 139, 157
Notley, Charles, 93
Nu'uanu Valley Plantation, 12, 20

O

O.R. & L. (O'ahu Railway and Land Company), 44-45, 47, 49, 51, 100, 166-167
O'ahu Sugar Company, 41, 45-46, 49-51, 141, 167, 178, 180-182, 188, 201-202
O'ahu, 26, 29, 39-51, 110, 116, 119, 136, 164, 166, 179

Oceanic Steamship Company, 200
Office of Price Administration, 197
Ogden, Maria, 207
Olokele Sugar Company, 138;
    plantation, 24-25, 33-35, 37, 201-202, 205
Olaa Sugar Company, 84, 92, 105-107, 143, 172
Oliver filter, 49
Oliver, Dr. Richard, 110
Olowalu (Maui), 53
Olowalu Company, 57, 60, 64;
    plantation, 139
Olsen, Olaf R., 29
Onomea (Hawai'i), 164
Onomea Sugar Company, 83, 101-102, 104, 126;
    plantation, 47, 78, 126, 137
'O'ōkala (Hawai'i), 80, 90, 96, 164
Ookala Sugar Company, Ltd., 96-97;
    plantation, 83, 96
Organic Act (1900), 71, 117, 129
Ormoc Sugar Company (Philippines), 90

P

Paalaa Mill, 120
Paauhau Sugar Company, 83, 76, 80, 92, 94, 139;
    independent mill, 120;
    plantation, 77, 93
Pa'auilo (Hawai'i), 77, 86, 92-95, 159, 164
Pacific Development Company, Ltd., 146
Pacific Guano & Fertilizer Company, 30
Pacific Sugar Mill Company, 76, 83, 92
Pāhala (Hawai'i), 109-110
Pahala Plantation, 47
Pahala Stock Farm, 111
Pāhoa (Hawai'i), 107
Pā'ia (Maui), 70, 72, 133
Paia Plantation Company, 45, 47, 61, 66, 68, 71, 142, 146, 173;
    mill, 133, 183
Pain, W.H, 57, 146
Palawai Development Company, 54, 57
Papa 'I'i, John, 49
Papa'aloa (Hawai'i), 76, 97
Papaikou Sugar Company, 83, 101-102, 104. See also Hitchcock & Company.
Parker Ranch, 85, 90
Parker, James, Esq., 85
Parker, John, 85
Parker, Rev. Benjamin, 208

Parker, Samuel, 93
Parsons, Judge Alfred W., 18
Patten, Maria, 207
Paukaa Sugar Company, 83, 101-102
Paulet, Lord George, 18
Pearl Harbor (Oʻahu), 49-50, 196
Peirce & Brewer, 137
Peirce, Henry, 28, 137-138, 169
Pepeʻekeo (Hawaiʻi), 164
Pepeʻekeo Sugar Company, 83, 99, 101, 104, 121, 139;
    plantation, 76, 78, 148
Perkins, R.C., 179
Pfluger, J.C., 139
Phelps, 208
Philippines, 90, 112, 123, 153, 171, 191
Piggly Wiggly, 135
Pineapple, 40, 53, 66, 141, 161
Pioneer Mill Company, 42, 44, 59-60, 63-64, 140-141, 180-181, 183, 200-203
Pitman, Benjamin, 63
Plantations, 3-6, 12-13, 126, 143;
    artesian wells, 44-45, 47, 49, 53, 55, 60, 63, 181;
    automation, 46-47, 49, 59, 77-79, 101, 104, 118, 131-133, 154, 176, 184-185, 199-200, 204;
    Caterpillar tractor, 81, 184;
    fertilizer, 30, 45, 79-80, 101, 113, 115, 151, 154, 175, 179;
    fluming, 77, 89-91, 93, 97-98, 101-102, 104, 107, 109-111, 113, 118, 121, 159, 183-184, 199;
    on Hawaiʻi (Big Island), 3, 13, 16-18, 75-113, 162;
    homesteaders, 115-117;
    hydroelectric power, 29, 36, 47, 92, 101, 103;
    independent farmers, 115-121, 127;
    irrigation 24, 28, 35, 44-45, 47, 49, 53, 55, 59, 62-63, 68-69, 72, 77, 79, 88, 91, 93, 180-181;
    on Kauaʻi, 7, 12, 16, 23-37, 162, 200;
    labor, 4, 11, 20, 26, 33, 46, 51, 59, 70-71, 75, 101, 113, 117, 123-133;
    on Lānaʻi, 12, 14, 53-54, 56-57;
    liming, 100;
    luna, 76, 132;
    management of, 26, 33, 76, 132, 149, 187;
    on Maui, 12-13, 15-16, 18-19, 31, 59-73, 162;

Plantations on Molokaʻi, 36, 53-56;
    on Oʻahu, 10-12, 15, 21, 39-51;
    pests & insects, 106, 175-176, 179-180, 204;
    plantation time, 33;
    production statistics, 6, 34, 43-44, 47, 49, 51, 60, 63-64, 67, 70, 72, 78, 82, 86, 97, 128, 145, 193, 201, 205;
    production costs, 183-185;
    radio systems, 176;
    ratooning, 35, 78, 91, 201;
    revenue, 130, 166;
    water wheels, 101;
    worker productivity, 185. *See also specific names of plantations.* *See also* Sugar industry; Sugarcane; Sugar mills.
Planters Convention, 153
Planters' Labor and Supply Company, 130, 153-155
Planters' Society, 153
Popohe, Stephen, 207
Port Allen, 33, 168
Porter Locomotive Works, 170
Portuguese:
    on plantations, 4, 11, 128-129;
    Madeira, 128
Princeville Plantation Company, 25, 30
Puakea Plantation, 82, 90
Puakea Ranch, 90
Puako Plantation, 82, 90, 186
Public education, 111, 131
Pulehu Plantation Company, 61, 71
Puna (Hawaiʻi), 92, 105, 107, 167
Puna Sugar Company, 106-107, 183. *See also* First Puna Sugar Company
Punahou School, 28
Purvis, William, 92
Puʻunēnē (Maui), 59, 66, 70, 72, 131
Puʻunene Mill, 58, 201

R

R.C. Janion, 89, 139
Railroad Museum (Hawaiʻi), 112
Railroads, 5, 11, 23, 32, 43-45, 47, 49, 51, 55, 62, 64, 66, 75, 78, 86, 88-89, 91-94, 96, 98, 100-102, 106-107, 109, 112-113, 131-132, 160, 164-169, 193
Railway Act, 44, 165, 168
Ransome & Rapier, 169
Reciprocity Sugar Company, 60, 67
Reciprocity Treaty (1876), 21, 28, 43, 45, 66-68, 84, 88, 91, 113, 117, 120, 125-126, 153-154, 161, 192, 196, 210

INDEX

Renton, George, 178
Renton, James, 88
Reynolds, Stephen, 15, 19-20, 136, 152
Rice, William Harrison, 28, 208
Richards, Mrs. William, 207
Richardson, C.E., 105
Rickard, W.H., 82, 91-92
Robertson, W.F., 76
Robinson, Aubrey, 33
Rogers, Edmund H., 208
Roney, John "Jack," 150, 190
Ross, Capt. James, 32
Royal Agricultural Society, 203
Royal Hawaiian Agricultural Society, 13, 18, 126, 151-153, 172
Royal Hawaiian Macadamia Nut Company, 141
Royal School, 43
Ruggles, Samuel, 207

S

S & W canned foods (Suessmann & Wurmser), 50
S.L. Austin & Company, 101-102, 126
Samoans, *See* South Sea islanders.
Samsing & Company, 18-19
San Francisco (California), 86, 91, 93, 135, 138, 141-142, 152, 155, 162, 191, 200, 210. *See also* California
Sandalwood, 14, 176
Schaefer, Frederick A., 91, 154
Schaefer, Frederick III, 136
Scotch Coast, 76, 92
Scott, John, 103-104, 178
Scottish immigrants, 76, 92
Searby, William, 182
Shepard, Stephen, 208
Shipman, Herbert, 107
Shipman, W.H., 105
Sinclair, Anne McHutchinson, 35
Sinclair, Eliza McHutchinson, 32-33, 35
Sinclair, Francis S., 32
Smith, A.H., 66
Smith, Dr. James, 37, 66, 208
Smith, Jared, 66
Smith, Rev. Lowell, 208
Smith, W.O., 66, 71
South Africa, 81
South Sea islanders: as plantation labor, 128
Spalding, Col. Andrew T., 99
Spalding, Col. Z.S., 31, 154, 156
Spalding, Philip, 138

Spaulding, Rev. Ephraim, 208
Spencer, Ambrose H., 27, 61
Spencer, Capt. O.B., 109
Spencer, Capt. Thomas, 102-103
Spencer, Charles, 109
Spreckels, Claus, 45, 68-69, 73, 93, 98, 103, 109, 129, 143, 156, 183, 200
Spreckels, J.D., 31
Star Mill Company, 82, 89;
   independent mill, 120
Starkey, Janion & Company, 139
Starr flour mill, 156
Stedman, Judge Alfred, 66
Steubenberg Company, 78
Stewart, Charles S., 207
Stockton, Betsey, 207
Stodart, William, 57
Stone, Delia, 207
Sugar Act, 189-190, 196
Sugar Equalization Bond, 196
Sugar Factors Company, Inc., 156
Sugar industry, 1-2, 4-7, 11, 21, 51, 73, 79, 81, 97, 113, 124-125, 129, 135, 146, 148, 150, 153, 157, 161, 187, 204-205;
   effects of annexation, 23, 36, 55, 71, 105, 123, 127-129, 154, 156, 196;
   beet sugar, 156, 160, 191-195, 202;
   effects of Civil War, 9-10, 12, 127, 191, 193;
   Cuba, 5, 153, 171, 191-193, 196;
   Florida, 195;
   Jamaica, 171;
   effects of Great Depression, 124, 189;
   Louisiana, 5, 12, 155, 171, 191-193, 195;
   marketing, 144, 191;
   Mexico, 171, 190, 195, 197;
   New York price, 210-211;
   Puerto Rico, 56, 171, 195;
   recessions, 137;
   Reciprocity Treaty, 21, 28, 43, 45, 66, 68, 84, 88, 91, 113, 117, 120, 125-126, 153-154, 161, 192, 196;
   revenues, 130;
   Santo Domingo, 171;
   sugar substitutes, 113, 194, 197;
   tariffs, 11, 23, 45, 71, 127, 129, 176, 190-196, 210;
   Texas, 195;
   treaties and legislation, 195-197. *See also* Plantations; Sugar mills; Sugarcane

Sugar Islander, 157
Sugar mills, 5, 12-13, 17, 22, 49, 51, 53, 55-57, 69, 71-72, 80, 87, 94, 171, 173, 193;
  centrifugals, 10, 56, 61, 128, 169, 183;
  hydroelectric power, 29, 98, 101, 159;
  independent mills, 115-121;
  machinery repair, 29, 160, 169;
  steam engine, 28, 62-64, 66, 86, 91, 128, 213;
  water-powered, 21, 66, 87. *See also* Plantations; Sugarcane; Sugar industry
Sugarcane: arrival in Hawai'i, 2;
  bagasse, 10, 29, 37, 59, 64, 69, 105, 160-161, 173, 176-177, 182, 199, 203;
  bulk sugar, 79, 157;
  burning cane trash, 80, 86, 96, 98, 107, 173;
  by-products, 160, 172-173, 205;
  Cane, 172;
  characteristics of plant, 4;
  early cultivation, 1-3;
  ethanol, 71, 161, 172-173, 176, 203;
  high-fructose corn syrup, 189, 194-195, 197;
  juice strainer, 103;
  pests and diseases, 175-176, 179-180, 204;
  refineries, 34, 50, 68, 81, 91, 93, 142-144, 150-151, 155, 171, 199;
  sugar manufacturing process, 9-10, 17, 45, 49, 61, 64-65, 69, 72, 100, 181-183, 212-214;
  transport, 5-6, 10, 32, 44, 46-47, 49, 51, 53, 57, 66, 75, 77-79, 81, 86, 91-94, 96, 101-102, 105, 110, 118, 151, 159, 161-169, 183-184, 189;
  varieties, 4, 79, 154, 175-178. *See also* Plantations; Sugar industry; Sugar mills.
Swanzy, Francis M., 23, 95, 146

T

Tahiti, Henry, 208
Tariffs, 11, 23, 45, 71, 127, 129, 176, 190-196, 210
Telegraph, 186
The Planters' Monthly, 154
Theo H. Davies & Co., Ltd., 7, 23, 36, 39, 59, 75, 78-81, 88-89, 92-93, 95, 97, 100, 115, 120, 124-125, 135-137, 139-140, 145-147, 149-150, 153, 159-160, 169-172

Thurston, Asa, 46, 207
Thurston, Lorrin, 70
Tinker, Rev. Rueben, 208
Titcomb, Charles, 177
Torbert, Linton L., 12-13, 18-20, 27-28, 31, 62, 64, 153
Tourism, 53, 64, 161, 202-203;
  resort development, 60, 64, 78, 105, 133
Trousseau, Dr. George, 92
Tsunami of 1946, 78, 93, 101, 107, 159
Turton, Henry, 42, 44, 63

U

U.S. Enemy Alien Property Custodian, 140
U.S. Food Administration, 196
'Ulupalakua (Maui), 12-13, 18, 31, 62
Ulupalakua Plantation (Makee Plantation), 60, 62, 137, 156, 168
Union Iron Works, 170
Union Mill & Plantation Company, 82, 86-89, 135, 139;
  independent mill, 120
United Cane Planters' Cooperative, 104
Unna, August, 62
Unna, Oscar, 67
USDA (Department of Agriculture), 115, 118

V

V. Knudsen & Estate, 25, 35
Vancouver, Captain (first name unknown), 1
Vida, Daniel, 89
Visitor industry. *See* Tourism
Von Holt, H.M., 168

W

W.G. Irwin & Company, 67, 98, 104, 138
Waiahole Ditch Company, 180
Waiakea Mill Company, 78, 84, 105, 115, 135, 139, 172, 182;
  independent mill, 120
Waiakea Plantation Company, 92, 105, 116
Wai'ale'ale Mountains (Kaua'i), 23-24
Waialua Agricultural Company, 41-42, 47-49, 172, 178, 181, 184, 201
Waialua Sugar Company, 141, 202;
  plantation, 133, 167
Wai'anae (O'ahu), 164
Waianae Sugar Company, 40-41, 43, 131
Waihee Sugar Company, 31, 60, 64-66;
  plantation, 64

Waikapu Sugar Company, 60, 66
Wailea Milling Company, 98, 183; independent mill, 120
Wailoa River, 105
Wailuku (Maui), 15, 47, 116, 166
Wailuku Sugar Company, 28, 60, 65-66, 182; plantation, 137
Waimanalo (Oʻahu), 164
Waimanalo Sugar Company, 39, 41, 43, 75, 162, 178
Waimea (Hawaiʻi), 18, 85
Waimea (Kauaʻi), 16-17, 34, 164
Waimea Sugar Company, 25, 35-36, 133; independent mill, 120
Wainaku (Hawaiʻi), 104
Wainaku Plantation, 84, 103-104. *See also* Hilo Sugar Company
Waiʻōhinu Plantation, 108
Waipahu (Oʻahu), 49
Waipahu Cultural and Garden Park, 51
Waipiʻo Peninsula (Oʻahu), 49
Waipiʻo Valley (Hawaiʻi), 77-78, 90-92, 165
Walker, Allen & Company, 145
Walker, Andrew, 76
Walker, J.S., 146
Ward Foods, Inc., 171
Ward, Mary, 208
Waterhouse & Company (Waterhouse Trust Company), 146
Watt, George, 111
Watt, John, 92
Webster, James, 100
West Hawaii Railway Company, 112, 166, 168
West Maui Plantation, 64
Western Sugar Refining Company, 156, 194

Weston, David M., 169
Whaling industry, 136
White, John, 13
Whitney, Samuel, 207
Widemann, Judge Hermann A., 43, 146
Wight, Dr. James, 85, 87, 90
Wilcox, Abner, 29-30, 208
Wilcox, Albert Spencer, 29, 43
Wilcox, George Norton, 30, 43
Wilder & Company, 146
Wilder Steamship Company, 160, 162-163
Wilder, Samuel G., 9-10, 19, 30, 86, 146, 160, 162, 164-166, 170
Wilder, Willie, 10
Wilfong, George W., 3, 18, 28, 62, 65, 85, 150, 164, 176
Wilkinson, John, 14
Wilkinson, W.H., 67-68
Williams, William, 105, 172
Winship, Captain Nathan, 26
Wishard, Leslie, 97
Wong Kwai, 146
Wong, Leong & Company, 54, 146
Wood, Dr. Robert W., 27, 31, 61, 140, 152
Wood, John W., 20
World War I, 140, 156, 196
World War II, 47, 49-50, 75, 86, 92-93, 99, 104-105, 109, 132, 138, 150, 164, 166-167, 171, 176, 184-185, 197, 199; martial law, 132
Wyllie, Robert Crichton, 30

Y

Young, Alexander, 100, 105, 135, 154, 169-170, 182

ABOUT FRANCIS S. MORGAN

(MARCH 19, 1919 - AUGUST 1, 1999)

FRANCIS S. MORGAN was born into a family with strong ties to the sugar industry. In 1850, they purchased Kualoa from King Kamehameha III and later built Oʻahu's first sugarmill in 1863 to centrifugally produce sugar. It was here that Morgan spent his childhood, attending Hanahauʻoli and Punahou schools. After graduating from Stanford University in 1941 and fighting for the Navy in World War II, Morgan returned to Hawaiʻi and followed in his grandfather's footsteps, working for Theo Davies where he eventually became Vice-President of Agriculture.

Always a faithful supporter of the sugar industry, Morgan bought Hamakua Sugar Company in 1984, the second largest sugar plantation in Hawaiʻi. Although he was nearing retirement, Morgan invested everything he had into this endeavor in the hopes of saving sugar on the Big Island and helping Hawaiʻi continue as a leading agricultural force. Despite his dedication and hard work, a string of bad weather, low sugar prices and unfortunate events ensued and the Hamakua Sugar Company was forced to close in 1993. An active member of the community and celebrated for his optimism and compassion, Francis S. Morgan is held in high regard by all who knew him.

ABOUT WILLIAM H. DORRANCE

(DECEMBER 3, 1921 - MARCH 28, 2000)

WILLIAM H. DORRANCE, V, was born on December 3, 1921 in Highland Park, Michigan. He attended the University of Michigan, earning B.S.E. and M.S.E. degrees in aeronautical engineering. His education was interrupted by World War II, during which he completed 33 combat missions as a B-17 pilot attached to the 8th Air Force. Returning to civilian life while retaining a reserve commission, he completed his education and embarked on an engineering and science career in the aerospace industry. He served successively as head of the Aerodynamics Section, University of Michigan Aeronautical Research Center; Lead Aerodynamicist, Project Atlas ICBM, Convair, San Diego; Senior Staff Scientist, Convair General Offices, San Diego; head of the Gas Dynamics Department, Aerospace Corporation, El Segundo, California; Director of Weapon System Plans, Aerospace Corporation, San Bernardino, California; Corporate Vice President, Conductron Corporation, Ann Arbor, Michigan; Chairman and Chief Executive Officer, Interface Systems Corporation, Ann Arbor, Michigan; and President, OCS, Inc., Ann Arbor, Michigan.

He published over twenty scientific papers in scholarly journals and a well-received technical book, authored or co-authored four patents on synthetic fuels production processes, and earned a Doctor of Science degree.

After moving to Oʻahu in 1986, Dr. Dorrance turned to researching and writing history. He published articles in *The Hawaiian Journal of History* and *Historic Hawaii* magazine, as well as in several military history journals. He authored *Fort Kamehameha, The Story of the Harbor Defenses of Pearl Harbor* and *Oʻahu's Hidden History*.